Methodological Issues in Controlled Studies on Effects of Prenatal Exposure to Drug Abuse

Editors:
M. Marlyne Kilbey, Ph.D.
Khursheed Asghar, Ph.D.

Research Monograph 114
1991

U.S. DEPARTMENT OF HEALTH AND HUMAN SERVICES
Public Health Service
Alcohol, Drug Abuse, and Mental Health Administration

National Institute on Drug Abuse
5600 Fishers Lane
Rockville, MD 20857

Associate Editors, NIDA

NORA CHIANG, Ph.D.
Medications Development Division

JOHN W. SPENCER, Ph.D.
Division of Clinical Research

LYNDA ERINOFF, Ph.D.
Division of Preclinical Research

PUSHPA V. THADANI, Ph.D.
Division of Preclinical Research

CORYL L. JONES, Ph.D.
Division of Epidemiology and
Prevention Research

CORA LEE WETHERINGTON, Ph.D.
Division of Clinical Research

ACKNOWLEDGMENT

This monograph is based on the papers and discussion from a technical review on "Methodological Issues in Controlled Studies on Effects of Prenatal Exposure to Drugs of Abuse" held on June 8-9, 1990, in Richmond, VA. The review meeting was sponsored by the National Institute on Drug Abuse and cosponsored by the National Institute of Child Health and Human Development.

COPYRIGHT STATUS

DHHS publication number (ADM)91-1837
Printed 1991

Preface

Prenatal exposure to drugs of abuse, now a public health concern of national importance, has adversely affected the lives of hundreds of thousands of babies born each year in the United States to drug-dependent mothers. The cost of providing intensive care to drug-exposed infants can be enormous. The cost of care and treatment of one infant could exceed $100,000 depending on the severity of sickness. Many infants born to drug-abusing mothers do not remain with the parents, and their placement outside the home excessively burdens the resources of the Nation's foster care provider agencies. The National Institute on Drug Abuse (NIDA) has assumed a lead role in supporting research to identify the prenatal effects of drugs of abuse on the behavioral, intellectual, and physical development of these infants and to determine the effects of drug abuse on reproductive outcome in the addicted mother. Moreover, NIDA is increasingly emphasizing research related to the prevention and treatment of developmental anomalies, which eventually would help reduce the suffering caused by this menace in the lives of babies, families, and society at large.

Methodological difficulties and the existence of confounding variables have been impeding progress in reaching the research goals identified above. Clearly, to deal with special problems of drug dependence, interaction and collaboration among different disciplines need to be engendered. Interaction is needed between those who have been studying human development for many years and those who are experienced in dealing with the problems associated with drug dependence. Therefore, NIDA sponsored two research technical reviews that focused on the experimental design issues inherent in research into the effects of prenatal exposure to drugs of abuse. The purpose of the technical reviews was to bring together panels of eminent researchers to consider how meaningful data can be best obtained and how to identify the kinds of research questions that can be addressed competently, given the current technological limitations.

This monograph presents the proceedings of the first NIDA technical review related to the conduct of controlled studies on the effects of prenatal exposure to drugs of abuse. Held June 8-9, 1990, at the Richmond Marriott in Richmond, VA, the technical review was cosponsored by the National Institute of Child

Health and Human Development. The following NIDA staff members participated in its planning and served as associate editors of this monograph: M. Marlyne Kilbey, Ph.D., Cochair (Dr. Kilbey served as Science Adviser to the Director of NIDA during calendar year 1989); Khursheed Asghar, Ph.D., Cochair; Nora Chiang, Ph.D.; Lynda Erinoff, Ph.D.; Coryl L. Jones, Ph.D.; John W. Spencer, Ph.D.; Pushpa V. Thadani, Ph.D.; and Cora Lee Wetherington, Ph.D.

We wish to express our appreciation of substantial advice and input provided in the planning of the technical review by the following NICHD staff members: Linda Wright, M.D.; Danuta Krotoski, Ph.D.; and Marian Willinger, Ph.D.

The second technical review, related to epidemiological, prevention, and treatment research on the effects of prenatal drug exposure on women and their children, was held July 25-26, 1990, at the Sheraton Inner Harbor Hotel in Baltimore, MD. The proceedings of this technical review are scheduled for publication in another NIDA monograph.

M. Marlyne Kilbey, Ph.D.
Chair
Department of Psychology
Wayne State University
Detroit, MI 48202

Khursheed Asghar, Ph.D.
Chief
Basic Sciences Research Review Branch
Office of Extramural Program Review
National Institute on Drug Abuse
Parklawn Building, Room 10-42
5600 Fishers Lane
Rockville, MD 20857

For sale by the U.S. Government Printing Office
Superintendent of Documents, Mail Stop: SSOP, Washington, DC 20402-9328
ISBN 0-16-035805-1

Contents

Session: Tracking Drug Effects Over the Lifespan

Drug Exposure to the Fetus—The Effect of Smoking

Betty R. Kuhnert

INTRODUCTION

Drugs are commonly abused in today's society. Often, they are abused by young women—frequently, the same young women who have unplanned pregnancies. Assessing the extent of exposure of the fetus to drugs of abuse and determining the effects of prenatal drugs on infant outcome are extremely difficult. The ideal study for obtaining this information would require knowledge of how much of a drug or drugs the mother took during pregnancy in order to correlate the exact amount of fetal drug exposure to neonatal outcome measures. This chapter presents general issues involved in assessing fetal drug exposure and reviews recent work on fetal exposure to tobacco smoke.

ASSESSING FETAL DRUG EXPOSURE

The first issue in an ideal study for assessing fetal drug exposure concerns measuring drug exposure. What is measured? Simply measuring the amount of drug ingested is not always enough because metabolites of some drugs also may cause adverse effects on the fetus. For example, meperidine (a narcotic analgesic) has an active metabolite, normeperidine, which actually causes more respiratory depression than the parent compound (Miller and Anderson 1954; Golub et al. 1988). Thus, in this case, both the parent compound and the active metabolite should be measured. Marijuana, for example, contains hundreds of ingredients and produces hundreds of metabolites (Szeto, this volume).

Rapidly metabolized drugs are another issue. Such drugs as 2-chloroprocaine, a local anesthetic, are rapidly metabolized primarily by plasma esterases, probably plasma cholinesterases. *In vitro*, the half-life of this drug is measured in seconds (O'Brien et al. 1979). Cocaine is predominately metabolized by hepatic enzymes but is also partially metabolized by these esterases. The cocaine half-life in humans is usually less than 1 hour (Kloss et al. 1984; Stewart et al. 1979; Inaba et al. 1978; Jatlow et al. 1979). When the drug is

1

unstable in the plasma, appropriate amounts of enzyme inhibitor must be added to the blood sample at the time of collection. In the case where the half-life of the drug is very short, a stable metabolite is usually measured (O'Brien et al. 1979; Kuhnert et al. 1980). Benzoylecgonine, a major metabolite of cocaine, is usually measured for the indication of cocaine exposure (Stewart et al. 1979; Inaba et al. 1978), and it has been described in one infant's urine for a period of several days (Chasnoff et al. 1986).

Measuring the drugs is often a problem because of the expense and the problems with detection limits if some time has elapsed since the drug was taken. Analytical methodologies can range from inexpensive immunoassay techniques, for example, using radioimmunoassay (RIA) or enzyme immunoassay (such as EMIT) for rapid screening, to sophisticated, time-consuming but more specific and sensitive gas chromatography/mass spectrometry for confirmation of nanogram or picogram levels of drugs. Other commonly used assay methods include thin-layer chromatography (TLC), gas-liquid chromatography (GLC), and high-performance liquid chromatography (HPLC).

The next issue to consider is what sample should be measured. Ideally, maternal blood samples and perhaps amniotic fluid samples should be measured during pregnancy. At birth, cord blood tells only what drug is present at that moment, not what is in the infant's tissues (Kuhnert et al. 1979). Neonatal urine can give a better indication of tissue levels, but only if the collection bags can be kept on and the skin stays intact long enough to get more than spot samples (Kuhnert et al. 1979). The rapid disappearance and then fluctuation of phencyclidine in neonatal urine has been documented in this way (Kuhnert et al. 1984). Maternal blood or urine taken at delivery also can be very informative (Kuhnert et al. 1984). Finally, an adhesive transcutaneous collection system that accumulates substances migrating from the blood to the skin was recently reported for use in preterm infants (Murphy et al. 1990). However, none of these samples will yield positive results unless drug exposure has been recent.

Accordingly, other noninvasive techniques for identifying past drug exposure have been suggested. Meconium from infants of drug-dependent mothers may test positive for drug metabolites, despite negative neonatal urine samples (Ostrea et al. 1989). Drug metabolites are thought to accumulate in meconium throughout gestation by direct deposition from bile, ingestion of metabolites in amniotic fluid, or both (Ostrea et al. 1989). Alternatively, benzoylecgonine has been reported in neonatal hair (Graham et al. 1989). Thus, hair analysis also may identify intrauterine exposure to drugs when maternal history is unclear or samples of body fluids test negative. However, at present, there are no generally accepted or standardized procedures for hair analysis for drugs of abuse, and laboratory analysis of hair is both laborious and tedious (Bailey 1989).

The final issue is how to measure neonatal neurobehavioral outcome after drug exposure. This remains controversial because many clinicians feel that the classical Brazelton exam (Brazelton 1973) is too time consuming and the data analysis required is too sophisticated if all of the confounding variables and pharmacologic variables are considered (Kuhnert et al. 1985).

The following review illustrates how some of the various methodologic issues can be dealt with in a study of the effect of smoking during pregnancy on neonatal outcome.

EFFECT OF SMOKING ON NEONATAL OUTCOME

Background

It is well known that smoking during pregnancy is harmful (Surgeon General's Report 1979; Abel 1980). The effects range from lesions in the placenta to abnormal behavior in the offspring (Kuhnert and Kuhnert 1985). The most common sign of fetal tobacco syndrome is decreased birth weight (Nieburg et al. 1985). But why cigarette smoking causes decreased birth weight, particularly in older parturients, is not clear (Cnattingius et al. 1985; Wen et al. 1990). Carbon monoxide and nicotine are obviously harmful components of cigarette smoke that may be related to decreased birth weight. Carbon monoxide binds to hemoglobin to form carboxyhemoglobin and cause fetal hypoxia, and nicotine causes a gamut of effects related to cholinergic agonists and catecholamine release.

But there are other components of cigarette smoke, including lead (Cogbill and Hobbs 1957), cadmium (Cd) (Lewis et al. 1972), and thiocyanate (SCN) (Pettigrew and Fell 1972), that may harm the fetus. Both lead and SCN can cause decreased birth weight. In addition, it has been suggested that cadmium may share responsibility for the decreased birth weight of infants of smokers (Webster 1978; Longo 1980). Smoking is the major source of cadmium in nonpolluted areas.

The adverse effects of cadmium come from its similarity in structure to zinc (Zn) and its ability to substitute for zinc in zinc-dependent enzymes, including alcohol dehydrogenase. The inhibition of this enzyme by cadmium from cigarette smoke may partially explain the reported potentiation of smoking on the effects of alcohol use during pregnancy (Fried and Makin 1987; Gusella and Fried

3

1984). However, studies in humans (Roels et al. 1978; Lauwerys et al. 1978) and animals (Parizek 1965; Levin and Miller 1980) have shown that very little cadmium actually crosses the placenta. Cadmium actually accumulates in the placenta and appears to be trapped there (Kuhnert et al. 1982; Van Hattum and de Voogt 1981; Miller and Gardner 1981).

Hypothesis

Animal studies had suggested the possibility of a cadmium-zinc interaction because low doses of cadmium resulted in growth retardation and malformations that were very similar to the same patterns seen in experimental zinc deficiency (Apgar 1985). It was thought that cadmium would induce the formation of binding proteins in the placenta that might also trap zinc. Support for this hypothesis came from the fact that many of the adverse effects of smoking during pregnancy are also found in mothers who are zinc-deficient during pregnancy (Jameson 1976; Lazebnik et al. 1988).

Methods

Testing the hypothesis in humans that smoking during pregnancy results in a cadmium-zinc interaction that may lead to zinc deficiency necessitated reliable quantification of the exposure to cigarette smoke. Fetal cadmium levels could not be used as an index of exposure because cadmium does not cross the placenta in proportion to the amount of smoking (Kuhnert et al. 1982). Thiocyanate, with its long half-life, has been shown to be a marker that correlates well with the number of cigarettes the mother smokes (Pettigrew et al. 1977; Bottoms et al. 1982). Furthermore, fetal SCN correlates well with maternal SCN (Bottoms et al. 1982).

The outcome measures included placental zinc, maternal and fetal measures of zinc status, placental cadmium and maternal whole blood cadmium, and birth weight (Kuhnert et al. 1987a). These variables had to be measured in the mother to eliminate any effects attributable to maternal zinc status. All elements were measured by sensitive atomic absorption spectrophotometry techniques.

The Cadmium-Zinc Interaction

Maternal indices turned out to be similar between smoking and nonsmoking groups (Kuhnert et al. 1987a, 1988a). This was particularly true for activity of maternal alkaline phosphatase (a zinc-dependent enzyme) and levels of zinc in plasma and red blood cells (RBCs). Thus, smoking did not appear to affect maternal zinc status.

4

As shown in figure 1, maternal whole blood cadmium was 65 percent higher; placental cadmium was 45 percent higher; and placental zinc was 10 percent higher in smokers (Kuhnert et al. 1987a). All three fetal indices of zinc status were significantly lower in the smoking group (figure 2) (Kuhnert et al. 1988a). The finding that cord blood RBC zinc was 9 percent lower in infants of smokers was in agreement with the hypothesis that smoking causes accumulated placental cadmium that traps zinc and results in a zinc-deficient fetus.

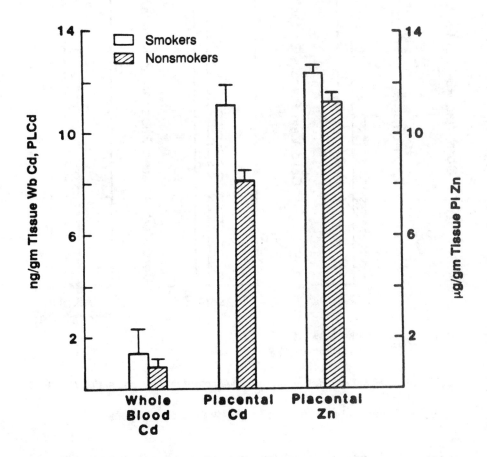

FIGURE 1.   *Effect of smoking on whole blood cadmium, placental cadmium, and placental zinc*

SOURCE: Kuhnert et al. 1987a, copyright 1987, Mosby-Year Book

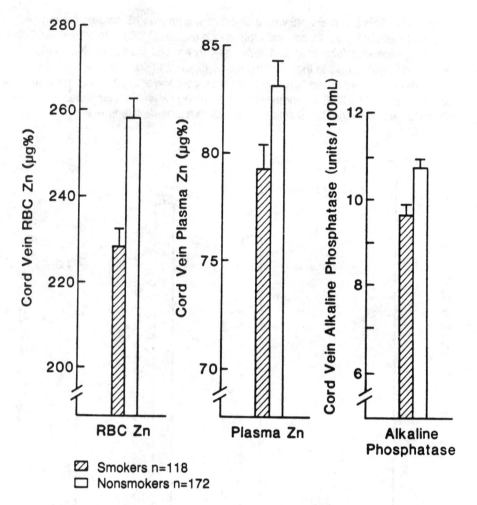

FIGURE 2. *Effect of smoking on the assessment of fetal zinc status ($\overline{X} \pm SEM$)*

SOURCE: Kuhnert et al. 1988a, copyright 1988, Wiley and Sons

The relationship between several indices of maternal and fetal zinc status also was disrupted by smoking. The only significant correlation between maternal and fetal indices of zinc status in nonsmokers was the weak positive relationship between maternal and fetal RBC zinc (r=0.25); but, in smokers, there was a weak negative correlation between maternal plasma zinc and cord vein plasma zinc (r=-0.20). This finding again suggests that maternal zinc stores are not as readily available to the fetus of the mother who smokes during pregnancy.

The clinical outcome measure was birth weight. As expected, there were significant differences in the means between the groups of smokers and nonsmokers (Kuhnert et al. 1987a, 1988a). Infants of smokers were almost 400 g (1 lb) lighter at birth. Cord vein RBC zinc (CVRBCZn) and the ratio of placental zinc to placental cadmium (Zn/Cd ratio) were positively related to birth weight in the smoking group. The correlations were r=0.30, p<0.05, and r=0.31, p<0.05, respectively. In contrast, maternal cadmium and SCN were negatively related to birth weight, but only in smokers (r=-0.35, p<0.05 and r=-0.33, p<0.05, respectively) (Kuhnert et al. 1987a, 1987b, 1988a). Furthermore, there was a significant negative correlation between maternal plasma zinc and birth weight in smokers (r=-0.29). The only significant correlation in the nonsmoking group was a correlation between cord vein RBC zinc and birth weight (r=0.30) (Kuhnert et al. 1988a). These data support the hypothesis that zinc is trapped in the placenta and that maternal zinc is therefore unavailable for fetal growth in smokers.

The relationship between cord vein RBC zinc and birth weight is more obvious when the whole range of birth weights in both groups together is considered (figure 3) (Kuhnert et al. 1988a). However, when this relationship is broken down by smoking status, an alteration in smokers is obvious (figure 4). Infants of nonsmokers always have higher cord vein RBC zinc levels for a given mean birth weight, suggesting that the infants of smokers may be marginally zinc deficient. That this is related to smoking is evident from the close relationship between SCN, the index of smoking exposure, and fetal cord vein RBC zinc (figure 5).

Maternal Age and Smoking

If the hypothesis of an interaction between zinc and cadmium were correct, one would expect that placental zinc would correlate with placental cadmium, especially since the Zn/Cd ratio correlated with birth weight. However, the findings were not so clear cut. A correlation was found but only in multiparous patients (r=0.41, p<0.01) (Kuhnert et al., in press). Why? The answer is related to a similar unanswered question: Why are older pregnant smokers more at risk for impaired fetal growth (Cnattingnius et al. 1985; Wen et al. 1990)?

Multiparous patients have been reported to be possibly deficient in some essential trace elements, such as chromium (Hambidge and Rodgerson 1969), but zinc stores were believed to be replenished after delivery (Rodriguez de la

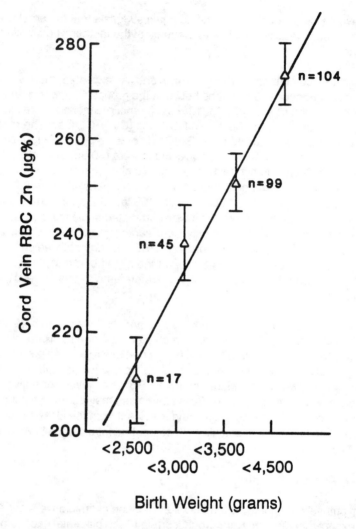

FIGURE 3. *Relationship between cord vein RBC zinc and birth weight*

SOURCE: Kuhnert et al. 1988a, copyright 1988, Wiley and Sons

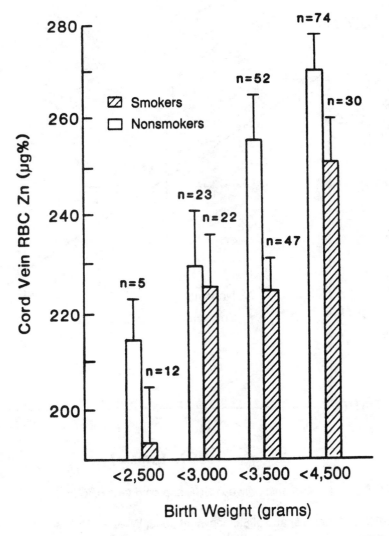

FIGURE 4. *Effect of smoking on the relationship between cord vein RBC zinc and birth weight*

SOURCE: Kuhnert et al. 1988a, copyright 1988, Wiley and Sons

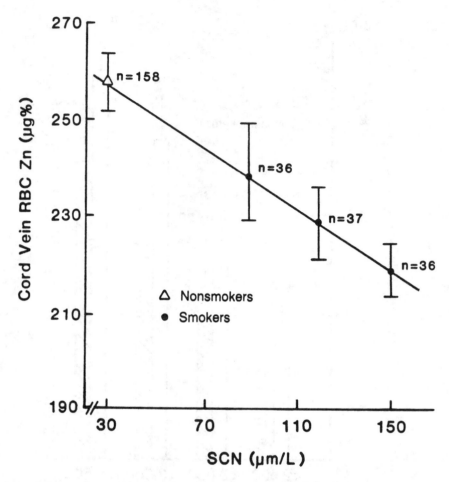

FIGURE 5. *Relationship between SCN and cord vein RBC zinc*

SOURCE: Kuhnert et al. 1988a, copyright 1988, Wiley and Sons

Nuez et al. 1981). However, when the various indices of zinc status were examined in relation to age or parity, placental zinc levels decreased with increased parity (figure 6) (Kuhnert et al. 1988b), and alkaline phosphatase activity also decreased with age ($r=-0.26$, $p<0.05$). These results are consistent with the depletion of body zinc stores with increasing parity and age.

On the other hand, placental cadmium increases with age and parity but only in smokers (figure 7) (Kuhnert et al. 1988b). These results are consistent with the

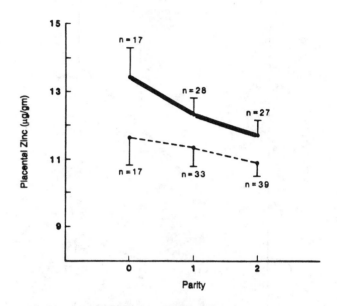

FIGURE 6. *Effect of smoking and parity on placental zinc (mean±SEM)*

NOTE: For clarity, only half of the standard error bars are shown. Black line=smokers; dashed line=nonsmokers.

SOURCE: Kuhnert et al. 1988b, copyright 1988, reprinted with permission from the American College of Obstetricians and Gynecologists

10-year half-life of Cd in the body (Telisman et al. 1986). The results also agree with information from autopsy tissues from smokers (Summer et al. 1986).

The relationship of the Zn/Cd ratio in the placenta with age and smoking status is shown in figure 8. It is obvious that smokers always have lower ratios than nonsmokers and that the ratio decreases with age. The Zn/Cd ratio was previously shown to be related to birth weight (Kuhnert et al. 1987b). Thus, the decrease in zinc with parity or age and the increase with cadmium in smokers (i.e., the Zn/Cd ratio) provides a partial explanation for the finding that older parturients are at higher risk for impaired fetal growth. It also attests to the toxicity of cadmium.

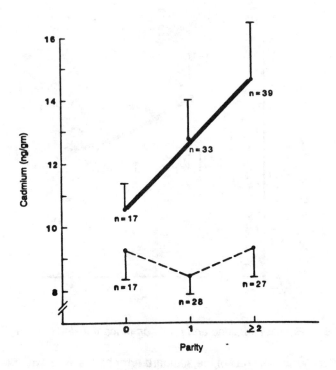

FIGURE 7.   *Effect of smoking and parity on placental cadmium (mean±SEM)*

NOTE: For clarity, only half of the standard error bars are shown. Black line=smokers; dashed line=nonsmokers.

SOURCE: Kuhnert et al. 1988b, copyright 1988, reprinted with permission from the American College of Obstetricians and Gynecologists

CONCLUSION

It is well known that smoking results in smaller infants, but the mechanism has been unclear, particularly in older women. Choosing the appropriate indicator of exposure to cigarette smoke and accurately measuring the appropriate outcome variables in the right samples with sensitive techniques has made it possible to suggest that infants of smokers are smaller because they may be marginally zinc-deficient. It also can be suggested that older parturients are at increased risk of bearing infants with decreased birth weight due to an altered placental zinc-to-cadmium ratio. Similar research strategies and methodologies could be used to measure the effects of exposure to other drugs of abuse during pregnancy.

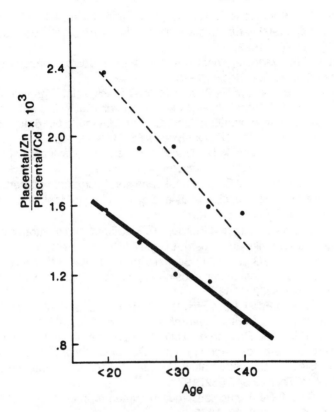

FIGURE 8.   *Effect of smoking and age on the ratio of placental zinc to placental cadmium*

NOTE: Black line=smokers; dashed line=nonsmokers

SOURCE: Kuhnert et al. 1988b, copyright 1988, reprinted with permission from the American College of Obstetricians and Gynecologists

REFERENCES

Abel, E. Smoking during pregnancy: A review of effects on growth and development of offspring. *Hum Biol* 52(4):593-625, 1980.
Apgar, J. Zinc and reproduction. *Annu Rev Nutr* 5:43-68, 1985.
Bailey, D.N. Drug screening in an unconventional matrix: Hair analysis. *JAMA* 262(23):3331-3330, 1989.

Bottoms, S.F.; Kuhnert, B.R.; Kuhnert, P.M.; and Reese, A.L. Maternal passive smoking and fetal serum thiocyanate levels. *Am J Obstet Gynecol* 144(7):787-791, 1982.

Brazelton, T.B. *Neonatal Behavioral Assessment Scale.* London: William Heinemann Medical Books, 1973.

Chasnoff, I.J.; Bussey, M.E.; Savich, R.; and Stack, A.M. Perinatal cerebral infarction and maternal cocaine use. *J Pediatr* 108(3):456-459, 1986.

Cnattingius, S.; Axelsson, O.; Eklund, G.; and Lindmark, G. Smoking, maternal age, and fetal growth. *Obstet Gynecol* 66:449-452, 1985.

Cogbill, E.C., and Hobbs, M.D. Transfer of metallic constituents of cigarettes to the main-stream smoke. *Tobacco* 144(19):24, 1957.

Fried, P.A., and Makin, J.E. Neonatal behavioral correlates of prenatal exposure to marijuana, cigarettes and alcohol in a low risk population. *Neurotoxicol Teratol* 9:1-7, 1987.

Golub, M.S.; Eisele, J.H.; and Kuhnert, B.R. Disposition of intrapartum narcotic analgesics in monkeys. *Anesth Analg* 67:637-643, 1988.

Graham, K.; Koren, G.; Klein, J.; Schneiderman, J.; and Greenwald, M. Determination of gestational cocaine exposure by hair analysis. *JAMA* 262(23):3328-3330, 1989.

Gusella, J.L., and Fried, P.A. Effects of maternal social drinking and smoking on offspring at 13 months. *Neurobehav Toxicol Teratol* 6:13-17, 1984.

Hambidge, K.M., and Rodgerson, D.O. Comparison of hair chromium levels of nulliparous and parous women. *Am J Obstet Gynecol* 103(3):320-321, 1969.

Inaba, T.; Stewart, D.J.; and Kalow, W. Metabolism of cocaine in man. *Clin Pharmacol Ther* 23:547-552, 1978.

Jameson, S. Effects of zinc deficiency in human reproduction. *Acta Med Scand* 593 (Suppl):1-89, 1976.

Jatlow, P.; Barash, P.G.; Van Dyke, C.; Radding, J.; and Byck, R. Cocaine and succinylcholine sensitivity: A new caution. *Anesth Analg* 58:235-238, 1979.

Kloss, M.W.; Rosen, G.M.; and Rauckman, E.J. COMMENTARY, cocaine-mediated hepatotoxicity. A critical review. *Biochem Pharmacol* 33(2):169-173, 1984.

Kuhnert, B.R.; Golden, N.L.; Syracuse, C.D.; Bagby, B.S.; and Kuhnert, P.M. Phencyclidine disposition in mother and neonate. *Res Commun Subst Abuse* 5(3):187-199, 1984.

Kuhnert, B.R., and Kuhnert, P.M. Placental transfer of drugs, alcohol, and components of cigarette smoke and their effects on the human fetus. In: Chiang, C.N., and Lee, C.C., eds. *Prenatal Drug Exposure: Kinetics and Dynamics.* National Institute on Drug Abuse Research Monograph 60. DHHS Pub. No. (ADM)87-1413. Washington, DC: Supt. of Docs., U.S. Govt. Print. Off., 1985. pp. 98-109.

Kuhnert, B.R.; Kuhnert, P.M.; Debanne, S.; and Williams, T.G. The relationship between cadmium, zinc, and birth weight in pregnant women who smoke. *Am J Obstet Gynecol* 157(5):1247-1251, 1987b.

Kuhnert, B.R.; Kuhnert, P.M.; Lazebnik, N.; and Erhard, P. The effect of maternal smoking on the relationship between maternal and fetal zinc status and infant birth weight. *J Am Coll Nutr* 7(4):309-316, 1988a.

Kuhnert, B.R.; Kuhnert, P.M.; Lazebnik, N.; and Erhard, P. The relationship between placental cadmium, zinc, and copper. *J Am Coll Nutr,* in press.

Kuhnert, B.R.; Kuhnert, P.M.; Prochaska, A.L.; and Gross, T.L. Plasma levels of 2-chloroprocaine in obstetric patients and their neonates after epidural anesthesia. *Anesthesiology* 53(1):21-25, 1980.

Kuhnert, B.R.; Kuhnert, P.M.; Tu, A.S.L.; and Lin, D.C.K. Meperidine and normeperidine levels following meperidine administration during labor. II. Fetus and neonate. *Am J Obstet Gynecol* 133(8):909-914, 1979.

Kuhnert, B.R.; Kuhnert, P.M.; and Zarlingo, T.J. Associations between placental cadmium and zinc and age and parity in pregnant women who smoke. *Obstet Gynecol* 71(1):67-70, 1988b.

Kuhnert, B.R.; Linn, P.L.; and Kuhnert, P.M. Obstetric medication and neonatal behavior—Current controversies. *Clin Perinatol* 12(2):423-439, 1985.

Kuhnert, P.M.; Kuhnert, B.R.; Bottoms, S.F.; and Erhard, P. Cadmium levels in maternal blood, fetal cord blood, and placental tissues of pregnant women who smoke. *Am J Obstet Gynecol* 142(8):1021-1025, 1982.

Kuhnert, P.M.; Kuhnert, B.R.; Erhard, P.; Brashear, W.T.; Groh-Wargo, S.L.; and Webster, S. The effect of smoking on placental and fetal zinc status. *Am J Obstet Gynecol* 157(5):1241-1246, 1987a.

Lauwerys, R.; Buchet, J.P.; Roels, H.; and Hubermont, G. Placental transfer of lead, mercury, cadmium, and carbon monoxide in women. I. Comparison of the frequency distributions of the biological indices in maternal and umbilical cord blood. *Environ Res* 15(2):278-289, 1978.

Lazebnik, N.; Kuhnert, B.R.; Kuhnert, P.M.; and Thompson, K.L. Zinc status, pregnancy complications, and labor abnormalities. *Am J Obstet Gynecol* 158(1):161-166, 1988.

Levin, A.A., and Miller, R.K. Fetal toxicity of cadmium in the rat: Maternal vs. fetal injections. *Teratology* 22:1-5, 1980.

Lewis, G.P.; Jusko, W.J.; and Coughlin, L.L. Cadmium accumulation in man: Influence of smoking, occupation, alcoholic habit and disease. *J Chronic Dis* 25(12):717-726, 1972.

Longo, L.D. Environmental pollution and pregnancy: Risks and uncertainties for the fetus and infant. *Am J Obstet Gynecol* 137(2):162-173, 1980.

Miller, J.W., and Anderson, H.H. The effect of N-demethylation on certain pharmacologic actions of morphine, codeine, and meperidine in the mouse. *J Pharmacol Exp Ther* 112:191-196, 1954.

15

Miller, R.K., and Gardner, K.A. Cadmium in the human placenta: Relationship to smoking. (Abstract.) *Teratology* 23:51, 1981.

Murphy, M.G.; Peck, C.C.; Conner, D.P.; Zamani, K.; Merenstein, G.B.; and Rodden, D. Transcutaneous theophylline collection in preterm infants. *Clin Pharmacol Ther* 47(4):427-434, 1990.

Nieburg, P.; Marks, J.S.; McLaren, N.M.; and Remington, P.L. The fetal tobacco syndrome. *JAMA* 253(20):2998-2999, 1985.

O'Brien, J.E.; Abbey, V.; Hinsvark, O.; Perel, J.; and Finster, M. Metabolism and measurement of chloroprocaine, an ester-type local anesthetic. *J Pharm Sci* 68:75-78, 1979.

Ostrea, E.M.; Brady, M.J.; Parks, P.M.; Asensio, D.C.; and Naluz, A. Drug screening of meconium in infants of drug-dependent mothers: An alternative to urine testing. *J Pediatr* 115(3):474-477, 1989.

Parizek, J. The peculiar toxicity of cadmium during pregnancy. An experimental "toxemia of pregnancy" induced by cadmium salts. *J Reprod Fertil* 9:111-112, 1965.

Pettigrew, A.R., and Fell, G.S. Simplified colorimetric determination of thiocyanate in biological fluids and its application to investigation of the toxic amblyopias. *Clin Chem* 18(9):996-1000, 1972.

Pettigrew, A.R.; Logan, R.W.; and Willocks, J. Smoking in pregnancy—Effects on birth weight and on cyanide and thiocyanate levels in mother and baby. *Br J Obstet Gynaecol* 84(1):31-34, 1977.

Public Health Service. Pregnancy and infant health. (Chapter 8.) *Smoking and Health, A Report of the Surgeon General.* U.S. Department of Health, Education, and Welfare. DHEW PHS Pub. No. 79-50066. Washington, DC: Supt. of Docs., U.S. Govt. Print. Off., 1979. pp. 8.1-8.93.

Rodriguez de la Nuez, A.; Sierrasesumaga Ariznavarreta, L.; Dura, T.; Sanchez-Dominguez, T.; Monreal, I.; and Zilla-Elizaga, I. Zinc en el periodo neonatal. Segunda parte. *Acta Paediatr Esp* 39(N449):95-98, 1981.

Roels, H.; Hubermont, G.; Buchet, J.P.; and Lauwerys, R. Placental transfer of lead, mercury, cadmium, and carbon monoxide in women. III. Factors influencing the accumulation of heavy metals in the placenta in the relationship between metal concentration in the placenta and in maternal and cord blood. *Environ Res* 16:236-247, 1978.

Stewart, D.J.; Inaba, T.; Lucassen, M.; and Kalow, W. Cocaine metabolism, cocaine, and norcocaine hydrolysis by liver and serum esterases. *Clin Pharmacol Ther* 25(4):464-468, 1979.

Summer, K.H.; Drasch, G.A.; and Heilmaier, H.E. Metallothionein and cadmium in human kidney cortex: Influence of smoking. *Hum Toxicol* 5:27-33, 1986.

Telisman, S.; Azaric, J.; and Prpic-Majic, D. Cadmium in blood as an indicator of integrated exposure to cadmium in the urban population. *Bull Environ Contam Toxicol* 36:491-495, 1986.

U.S. Department of Health, Education, and Welfare. DHEW PHS Pub. No. 79-50066. Washington, DC: Supt. of Docs., U.S. Govt. Print. Off., 1979. pp. 8.1-8.93.

Van Hattum, B., and de Voogt, P. An analytical procedure for the determination of cadmium in human placentae. *Int J Environ Anal Chem* 10:121-133, 1981.

Webster, W.S. Cadmium-induced fetal growth retardation in the mouse. *Arch Environ Health* 33:36-42, 1978.

Wen, S.W.; Goldenberg, R.L.; Cutter, G.R.; Hoffman, H.J.; Cliver, S.P.; Davis, R.O.; and DuBard, M.B. Smoking, maternal age, fetal growth, and gestational age at delivery. *Am J Obstet Gynecol* 54:53-58, 1990.

ACKNOWLEDGMENT

The research described here was supported in part by U.S. Public Health Service, National Institutes of Health grants 5MO1-RR-00210, NO1-RR-8-2212, RO1-HD-13359, and RO1-DAU-2903.

AUTHOR

Betty R. Kuhnert, Ph.D., M.B.A.
Associate Professor, Reproductive Biology
Perinatal Clinical Research Center
Cleveland Metropolitan General Hospital
Case Western Reserve University
3395 Scranton Road
Cleveland, OH 44109

Present title and address

Associate Director
Clinical Communications
Clinical Research and Development
Wyeth-Ayerst Research
P.O. Box 8299
Philadelphia, PA 19101

Pharmacokinetic Correlates of Fetal Drug Exposure

C. Lindsay DeVane

INTRODUCTION

Essentially all drugs taken by a pregnant woman reach her fetus. The consequences of fetal drug exposure may be inconsequential, disastrous, or, in most cases, unknown. Pharmacokinetic studies attempt to quantitate the degree of fetal drug exposure. Factors that determine the degree of fetal drug exposure include maternal absorption, distribution, and elimination; bidirectional placental transfer; placental disposition; and fetal distribution and elimination. A major determinant of fetal relative to maternal drug exposure is the lipid solubility of the drug or chemical of interest. Most xenobiotics possess sufficient lipid solubility so that the placenta does not limit drug transfer to the fetus, and fetal exposure becomes limited only by blood flow. Ironically, the neonatal period may be associated with slower elimination of fetally received drugs because of the abrupt cessation of maternal contributions to drug elimination at the time of birth.

The accurate measurement of fetal exposure to a maternally administered drug is crucial to establishing the relationship between maternal drug use and fetal effects. This is a major objective of pharmacokinetic studies, along with assessing the risk of potential fetal harm from xenobiotic exposure. In addition, an important aim of pharmacokinetic studies is to predict drug exposure of the fetus given a specific maternal exposure. This is important not only in establishing thresholds that are associated with hazardous effects on the fetus from maternal drug ingestion, but also in developing guidelines to treat the fetus pharmacologically with appropriate maternally administered drug-dosage regimens as medical science extends treatment to the preterm fetus (Cagnazzo and D'Addario 1989).

With the advent of methodology for the specific and sensitive measurement of plasma drug concentrations during the 1960s and 1970s, there has been an increased emphasis on pharmacokinetic studies of placental drug transfer (Nau and Scott 1987). This chapter reviews problems and design considerations

18

inherent in conducting pharmacokinetic studies of fetal drug exposure and potential methods for minimizing these obstacles in the analysis of data. The focus is on neither animal nor human studies exclusively, but on general principles involved in all studies of fetal drug exposure.

PROBLEMS IN PLACENTAL TRANSFER STUDIES

Factors Contributing to Intersubject Variability

The list below enumerates the potential factors contributing to intersubject variation in fetal drug exposure. The degree of variability is often large, both between and within individuals. Although it is generally assumed that variability in pharmacological/toxicological response is the result of pharmacokinetics, it is reasonable to assume that the pharmacodynamic response also may vary. Much less is known about this source of variability in the toxicological response to maternally administered drugs than about the sources of pharmacokinetic variability.

- Maternal factors

    - Overall state of health
    - Cardiovascular, renal, hepatic, and endocrine function
    - Acid-base balance
    - Concentration of plasma drug-binding proteins
    - Presence or absence of plasma drug-binding displacers
    - Gestational age

- Fetal factors

    - Gestational age
    - Serum/plasma drug-binding proteins
    - Hepatic and renal development

- Other factors

    - Input rate of drug and size of dose
    - Functional state of placenta

The dynamic physiological status of the mother and fetus during pregnancy results in changes in numerous plasma constituents, including the major drug-binding proteins (Hytten and Chamberlain 1980). These changes directly affect fetal drug exposure. Both albumin and alpha-1-acid glycoprotein concentrations become reduced during the course of pregnancy. This effect implies that highly protein-bound acidic and basic drugs may have an increased free fraction or concentration. The mean change of albumin from the third month of gestation to the ninth in 27 women was from 44±5 g/L to 32±5 g/L (Haram et al. 1983). Alpha-1-acid glycoprotein changed from 0.72±0.21 to 0.50±24 g/L during pregnancy. The widely held assumption that only unbound drug is able to pass the placenta predicts that a diffusion equilibrium can be expected to exist at steady-state between free drug concentration in maternal plasma and fetal plasma. Reduced maternal binding as a result of either the presence of binding displacers or reduced binding proteins would allow more free drug to pass the placenta. In addition, if drug binding is greater on the fetal side when equilibrium of free drug across the placenta is established, then total drug concentration would be greater in the fetal plasma, even though the free concentration should be equivalent to that of the maternal side. This reasoning is consistent with several observations of high-plasma diazepam and N-desmethyldiazepam concentration in maternal and fetal plasma (Gamble et al. 1977; Hamar and Levy 1980; Kuhnz and Nau 1983).

Collection of Data at Appropriate Intervals

Human studies of fetal drug exposure are limited by ethical and practical considerations. Generally, the data of many pharmacokinetic studies in humans has provided descriptive information involving determinations of maternal and fetal drug exposure at only a single time point. Ethical considerations prohibit sampling from humans during pregnancy, except in a few circumstances where the benefits of drug exposure are judged to outweigh the risks of maternal drug administration. Often, pharmacokinetic studies consist of data from a limited number of sample times for the determination of when and how much of the drug is transferred to the fetus. Several researchers have emphasized the inability to draw valid conclusions about the extent of fetal drug exposure when samples are limited. For this reason, *in vivo* animal models have become a major research tool. Depending on whether the fetal drug plasma concentration is below, equal to, or greater than maternal plasma drug concentration at the time of sampling, the conclusion reached that placental transfer is either minimal or extensive could be very misleading. As illustrated in figure 1, the concentration of cocaine in the fetal lamb exceeds that in the pregnant ewe for approximately 4 minutes following an intravenous (IV) maternal cocaine dose (DeVane et al., in press). A single sample taken before or after 4 minutes would suggest opposite conclusions about the degree of placental passage of cocaine. Therefore, the area under the concentration-time curve (AUC) has been used as a better index for drug exposure after a single dose. It is important in the assessment of placental transfer to collect an adequate number of samples to better define the extent of drug exposure. Obviously, the ability to estimate pharmacokinetic parameters improves as the number of data points increases.

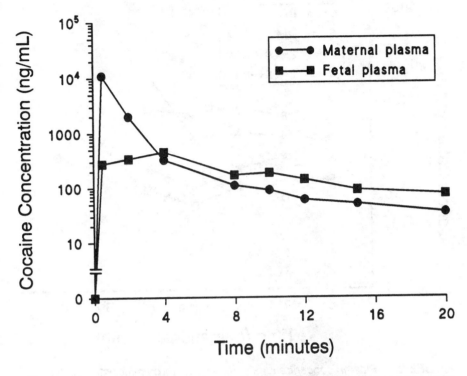

FIGURE 1. *Plasma concentration vs. time course of cocaine in a ewe and its fetus following a 2 mg/kg IV bolus dose to the ewe*

SOURCE: Data taken from DeVane et al., in press

In many studies, the time of sampling may occur randomly, either by necessity or by temporary convenience. The number of observations may vary widely between individuals. Also, depending on the drug or chemical of interest, the emphasis may shift from single-dose situations to steady-state conditions. In figure 2, the plasma concentrations of imipramine (IMI) (50 mg/day oral administration) and its three major pharmacologically active metabolites in a pregnant woman with panic disorder can be seen to remain relatively stable during the final 3 months of gestation (Ware and DeVane 1990). Cord plasma at delivery contained all four drugs, but in lower concentration than in maternal plasma. These data also suggest a postdelivery change in desipramine (DMI) disposition, with increased concentration in both maternal plasma and breast milk after delivery. Apart from documenting fetal drug exposure, only limited

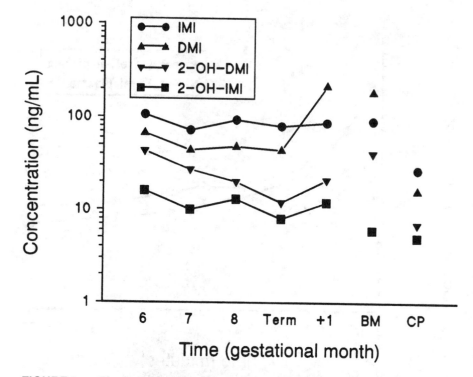

FIGURE 2. *Plasma concentrations of IMI and its three major metabolites (DMI; 2-hydroxy-imipramine, 2-OH-IMI; 2-hydroxy-desipramine, 2-OH-DMI) following 50 mg/day oral administration in a pregnant woman. Concentrations are also shown for breast milk (BM) at the time of delivery and from a sample of plasma obtained from the infant's cord blood (CP).*

information from data of this type can be extrapolated to other pregnant women receiving IMI therapy.

INTERSPECIES DIFFERENCES IN DRUG DISPOSITION

Active Metabolites

The assessment of fetal drug exposure is complicated by recognition that many, if not most, drugs produce biologically active metabolites. Thus, measurement of fetal drug exposure should include the contribution of pharmacologically active metabolites. Figure 3 shows the maternal plasma and whole fetal tissue concentrations of DMI, the demethylated metabolite of the tricyclic antidepressant IMI, following an intraperitoneal (IP) injection of 30 mg/kg IMI to pregnant rats (DeVane and Simpkins 1985). Following an oral dose, DMI is extensively formed in humans by presystemic elimination of IMI in the liver. Steady-state DMI concentrations usually exceed those of IMI during chronic therapy. However, as shown in figure 2, there are exceptions to this generalization, as plasma DMI was lower than was IMI during pregnancy. The rapid appearance of DMI in the maternal rat plasma (figure 3) and parallel decline in the fetus suggest both maternal formation of DMI and elimination with equilibrium of drug distribution in the fetus. Even when human data are limited, if combined with animal data, insight may be gained into fetal drug exposure during gestation.

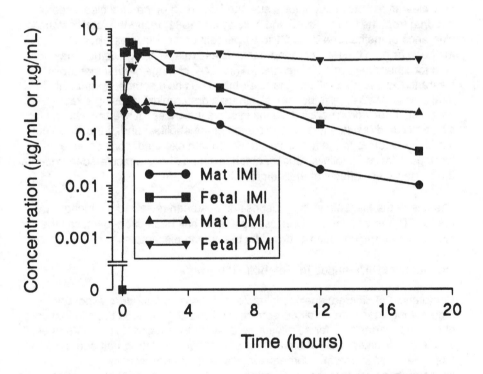

FIGURE 3. *IMI and DMI concentrations in pregnant rat plasma (Mat. IMI; Mat. DMI) and whole fetal tissues following IP administration of 30 mg/ kg IMI*

The issue of active metabolites is further complicated by the fact that maternally administered drugs may be biotransformed in several major sites, including the maternal liver, placenta, and fetal liver. Renal clearance by the fetus is also possible. By directly infusing cocaine into the fetal lamb, DeVane and colleagues (in press) were able to measure ecgonine methylester and benzoylecgonine, two major metabolites of cocaine, in the fetal circulation. Their concentrations were higher than in the maternal circulation, implying cocaine metabolism by the fetal liver.

More rigorous experiments are needed to define the precise contribution of fetal metabolism to the overall fetal disposition of a maternally administered drug. Although contribution of fetal drug clearance to the overall total body clearance (including both fetal and maternal clearance) may be negligible (Levy 1981), fetal clearance may account for a substantial portion of the total clearance of the drug from the fetus. Szeto and colleagues (1982) found the fetal metabolic clearance of methadone to be 21 to 51 percent of the total clearance of methadone from the fetal compartment. These relatively high values may not hold for other drugs or other species. This 2.4-fold range of fetal metabolic clearance values also reflects the role of the fetus as a source of variability in fetal drug exposure. A fetus may eliminate a drug rapidly, causing a rapid decrease in fetal drug concentrations in some instances. Nevertheless, this situation could result in fetal accumulation of metabolites; and, if these are not rapidly transferred to the maternal circulation and excreted, considerable teratogenicity could follow. Such a mechanism has been speculated to underlie the teratogenetic effects of thalidomide (Juchau 1989).

The role of the placenta in drug disposition has been reviewed by Juchau (1976). The in vitro-isolated perfused placenta has been used to assess the extent of biotransformation of drugs by the human placenta.

Quantitative Differences in Metabolic Pathways

Comparison of different species is useful in assessing fetal drug exposure. Figure 4 includes data obtained from several investigations on the elimination of cocaine, normalized for administered dose, in the pregnant rat (DeVane et al. 1989), dog (Kanter et al., submitted for publication), and pregnant sheep (DeVane et al., in press). Comparison also is made with cocaine concentrations calculated from pharmacokinetic parameters in humans, as reported by Chow and coworkers (1985). Some differences can be appreciated in the rate of cocaine's elimination from plasma among these species. In pregnant sheep, cocaine had a mean half-life of 5.0 minutes in the ewe and 4.3 minutes in the fetal lamb. Khan and coworkers (1987) attributed the rapid clearance of cocaine in the sheep (mean half-life of 12.9 minutes) to pulmonary

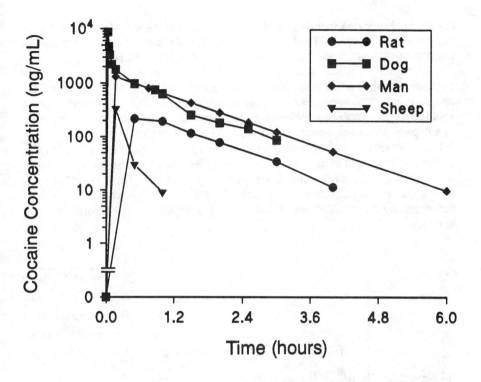

FIGURE 4. *Cocaine disposition in different species. Plasma concentrations are shown for the pregnant rat (DeVane et al. 1989), dog (Kanter et al., submitted for publication), pregnant ewe (DeVane et al., in press), and human (Chow et al. 1985). The curve for humans is calculated from mean pharmacokinetic parameters. Concentrations have been normalized to a 3 mg/kg dose. Route of administration was IP in rat and IV in all other species.*

clearance not occurring in other species (half-life in humans of 48 minutes). Although the ovine maternal-fetal model has been useful for studying several drugs (Szeto 1982), the clearance pathways of cocaine in this species may make it less suitable for studying fetal drug exposure of this particular drug of abuse.

DeVane and colleagues (1989) found in rodent studies that the AUC for norcocaine was only 3.1 percent of that of cocaine in maternal plasma; however, norcocaine was present in substantial concentration in whole fetal tissues compared with maternal plasma. The tissue concentration vs. time curves of norcocaine in the fetal rat compared with those in maternal plasma can be seen in figure 5. Thus, the near absence of a metabolite in the maternal plasma cannot be taken as evidence of a lack of fetal metabolite exposure.

In contrast to the rodent data, DeVane and coworkers (in press) have been unable to quantitate norcocaine in pregnant sheep using a high performance liquid chromatography assay with a sensitivity of 1 ng/mL and cocaine doses up to 4 mg/kg. However, norcocaine has been found in the urine of cocaine-exposed infants (Chasnoff and Lewis 1988), suggesting that this metabolite is potentially important in humans. Norcocaine has been found to have some of the pharmacologic activity of cocaine (Hawks et al. 1975). Thus, interspecies differences in drug disposition may be important considerations, both quantitatively and qualitatively, in assessing the consequences of fetal drug exposure.

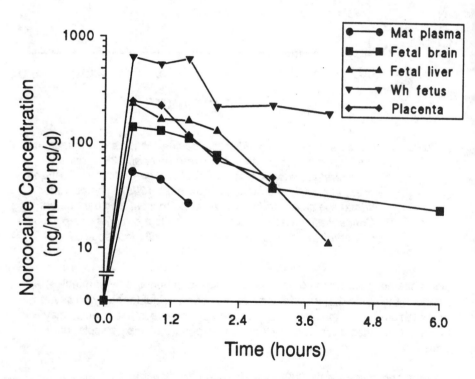

FIGURE 5.   *Time course of norcocaine concentrations in maternal plasma and fetal tissues of the fetal rat following a 30 mg/kg IP dose*

EXPERIMENTAL REQUIREMENTS

Basic Considerations In Study Design

The fetal-drug-exposure problem is complicated by an uncertain knowledge of how to best express fetal exposure and to compare exposure between drugs and species. The area under the plasma or tissue concentration vs. time curve is widely believed to be an accurate representation of fetal exposure. DeVane and colleagues (1991) found that the same mg/kg dose of phenobarbital and phenytoin administered to rats resulted in an identical ratio of AUC in fetus to AUC in maternal plasma (AUC-F/AUC-M) of 0.77. This finding suggests that the rat fetus received an identical proportional exposure relative to the maternal plasma concentration of either of these drugs. However, phenytoin has more teratogenic potential than does phenobarbital when used as an anticonvulsant by pregnant women. Thus, in terms of pharmacodynamic and toxicologic implications, the free drug concentration should be considered rather than the total drug in plasma (plasma protein bound plus free).

In the commonly used two-compartment pharmacokinetic model, where the fetus has minimal ability to eliminate drugs, at steady-state the fetal plasma concentration should be equal to the maternal plasma concentration when referenced to free, nonprotein bound drug. Such models, discussed in more detail below, also consider the maternal and fetal compartments to exist with homogeneous drug distribution. However, this is a simplification, as neither the fetus nor the mother behave as a homogeneous compartment. Table 1 shows AUC values found for various fetal tissues for different drugs administered to pregnant Sprague-Dawley rats at a dose of 30 mg/kg. The fetal drug distribution is both uneven and inconsistent between drugs. It therefore appears that maternal and fetal tissue concentrations are dictated by binding to tissue components. As suggested by differences in teratogenic potential among drugs, most of this binding is probably nonspecific and pharmacodynamically irrelevant. Nevertheless, the degree of fetal drug exposure can be predicted by physiochemical properties of drugs. In figure 6, the relationship between the AUC of the whole rat fetus to the AUC in the dam strongly correlates with the logarithm of the octanol-water partition coefficient of the administered drug (Leo et al. 1971). Several researchers have found positive relationships between lipid solubility and biological activity (Kubinyi 1979; Manners et al. 1988).

As mentioned above, phenytoin and phenobarbital had the same relative fetal exposure referenced to total maternal plasma concentration, although the partition coefficient for phenytoin is greater. By taking literature values for free drug concentration, the inset in figure 6 shows a much stronger relationship

TABLE 1.   *Fetal rat tissue exposure to various drugs**

Drug Administered	Tissue			
	Whole Fetus	Placenta	Fetal Liver	Fetal Brain
IMI	14.9 (7.5)	53.3 (26.9)	32.9 (16.6)	33.5 (16.9)
Phenytoin	57.7 (0.8)	74.6 (1.0)	90.2 (1.2)	67.6 (0.9)
Phenobarbital	586.0 (0.8)	659.0 (0.9)	495.0 (0.6)	390.0 (0.5)
Morphine	12.9 (2.5)	141.0 (27.0)	135.0 (26.0)	23.8 (4.5)
Cocaine	130.6 (3.3)	98.3 (25.1)	81.3 (20.7)	5.6 (1.4)

*Values are AUC in mcg/mL hr following a dose of 30 mg/kg IP. AUC ratios to maternal plasma appear in parentheses.

between fetal exposure when referenced to free plasma concentration in the dam. In many cases, fetal drug exposure referenced to free drug concentration will be unity, and differences between total (free and bound) drug in AUC ratios may have little significance (Levy 1981). If this reasoning is correct, then future studies should consider free drug concentration in maternal plasma as a primary determinant of fetal drug exposure.

Idealized Data for Parameter Estimation

Ideally, the extent of fetal drug exposure given a maternal drug dose should be known. Assessment of differences between single exposure and steady-state conditions would be desirable, as would some evaluation of linearity. The relative contribution of fetal clearance to maternal clearance should be determined, as well as the separate contributions of fetal liver, renal, and placenta processes. In addition, it would be desirable to know how perturbations in the mother affect fetal drug exposure. These would include changes in maternal serum constituents and other physiological changes that normally occur during pregnancy (Hytten and Chamberlain 1980; Notarianni 1990) that affect the relative risk of fetal exposure at different times of pregnancy.

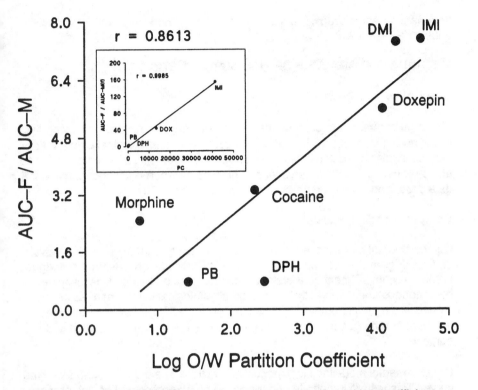

FIGURE 6. *The relationship between log octanol/water partition coefficient (PC) and ratio of area under the fetal tissue concentration vs. time curve (AUC-F) to maternal plasma concentration vs. time curve (AUC-M) in rats after IP administration of several drugs. The inset shows the relationship between PC and the AUC ratio for calculated free concentration in maternal plasma (AUC-F/AUC-M[f]).*

Ultimately, fetal drug exposure must be related to pharmacological effects. In doing so, effect-concentration pairs of data should be collected under circumstances in which concentrations are both rising and falling in the maternal organism, at steady-state. Because of the variability in fetal drug exposure, sample size in animal studies needs to be adequate to define the extent of variability. It should be ensured that sampling does not alter either the pharmacokinetics or the pharmacodynamics of the drug. All active metabolites should be measured. When appropriate in pharmacodynamic studies, the effect of placebo should be determined. Route of administration can be important for some drugs. Finally, factors contributing to intersubject variability should be assessed.

METHODS FOR ANALYSIS OF PHARMACOKINETIC DATA

Descriptive Approach

The most common approach to analysis of pharmacokinetic data is descriptive, including a history of maternal drug exposure, any pharmacokinetic data that may be available (such as plasma or urine drug/metabolite concentrations), and any pharmacodynamic observations. This type of report is illustrated by the IMI data described above (figure 2) (Ware and DeVane 1990).

Compartmental Models

Compartmental modeling is the classical approach to pharmacokinetic analysis of data. Figure 7 is a compartmental model proposed by Krauer and colleagues (1980). A compartment consists of tissues that can be treated kinetically as a homogenous unit. Generally, there is no physiological counterpart, as all models are an approximation of biological systems. However, a model need not be any more complex than required to serve the scientist's function and purpose.

Compartmental modeling fits exponential functions to a drug concentration time curve. Tissues are lumped together and the body represented as one or more large compartments, generally termed a central, or shallow, compartment and peripheral, or deep, compartment(s). Following drug administration, rapid equilibrium is reached between the tissues of central compartment and the blood, while slow equilibrium is reached between tissues of the peripheral compartment(s) and the blood.

The simplest maternal-fetal compartmental model would consist of a maternal and a fetal unit. Consistent with observations that the human fetal liver can metabolize various xenobiotics (Pacifici et al. 1987), elimination could occur from both the maternal and the fetal compartments. An intercompartmental clearance or rate constant describes the transfer of drug across the placenta. Maternal and fetal plasma concentration versus time data are necessary to derive estimates of all parameters of this model. Following separate constant rate IV infusions to the mother and fetus, both the maternal and the fetal steady-state free drug concentrations are measured. Experimental data for several narcotic agonists have been obtained using this approach by Szeto and colleagues (1982).

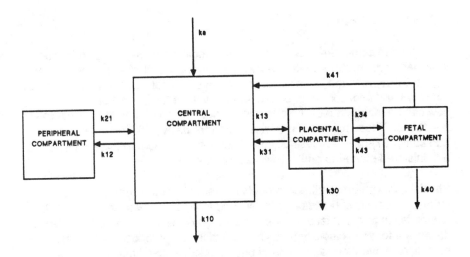

FIGURE 7. *Maternal-fetal compartmental pharmacokinetic model consisting of a maternal central and peripheral compartment and a placental and fetal compartment. Rate constants (kii) describe transfer between compartments or absorption into the central compartment (ka).*

Several disadvantages of compartment modeling are apparent. This empirical approach does not describe a physiological system with large tissue-to-tissue concentration differences as shown in table 1. Such models may be inadequate if the drug has a specific target organ. Compartmental models do not permit extrapolation from species to species. The volume of distribution and transfer rate constants are based on mathematics rather than on actual anatomy and physiology.

The assumption of compartmental models of kinetic homogeneity does not mean that drug concentrations in all tissues of compartments are equal but, instead, that any change in plasma concentration reflects a change in the central compartment. Peripheral compartments are hybrids of several physiological units. Tissues may be in the peripheral or central compartment, depending on distribution properties of the drug. Drug elimination is assumed to be first order, as are drug transfers between compartments. Whether a distribution phase is apparent after rapid maternal drug administration depends on the frequency with which blood samples are taken. The two or three compartment models often fail, especially when several species are scaled, to account for metabolites, or the administration of other drugs.

Physiological Models

In contrast to compartmental models, physiological models incorporate blood flow, perfusion, organ size, and anatomical arrangement of all relevant organs. Figure 8 illustrates the basic concept of a physiological model incorporating a placental and fetal compartment. Literature values for organ size and blood flow can be incorporated with observed concentration data to fit the data to equations. These models (Gabrielsson and Paazlow 1983; Gabrielsson and Larsson 1987) have successfully predicted fetal exposure to maternally administered morphine and salicylic acid in the rat.

Physiological pharmacokinetic models are far better than compartmental models to identify sources of variability and to predict how such variability is expressed in terms of fetal drug exposure. Obviously, the amount of data necessary for physiological modeling far exceeds that for compartmental modeling. Nevertheless, the use of physiologically based models represents progress in developing insight into the sources of variability that affect placental drug transfer and fetal drug exposure. However, once sources of variablity are identified, the problem remains of assessing their significance in regard to overall fetal health.

Combined Pharmacokinetic-Pharmacodynamic Models

The lack of pharmacologic response data in most pharmacokinetic studies of placental transfer greatly limits the ability to utilize pharmacokinetic data. The combined kinetic-effect models (Holford and Sheiner 1982; Schwartz et al. 1989) offer very attractive approaches for relating pharmacokinetic data on fetal drug exposure with pharmacodynamic events. Theoretically, this approach is capable of relating a concentration at an "effect" site with pharmacological effects, but it has not yet been applied to studies of fetal drug exposure.

METHODS FOR MINIMIZING PROBLEMS IN PHARMACOKINETIC STUDIES

Obtaining Sufficient Data

Pharmacokinetic studies must be designed to obtain sufficient data to characterize the maternal and fetal drug exposure. When only a few data points are obtained, the estimates of kinetic parameters (half-life, clearance, AUC) will be unreliable.

Obtaining serial blood or plasma samples is difficult or impossible in small laboratory animals. For this reason, much information on placental transfer has been obtained using the pregnant ewe (Szeto 1982). This preparation allows

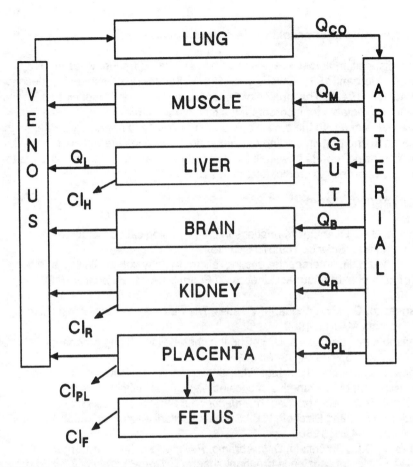

FIGURE 8. *Maternal-fetal physiological pharmacokinetic model. Compartments are connected by blood flows (Q) between the venous and arterial blood, with elimination by clearance (Cl) from various organs and tissues.*

cannulation of fetal blood vessels in order to serially collect simultaneous blood samples from the fetus and the mother during transfer experiments. In addition, the fetal lamb is not sacrificed and can be used in repeated experiments, providing the additional advantage of being able to use a fetus as its own control. This is a suitable model for application of the combined pharmacokinetic-pharmacodynamic approach discussed above.

Extrapolating Pharmacokinetics Across Species

Drug disposition across species has been estimated frequently using body weight (Mordenti 1986; Owens et al. 1987) after the relationships first described by Adolph (1949). The studies of Boxenbaum (1982) and Dedrick and Bischoff (1980) are notable for incorporating a time variable, maximum lifespan potential, along with the physiological pharmacokinetic approach in relating the clearance and protein binding of several drugs among different species. With the increasing reports of values for fetal drug clearance, it may be possible to use this approach to predict fetal drug exposure.

REFERENCES

Adolph, E.F. Quantitative relations in the physiological constitutions of mammals. *Science* 109:579-585, 1949.

Boxenbaum, H. Interspecies scaling, allometry, physiological time, and the ground plan of pharmacokinetics. *J Pharmacokinet Biopharm* 10:201-227, 1982.

Cagnazzo, G., and D'Addario, V., eds. *The Fetus as Patient*. Amsterdam: Excerpta Medica, 1989.

Chasnoff, I.J., and Lewis, D.E. Cocaine metabolism during pregnancy. *Pediatr Res* 23[Suppl]:257A, 1988.

Chow, M.J.; Ambre, J.J.; Ruo, T.I.; Atkinson, A.A., Jr.; Bowsher, D.J.; and Fischman, M.W. Kinetics of cocaine distribution, elimination, and chronotropic effects. *Clin Pharmacol Ther* 38:318-324, 1985.

Dedrick, R.L., and Bischoff, K.B. Species similarities in pharmacokinetics. *Fed Proc* 39:54-59, 1980.

DeVane, C.L.; Burchfield, D.J.; Abrams, R.M.; Miller, R.L.; and Braun S.B. Disposition of cocaine in pregnant sheep. I. *Dev Pharmacol Ther*, in press.

DeVane, C.L., and Simpkins, J.W. Pharmacokinetics of imipramine and its major metabolites in pregnant rats and their fetuses following a single dose. *Drug Metab Dispos* 13:438-442, 1985.

DeVane, C.L.; Simpkins, J.W.; Miller, R.L.; and Braun, S.B. Tissue distribution of cocaine in the pregnant rat. *Life Sci* 45:1271-1276, 1989.

DeVane, C.L.; Simpkins, J.W.; and Stout, S.A. Distribution of phenobarbital and phenytoin in pregnant rats and their fetuses. *Epilepsia* 32:250-256, 1991.

Gabrielsson, J.L., and Larsson, K.S. The use of physiological pharmacokinetic models in studies on the disposition of salicyclic acid in pregnancy. In: Hau, H., and Scott, W.J., Jr., eds. *Pharmacokinetics in Teratogenesis*. Vol. II. Boca Raton, FL: CRC Press, 1987. pp. 13-26.

Gabrielsson, J.L., and Paalzow, L.K. A physiological pharmacokinetic model for morphine disposition in the pregnant rat. *J Pharmacokinet Biopharm* 11:147-163, 1983.

Gamble, J.A.S.; Moore, J.; Lamki, H.; and Howard, P.J. A study of plasma diazepam levels in mother and infant. *Br J Obstet Gynaecol* 84:588-591, 1977.

Hamar, C., and Levy, G. Serum protein binding of drugs and bilirubin in newborn infants and their mothers. *Clin Pharmacol Ther* 28:58-63, 1980.

Haram, K.; Augensen, K.; and Elsayed, S. Serum protein pattern in normal pregnancy with special reference to acute-phase reactants. *Br J Obstet Gynaecol* 90:139-145, 1983.

Hawks, R.L.; Kopin, I.J.; Colburn, R.W.; and Thoa, N.B. Norcocaine: A pharmacologically active metabolite of cocaine found in brain. *Life Sci* 15:2189-2195, 1975.

Holford, N.H.G., and Sheiner, L.B. Kinetics of pharmacologic response. *Pharmacol Ther* 16:143-166, 1982.

Hytten, F.E., and Chamberlain, G. *Clinical Physiology in Obstetrics*. Oxford, England: Blackwell Scientific, 1980.

Juchau, M.R. Drug biotransformation reaction in the placenta. In: Mirkin, B.L., ed. *Perinatal Pharmacology and Therapeutics*. New York: Raven Press, 1976. pp. 29-39.

Juchau, M.R. Bioactivation in chemical teratogenesis. *Annu Rev Pharmacol Toxicol* 29:165-187, 1989.

Kanter, R.J.; DeVane, C.L.; and Epstein, M.L. Electrocardiographic and electrophysiologic effects of very high-dose cocaine on dogs. *Am J Cardiol*, submitted for publication.

Khan, M.; Gupta, P.K.; Cristie, R.; Nangia, A.; Winter, H.; Lam, F.C.; and Perrier, D.G. Determination of pharmacokinetics of cocaine in sheep by liquid chromatography. *J Pharm Sci* 76:39-43, 1987.

Krauer, B.K.; Krauer, F.; and Hytten, F.E. Drug disposition and pharmacokinetics in the maternal-placental-fetal unit. *Pharmacol Ther* 10:301-328, 1980.

Kubinyi, H. Lipophilicity and biological activity. *Arzneimittelforschung* 29:1067-1080, 1979.

Kuhnz, W., and Nau, H. Differences in in vitro binding of diazepam and N-desmethyldiazepam to maternal and fetal plasma proteins at birth: Relation to free fatty acid concentration and other parameters. *Clin Pharmacol Ther* 34:220-226, 1983.

Leo, A.; Hansch, C.; and Elkins, D. Partition coefficients and their uses. *Chem Rev* 71:525-616, 1971.

Levy, G. Pharmacokinetics of fetal and neonatal exposure to drugs. *Obstet Gynecol* 58(5, Suppl):9S-16S, 1981.

Manners, C.N.; Payling, D.W.; and Smith, D.A. Distribution coefficient, a convenient term for the relation of predictable physico-chemical properties to metabolic processes. *Xenobiotica* 18:331-350, 1988.

Mordenti, J. Man versus beast: Pharmacokinetic scaling in mammals. *J Pharm Sci* 75:1028-1040, 1986.

Nau, H., and Scott, W.J., Jr., eds. *Pharmacokinetics in Teratogenesis.* Vols. I and II. Boca Raton, FL: CRC Press, 1987.

Notarianni, L.J. Plasma protein binding of drugs in pregnancy and neonates. *Clin Pharmacokinet* 18:20-36, 1990.

Owens, S.M.; Hardwick, W.M.; and Blackall, D. Phencyclidine pharmacokinetic scaling among species. *J Pharmacol Exp Ther* 242:96-101, 1987.

Pacifici, G.M.; Peng, D.; Bistoletti, P.; Mellgren, A.; and Rane, A. Morphine glucuronidation in human fetal liver cultures and isolated hepatocytes. In: Nau, H., and Scott, W.J., Jr., eds. *Pharmacokinetics in Teratogenesis.* Vol. II. Boca Raton, FL: CRC Press, 1987. pp. 219-224.

Schwartz, J.B.; Verotta, D.; and Sheiner, L.B. Pharmacodynamic modeling of verapamil effects under steady-state and nonsteady-state conditions. *J Pharmacol Exp Ther* 251:1032-1038, 1989.

Szeto, H.H. Pharmacokinetics in the ovine maternal-fetal unit. *Annu Rev Pharmacol Toxicol* 22:221-243, 1982.

Szeto, H.H.; Umans, J.G.; and Rubinow, S.I. The contribution of transplacental clearances and fetal clearance to drug disposition in the ovine maternal-fetal unit. *Drug Metab Dispos* 10:382-386, 1982.

Ware, M.R., and DeVane, C.L. Treatment of panic disorder during pregnancy with imipramine. *J Clin Psychiatry* 51:482-484, 1990.

ACKNOWLEDGMENT

Preparation of this chapter was supported in part by National Institute of Child Health and Human Development grant HD-14075 and National Institute on Drug Abuse grant DA-05170.

AUTHOR

C. Lindsay DeVane, Pharm.D.
Professor of Pharmacy and Psychiatry
Department of Pharmacy Practice
University of Florida
Box J-486
Gainesville, FL 32610

36

allude

Discussion: Methodological Issues in Controlled Studies on Effects of Prenatal Drugs

Hazel H. Szeto

INTRODUCTION

The primary concern in the use of both licit and illicit drugs during pregnancy is the adverse effects that these drugs may produce on the developing fetus. Over the past 10 years, there has been a dramatic increase in clinical and basic research on the impact of substance abuse on the fetus. These investigations have progressed from simply determining if a certain drug "crosses the placental barrier" and the adverse effects seen in the neonate to highly sophisticated studies determining the mechanisms of drug action on the fetus. Kuhnert and DeVane (this volume) allude to the fact that the placenta does not serve as a barrier to exclude drugs from the fetus. This is particularly true for drugs that are readily distributed to the central nervous system, as are the drugs of abuse.

Kuhnert (this volume) proposes to correlate the extent of fetal drug exposure to neonatal outcome measures. However, the extent of fetal drug exposure in the human can be rather difficult to ascertain. Some of the difficulties have been outlined by Kuhnert. Although the presence of drug or metabolites in cord blood, amniotic fluid, or neonatal urine may indicate that the fetus has been exposed to the drug at some time prior to sample collection, it does not reveal the frequency of drug use nor the overall extent of fetal drug exposure throughout gestation. The quantitation of drug or metabolites in meconium or neonatal hair would certainly help in determining drug exposure for drugs that are eliminated rapidly, but it does not provide any quantitative measure of the extent of fetal drug exposure throughout gestation. Thus, even given adequate analytical methods, the interpretation of such drug levels is still very limited.

The choice of compound to quantitate is also a problem, particularly for exposure to either nicotine or marijuana smoke. Both these substances contain a large number of ingredients besides the main pharmacological ingredient.

More than 60 cannabinoids have been identified in marijuana smoke, and it is not known which of these is(are) the pharmacologically relevant compound(s). To date, there has not been a good example of a correlation between the extent of fetal drug exposure and neonatal outcome in the clinical setting as most of the reports have attempted to correlate only the extent of reported drug use and neonatal outcome.

DeVane (this volume) also addresses the need to relate fetal drug exposure to pharmacodynamic effects. Furthermore, it was suggested that an understanding of the pharmacokinetics of a drug in the maternal-fetal unit may help in the interpretation of single time-point drug levels in the clinical setting. It is quite obvious that detailed pharmacokinetics studies can only be obtained using suitable animal models. DeVane points out the problems in interpreting data from different species. Despite these difficulties, pharmacokinetics studies in animal models have contributed significantly to the understanding of maternal-fetal drug disposition. Some of the more important findings are highlighted in this chapter.

MECHANISMS OF DRUG ACTION ON THE FETUS

First, the potential mechanisms by which maternal drug use may affect fetal development must be addressed. Kuhnert and DeVane already have pointed out that a drug may exert direct action on the fetus via placental drug transfer. In this case, it can be assumed that the magnitude of adverse effect should be a function of the extent of fetal drug exposure. However, a drug also may adversely affect the fetus by indirect action on placental function, including possible effects on placental perfusion and the diffusion of oxygen and nutrients across the placental membranes (e.g., the well-known effects of cocaine on maternal hemodynamics and uterine vascular resistance). Intravenous administration of cocaine to maternal sheep produced dose-dependent increases in maternal blood pressure and heart rate, decreases in uterine blood flow, and fetal hypoxemia, tachycardia, and hypertension (Woods et al. 1987). While the fetal tachycardia and hypertension are largely due to placental transfer of cocaine and a direct action on the fetus, the hypoxemia was secondary to the reduction in uterine blood flow. This was confirmed by direct administration of cocaine to the fetus. Cocaine is thought to act on uterine blood vessels by blocking reuptake of norepinephrine, thereby potentiating the vasoconstrictive actions of norepinephrine. In this case, the magnitude of fetal hypoxemia would be more a function of maternal drug levels than of fetal drug levels; the reduction in uterine perfusion may reduce the distribution of cocaine to the fetus, as its distribution is most likely flow-dependent.

38

A similar situation has been demonstrated in studies of the effects of tobacco and marijuana smoking. Intravenous administration of nicotine to maternal sheep increased fetal blood pressure, decreased fetal heart rate and fetal pO_2, and suppressed fetal breathing movements (Manning et al. 1978). On the other hand, direct administration of nicotine to the fetus induced a burst of fetal breathing movements, no change in blood gases, and an increase in blood pressure and heart rate. These findings suggest that the suppression of fetal breathing movements following maternally administered nicotine was most likely due to fetal hypoxemia as a result of uterine vasoconstriction.

Introduction of marijuana smoke to pregnant sheep caused significant reductions in maternal respiratory rate and arterial pO_2 (Clapp et al. 1986). This maternal hypoxemia resulted in a significant reduction in fetal oxygen tension, which remained depressed even after maternal pO_2 values had returned to control levels. The prolonged reduction in fetal pO_2 suggests that either placental gas transfer or fetal oxygen consumption also was affected by marijuana smoke inhalation. Therefore, although the extent of fetal drug exposure is important, fetal development also may be affected indirectly by the drug's action on placental function.

NEW FINDINGS ON MATERNAL-FETAL PHARMACOKINETICS OF DRUG ABUSE

Some important findings have come from maternal-fetal pharmacokinetics studies. First, it has been clearly demonstrated that all drugs studied to date are distributed to the fetus with relative ease, although there are some differences in their rate and extent of transfer. Ethanol is distributed very rapidly between the mother and fetus, and maternal and fetal concentrations are virtually superimposable up to 14 hours after 1-hour infusion of ethanol to the mother (Brien et al. 1985). The placental transfer of most opioid drugs also was found to be very rapid, with peak fetal blood levels occurring in less than 10 minutes (Szeto et al. 1978, 1981; Golub et al. 1986). The placental transfer of cocaine also has been shown to be very rapid (Woods 1989). On the other hand, the placental transfer of tetrahydrocannabinol (THC) following marijuana smoke inhalation was found to be much slower, with peak fetal levels not seen until 1.5 to 2 hours after smoke exposure (Abrams et al. 1985). The reason for this apparently slow distribution of such an extremely lipid soluble compound is not known, but it may be because of the extensive binding of THC to maternal plasma proteins.

Another major finding from these pharmacokinetics studies is that the placenta plays the major role in drug elimination from the fetus. For all drugs that have been studied, the elimination half-life in the fetus is identical to that in the

39

mother, suggesting that elimination of these drugs from the fetus is largely dictated by maternal elimination characteristics. This is in contrast to the old idea that the fetus may act as a "sink" for drugs because of inadequate drug-elimination capacity. The immature drug-elimination system is only a problem upon removal of the placenta, such as at the time of birth. This has been very elegantly demonstrated for ethanol, where the decline in ethanol concentration in the sheep fetus has been shown to be similar to that in maternal plasma but is much slower in the newborn (Cumming et al. 1984).

Not only have recent studies revealed that the fetus does not act as a sink for drugs, but also most studies have found that fetal plasma drug levels tend to be significantly lower than maternal plasma levels, even at steady state after continuous drug infusion (Szeto 1982). Pharmacokinetics modeling suggests that this lack of equilibrium between mother and fetus can be explained only by the presence of fetal drug elimination (Szeto et al. 1982a). Although early *in vitro* metabolism studies in fetal rats indicated that the fetus has negligible capacity to eliminate drugs, recent functional studies in the fetal lamb have revealed varying degrees of renal and hepatic drug elimination (Szeto et al. 1979, 1980; Olsen et al. 1988). Drugs that are excreted renally can be found in amniotic fluid (Szeto et al. 1979). There is even evidence that metabolites of fetal origin such as morphine-3-glucuronide may accumulate in fetal plasma because of their polar nature (Olsen et al. 1988).

Pharmacokinetics studies have clearly helped in understanding the factors that determine the extent of fetal drug exposure. However, these findings also raise further questions, some of which are addressed below.

QUESTIONS FOR FUTURE INVESTIGATION

1. Does the extent of fetal drug exposure change as a function of gestational age? Pharmacokinetics modeling suggested that the extent of fetal drug exposure depends on both placental and fetal clearance of the drug (Szeto 1982). For the same drug, placental clearance may be affected by changes in plasma protein binding and placental perfusion. Gestational age-dependent changes in plasma protein binding have been demonstrated in both maternal and fetal plasma. For instance, it was found that the extent of methadone binding in fetal plasma increases with gestational age (Szeto et al. 1982b). Fetal binding was initially much lower than maternal binding, but it increased significantly in the last 2 weeks of gestation, reaching the level of maternal binding by the time of birth. How would this affect drug distribution between the maternal and fetal compartments throughout gestation? Placental perfusion also can change throughout pregnancy. How would these changes affect the extent of fetal

drug exposure? Would the effects depend on the degree of plasma protein binding of the drug and on whether the distribution is flow- or diffusion-limited? Although there has been much speculation on these issues, there have not been any systematic studies addressing these points.

Furthermore, the extent of fetal drug exposure can be expected to change with progressive maturation of fetal drug-elimination systems. The contribution of fetal drug clearance to the overall clearance of methadone from the fetal compartment has been found to increase throughout the third trimester until 2 weeks prior to birth, while it remained constant for morphine prior to birth (Szeto et al. 1982c). However, there has been no longitudinal study of the extent of fetal exposure to any of the drugs of abuse throughout pregnancy, and there have been no attempts to correlate extent of fetal drug exposure to fetal drug-elimination capacity. This is clearly an area that deserves more attention.

2. Although studies to date have clearly demonstrated the important role that the placenta plays in the elimination of drugs from the fetal compartment, what are the consequences of polar metabolites that are generated by the fetus? The fetal-maternal clearance of these polar metabolites can be expected to be rather restricted. Morphine-3-glucuronide has been shown to accumulate in fetal plasma following morphine administration to the mother (Olsen et al. 1988); and there is some evidence that this metabolite may be pharmacologically active. Another interesting case may be the comparison of the extent of fetal drug exposure to heroin vs. methadone. Heroin is hydrolyzed rapidly in plasma to 6-monoacetylmorphine and morphine. Szeto and colleagues (1982c) showed that the extent of fetal exposure to methadone is threefold higher than that to morphine because of the lower placental clearance of morphine from mother to fetus due to its relative lower lipophilicity. When heroin is administered to the mother, it can be expected to be rapidly distributed to the fetus because of its lipid solubility. Once in the fetal compartment, it may be rapidly hydrolyzed to 6-monoacetylmorphine and morphine. Because of the relatively low placental clearance of morphine, it may be expected to accumulate in the fetus. Thus, the extent of fetal opiate exposure may be higher for heroin than for methadone. This hypothesis needs to be tested.

3. What is the fate of drug or metabolites excreted into amniotic fluid? Will the dynamics be different for lipid-soluble vs. polar compounds? Many investigators have suggested that drugs in amniotic fluid are swallowed by the fetus and undergo enterohepatic recirculation. The dynamics of this potential pathway have not been investigated. Previous data suggest that for lipid-soluble compounds, the majority of the drug is distributed back into the maternal circulation via diffusion across the amnion (Szeto et al. 1978).

But what about polar metabolites such as morphine-3-glucuronide? How much of this can be absorbed from the gastrointestinal tract in the fetus, and is there any β-glucuronidase activity? Although drug levels can be readily determined in amniotic fluid samples obtained in humans during amniocentesis, they can only be interpreted if there is a clear understanding of the dynamics of drugs in this fluid compartment.

4. Some rather sophisticated compartmental models have been proposed for the maternal-placental-fetal unit. Other researchers have even included the amniotic fluid as a separate compartment. The number of unknown kinetic constants and compartment volumes far exceeds the information that can be obtained experimentally. To date, only a simple two-compartment model (with mother and fetus each being treated as a homogenous compartment) has been solved (Szeto et al. 1982a). New experimental approaches would be necessary to make these more complicated models worthwhile. Can it be done? What additional information would they provide? And would the efforts be worth it?

5. The physiological modeling presented by DeVane (this volume) obviously has many advantages because it does not assume that the mother and fetus are homogenous compartments. However, the disadvantages are that the blood flows to the various organs must be determined in the same species, and it must be assumed that the drug that is being studied does not change any of the flow parameters. This may be rather difficult because many of the drugs of abuse tend to alter uterine-placental perfusion. Furthermore, such a model would have to be further modified to include drug elimination from the fetus and umbilical blood flows. As it stands, this model puts heavy emphasis on the maternal side only, disregarding the complexity of the fetal side. However, such models would be extremely useful in predicting the effects of blood-flow changes on the extent of fetal drug exposure.

6. Finally, Kuhnert and DeVane have indicated that the goal is to correlate the extent of fetal drug exposure with pharmacodynamic responses in the fetus. To date, there has been only one example where a clear correlation between maternal-fetal pharmacokinetics and magnitude of fetal response has been demonstrated. Pharmacokinetics studies in the pregnant ewe have shown that the extent of fetal exposure to methadone is threefold higher than with morphine (Szeto et al. 1982c). It has now been demonstrated that the magnitude of neurobehavioral effects in the fetal lamb is also three times greater following maternal methadone administration compared with morphine administration (Umans and Szeto

1983). It would be important to obtain more experimental evidence such as this to document a clear dose-response relationship in the fetus.

A final point concerns the development of tolerance upon chronic exposure to many of the drugs of abuse. Tolerance has been demonstrated to develop rapidly in the fetus with constant-rate administration of morphine to the mother (Szeto et al. 1988). In such instances, any relationship between dose and response would be expected to fall apart. Furthermore, intermittent drug exposure also may result in intermittent withdrawal between doses (Umans and Szeto 1985) and may have a detrimental impact on fetal development and pregnancy outcome. Thus, the total impact of maternal drug abuse may be very complicated and not solely dependent on the extent of fetal drug exposure.

REFERENCES

Abrams, R.M.; Cook, C.E.; and Davis, K.H., Niederreiher, K; and Szeto H.H. Plasma THC in pregnant sheep and fetus after smoking a marijuana cigarette. *Alcohol Drug Res* 6:361-369, 1985.
Brien, J.F.; Clarke, D.W.; Richardson, B.; and Patrick, J. Disposition of ethanol in maternal blood, fetal blood, and amniotic fluid of third trimester pregnant ewes. *Am J Obstet Gynecol* 152:583-590, 1985.
Clapp, J.F.; Wesley, M.; Cooke, R.; Pekala R.; and Holstein, C. The effects of marijuana smoke on gas exchange in ovine pregnancy. *Alcohol Drug Res* 7:85-92, 1986.
Cumming, M.E.; Ong, B.Y.; Wade, J.G.; and Sitar, D.S. Maternal and fetal ethanol pharmacokinetics and cardiovascular responses in near-term pregnant sheep. *Can J Physiol Pharmacol* 62:1435-1439, 1984.
Golub, M.S.; Eisele, J.H.; and Anderson, J.H. Maternal-fetal distribution of morphine and alfentanil in near-term sheep and rhesus monkeys. *Dev Pharmacol Ther* 9:12-22, 1986.
Manning, F.A.; Walker, D.; and Feyerabend, C. The effect of nicotine on fetal breathing movements in conscious pregnant ewes. *Obstet Gynecol* 52:563-568, 1978.
Olsen, G.D.; Sommer, K.M.; Wheeler, P.L.; Boyea, S.R.; Michelson, S.P.; and Cheek D.B.C. Accumulation and clearance of morphine-3-glucuronide in fetal lambs. *J Pharmacol Exp Ther* 247:576-584, 1988.
Szeto, H.H. Pharmacokinetics in the ovine maternal-fetal unit. *Ann Rev Pharmacol Toxicol* 22:221-243, 1982.
Szeto, H.H.; Mann, L.I.; Bhakthavathasalan, A.; Liu, M.; and Iuturrisi, C.E. Meperidine pharmacokinetics in the maternal-fetal unit. *J Pharmacol Exp Ther* 206:448-459, 1978.

Szeto, H.H.; Kaiko, R.F.; Clapp, J.F.; Larrow, R.W.; Mann, L.I.; and Iuturrisi, C.E. Urinary excretion of meperidine by the fetal lamb. *J Pharmacol Exp Ther* 209:244-248, 1979.

Szeto, H.H.; Clapp, J.F.; Larrow, R.W.; Inturrisi, C.E.; and Mann, L.I. Renal tubular secretion of meperidine by the fetal lamb. *J Pharmacol Exp Ther* 213:346-349, 1980.

Szeto, H.H.; Clapp, J.F.; Larrow, R.W.; Hewitt, J.; Iuturrisi, C.E.; and Mann, L.I. Disposition of methadone in the ovine maternal-fetal unit. *Life Sci* 28:2111-2117, 1981.

Szeto, H.H.; Umans, J.G.; and Rubinow, S.I. The contribution of transplacental clearances and fetal clearance to drug disposition in the ovine maternal-fetal unit. *Drug Metab Dispos* 10:382-386, 1982a.

Szeto, H.H.; Umans, J.G.; Umans, H.R.; and McFarland, J.W. The relationship between maternal and fetal plasma protein binding of methadone in the ewe during the third trimester. *Life Sci* 30:1271-1279, 1982b.

Szeto, H.H.; Umans, J.G.; and McFarland, J.W. A comparison of morphine and methadone disposition in the maternal-fetal unit. *Am J Obstet Gynecol* 143:700-706, 1982c.

Szeto, H.H.; Zhu, Y.S.; Cox, M.J.; Amione, J.; and Clare, S. Prenatal morphine exposure and sleep-wake disturbances in the fetus. *Sleep* 11:121-130, 1988.

Umans, J.G., and Szeto, H.H. Precipitated opiate abstinence in utero. *Am J Obstet Gynecol* 151:441-444, 1985.

Umans, J.G., and Szeto, H.H. Effects of opiates on fetal behavioral activity in utero. *Life Sci* 33:639-642, 1983.

Woods, J.R. Pharmacokinetics of cocaine: Fetal lamb studies. *Ann N Y Acad Sci* 1989.

Woods, J.R.T.; Plessinger, M.A.; and Clark, K.E. Effects of cocaine on uterine blood flow and fetal oxygenation. *JAMA* 257:957-961, 1987.

AUTHOR

Hazel H. Szeto, M.D., Ph.D.
Associate Professor
Department of Pharmacology
Cornell University Medical College
1300 York Avenue
New York, NY 10021

Selected Methodologic Issues in Investigations of Prenatal Effects of Cocaine: Lessons From the Past

Barry Zuckerman

INTRODUCTION

The perinatal cocaine epidemic has emerged rapidly. In the most systematic study to date on cocaine use during pregnancy, 18 percent of women receiving prenatal care at Boston City Hospital used cocaine at least once during pregnancy (Zuckerman et al. 1989a). Less systematic surveys at other hospitals, mostly in urban settings, demonstrate somewhat lower rates. However, because urine assessments conducted at delivery fail to identify many women who used cocaine earlier in pregnancy, these rates may somewhat underestimate the use of cocaine during pregnancy.

Pregnancies of women who use cocaine are at risk not only because of cocaine use but because of poor nutrition; sexually transmitted diseases; use of cigarettes, marijuana, alcohol, and other illicit drugs; and lack of prenatal care. Understandably, as preliminary investigations indicate, infants born to mothers who use cocaine have a high likelihood of low birth weight, microcephaly, prematurity, neurobehavioral dysfunction, and rare but catastrophic events such as cerebral vascular accidents, necrotizing enterocolitis, malformations, and *abruptio placentae*. The association between cocaine and these outcomes has biologic plausibility because of the known pharmacologic actions of cocaine. However, with few exceptions, these early studies have significant methodologic flaws that prevent meaningful conclusions regarding the independent effect of cocaine use during pregnancy.

Information based on good science is needed to make sound clinical, public health, and public policy decisions. Professionals and the media also have an important responsibility to ensure the dissemination of accurate information. A recent review of abstracts submitted for presentation at the annual meeting of the Society for Pediatric Research (Koren et al. 1989) showed that it was much more likely that a paper on cocaine use during pregnancy would be accepted for presentation if there were positive findings between cocaine exposure and adverse outcomes compared to a paper reporting negative findings. In the media, cocaine-exposed babies are depicted as "addicted" when in fact a withdrawal syndrome has not been documented. Untoward consequences of this misinformation include a national adoption agency declaring that cocaine-exposed infants are not adoptable. Clinical decisions are also adversely effected. Early reports from a convenience sample of infants of cocaine-using mothers suggest an extraordinarily high rate (15 percent) of sudden infant death syndrome (SIDS) (Chasnoff et al. 1989). If this report were accurate, cocaine-exposed infants would need to be maintained on home monitors. Resulting increased maternal anxiety might lead in turn to self-medication with drugs and difficulty in attachment. However, this report was not supported by the only systematic investigation of prenatal cocaine exposure and SIDS, which showed no increase in SIDS (Bauchner et al. 1988).

Scientific standards for investigations are well known and are not reviewed extensively here. This chapter identifies selected methodologic issues that have plagued investigations of the impact of prenatal use of drugs. These methodologic problems are the lack or incomplete control of potentially confounding variables, reliance on self-report in identifying drug users, and use of biased samples. The importance of identifying intervening variables, especially protective factors that influence outcome, also is emphasized.

LESSONS LEARNED FROM PRENATAL ALCOHOL RESEARCH

Attributing Cause

The original description of fetal alcohol syndrome (FAS) (Jones et al. 1973) was based on very careful descriptions of the physical characteristics of the children. However, the extent to which health habits and other characteristics of the mothers were documented varied widely. This tendency to record the physical characteristics of offspring more completely than maternal characteristics is also found in many of the approximately 250 reported cases that served as a basis for the development of criteria for FAS. Clinicians and investigators who believe the key component to be alcohol may pay more attention to a mother's alcohol consumption than to her other habits.

Evidence from three lines of investigation has raised questions regarding the specificity of alcohol as causing FAS (Zuckerman and Hingson 1986). First, the facial dysmorphology that some investigators consider to be the most striking aspect of FAS has been demonstrated to resemble the facial appearance of children born to mothers with phenylketonuria (Lipson et al. 1981). Children of epileptic women who used phenytoin (Dilantin) during pregnancy also have a similar appearance (Hill 1976). The facial appearance of FAS may not be as distinct as originally thought. In one study, one of seven experts on FAS could

46

not identify children with FAS based on pictures of their faces (Clarren et al. 1987).

Second, the similarity of appearance to infants exposed to the three agents mentioned above is consistent with the results of studies using mice suggesting that any teratogen exposure during the gastrulation stage of embryogenesis can result in craniofacial, brain, and eye defects corresponding to those noted in severe forms of FAS (Sulik 1984).

Third, factors other than alcohol have been associated with features compatible with FAS (CFAS). Because FAS is rare, Hanson (Hanson et al. 1978) developed criteria for classifying infants as CFAS in an attempt to identify an association between lower levels of drinking and less extensive dysmorphology. In the only study (Hingson et al. 1982) that attempts to identify any association between CFAS and factors other than alcohol, 2.2 percent of 1,384 infants examined had CFAS. When other confounding variables were controlled, marijuana use during pregnancy, weight gain less than 5 pounds, and exposure to x-rays increased the risk that an infant would be born with CFAS. In contrast, there was no increased risk for women who averaged two or more drinks daily. These three lines of investigations suggest that the dysmorphology of FAS may reflect a common pathway of numerous agents or a combination of agents rather than a specific teratogenic effect of alcohol. It is possible that the initial naming of the syndrome for its hypothesized cause may have resulted in the neglect of important research questions; investigators may be failing to consider the influence of maternal health or other drug use. Thus, while initial uncontrolled observations are important, the observer should describe in detail not only the outcome but also all possible factors that may have independently or synergistically contributed to that outcome.

A similar type of problem with causal attribution now can be seen in attributing the neurobehavioral dysfunction of cocaine-exposed infants to withdrawal ("crack-addicted babies"). Although neurobehavioral dysfunction has been shown to be associated with prenatal cocaine exposure (Chasnoff et al. 1985), a withdrawal syndrome has not been demonstrated. Other possible explanations of neurobehavioral dysfunction include acute direct toxic effect of cocaine on the central nervous system (CNS) (Mittleman et al. 1989), neurotransmitter (especially norepinephrine) elevations (Ward et al. 1989), or structural CNS damage (Dixon and Bejar 1989).

Confounding Variables

Efforts to identify and to confirm the effects of a single substance such as cocaine are complicated because it is unusual for humans to use or to abuse only one drug. Assessing the independent effect of any drug or health variable requires carefully designed studies with samples large enough to allow multivariate data analysis and statistical control for confounding variables. Unless confounding variables are controlled, study findings may either overestimate the magnitude of a specific substance or demonstrate a significant association where none exists.

Two of the most frequently cited studies showing an association between small amounts of alcohol consumption and lower birth weight did not control for important potentially confounding variables. Little (1977) found that one ounce of absolute alcohol (two drinks) per day consumed before pregnancy was associated with an average decrease of 90 grams at birth weight. Drinking that amount during months 5 to 8 of pregnancy was associated with a decrease of 160 grams at birth weight. The effects of maternal age, height, parity, cigarette use, and gestational age and sex of the child were held constant through regression analysis. However, other potentially important variables, including maternal illness during pregnancy, prepregnancy weight, maternal weight gain, and marijuana use, were not examined. A more recent study (Mills et al. 1984) demonstrates that drinking an average of one to two drinks per day reduced infant birth weight by 83 grams. Although this study controlled many variables and had fewer methodologic limitations than most studies, it did fail to control for weight gain and marijuana consumption during pregnancy. The unexplored variables in both studies may explain the small differences in birth weight.

This possibility is illustrated by data from a study conducted at Boston City Hospital (Hingson et al. 1982). Infants whose mothers drank two or more drinks per day weighed 220 grams less (p<.04) than infants whose mothers did not drink alcohol during pregnancy. When confounding variables were controlled in the statistical analysis, the birth weight difference was only 51 grams and was not statistically significant. On the other hand, women who smoked marijuana during pregnancy delivered infants who weighed 300 grams less than infants of mothers who did not smoke marijuana. When confounding variables were controlled, the weight was 105 grams less, but this difference remained statistically significant. The role of marijuana may be critical because it is frequently used by women who drink alcohol (Zuckerman et al. 1989a; Hingson et al. 1982). The inconsistency of findings between alcohol consumption and decreased birth weight compared with the consistency of findings between cigarette smoking and lowered birth weight suggests that control for confounding variables is one of many important methodologic problems (Zuckerman and Hingson 1986; Stein and Kline 1983; Roman et al. 1988) in investigations of alcohol consumption during pregnancy. Many studies that control for potentially confounding variables do not demonstrate a significant association between two or fewer drinks per day and lower infant birth weight (Zuckerman et al. 1989a; Hingson et al. 1982; Marbury et al. 1983; Tennes and Blackard 1980; Grisso et al. 1984; Kline et al. 1987).

Determining the independent effect of cocaine is also complicated by the tendency of cocaine users to use other drugs and practice peer health behavior. Thus, in one study (Zuckerman et al. 1989a), while infants of mothers who had a positive urine assay for cocaine during pregnancy were 400 grams smaller in birth weight compared with infants of mothers who did not use cocaine, only 25 percent of the weight decrement could be attributed directly to cocaine. The remainder was attributable to the effects of cigarettes and marijuana, other drugs, and poor nutrition.

LESSONS FROM PRENATAL MARIJUANA RESEARCH: THE VALIDITY OF SELF-REPORT

Studies in humans on the effect of smoking marijuana during pregnancy show conflicting findings (Hingson et al. 1985). One possible explanation for the inconsistency of study results is the reliance by these studies on maternal self-report. In the absence of the ascertainment of marijuana use through a biologic marker such as urine testing, the number of marijuana users may have been underestimated and some users misclassified as nonusers. This could result in obscuring significant associations between marijuana use and neonatal outcomes.

Hingson and colleagues (1986) conducted an investigation to explore the validity of self-reported marijuana use during pregnancy by randomly allocating pregnant women into a group who were told their urine would be tested for marijuana and another group not so tested. Women told that they would be tested reported using more marijuana than did untested women. Moreover, urine assays identified more women who used marijuana during pregnancy than were willing to admit it in the interview, even after being told their urine would be tested.

Based on this evidence, Zuckerman and coworkers (1989a) conducted an investigation on the effect of marijuana use during pregnancy by identifying use by both self-report and urine assay for marijuana. Of 1,226 women, 331 (27 percent) were classified as marijuana users on the basis of the interview, urine assay, or both. After potentially confounding variables were controlled for, the infants of women who had a positive urine assay for marijuana were found to weigh 79 grams less at birth (p=.04) and to be .5 centimeters shorter (p=.02) than the infants of nonusers. To determine whether this finding was comparable with those of other investigations that did not use urine assays, the multiple regression analyses were repeated with the use of marijuana based solely on interview findings. Of the 202 women whose samples were positive for marijuana, 53 denied using it. Thus, 16 percent (53 of 331) of the women who did not report marijuana use were identified as users with the urine assay alone. On the basis of self-report alone, these women were misclassified as nonusers. When the same potentially confounding variables were controlled for, infants of women who reported marijuana use weighed only 15 grams less (p=.66) and were .37 centimeters shorter (p=.06) than the infants of those who did not report use. These data support the importance of the use of biologic markers to ascertain marijuana use and suggest that, without urine assays, the number of marijuana users in previous studies may have been underestimated. The misclassification of users as nonusers potentially obscures significant relationships between marijuana use and fetal growth.

Zuckerman and colleagues (1989b) also have shown that women 19 years and younger have a different rate of denial for marijuana (12 percent) compared with cocaine (35 percent). This difference in underreporting was not seen for adult pregnant women (17 percent for marijuana and 20 percent for cocaine), indicating that adolescents may have different drug-specific attitudes as well as different perceptions of the acceptability of reporting drugs. Thus, studies may have different rates of underreporting because of varying proportions of young women in the study.

LESSONS FROM PRENATAL COCAINE STUDIES: PROBLEM WITH BIASED SAMPLES

An important methodologic problem common among the published reports regarding cocaine use during pregnancy is the use of potentially biased samples of cocaine-using pregnant women. Some studies recruit women from special prenatal chemical dependency programs, whereas other studies identify cocaine-exposed infants by testing the infant's urine at birth. Testing urines at birth may result in users (women who used during pregnancy but denied use and had a negative urine because they did not use within 3 days of delivery) being misclassified as nonusers. Some studies only evaluate urines of newborns meeting certain clinical criteria, which potentially introduces an even greater bias. Data from the Boston City Hospital study (Zuckerman et al. 1989a) provide an opportunity to explore this potential bias. Only 25 percent of women who acknowledged cocaine use during pregnancy had a positive urine at the time of delivery. Among women who self-reported use, those who had a positive urine at the time of delivery were heavier users compared with women users who did not have a positive urine at the time of delivery (table 1). Twenty-six percent of women with a positive postpartum urine used daily compared with 9 percent of users who had negative urine postpartum (p<.001). To determine whether the findings of Zuckerman and colleagues' study (1989a) in which urines were collected prenatally and postpartum were comparable with investigations that depend on urines from newborns (similar to maternal postpartum urines), the multiple regression analysis was repeated with cocaine exposure defined solely by positive postpartum urine assay. Women who had a

50

positive urine prenatally and a negative urine postpartum were thereby misclassified as nonusers. When the same confounding variables were controlled, infants of women with positive postpartum urines had a 23-percent further decrease in birth weight (from 93 grams to 115 grams) compared with published results. Bias could have been introduced in both directions. Women with positive urines postpartum are heavier users, which could result in a greater decrease in birth weight in the postpartum cocaine-exposed group. This potentially could be counterbalanced by a decrease in birth weight among the nonusing cocaine group because nonusers were misclassified as users. This could result in decreasing the difference between the cocaine-exposed and nonexposed group. Based on the data, the net effect shows a greater detrimental effect in the postpartum cocaine-exposed group. Therefore, infants who are identified at the time of birth only by positive urines represent the tip of the iceberg and skew findings toward mothers who were more frequent cocaine users and infants with lower birth weight.

TABLE 1.   *Comparison of frequency of cocaine use between women with positive and negative urines postpartum (among self-reported cocaine users)*

Urines	Less Than Once a Month (%)	1 to 3 Times a Month (%)	1 to 2 Times a Week (%)	3 to 6 Times a Week (%)	Daily (%)
Negative (n=128)	44	17	20	10	9
Positive (n=35)	11	11	32	20	26

p<.0001

It is important to note that even in the Boston City Hospital study, a significant association was demonstrated only between women who had a positive urine assay for cocaine and impaired fetal growth and smaller head circumference. There was no significant association among women who reported use but had a negative urine assay. These women were less frequent users. Also, had the cocaine users been combined regardless of means of identification, a significant association would not have been found between cocaine use during pregnancy and poor fetal growth or smaller head circumference when confounding variables are controlled.

Important biases also may be introduced in investigations of women participating in special prenatal chemical-dependency programs. Women in such programs may be different in the amount, type, chronicity, and variety of drugs used; amount of prenatal care; use of Special Supplemental Food Program for Women, Infants, and Children; and presence of other risk factors compared with women who were not in such programs.

An example of a bias introduced from this type of convenience sample is initial early reports of a 15-percent rate of SIDS among children born to known cocaine-using mothers (Chasnoff et al. 1987). Data from the Boston City Hospital study obtained from a general prenatal clinic population showed there was no significant difference in the prevalence of infants with SIDS between mothers who used cocaine during pregnancy compared with infants from the same population whose mothers did not use cocaine (Chasnoff et al. 1989).

CONCLUSION

Initial observations of possible adverse effects of any drug used prenatally should be followed by systematic investigations. Attention to methodologic issues described in this chapter, other chapters in this volume, and well-accepted scientific standards (Feinstein 1988) will improve the accuracy of information generated from investigations of prenatal drug use. Limitations in study design should be identified and their implications acknowledged. Replication of study results with different populations and different methods further assures the validity of the findings, for all studies will have some limitations. Good clinical care and good public health policy depend on good information.

REFERENCES

Bauchner, H.; Zuckerman, B.; McClain, M.; Frank, D.; Fried, L.; and Kayne, H. Risk of sudden infant death syndrome among infants with in utero exposure to cocaine. *J Pediatr* 13:831-834, 1988.

Chasnoff, I.J.; Burns, K.A.; and Burns, W.J. Cocaine use in pregnancy: Perinatal morbidity and mortality. *Neurotoxicol Teratol* 9:291-293, 1987.

Chasnoff, I.J.; Burns, W.J.; Schnoll, S.H.; and Burns, K.A. Cocaine use in pregnancy. *N Engl J Med* 313(11):666-669, 1985.

Chasnoff, I.J.; Hunt, C.E.; Kletter, R.; and Kaplan, D. Prenatal cocaine exposure is associated with respiratory pattern abnormalities. *AJDC* 143:583-587, 1989.

Clarren, S.; Sampson, P.; Larsen, J.; Donnell, D.; Barr, H.; Bockstein, F.; Martin, D.; and Streissguth, A.P. Facial effects of fetal alcohol exposure: Assessments by photographs and morphometric analysis. *Am J Med Gen* 26:651-666, 1987.

Dixon, S.D., and Bejar, R. Echoencephalographic findings in neonates associated with maternal cocaine and methamphetamine use: Incidence and clinical correlates. *J Pediatr* 115:770-778, 1989.

Feinstein, A.R. Scientific standards in epidemiologic studies of the menace of daily life. *Science* 242:1257-1263, 1988.

Grisso, J.A.; Roman, E.; Inskip, H.; Varel, V.; and Donovan, J. Alcohol consumption and outcome of pregnancy. *J Epidemiol Community Health* 38:232-235, 1984.

Hanson, J.W.; Streissguth, A.P.; and Smith, D.W. The effects of moderate alcohol consumption during pregnancy on fetal growth and morphogenesis. *J Pediatr* 92:457-460, 1978.

Hill, R.M. Fetal malformations and antiepileptic drugs. *Am J Dis Children* 130:923-925, 1976.

Hingson, R.; Alpert, J.; Day, N.; Dooling, E.; Kayne, H.; Morelock, S.; and Zuckerman, B. Effects of maternal drinking and marijuana use on fetal growth and development. *Pediatrics* 70:539-546, 1982.

Hingson, R.; Zuckerman, B.; Amaro, H.; Frank, D.; Kayne, H.; Sorenson, J.R.; Mitchell, J.; Parker, S.; Morelock, S.; and Timperi, R. Maternal marijuana use and neonatal outcome. Uncertainty posed by self-reports. *Am J Pub Health* 76:667-669, 1986.

Hingson, R.; Zuckerman, B.; Frank, D.A.; Kayne, H.; Sorenson, J.R.; and Mitchell, J. Effects on fetal development of maternal marijuana use during pregnancy. In: Harve, D.J., ed. *Marijuana '84, Proceedings of the Oxford Symposium on Cannabis.* Oxford, England: IRL Press, 1985.

Jones, K.L.; Smith, D.W.; Ulleland, C.N.; and Streissguth, A.P. Pattern of malformation in offspring of chronic alcoholic women. *Lancet* 1:1267-1271, 1973.

Kline, J.; Stein, Z.; and Hutzler, M. Cigarettes, alcohol and marijuana: Varying associations with birthweight. *Int J Epidemiol* 16:44-51, 1987.

Koren, G.; Graham, H.; Shear, H.; and Einarson, T. Bias against the null hypothesis: The reproductive hazards of cocaine. *Lancet* 2(8677):1440-1442, 1989.

Lipson, A.H.; Yu, J.S.; O'Halloran, M.T.; and Williams, R. Alcohol and phenylketonuria. *Lancet* 1:717-718, 1981.

Little, R. Moderate alcohol use during pregnancy and decreased infant birth weight. *Am J Public Health* 67:1154-1156, 1977.

Marbury, M.C.; Linn, S.; Monson, R.; Schoenbaum, S.C.; Stubblefield, P.G.; and Ryan, K.J. The association of alcohol consumption with outcome of pregnancy. *Am J Public Health* 73:1165-1168, 1983.

Mills, J.L.; Graubard, B.I.; Harley, M.S.; Rhoads, G.G.; and Berrendes, H.W. Maternal alcohol consumption and birthweight. *JAMA* 252:1875-1879, 1984.

Mittleman, R.; Lofino, J.; and Hern, W. Tissue distribution of cocaine in a pregnant woman. *J Forensic Sci* 34:481-486, 1989.

Roman, E.; Beral, V.; and Zuckerman, B.S. Review of the relationship between alcohol consumption and pregnancy outcome in humans. In: Kalter, H., ed. *Issues and Reviews in Teratology.* Vol. 4. 1988. pp. 205-235.

Stein, Z., and Kline, J. Smoking, alcohol, and reproduction. *Am J Public Health* 73:1154-1156, 1983.

Sulik, K.K. Critical periods for alcohol teratogenesis in mice with special reference to the gastrulation stage of embryogenesis. In: *Mechanisms of Alcohol Damage in Utero. Ciba Foundation Symposium 105.* London: Pittman, 1984. pp. 124-141.

Tennes, K., and Blackard, C. Maternal alcohol consumption, birthweight, and minor physical anomalies. *Am J Obstet Gynecol* 138:774-780, 1980.

Ward, S.L.; Bautista, D.B.; Buckley, S.; Schuetz, S.; Wachsman, L.; Bean, X.; and Warburton, D. Circulating catecholamines and adrenoreceptors in infants of cocaine abusing mothers. *Ann N Y Acad Sci* 562:349-350, 1989.

Zuckerman, B.S.; Amaro, H.; and Cabral, H. The validity of self-reported marijuana and cocaine use among pregnant adolescents. *J Pediatr* 115:812-815, 1989b.

Zuckerman, B.; Frank, D.; Hingson, R.; Amaro, H.; Levenson, S.; Parker, S.; Vinci, R.; Aboagye, K.; Fried, L.; Cabral, H.; Timperi, R.; and Bauchner, H. Effects of maternal marijuana and cocaine use on fetal growth. *N Engl J Med* 320:762-768, 1989a.

Zuckerman, B.S., and Hingson, R. Alcohol consumption during pregnancy: A critical review. *Dev Med Child Neurol* 28:649-661, 1986.

ACKNOWLEDGMENT

This work was supported by the Harris Foundation.

AUTHOR

Barry Zuckerman, M.D.
Professor of Pediatrics
Department of Pediatrics and Public Health
Boston University School of Medicine
Director
Division of Developmental and Behavioral Pediatrics
Boston City Hospital
Talbot 214
818 Harrison Avenue
Boston, MA 02118

Methodological Issues in Studying Cocaine Use in Pregnancy: A Problem of Definitions

Ira J. Chasnoff

INTRODUCTION

Rigorous clinical investigation is a tedious process, requiring strict attention to methodologic details that can influence the ultimate outcome of the research. Unfortunately, the difficulties inherent in working with any substance-abusing population afflict the planning and implementation of most projects that hope to evaluate the impact of maternal cocaine use on pregnancy and neonatal outcome. In addition, the emotional, legal, and financial issues surrounding drug use in general, and perinatal cocaine use in particular, have been reflected in a flood of reports of drug-related effects, which, in some cases, have not been substantiated through well-conceived, well-executed studies.

REVIEW OF HUMAN STUDIES

The earliest case report of cocaine use in pregnancy concerned two pregnancies complicated by *abruptio placentae* (Acker et al. 1983). In 1985 Chasnoff and colleagues published the first clinical study of cocaine use in pregnancy, in which outcomes of 23 infants were reported. Women were enrolled prenatally and tracked with urine toxicologies throughout pregnancy. One group of cocaine-using women also used opiates, and one group used cocaine but not opiates. A third group of women used opiates but not cocaine, and a fourth group of drug-free women was identified. No differences in birth weight, length, head circumference, or Apgar scores were found, but *abruptio placentae* and marked neurobehavioral deficiencies were noted in some of the cocaine-exposed population, and in two of these infants genitourinary tract anomalies also were found.

A small study by Madden and coworkers (1986) of eight infants who were identified at birth because of their mothers' positive urine toxicologies for cocaine concluded that there was no evidence of negative effects on the pregnancies or infants, but two women who also admitted to alcohol use had small-for-gestational-age infants. No control group was used.

The outcome of 160 pregnancies in which women used cocaine were reported by Bingol and colleagues in 1987. The women were identified through questioning at delivery by a genetic counselor. Fifty mothers admitted to using cocaine only; 110 women used multiple drugs, including cocaine; and a third group of 340 drug-free women were identified. A single urine toxicology on the infant at delivery was used to confirm placement in the appropriate study or control group. The two groups of cocaine-using women generally had an increased incidence of *abruptio placentae* with stillbirths, and their live-born infants were of lower mean birth weight and head circumference; however, only the first group was statistically different from the drug-free group. The infants in the cocaine-only group also displayed an increased incidence of malformations (three with central nervous system/cranial defects and two with cardiac anomalies).

MacGregor and colleagues (1987) reported on 70 women who were identified as cocaine users during the early prenatal period and were followed in a program designed to deliver comprehensive services to substance-abusing pregnant women. Twenty-four of the women used cocaine only, 20 used cocaine and marijuana, 22 used cocaine and opiates, and 4 used cocaine plus various other illicit substances. Seventy women selected from the general obstetric clinic population served as drug-free controls. These women were similar in several prenatal parameters, except that the cocaine-using women had a significantly higher rate of alcohol use. The cocaine- and cocaine/polydrug-exposed pregnancies showed a significant decrease in gestational age and birth weight, with a significantly higher rate of premature labor and delivery and of small-for-gestational-age infants. Comparison of the 24 cocaine-only-exposed pregnancies with the 46 cocaine/polydrug-exposed pregnancies demonstrated no differences between the two groups' outcomes.

In a study from California, Oro and Dixon (1987) reported 110 neonates identified by retrospective interview at the time of delivery as having been exposed to cocaine, methamphetamines, heroin, or methadone during the pregnancy. Forty-five women served as controls, who were matched for age, prenatal care, and race but not for cigarette or alcohol exposure. It was found that the drug-exposed infants had a high incidence of prematurity and intrauterine growth retardation and a significant decrease in gestational age, birth weight, length, and head circumference. There was also a higher rate of perinatal complications in the drug-using groups. Significant neurobehavioral changes were documented in the drug-exposed groups using a drug-withdrawal scoring system.

A series of smaller studies reported cocaine-using women ascertained by various methods. Ryan and coworkers (1987) reported on 50 women enrolled in a drug treatment program who were using cocaine plus heroin and methadone and compared them with 50 women in the same program who were using heroin and methadone but not cocaine and with 50 women who had no history of drug use. Urine toxicologies were used to determine cocaine use, but it is not clear if the drug-free controls had urines tested. The cocaine-exposed infants demonstrated a significant decrease in birth weight, head circumference, length, and Apgar scores compared with the control population.

Chouteau and colleagues (1988) identified 361 women at the time of delivery who had had no prenatal care and divided them into two groups based on a single urine toxicology at the time of delivery. One hundred forty-three women had a positive urine for cocaine and 218 did not. Both groups had evidence for a high rate of polydrug use, including alcohol and tobacco, but these factors were not controlled for. There was no difference in the rate of *abruptio placentae* between the two groups. The women with a positive urine toxicology for cocaine, however, had a significantly higher rate of infants born prematurely and at a birth weight less than 2,500 grams.

Cherukuri and coworkers (1988) identified a group of crack-using women when they entered the hospital for delivery. Fifty-five women admitted having used crack during the pregnancy, and they were compared with 55 women who denied any crack use. Assignment to drug-using and control groups and evaluation of substance use or abuse relied on recall history, and no urine toxicologies were performed. There was a significant decrease in gestational age and birth weight in the crack-identified group, and the authors concluded that crack-exposed infants were 3.6 times more likely to be growth retarded and 2.8 times more likely to have a head circumference less than the 10th percentile for gestational age.

Little and colleagues (1989) also relied on self-report to identify 53 cocaine-exposed pregnancies. A group of 100 drug-free women was selected based on self-report to serve as controls. Growth parameters of the cocaine-exposed infants were significantly reduced, and an increased rate of malformations was reported; however, the polydrug use patterns of the drug-using women were not considered in the analysis of data.

Chasnoff and coworkers (1989) evaluated 75 pregnancies, dividing them into two groups: The first had used cocaine only in the first trimester (n=23), and the second had used cocaine throughout the pregnancy (n=52). None of the women used opiates. A third group of drug-free controls (n=40) was identified to serve as comparison. All three groups of women had been ascertained in the early prenatal period and had histories as well as urine toxicologies tracked through the time of delivery. The drug-using women all had been referred for drug abuse treatment into the hospital-based center. The infants exposed to cocaine throughout the pregnancy had a significantly reduced gestational age and birth weight, length, and head circumference in addition to a significantly higher rate of intrauterine growth retardation. Infants exposed in only the first trimester had no reduction in gestational age and had normal growth parameters. Both groups of infants, however, demonstrated significant impairment in orientation, motor, and state-regulation neurobehaviors. Regression analyses to evaluate effects of secondary drug use were not performed, although the two cocaine-using groups were similar in their use of alcohol and marijuana, and all three groups had similar patterns of cigarette use.

Zuckerman and colleagues (1989) identified 1,226 pregnant women during the prenatal period and evaluated the impact of cocaine and/or marijuana on pregnancy outcome. Controlling for tobacco and alcohol effects, it was found that cocaine use in 216 women was independently associated with decreased birth weight and head circumference. Other complications of pregnancy were not addressed.

Burkett and coworkers (1990) reviewed obstetric charts for 139 women who were identified on voluntary self-report as cocaine users. Ninety-two percent of the cocaine-using women used multiple drugs in addition to the cocaine. No control or comparison group was used, but it was concluded that the cocaine-using women were at high risk for perinatal complications: More than 30 percent had a sexually transmitted disease; 63.9 percent had precipitous labor; 20.5 percent had meconium-stained fluid, 36 percent had infants weighing less than 2,500 grams; and 32 percent of the infants were small for gestational age. Placental abruptions were not assessed.

Thus, in reviewing the current scientific literature on the effects of cocaine on pregnancy and neonatal outcome, it becomes evident that many of the methodologic difficulties revolve around a lack of precision in the definition of maternal drug use and the variables to be studied. In addition, other complicating factors in pregnancy have not been assessed so that their contribution to outcome variables could be determined.

DEFINITION OF THE POPULATION

The cocaine-using population is a chaotic one, prone to abrupt changes in lifestyle and drug use patterns. Many studies suffer at inception with the lack of a specific definition for the drug-using population to be evaluated. The pregnant woman tends to identify cocaine as the primary drug of abuse, but further investigation reveals the use of multiple other drugs, including marijuana, alcohol, and heroin. In addition, this polydrug use pattern may vary widely through the tenure of the pregnancy, with binge use of cocaine accompanied by continuous or intermittent use of the other substances. Some research (Madden et al. 1986; Cherukuri et al. 1988; Chouteau et al. 1988; Hume et al. 1989) identified the population under study as cocaine-using women but did not delineate other drugs used. One study (Ryan et al. 1987) labeled the women as cocaine abusers, but in actuality, all of the women were opiate users on methadone maintenance who also used cocaine. Two studies (MacGregor et al. 1987; Little et al. 1989) identified other drugs used by the cocaine-using women in their populations but did not take these secondary drug use patterns into account when analyzing the pregnancy outcome data. Some studies have used comparison groups with similar patterns of secondary drug use (Chasnoff et al. 1985, 1987, 1989; Bingol et al. 1987; Oro and Dixon 1987) but did not use statistical analyses capable of determining the relative impact of the multiple drugs. The relatively small number of subjects in these studies makes these types of analyses difficult.

The timing of the identification of the population to be evaluated varies from one study to the next along the prenatal and postpartum continuum. Studies by several groups that identified women retrospectively at the time of delivery (Cherukuri et al. 1988; Little et al. 1989; Burkett et al. 1990) relied on historical recall by women to review drug use patterns. Other studies (Madden et al. 1986; Oro and Dixon 1987; Bingol et al. 1987; Chouteau et al. 1988) relied on a single urine toxicology at the time of delivery to identify the "cocaine-using" population. The lack of prospective evaluation impedes accurate ascertainment of drug-using women, and one negative urine toxicology at the time of delivery does not assure the drug-free status of the woman throughout the pregnancy.

Other research (Chasnoff et al. 1985, 1987, 1989; Ryan et al. 1987; MacGregor et al. 1987; Frank et al. 1988; Hume et al. 1989; Zuckerman et al. 1989) identified women during the prenatal period and tracked the women's drug use patterns throughout the pregnancy. These studies had the advantage of being able to identify more specifically the patterns and timing of drug use, but they still could not accurately ascertain the amount of drug used at each instance. This aspect has particularly impeded the establishment of dose-effect relationships for pregnancy complications associated with cocaine use.

The setting of the project also can affect the recruitment of study subjects and thus the definition of the population under investigation. In some research (Chasnoff et al. 1985, 1987, 1989; Ryan et al. 1987; MacGregor et al. 1987), the groups studied were all women referred for drug abuse treatment services within a hospital-based program. Thus, these study results cannot necessarily be extrapolated to women who receive no prenatal care (and are therefore probably more dysfunctional than those in treatment) or to women whose more moderate or minimal use does not initiate referral into a substance abuse treatment program. Zuckerman and colleagues (1989) identified women receiving prenatal care but did not collect information regarding past or present drug abuse treatment.

Women identified as cocaine users in a community setting will receive interventions that vary according to the whim of the individual practitioner. Only pregnant women who are perceived to be at greatest risk from their substance use will be referred to clinical research programs, again affecting the definition of the population to be studied. These issues are especially pertinent given recent evidence that cocaine use occurs at a significant rate in the middle-class population of women seeking care in the private health care setting (Chasnoff et al. 1990).

DEFINITION OF THE DRUG

The drug under study, although labeled "cocaine," may take many forms and may be used in different ways (inhaled, smoked, freebased, injected). The concentration of cocaine may vary from one community to another and, in fact, may vary within a community or over a particular timeframe, as in the 40 weeks of pregnancy. Contaminants with which the cocaine is processed may in themselves have an impact on pregnancy, although no studies have addressed this issue. Economic realities for the pregnant woman also may influence the frequency, timing, and purity of the cocaine she uses as well as the interim use of other drugs.

The dose of cocaine used also can vary over a period of time for the individual. As noted above, polydrug use patterns predominate among cocaine users, but studies are often not designed to take this fact into account. One aspect of this problem is that, at the national level, societal and political concerns have tended to focus on one particular drug at a time. Research priorities are vulnerable to these concerns, so that research proposals and articles accepted for publication tend to focus on that one drug rather than the spectrum of substance use and abuse in pregnancy. This further fragments attempts to understand the interactive and/or additive effects of multiple drugs.

DEFINITION OF THE ENVIRONMENT

In studies of cocaine use in pregnancy, the most difficult problem to overcome is that of other variables in the maternal and fetal environments. The biologic outcome variables (e.g., frequency of low birth weight) may be affected by nutritional factors, previous pregnancy history, and maternal health, to name a few. The frequencies of congenital malformations are known to vary according to maternal age, race, geographic location, and maternal health. If these confounding variables are ignored, their presence in abnormal pregnancy outcomes may be spuriously attributed to drug use simply because these high-risk women also were more likely to use drugs. Conversely, improper consideration of these variables could obscure a drug effect if, for example, the "control group" values are abnormal because of factors increasing risk.

Few of the cited studies thoroughly assessed any of these factors, although some (Chasnoff et al. 1985, 1987, 1989; Bingol et al. 1987; Ryan et al. 1987; MacGregor et al. 1987; Little et al. 1989; Zuckerman et al. 1989) used as controls women from the same obstetric population as their study group to reflect a similar socioeconomic background. Chasnoff and colleagues (1985, 1987, 1989) and Zuckerman and colleagues (1989) used weight gain during pregnancy as a rough indicator of nutritional status, but no studies have assessed the impact of violence on pregnancy outcome—an important aspect of many of these women's lives.

The genetic makeup of the woman and the efficiency at which the pregnant woman may metabolize and excrete cocaine are other areas that could have a profound influence on pregnancy and the fetus, but researchers are not even close to understanding these issues. Differences in fetal susceptibility to drug effects are also of prime importance to the expression of outcome, as has been demonstrated in studies of discordant teratogenesis found in dizygotic twins exposed to alcohol *in utero* (Christoffel and Salafsky 1975; Chasnoff 1985). The mechanism underlying this difference in susceptibility could involve discordance of fetal and placental vasculature (Fogel et al. 1965), different rates of organogenesis with resultant differences in susceptibility to teratogenesis at different times (Lenz 1966), or different rates of drug degradation and elimination on the part of each fetus (Seppala et al. 1971). Whatever the mechanism, it is clear that current debates regarding "threshold" amounts of cocaine that can affect pregnancy outcome are futile, because individual fetal susceptibility is an important yet unpredictable factor in the outcome of the fetus passively exposed to the drug.

DEFINITION OF APPROPRIATE COMPARISON GROUPS

The most difficult aspect of developing comparison groups is assuring that the women selected are in fact drug-free. Most studies (Bingol et al. 1987; Oro and Dixon 1987; Chouteau et al. 1988; Cherukuri et al. 1988; Little et al. 1989; Burkett et al. 1990) have relied on ascertainment of controls retrospectively at the time of delivery, relying on a negative history or one negative urine toxicology to define drug-free status. Cocaine use even 72 hours prior to delivery would thus not show up in the urine toxicology but could well affect the outcome of the pregnancy and the infant. Some researchers have stated that the mistaken inclusion of drug-using women in the drug-free comparison group could obliterate significant differences for the cocaine-using group. However, another way to look at this problem is that if cocaine-exposed neonates did not get identified as drug-exposed because they were asymptomatic (as could have happened in any of the studies just mentioned), their more "normal" outcome could ameliorate the overall negative outcome of the cocaine-exposed group. This speaks to the importance of prenatal identification of control subjects, so that their drug-free status throughout pregnancy can be documented.

In addition, although a control group may be demographically similar to the group under study, there is little one can do to control for the drug-seeking environment in which most of the women under study live. Some studies (Little et al. 1989; Burkett et al. 1990), when they have ascertained controls and study populations at the time of delivery, have included women who had no prenatal care, usually in the substance-using group. Thus, many women in the drug-using group will have had no prenatal care, whereas most of the women in the drug-free group have had prenatal care—a major factor in predicting pregnancy outcome.

DEFINITION OF APPROPRIATE OUTCOME MEASURES

Some of the inconsistency as to outcomes found in various studies may be traced to inadequate appreciation of the biologic expression of cocaine's action on the pregnancy and the fetus. Through a review of the current literature, it appears that cocaine has two modes of action. The first is the indirect effect of cocaine mediated through its pharmacologic action, which causes maternal and fetal vasoconstriction and tachycardia (Woods et al. 1987) and stimulates the pregnant uterus to contract (Lederman et al. 1978). This stimulation of the uterus results in the high rate of prematurity seen in these pregnancies. Other fetal outcomes, especially growth retardation, microcephaly, and congenital anomalies, are mediated through the intrauterine hypoxia and malnutrition induced by the vasoconstriction (Woods et al. 1987). Thus, one does not see malformations but does see evidence for fetal disruptions in pregnancies complicated by cocaine use (Van Allen 1981; Hoyme et al. 1990).

On the other hand, the second mode of action is the direct effects of cocaine induced by its interference with dopamine, norepinephrine, and serotonin reuptake engender increased neurotransmission and central nervous system irritability that may result in direct toxicity to the developing central nervous system of the fetus. This would explain the variations in neurobehavior seen in these infants and also is consistent with studies showing that maternal use of cocaine in the first trimester only can still result in neurobehavioral deficiencies in the newborn infant (Chasnoff et al. 1989). Thus, it would appear that the indirect effects of cocaine could be ameliorated through intervention (i.e., cessation of the woman's cocaine use in pregnancy resulting in a decreased rate of obstetric complications). This is consistent with the work of Chasnoff and coworkers (1989) and Zuckerman and coworkers (1989). However, it also appears that cessation of cocaine use would not reverse the direct effects of cocaine, resulting in toxicity to the fetal central nervous system. Methodologic issues thus arise when techniques for identification of a study population intermix women who used cocaine only early in pregnancy with women who used cocaine throughout the pregnancy.

CONCLUSION

Although all the studies completed thus far have suffered from many of the methodologic issues discussed here, they have been of great value in defining key risk factors and general clinical outcome. With the information now available, it appears safe to conclude that placental dysfunction due to cocaine's vasoconstrictive activity increases risk for intrauterine growth retardation and prematurity; fetal disruption due to acute cocaine-induced vascular compromise places the fetus at risk for structural anomalies; and neurotoxicity due to cocaine's action on monoaminergic neurons places the infant at risk for neurobehavioral abnormalities. Given the extreme difficulty that studies have in establishing experimental control over the myriad confounding variables that can influence pregnancy outcome and the status of the child, what are now needed are studies designed so that sophisticated analytical techniques can be used to establish statistical control over the additive and/or interactive effects of demographic and lifestyle characteristics that place the cocaine-using pregnant woman and her child at risk.

REFERENCES

Acker, D.; Sachs, B.P.; Tracey, K.J.; and Wise, W.E. Abruptio placentae associated with cocaine use. *Am J Obstet Gynecol* 146:220-221, 1983.
Bingol, N.; Fuchs, M.; Diaz, V.; Stone, R.K.; and Gromisch, D.S. Teratogenicity of cocaine in humans. *J Pediatr* 110:93-96, 1987.
Burkett, G.; Yasin, S.; and Palow, D. Perinatal implication of cocaine exposure. *J Reprod Med* 35:35-42, 1990.
Chasnoff, I.J. Fetal alcohol syndrome in twin pregnancy. *Acta Genet Med Gemellol (Roma)* (34:229-232, 1985.

63

Chasnoff, I.J.; Burns, K.A.; and Burns, W.J. Cocaine use in pregnancy: Perinatal morbidity and mortality. *Neurotoxicol Teratol* 9:291-293, 1987.

Chasnoff, I.J.; Burns, W.J.; Schnoll, S.H.; and Burns, K.A. Cocaine use in pregnancy. *N Engl J Med* 313:666-669, 1985.

Chasnoff, I.J.; Griffith, D.R.; MacGregor, S.; Dirkes, K.; and Burns, K.A. Temporal patterns of cocaine use in pregnancy. *JAMA* 261(12):1741-1744, 1989.

Chasnoff, I.J.; Landress, H.J.; and Barrett, M.E. The prevalence of illicit-drug or alcohol use during pregnancy and discrepancies in mandatory reporting in Pinellas County, Florida. *N Engl J Med* 322:1202-1206, 1990.

Cherukuri, R.; Minkoff, H.; Feldman, J.; Parekh, A.; and Glass, L. A cohort study of alkaloid cocaine ("crack") in pregnancy. *Obstet Gynecol* 72:147-151, 1988.

Chouteau, M.; Namerow P.B.; and Leppert, P. The effect of cocaine abuse on birth weight and gestational age. *Obstet Gynecol* 72:351-354, 1988.

Christoffel, K.K., and Salafsky, I. Fetal alcohol syndrome in dizygotic twins. *J Pediatr* 87:963-967, 1975.

Fogel, B.J.; Nitkowsky, H.M.; and Gruenwald, P. Discordant abnormalities in monozygotic twins. *J Pediatr* 66:64-72, 1965.

Frank, D.A.; Zuckerman, B.S.; Amaro, H.; Aboagye, K.; Bauchner, H.; Cabral, H.; Fried, L.; Hingson, R.; Kayne, H.; Levenson, S.M.; Parker, S.; Reece, H.; and Vinci, R. Cocaine use during pregnancy: Prevalence and correlates. *Pediatrics* 82:888-895, 1988.

Hoyme, H.E.; Jones, K.L.; Dixon, S.D.; Jewett, T.; Hanson, J.W.; Robinson, L.K.; Msall, M.E.; and Allanson, J.E. Prenatal cocaine exposure and fetal vascular disruption. *Pediatrics* 85:743-747, 1990.

Hume, R.F.; O'Donnell, K.J.; Stanger, C.L.; Killam, A.P.; and Gingras, J.L. In utero cocaine exposure: Observations of fetal behavioral state may predict neonatal outcome. *Am J Obstet Gynecol* 161:685-690, 1989.

Lederman, R.P.; Lederman, E.; Work, B.A., Jr.; and McCann, D.S. The relationship of maternal anxiety, plasma catecholamines, and plasma cortisol to progress in labor. *Am J Obstet Gynecol* 132:495-500, 1978.

Lenz, W. Malformations caused by drugs in pregnancy. *Am J Dis Child* 112:99-105, 1966.

Little, B.B.; Snell, L.M.; Klein, V.R.; and Gilstrap III, L.C. Cocaine abuse during pregnancy: Maternal and fetal implications. *Obstet Gynecol* 73:157-160, 1989.

MacGregor, S.N.; Keith, L.G.; Chasnoff, I.J.; Rosner, M.A.; Chisum, G.M.; Shaw, P.; and Minogue, J.P. Cocaine use during pregnancy: Adverse perinatal outcome. *Am J Obstet Gynecol* 157:686-690, 1987.

Madden, J.D.; Payne, T.F.; and Miller, S. Maternal cocaine use and effect on the newborn. *Pediatrics* 77:209-211, 1986.

Oro, A.S., and Dixon, S.D. Perinatal cocaine and methamphetamine exposure: Maternal and neonatal correlates. *J Pediatr* 111:571-578, 1987.

Ryan, L.; Ehrlich, S.; and Finnegan, L. Cocaine abuse in pregnancy: Effects on the fetus and newborn. *Neurotoxicol Teratol* 9:295-299, 1987.

Seppala, M.; Raiba, N.C.R.; and Tamminen, V. Ethanol elimination in a mother and her premature twins. *Lancet* 1:1188-1189, 1971.

Van Allen, M.I. Fetal vascular disruption: Mechanisms and some resulting birth defects. *Pediatr Ann* 10:219-233, 1981.

Woods, J.R.; Plessinger, M.A.; and Clark, K.E. Effect of cocaine on uterine blood flow and fetal oxygenation. *JAMA* 257:957-961, 1987.

Zuckerman, B.; Frank, D.A.; Hingson, R.; Amaro, H.; Levenson, S.M.; Kayne, H.; Parker, S.; Vinci, R.; Aboagye, K.; Fried, L.E.; Cabral, H.; Timperi, R.; and Bauchner, H. Effects of maternal marijuana and cocaine use on fetal growth. *N Engl J Med* 320:762-768, 1989.

AUTHOR

Ira J. Chasnoff, M.D.
Associate Professor of Pediatrics and Psychiatry
Northwestern University Medical School
President
National Association for Perinatal Addiction Research and Education
Suite 200
11 East Hubbard Street
Chicago, IL 60611

Use of Birth Defects Monitoring Programs for Assessing the Effects of Maternal Substance Abuse on Pregnancy Outcomes

M. Louise Martin and Larry D. Edmonds

INTRODUCTION

Birth defects are the fifth leading cause of years of potential life lost before age 65 and are the leading cause of infant mortality; they are directly responsible for 21 percent of all infant deaths in the United States (Centers for Disease Control 1989).

From a public health perspective, studying the causes of birth defects and other adverse pregnancy outcomes is important because some causes are entirely preventable. Adverse pregnancy events influenced or caused by maternal ingestion of alcohol, cocaine, and other licit and illicit substances are preventable. To prevent those defects, however, researchers must know (1) the kind and extent of adverse events that are due to a particular agent, (2) the population that is susceptible, and (3) the overall impact of the agent on the public's health.

One way to gain this knowledge is through surveillance systems constructed to monitor or survey birth defects and other adverse pregnancy outcomes. The data gathered through such systems provide a unique source for generating and testing hypotheses about congenital malformations and a variety of maternal and environmental exposures. Data from birth defects surveillance programs have been used to supplement information gained through clinical studies, to test hypotheses generated through clinical studies, and to assess local and national trends in health events for the purpose of correlating changing health trends with shifts in cultural, social, and environmental exposures.

For more than 20 years, the Division of Birth Defects and Developmental Disabilities, Centers for Disease Control (CDC), has conducted two well-known surveillance programs, the Metropolitan Atlanta Congenital Defects Program (MACDP) and the national Birth Defects Monitoring Program (BDMP), to monitor trends in the occurrence of congenital defects and for use in epidemiological studies (Edmonds et al. 1981). Recently, data from these programs have been used to examine maternal substance abuse and its effects on the developing fetus.

Descriptive and epidemiological studies using birth defects surveillance systems contribute significantly to understanding of the etiologies and patterns in birth defect occurrence in populations. In addition, surveillance data gathered in a properly monitored program act as early warnings of new teratogens in the study population.

FUNCTIONS AND ATTRIBUTES OF SURVEILLANCE SYSTEMS

A good health surveillance system maximizes its resources by addressing many needs of the community. The multiple functions of a strong surveillance system constructed to monitor or survey birth defects and other adverse pregnancy outcomes may include (1) developing baseline data so that rates of birth defects and trends in defect rates can be calculated, (2) identifying geographic areas of concern (areas where clusters of defects occur) that may warrant indepth epidemiological investigation, (3) conducting etiologic studies to identify causes of birth defects, (4) planning and evaluating health care programs and services, (5) identifying children in need of special services, and (6) supporting education and advocacy for special health care needs.

The functions of a birth defects surveillance program and the appropriate use of its data depend heavily on the program's characteristics and methods. A good surveillance system has several key characteristics: (1) It has more than one function so that surveillance resources are maximized; (2) it has representative (population-based) coverage so that information gained can be applied or "generalized" to the public at large; (3) its diagnostic data are accurate and precise; (4) its data are reported in a timely manner; (5) its personal identifiers link maternal and paternal records so that cases of disease among infants or events of interest can be followed or, when necessary, coupled with parental exposures; (6) it has case ascertainment (which may require data from multiple sources) that is comprehensive so that underreporting is minimized; (7) it measures many reproductive outcomes; (8) its nosologic methods are etiologically meaningful; (9) it provides a large historic database for comparing rates and for analyzing trends; (10) it can link birth defects data with exposure data; (11) its methods of data collection make followup studies easy to do; (12) its statistical analyses are appropriate; and (13) its patient records are kept confidential.

As the functions and attributes of surveillance systems vary, so too do the quality of the data and the procedures for generating those data. Researchers using any surveillance data must have a thorough knowledge of the quality of these data to interpret them correctly and to extrapolate results. Researchers reviewing scientific literature describing studies based on surveillance data should be aware of the strengths and limitations inherent in the data.

DATA SOURCES FOR BIRTH DEFECTS SURVEILLANCE

Numerous data sources are employed in birth defects surveillance systems; frequently, they include birth and death certificates, hospital discharge summaries, special surveys of existing medical data, special clinic notes, laboratory reports, parental interview data, and environmental data. Each data source has its strengths and limitations. For example, birth and death certificates are useful in that they provide complete coverage of a population of study (thus reducing the likelihood of selection bias) and provide both infant medical data and parental information (allowing correlation with selected parental characteristics or exposures). They are less useful for surveillance tasks that require rapid reporting (because of delay in processing) and for case identification (since they generally have lower rates of case ascertainment and have less complete or accurate information). Newborn hospital discharge summaries are generally more complete and available more quickly than are birth or death certificates, but they provide little or no maternal information. In addition, because newborn hospital discharge data only cover the newborn period, data on defects ascertained after that period are usually missing.

One important difference among data sources is in the quality of case ascertainment. Table 1 illustrates this difference, showing a comparison of rates of major birth defects by source of data.

TABLE 1. *Rates of major birth defects by data source*

Source of Data	Rate Per 10,000 Births
Birth certificates (NCHS[a] 1982-1983)	88.9
Newborn hospital discharge (BDMP[b] 1982-1985)	282.5
Mandatory hospital reporting (Nebraska[c] 1982-1985)	248.0
Linked data sources (Missouri[d] 1982-1987)	336.0
Active hospital surveillance (MACDP[e] 1982-1987)	415.0
(Iowa[f] 1983-1986)	549.0
Physical examination of infant (CPP[g] 1959-1965)	830.0

ᵃ Public use data tape documentation: Birth certificates, 1982-83. Hyattsville, MD: National Center for Health Statistics (1983)
ᵇ Birth Defects Monitoring Program, Division of Birth Defects and Developmental Disabilites, Center for Environmental Health and Injury Control, Centers for Disease Control
ᶜ Nebraska Birth Defects Registry, Division of Health Data and Statistical Research, State Department of Health
ᵈ Missouri Division of Health Resources, Missouri Department of Division of Health
ᵉ Metropolitan Atlanta Congenital Defects Program, Division of Birth Defects and Developmental Disabilities, Center for Environmental Health and Injury Control, Centers for Disease Control
ᶠ Iowa Birth Defects Registry, Iowa Health Registry, University of Iowa Department of Pediatrics and the Department of Health
ᵍ The Collaborative Perinatal Project of the Collaborative Study of Cerebral Palsy, Mental Retardation, and Other Neurological and Sensory Disorders of Infancy and Childhood, from the National Institute of Neurological Diseases and Stroke, National Institutes of Health

BASIC DESIGN ISSUES IN BIRTH DEFECTS SURVEILLANCE

In surveying for birth defects generally and for those attributable specifically to substances of abuse, researchers must understand the basic design issues with which they must contend. For example, researchers must consider the following:

1. Population at risk—Will the surveillance system "capture" this group?

2. Outcomes to include in the case definition—Are nosologic and data collection methods suitable for finding cases as defined in the study?

3. Methods to use for case ascertainment—Are the data sources adequate to capture defined cases from the appropriate populations?

4. Dilemma between the need for confidentiality and the need for personal identifiers—Does the ability to link data sources or to track records over time add significantly to the quality of the surveillance and to the data?

5. Data to collect and by what methods—Will the surveillance system provide adequate descriptive data to facilitate study comparisons of interest?

6. Procedures for data coding, analysis, and reporting and the quality of data resulting from these procedures—Do these have limitations that influence the data quality adversely?

69

7. Need for followup studies and the procedures for conducting followup—
    Does the surveillance system facilitate or preclude followup studies?

METHODS OF CASE ASCERTAINMENT: ACTIVE AND PASSIVE SYSTEMS

Cases in birth defects surveillance systems are ascertained actively or
passively. In active surveillance, trained surveillance staff actively seek cases
in hospitals, clinics, or other facilities by systematically reviewing medical and
other health or social records. In some active surveillance systems, such as the
Collaborative Perinatal Project (Myrianthopoulus and Chung 1974), personnel
performed complete medical examinations of each case infant. In CDC's
MACDP, multiple sources of information, such as vital records and medical
charts in obstetric and pediatric hospitals, cytogenetic laboratories, and genetics
clinics, are used to identify cases (Edmonds et al. 1981).

Active surveillance systems with multiple sources of existing medical data
include the following as their strengths: (1) reporting of defects is fairly
complete, (2) data are provided in a timely fashion, (3) diagnoses are generally
complete and accurate, (4) followup studies are possible, and (5) information is
collected and available on both the infant and the mother. The latter is
especially important for assessing influences on the infant because of maternal
conditions and exposures. Active surveillance systems, however, are limited in
that they are often expensive and because their high cost may limit their range
of catchment to small populations. In addition, because they are generally
based on small populations, it takes much time to generate adequate baseline
data for reliable prevalence rates and to detect and monitor trends.

In passive surveillance systems, cases are identified through reports submitted
to the surveillance program by staff in hospitals, clinics, or other health care
facilities. Those reporting the data may do so voluntarily or because they are
required to do so by law or regulation. CDC's national BDMP is a passive

system; its information comes from hospital discharge data on newborns and is
provided voluntarily by the contributing hospitals. The data in other systems are
gathered through legislatively mandated reports of birth defects, through linked
data from multiple sources, and through vital statistics sources only (Flynt et al.
1987).

In general, the strengths of passive systems are that they can cover populations
from a larger geographic area and therefore have data on a greater number of
cases than do active systems, and they are less expensive to conduct and
manage. Passive systems are, however, limited more than active systems by
incomplete data, inadequate data for followup studies, and greater delays in
reporting data.

70

An important factor for researchers to consider when interpreting data derived from these two types of surveillance systems is that the data, like the sources, differ in how thoroughly cases are ascertained. Table 2 shows select birth defects prevalence rates per 10,000 births by method of ascertainment. Comparing two well-known passive systems with three reputable active systems highlights that, in virtually all cases, active surveillance programs have better systems for diagnosing and ascertaining cases of birth defects. Also noteworthy is that ascertaining cases of apparent defects, such as anencephaly and cleft lip and palate, is better in both active and passive systems than is ascertaining cases with more covert malformations, such as congenital cardiac and renal anomalies.

CHARACTERISTICS OF TWO BIRTH DEFECTS SURVEILLANCE SYSTEMS

We will use two well-known surveillance systems operated by CDC to discuss the data used for assessing pregnancy outcomes. Table 3 is a comparison of these two systems and shows that the active system (MACDP) has a smaller population (about 1/20th the number of births reported to BDMP) and covers a smaller geographic area (Metropolitan Atlanta versus the Nation as a whole). MACDP reports data faster and has an extended period for diagnosing and ascertaining cases (it includes infants up to 1 year of age rather than newborns only). For most cases, the active system has a greater sensitivity and predictive value positive than does the passive system; it contains maternal information, and researchers can use its data more easily for followup studies. These surveillance systems have been used to augment information derived from clinical research on birth defects and other adverse pregnancy outcomes.

USE OF SURVEILLANCE SYSTEMS FOR ASSESSING RISK OF BIRTH DEFECTS ARISING FROM MATERNAL SUBSTANCE ABUSE

BDMP

In 1974 CDC began BDMP, the first nationwide system for monitoring congenital malformations. BDMP was to function primarily as an early warning system to identify new teratogens in the population and to alert public health officials to any changing trends in birth defects or unusual geographic differences within participating areas of the United States.

CDC purchases hospital discharge data from two sources, the Commission on Professional and Hospital Activities and the MacDonnell Douglas Hospital Information Service (MDHIS). Annually through these data, CDC follows about 1 million births (25 percent of the total in the United States) from a nonrandom, hospital-based sample of U.S. births. The information gathered is collected and

TABLE 2. *Comparison of birth defect rates per 10,000 births by method of ascertainment*

Birth Defect	Passive			Active	
	NCHS[a]	BDMP[b]	MACDP[c]	IOWA[d]	CBDMP[e]
Anencephaly	1.5	2.9	3.3	3.9	3.3
Spina bifida	3.2	4.8	6.6	7.3	7.1
Cleft lip +/- cleft palate	5.9	9.1	9.9	12.1	11.1
Hypoplastic left heart	0.3	0.8	3.2	3.8	3.0
Down's syndrome	3.6	8.5	9.6	10.1	9.7

[a] Public use data tape documentation: Birth certificates, 1982-83. Hyattsville, MD: National Center for Health Statistics (1983)
[b] Birth Defects Monitoring Program (1982-1985). Division of Birth Defects and Developmental Disabilities, Center for Environmental Health and Injury Control, Centers for Disease Control
[c] Metropolitan Atlanta Congenital Defects Program (1983-1987), Division of Birth Defects and Developmental Disabilities, Center for Environmental Health and Injury Control, Centers for Disease Control
[d] Iowa Birth Defects Registry, Iowa Health Registry, University of Iowa Department of Pediatrics and the Department of Health
[e] California Birth Defects Monitoring Program (1983-1985). California Department of Health Services

coded uniformly from hospital discharge data, making BDMP the largest single set of uniformly collected and coded data on birth defects among U.S. newborns.

From these data, CDC generates prevalence rates and maintains historic databases from which trends in birth defects can be monitored. Data are monitored quarterly, and trends in rates are evaluated by CUSUM methods for statistical significance. Data also have been used for descriptive and epidemiological studies.

Using a subset of these data, CDC has also generated a linked record system that allows us to generate hypotheses concerning maternal exposures and infant outcomes.

TABLE 3. *Characteristics of two birth defects surveillance systems, Centers for Disease Control*

Characteristic	MACDP[a]	BDMP[b]
Population	35,000/year	1,000,000/year
Database	1968-present (609,000 births)	1970-present (19 million births)
Time between birth and report	1-6 months	6-12 months
Nosology	6 digit BPA/CDC[c]	ICD-9-CM[d]
Precise diagnosis	Written description	ICD code
Case definition	Diagnosis in first year	Newborn diagnosis
Sensitivity	90-100%	60-90%
PVP[e]	90-100%	45-100%
Ascertainment	Multiple source	Newborn discharge
Maternal data	Yes	No
Followup	Yes	Difficult

[a] Metropolitan Atlanta Congenital Defects Program, Division of Birth Defects and Developmental Disabilities, Center for Environmental Health and Injury Control, Centers for Disease Control
[b] Birth Defects Monitoring Program, Division of Birth Defects and Developmental Disabilities, Center for Environmental Health and Injury Control, Centers for Disease Control
[c] British Paediatric Association/Centers for Disease Control; the coding is a CDC modification of the BPA coding scheme
[d] ICD-9-CM: International Classification of Diseases, 9th Edition, Clinical Modification
[e] Predictive value positive

BDMP: Monitoring Trends. From BDMP-generated rates, we can follow birth defect trends in time and place for large populations and geographic regions; we can also make comparisons among rates for select groups of infants. Table 4 shows rates of selected defects among designated racial or ethnic groups in the United States (Chavez et al. 1989). One syndrome routinely monitored is fetal alcohol syndrome (FAS). Compared with the risk for FAS among white infants, Hispanic infants have about the same risk, black infants have a sixfold greater risk, American Indian infants have a 30-fold greater risk, and Asian infants have one-third the risk. These data illustrate that monitoring trends of defects among subgroups is epidemiologically rewarding; the groups identified as being at increased risk can be targeted for prevention and intervention programs; those with lower relative risks can be studied for behavioral, physiological, and genetic factors that protect them from alcohol-related adverse events.

BDMP and MDHIS: Linking Maternal and Infant Records. Since 1982 CDC has accumulated discharge data on almost 3 million infants born in hospitals that subscribe to MDHIS and on women who gave birth in those hospitals. To

TABLE 4. *Rates (per 10,000 births) of major congenital malformations by race/ethnicity, United States, 1981-86*

Malformation	Black	Hispanic	American Indian	Asian	White
Anencephaly	2.1	4.4	3.6	4.4	3.0
Patent ductus arteriosus	49.9	20.7	33.5	25.1	26.5
Cleft palate/ no cleft lip	3.7	3.7	9.8	4.6	5.9
Cleft lip +/- cleft palate	4.4	8.6	17.5	12.9	9.7
FAS	6.0	0.8	29.9	0.3	0.9
Down's syndrome	6.5	11.6	6.7	11.3	8.5
Total	179.9	144.4	222.0	157.8	189.8

SOURCE: Centers for Disease Control 1988

ensure patient confidentiality, no data have personal identifiers; this need for confidentiality, however, limits the usefulness of the data because there is no direct link between maternal and infant records. To enhance the usefulness of the data, yet continue to maintain patient confidentiality, CDC has developed a probabilistic model for linking infant and maternal records anonymously. The linking algorithm relies on a weighted scoring system that assigns numeric values to demographic and clinical variables. Table 5 is a list of some of these variables and the maximum scores assigned for concordance between the infant and the imputed maternal record. The minimum score for considering a pair as matching is seven. Each match is the best match that can be achieved for the pair. Validation studies have shown that 98 percent of infants and mothers match; 95 percent of these are true matches (Heuther 1990).

TABLE 5. *Variables used to link maternal and infant records, BDMP[a] 1982-present*

Variable	Score
ZIP Code	3
Race	2
Religion	2
Twin status	5
Prematurity status	2
Same pay source	1
Physician	1
Surgeon	1
Hours between admissions	4 (maximum)
Same discharge hour	6 (maximum)

[a] From the Division of Birth Defects and Developmental Disabilities, Center for Environmental Health and Injury Control, Centers for Disease Control

The authors have used this linked data set to examine pregnancy outcomes of women with specific medical conditions and environmental exposures coded on their hospital records when their infants were delivered. We have compared the birth outcomes of mothers with the exposures of interest with the outcomes of all mothers in the data set. Several examples illustrate how the data can be used for different maternal exposures.

Maternal Lithium Use and Ebstein's Anomaly. It had been suggested that women taking lithium for manic-depressive disorder were at an increased risk of having an infant with a rare cardiac defect, Ebstein's anomaly. Edmonds and

Oakley (1990) reported on a case-control study conducted at CDC with BDMP data. They identified 53 infants with cases of Ebstein's anomaly coded on their records and reviewed the medical records of these infants. They determined that infants that had false-positive cases (6 miscoded and 13 coded "rule-out Ebstein's" for which diagnoses were never confirmed). Thirty-four infants had confirmed cases. Edmonds and Oakley reviewed hospital and physician records for those 34 infants and for 34 control infants. No infants had mothers with a reported exposure to lithium during pregnancy or history of manic-depressive disease. Edmonds and Oakley corroborated their findings using the MDHIS maternal-infant linked data set: Of the 34 infants whose records indicated they had Ebstein's anomaly, none were born to the 88 women whose records indicated they suffered from manic-depressive disorder.

Maternal Alcohol Dependence. Another example of how these data can be used for maternal exposures is illustrated in table 6, which shows selected outcomes for infants born to 276 mothers whose records had codes for alcohol dependence. As might be expected, these infants were at a higher (1,110-fold) risk of having FAS than were other infants whose records were in the data set. Infants of alcohol-dependent mothers were also at a 12.6-fold higher risk of having microcephaly and at a 5.3-fold higher risk of having oral clefts.

TABLE 6. *Association of maternal alcohol dependence with selected birth defects: Preliminary Data, BDMP[a]*

Rates Per 10,000 Births

Birth Defect	Exposed	Overall	Relative Risk
Microcephaly	36.2	2.9	12.6
FAS	1,775.4	1.6	1,110.0
Oral clefts	72.4	13.6	5.3

[a] From the Division of Birth Defects and Developmental Disabilities, Center for Environmental Health and Injury Control, Centers for Disease Control

Maternal Cocaine Dependence. We also have used the data set to look at pregnancy outcomes of mothers whose records show they were cocaine-dependent at the time of delivery. Table 7 shows selected outcomes for infants born to these mothers. These infants were 113 times more likely to have microcephaly than were other infants with records in the data set. They were also 154 times more likely to suffer from FAS, 24 times more likely to have an atrial septal defect, and 3 times more likely to have a ventricular septal defect.

76

Interpreting data from this data set must proceed with caution: Record-linkage systems, such as this, are enticing because they are relatively inexpensive, provide large sample sizes, and can be useful for exposures that are difficult to ascertain. They are limited, however, by the degree of accuracy and completeness of the linkage, by concerns about breach of confidentiality, and by the potential for misclassification of exposures. For this data set, in particular, limitations also include (1) lack of data on stillborns, (2) lack of detailed information on maternal conditions and therapies, and (3) diagnoses of birth defects only through the newborn period. Despite the limitations, such data sets are excellent for generating hypotheses but should be complemented by followup studies of medical records.

TABLE 7.   *Association between maternal cocaine dependence and selected birth defects: Preliminary Analysis, BDMP[a]*

Birth Defect	Rates Per 10,000 Births		
	Exposed	Overall	Relative Risk
Microcephaly	327.9	2.9	113.1
FAS	245.9	1.6	153.7
Ventricular septal defect	41.0	14.4	2.8
Atrial septal defect	41.0	1.7	24.1

[a] From the Division of Birth Defects and Developmental Disabilities, Centers for Disease Control

MACDP Surveillance Data

The MACDP is a collaborative effort between the CDC, the Georgia Mental Health Institute, and Emory University School of Medicine. The MACDP, like the BDMP, is multifunctional. It has two main objectives: (1) to monitor births of malformed infants for changes in prevalence or other unusual patterns suggestive of environmental influences and (2) to develop a case registry for use (a) in epidemiological and genetic studies, such as descriptive epidemiologic studies; (b) in generating and testing hypotheses; and (c) in conducting case-control and family studies. Since 1967 the MACDP has collected data systematically, including identification, demographic, clinical, and diagnostic information as well as information prior maternal illnesses and pregnancy history. Cases of birth defects are ascertained by reviewing maternal and infant medical records from multiple sources, including birth hospitals, pediatric hospitals, cytogenetic laboratories, specialty clinics, and vital records. Data are analyzed quarterly, and trends in rates are evaluated by CUSUM methods for statistical significance. An added component of the MACDP is the Atlanta Case Control Study (described later). MACDP data have been used extensively in descriptive studies of selected birth defects, including trends in the clinical characteristics of infants with spina bifida (Adams et al. 1985), in the incidence of pyloric stenosis (Lammer and Edmonds 1987), in the epidemiology of early amnion rupture spectrum (Garza et al. 1988), and in the impact of prenatal diagnosis of Down's syndrome, selected midline defect associations, and coarctation of the aorta (Martin et al. 1990). Using the MACDP data, researchers are currently conducting two studies to explore an association of selected birth defects and cocaine abuse during pregnancy.

Gastroschisis Cluster Investigation. The first study is a case-control study of gastroschisis in the Atlanta metropolitan area. In 1988 CDC identified a cluster of infants affected by gastroschisis by monitoring MACDP trends in birth defects. During that year, 18 infants with gastroschisis were born when only 6 were expected. The observed-to-expected ratio was 3.0 (p=0.00004). Figure 1 shows the prevalence of gastroschisis-affected births in Atlanta from 1968 through 1988. Because cocaine use during pregnancy is believed to produce vascular disruption defects, one of which may be gastroschisis, one hypothesis

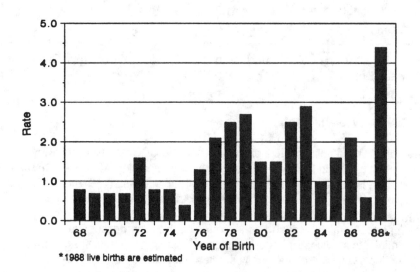

* 1988 live births are estimated

FIGURE 1. *Gastroschisis: Trends in reported incidence among live births and stillbirths: MACDP, January 1968-December 1988 (rates per 10,000 live births)*

78

to be tested in this case-control study is that maternal use of cocaine in pregnancy may be associated with the increase in gastroschisis. Mothers of case and control infants are currently being interviewed concerning a variety of exposures during pregnancy, including use of cocaine in its various forms and routes of administration (Lynberg, manuscript in progress).

Trends in Vascular Disruption Defects. Because it has been reported that the incidence of cocaine use among women of childbearing age has been increasing in the United States (Miller et al. 1984; Johnston et al. 1987), we hypothesized that if maternal cocaine use caused vascular disruption, then a concomitant increase in the prevalence of these defects should occur. Martin and colleagues (1990) used MACDP surveillance data to examine trends for vascular disruption defects. The infants selected were born between January 1, 1968, and December 31, 1989, with vascular disruptions involving two or more organ systems; defects of interest included gastroschisis, porencephaly, intestinal atresia, renal agenesis/dysgenesis and other urinary anomalies, and transverse limb reductions. Figure 2 shows the 3-year moving average of birth prevalence of infants with vascular disruption defects in two or more organ systems during the study period. Preliminary analysis for trends showed no significant increase in births over the time period of study (Chi square for linear trend=1.16, p=0.28). In addition, the relative risk (RR) was not significantly different for race (RR for blacks [whites as referent]=0.68, 95 percent confidence interval [CI]=0.42-1.11). Further analysis is under way. Although no detectable "epidemic" of multiple vascular disruption defects has occurred in Atlanta during the study period, further epidemiologic studies are clearly indicated to establish whether cocaine is a human teratogen and, if so, to evaluate patterns of birth defects related to its teratogenic effects.

Atlanta Birth Defects Case Control Study. The Atlanta Birth Defects Case Control Study is a special component of the MACDP. Data for the Atlanta Birth Defects Case Control Study were collected from parents of babies with cases of major congenital anomalies and from a group of parents of randomly selected control babies without birth defects. Case infants were ascertained through the MACDP data for 1968 through 1980. Through computer-assisted telephone interviews, MACDP data for case infants were supplemented with detailed maternal interview data collected from 1982 through 1983. Nearly 5,000 mothers of case infants and more than 3,000 mothers of control infants responded to questions regarding family history, demographics, health, and maternal exposures (overall response rate 71 percent). Details of the studies have been described elsewhere (Erickson et al. 1984).

Data from this case control study were used by Chavez and coworkers (1989) to investigate the association between genitourinary tract malformations and

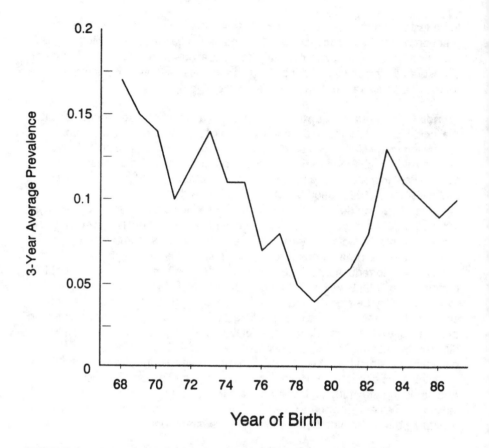

Year of Birth

FIGURE 2. *Three-year moving average, prevalence of two vascular disruptions in infants, 1968-89*

cocaine use during pregnancy. Among the case infants, 276 were identified with urinary anomalies and 791 with genital anomalies; among a group of control infants (frequency matched to case infants by race, hospital of birth, and calendar quarter of birth), they found 2,630 with urinary anomalies and 2,965 with genital anomalies (table 8). Maternal cocaine use was defined as use at any time from 1 month before pregnancy through the first 3 months of pregnancy. Chavez and coworkers found a statistically significant association between reported cocaine use and an increased risk for urinary tract defects. Infants of mothers who admitted to cocaine use were at a 4.39-fold higher risk of having urinary tract abnormalities (95 percent CI: 1.12-17.24). No significant association with genital organ defects was noted. This study was the first population-based case-control study of maternal cocaine use and congenital urogenital anomalies.

Several limitations of the Chavez and coworkers' study are noteworthy: (1) The number of urogenital anomalies identified among babies of cocaine-using women was small; and the confidence limits, although excluding unity, were wide. The results, as the investigators pointed out, should be viewed as tentative until confirmed or refuted by larger studies. (2) Cocaine use was classified on the basis of maternal self-report. Classifying maternal cocaine exposure on the basis of self-report has been controversial and has led to criticisms of exposure misclassification (Valanis et al. 1988; Zuckerman et al. 1989). (3) The prevalence of cocaine exposure during the study period (1968-1980) is probably lower than exposure prevalence during the latter part of the 1980s; using 1968-1980 figures may cause researchers to underestimate current drug use. (4) The study period predated "crack" cocaine; if different routes of cocaine administration have different pathogenetic effects on the developing fetus, those differences may not be reflected in the results of this study.

SUMMARY

We have attempted to demonstrate that birth defects surveillance systems are a unique adjunct to clinical research data on maternal exposures, including substances of abuse. Surveillance system data reflect the experiences of the populations from which they are drawn and the characteristics of the people in

TABLE 8. *Association between maternal cocaine use and urogenital anomalies in infants*

Anomaly	Maternal Cocaine Use		No Maternal Cocaine Use		Odds Ratio (95% CI)
	Cases	Controls	Cases	Controls	
All urinary tract defects	3	7	273	2,630	4.39 (1.12-17.24)
All genital organ defects	4	8	787	2,965	2.26 (0.67-7.62)

SOURCE: Chavez et al. 1989

81

those populations. Sensitive systems may reveal trends in health status and changes in behavioral, cultural, social, or environmental exposures. They can be used to monitor changing trends, to identify clusters for investigation, to generate and test hypotheses, and to conduct epidemiological studies.

For researchers to interpret data derived from surveillance systems appropriately and wisely, they need a thorough knowledge of the data sources, the data-collection procedures, and the intent of the surveillance systems. Researchers using surveillance data should have a thorough understanding of the quality of their data and the methodologic subtleties that bear on its interpretation; researchers reviewing scientific literature based on surveillance data should be aware of the strengths and limitations inherent in the data.

REFERENCES

Adams, M.M.; Greenberg, F.; Khoury, M.J.; Marks, J.S.; and Oakley G.P. Trends in clinical characteristics of infants with spina bifida: Atlanta, 1972-79. *Am J Dis Child* 139:514-517, 1985.

Centers for Disease Control. Contributions of birth defects to infant mortality—United States, 1986. *MMWR* 38:633-635, 1989.

Chavez, G.F.; Cordero, J.F.; and Becerra, J.E. Leading major congenital malformations among minority groups in the United States, 1981-1986. *JAMA* 261:205-208, 1989.

Chavez, G.F.; Mulinare, J.; and Cordero, J.F. Maternal cocaine use during early pregnancy as a risk factor for congenital urogenital anomalies. *JAMA* 262(6):795-798, 1989.

Edmonds, L.D.; Layde, P.M.; James, L.M.; Flynt, J.W.; Erickson, J.D.; and Oakley, G.P. Congenital malformation surveillance: Two American systems. *Int J Epidemiol* 10:247-252, 1981.

Edmonds, L.D., and Oakley, G.P. Ebstein anomaly and maternal lithium exposure during pregnancy. (Abstract.) *Proceedings of the Third International Conference of Teratogen Information Services.* Park City, UT: Third International Conference of Teratogen Information Services, 1990.

Erickson, J.D.; Mulinare, J.; McClain, P.W.; Fitch, T.G.; James, L.M.; McClearn, A.B.; and Adams, M.J. *Vietnam Veterans' Risks for Fathering Babies with Birth Defects.* Atlanta, GA: Centers for Disease Control, 1984.

Flynt J.W.; Norris, C.K.; Zaro, S.; Kitchen, S.B.; Kotler, M.; and Ziegler, A. *State Surveillance of Birth Defects and Other Adverse Reproductive Effects.* Atlanta, GA: Centers for Disease Control, 1987.

Garza, A.; Cordero, J.F.; and Mulinare, J. Epidemiology of early amnion rupture spectrum of defects: Atlanta, 1968-1982. *Am J Dis Child* 142:541-544, 1988.

Heuther, C.A. "Qualitative Assessment of CDC's Birth Defects Monitoring Program Data Sets." Centers for Disease Cntrol, Atlanta, GA, 1990.

Johnston, L.D.; O'Malley, P.M.; and Bachman, J.G. *National Trends in Drug Use and Related Factors Among American High School Students and Young Adults, 1975-1986.* National Institute on Drug Abuse. DHHS Pub. No. (ADM)87-1539. Washington, DC: Supt. of Docs., U.S. Govt. Print. Off., 1987.

Lammer, E.J., and Edmonds, L.D. Trends in pyloric stenosis incidence. *J Med Genet* 24:482-487, 1987.

Martin, M.L.; Adams, M.M.; and Mortensen, M.L. The descriptive epidemiology of selected malformations of the aorta: Atlanta, 1970-1983. *Teratology* 42(3):273-283, 1990.

Miller, J.D.; Cisin, I.H.; and Gardner-Keaton, H. *National Survey on Drug Abuse: Main Findings 1982.* National Institute on Drug Abuse. DHHS Pub. No. (ADM)84-1263. Washington, DC: Supt. of Docs., U.S. Govt. Print. Off., 1984.

Myrianthopoulos, N.C., and Chung, C.S. *Report from the Collaborative Perinatal Project: Congenital Malformations in Singletons: Epidemiologic Survey.* Birth Defects: Original Article Series. The National Foundation, March of Dimes. New York: Stratton Intercontinental Medical Book Corp, 1974. pp. 1-59.

Valanis, B.; Waage G.; Dworkin, L.; and Romig, K. Prevalence of drug use during pregnancy by source of data used. *Am J Epidemiol* 128:944, 1988.

Zuckerman, B.; Frank, D.A.; Hingson, R.; Amaro, H.; Levenson, S.M.; Kayne, H.; Parker, S.; Vinci, R.; Aboagye, K.; Fried, L.E.; Cabral, H.; Timperi, R.; and Bauchner, H. Effects of maternal marijuana and cocaine use on fetal growth. *N Engl J Med* 320:762-768, 1989.

AUTHORS

M. Louise Martin, M.S., D.V.M.
Epidemiologist

Larry D. Edmonds, M.S., D.V.M.
Epidemiologist

Birth Defects and Genetic Diseases Branch
Division of Birth Defects and Developmental Disabilities
Center for Environmental Health and Injury Control
Centers for Disease Control
1600 Clifton Road, N.E., F-37
Atlanta, GA 30333

Discussion: Methodologic Issues in Assessment of Pregnancy Outcomes

Ronald A. Chez

INTRODUCTION

Birth defects monitoring programs for assessing the effects of maternal substance abuse on pregnancy outcome are aimed at enhancing the capacity to prevent such outcomes. As reviewed by Martin and Edmonds (this volume), appropriate surveillance systems feature at least 13 key characteristics and methodologic attributes. The source of data remains the crux, however, because of the strengths and weaknesses of each data source. An example is estimating the rates of major birth defects. Using birth certificates as a source of data provides a rate of one-tenth the rate of 830 per 10,000 births found on physical examination during the first year of life. Examinations done as the infant progresses through childhood and puberty yield an even higher rate.

Consideration of these basic design issues highlights the differences between active and passive surveillance. In analyzing the strengths and weaknesses of each method, accuracy is the dominant area of disparity. Contrasting the Metropolitan Atlantic Congenital Defects Program, an active program that examines children up to 1 year of age, with the National Birth Defects Monitoring Program, a passive program, emphasizes their differences, including sensitivity and predictive value (Martin and Edmonds, this volume).

Some fundamental questions related to design need to be addressed. Without answers, an inability to recognize the presence of birth defects with any alacrity will continue. The first question concerns how one recognizes birth defects. Phocomelia was recognized rapidly because it was relatively rare and its features were overt. In contrast, an increased incidence of urinary tract disorders, cerebral palsy, mental retardation, or a number of other conditions with multifactorial origins would have delayed or prevented recognition of the causal relationship between phocomelia and thalidomide use in mothers.

Extend this notion to ask whether the maternal use of a teratogen resulting in a modification of intellectual, psychological, sociological, or learning behaviors would be identified. These disabilities may not be manifest until a child enters school. Question also the likelihood of recognizing a teratogen resulting in a marked increase in the incidence of carcinoma of the cervix, gallbladder disease, or emphysema, all relatively common diseases.

The diethylstilbestrol (DES) exposure in pregnancy experience is similar to the phocomelia example. Again, the rarity of the lesions (adenosis and carcinoma of the vagina and changes in the anatomical and functional capacity of the cervix and uterus) enhanced recognition of the causal relationship. If, instead, DES exposure had resulted in an increase of infertility per se or menstrual dysfunction or premature rupture of the membranes, most likely the role of DES would not have been identified.

DATA DEFICIENCIES

The reliability of research data that depend on history-taking and physical examination by direct-care health professionals is also questionable. There are always deficiencies in creating a medical record, including the discharge summary. Regardless of the time of day, the intellectual interest, the capacity of the patient to communicate, and the curiosity and thoroughness of the examiner, too many data are always lacking. Without a specifically trained and focused investigator who has no clinical responsibility but to obtain data related to causation to test a specific hypothesis, medical records will always be an unsatisfactory source of data.

Also important is how the questions are asked to ensure that reliable data are obtained. A relevant example relates to identification of alcohol use in pregnancy. Questions related to quantity of alcoholic beverages consumed daily are neither as sensitive nor as specific as those related to changes in the woman's tolerance to alcohol (Martier et al. 1990). Also, it is necessary to be alert to pejorative connotations in the construct of the questions and to prejudices that the questioner may manifest verbally and nonverbally. Finally, the patient's own perceptions of her behavior, local societal values, and the stigma and guilt about the appropriate or correct answers will affect her willingness, her candor, and the veracity of her responses.

Another consideration is the extent to which this research depends on patient self-reports. Because this is a medicine-taking society, women who take over-the-counter medications may not think of them as medications and may not include them in a drug history. Large numbers of women take nonprescription appetite suppressants, antiemetics, tranquilizers, analgesics, antihistamines, supplemental minerals, and vitamins periconceptionally (Piper et al. 1987). Women also are exposed unwittingly to environmental toxins and pollutants, both in the home and at work. Most are not recognized. In other words, during embryogenesis, a human fetus has the potential to be exposed to a number of exogenous agents, not all of which are recognized or remembered by its mother.

There is a current debate in this country as to whether the use of periconceptional multivitamins can decrease the incidence of neural tube defects. Competent clinical investigators have published exactly opposite interpretations. One group, headed by Mills, indicates that multivitamins have no value; the other group, headed by Milunsky, indicates that the incidence can be decreased by 75 percent (Mills et al. 1989; Milunsky et al. 1989). Both sets of data were collected through recall of the patients' use of vitamins; the timing and manner of data collection are the dominant differences between these two studies. This is a specific example of the varying effect of when in pregnancy the interview (and therefore the self-reporting) is solicited. In this case, further bias is probable because of the selective and focused memory of a mother when a neural tube defect is found at birth or prenatally with ultrasound.

A separate issue relates to cross-sectional vs. longitudinal studies. Many practical reasons exist for performing cross-sectional studies; without longitudinal studies, however, it is not possible to evaluate the full spectrum of physical, mental, intellectual, behavioral, and psychological functioning in those exposed to possible toxins or teratogens. Major deterrents are the cost and the logistics of such studies. An additional deterrent applies specifically to substance abuse. Criminalization of substance abuse with punitive sanctions has made anonymity a basic requirement of this research area. The additional factors of a mobile society, the demands of tracking people through many years of life, and the relatively low priority most people place on providing health information to researchers, all make a longitudinal study seem a utopian, unrealistic dream. Longitudinal and prospective are the two key words. Innovative and creative research techniques are the challenge for this high-priority goal as is the development of viable, alternative methodologies.

Zuckerman ("Selected Methodologic Issues," this volume) reported data from a number of published studies that exemplify bias, sampling error, and inappropriate conclusions. The lessons derive not only from cocaine, but also from alcohol and marijuana research. The common threads are dependency on self-reporting and the lack of biologic markers to quantify amount and duration of drug exposure. Flexible laboratory monitoring is not available as it is for the pregnant insulin-dependent diabetic woman. For that patient, a glucometer can measure current plasma glucose levels daily. Data are recorded on a memory chip that is reviewed when the patient returns to the office. Glycosylated blood hemoglobin levels integrate information about blood glucose levels over 8 to 12 weeks. Glycosylated blood albumin levels provide similar information about albumin integrated over 3 to 4 weeks. These biochemical markers decrease dependence on the patient's memory or reporting. The preliminary data obtained from research on meconium analysis is an important advance in quantifying past exposure to cocaine (Ostrea et al. 1988). A search for other laboratory aids in the field of substance abuse is critical.

There is a temptation to evaluate data from the point of view of biologic plausibility. Fetal alcohol syndrome is an example of not making this too strong a test of credibility. Alcohol is used by all cultures and tribes. A high use rate of wine and beer exists in Europe and this country, yet the estimates of adverse outcome in alcoholic pregnancy in studies from the United States and Europe have failed to show an incidence higher than 50 percent (Danis and Keith 1983). This suggests that there are moderating variables, including genetic susceptibility, individual metabolism, and a threshold for anomalies. Recent articles on allelic genes for alcoholism and differences in alcohol dehydrogenase levels in women compared with men emphasize susceptibility (Blum et al. 1990; Frezza et al. 1990); however, many authorities interdict any alcohol ingestion during pregnancy. The data do not allow this extrapolation. The data also do not define a universal threshold. The incidence of minor or major anomalies can be shown to relate to the number of drinks per day, but whether this number is two, four, or six remains in doubt. The challenge is to define the specificity, the critical period, and the threshold for alcohol teratogenicity (Ernhart et al. 1987).

A recent article dealt cogently with the prediction and risk of fetal hydantoin syndrome (Buehler et al. 1990). The human fetus has a variable response when exposed to hydantoin during pregnancy. The maternal ingestion of this drug results in elevated levels of its toxic intermediary metabolites. These are normally eliminated by epoxide hydrolase, whose activity level is regulated by a single gene with two allelic forms. According to this preliminary study, low epoxide hydrolase activity in the fetus of a woman taking phenytoin monotherapy will result in clinical findings compatible with the fetal hydantoin syndrome. In contrast, the syndrome will not manifest in a fetus with high enzyme activity. This study is important because it will eventually help to identify fetuses at increased risk when their mothers ingest hydantoin. It also provides insight into a biologic basis for variations in fetal susceptibility similar to the lack of universality of adverse impact that characterizes most teratogens.

CONFOUNDING VARIABLES

Investigations into the relationship between use or abuse of teratogens and adverse perinatal outcome address cause and effect; yet in many studies, a number of potential contributing variables have not been examined. In terms of epidemiologic principles, such investigations are asking about determinants or etiologic factors on the causal pathway to consequences or outcomes. The research problem is one of identifying and factoring the effects of mediating and confounding variables and effect modifiers. Mediating variables, both as direct and indirect determinants, affect the magnitude of the cause-and-effect relationship. Effect modifiers are factors that modify the magnitude of the determinant's affect on outcome. Confounding variables, although they are not on the direct line of cause and effect, can bias its strength by distorting the apparent relationship.

In clinical obstetrics, the recurring examples that exemplify these principles are intrauterine growth retardation and premature rupture of membranes/premature labor. Consider the established determinants of intrauterine growth and gestational duration. The major etiologic categories for intrauterine growth retardation are maternal, placental, and fetal. Each of these divisions has immunologic, genetic, chromosomal, endocrine, and infectious disease subcategories. The direct variables include infant sex, racial and ethnic origin, maternal height, prepregnancy weight, paternal height and weight, maternal birth weight, parity, history of prior infant with low birth weight, gestational weight gain, caloric intake, general morbidity, cigarette smoking, and alcohol consumption (Kramer 1987). With regard to gestational duration, the direct determinants that have been established are prepregnancy weight, prior history of prematurity or cigarette smoking, and *in utero* DES exposure (Kramer 1987). Other etiologic categories for preterm birth include personal demographic features; maternal behaviors, including stress, work, fatigue, and intercourse; and personal hygiene and environmental conditions, including inadequate social support systems.

These long lists illustrate the difficulties in establishing a causal pathway for either of these outcomes. The result is underestimated determinants, misclassified effect modifiers, unrecognized outcomes, and undocumented confounding variables. In this environment, valid conclusions cannot be forthcoming.

The review of human studies by Chasnoff (this volume) helps identify methodologic difficulties that fundamentally revolve around lack of consistency in the definitions of cocaine use and adverse outcome. The narrow focus of investigators when validating their hypotheses almost ensures that confounding and mediating variables cannot be identified or recognized. Furthermore, the polydrug use pattern of patients (including the use of nicotine, with its long list of adverse pregnancy outcomes) is frequently not recognized because information about it is not sought and because many drugs cannot be identified in the absence of biologic markers.

There can be uncertainty about the timing of a prenatal insult and subsequent adverse pregnancy outcomes. The putative effects of a teratogen in pregnancy can involve assaults to the egg or sperm prior to conception, conception itself with mutagenicity, the embryo with teratogenicity, embryotoxicity via fetal growth and development, and newborn morbidity. Identifying the time of impact requires tracking of patients. This strategy, a variation of the longitudinal study, is essential to the clarification of fetal abnormalities associated with drug use.

There is a finite period of human embryogenesis; however, this timeframe may be too narrow. Freinkel (1980) has posited that hyperglycemia during the second trimester has an adverse effect on subsequent intellectual, behavioral, and psychological development in the offspring of a diabetic mother. It is known that the central nervous system continues to develop throughout the fetal life and on into infancy; that neuronal differentiation, axonal growth, synapse formation, process elimination, and myelinization continue throughout postnatal life for many months; and that some of the adverse impact of alcoholism on fetal growth can be decreased by modifying drinking behaviors even as late as the third trimester. It is also known that establishing positive health practices in women with insulin-dependent diabetes mellitus and with epileptics using antiseizure medications prior to conception will decrease the incidence of congenital malformations. The establishment of dose-effect relationships for pregnancy complications requires obtaining data from preconception to the postnatal period.

This research also requires the use of short- and long-term biochemical and biophysical laboratory markers. A woman who has a single exposure to cocaine at term in an attempt to precipitate the onset of labor will have a positive urine screen at delivery. As such, she will be labeled as a cocaine user during pregnancy and her data will be incorrectly combined with that from women with other patterns of cocaine use. Chasnoff (this volume) emphasizes the importance of quantifying the insult. The inability to ascertain what is actually being used by the patient is a major concern in identifying causation. Additional confounding factors relate to route, frequency, duration, and timing of use; to peak maximum blood levels; and to the purity of the substance used. The same comments apply to identifying the impurities contaminating the substance of abuse and their effect on the pregnancy. Such pharmacokinetic questions constitute the crux of the dose-response relationships.

Another variable is the physiology and function of the placenta. Drugs of abuse can cause placental dysfunction, either via modification of metabolic pathways or by curtailing the vascular supply of substrates and oxygen to and from the placenta. Moreover, the location of the implantation site of the placenta in the uterus, the normal physiological senescence of the placenta late in pregnancy, and the possibility of disease of the placenta (such as infection) are all confounding variables that cannot be quantitated.

A necessary part of clinical research is to define an appropriate comparison group, but what is really known about the people assigned to control groups? The same questions of teratogen exposure, nutrition, confounding and mediating variables, and lack of biologic markers all apply to the control group. The factors that influence pregnancy outcome include social status, psychological stress, genetic makeup, infection and environmental hazards, health and physiologic state during pregnancy, childhood experiences, sociocultural pattern, health practices, and motivation to seek and use prenatal care.

Considering this long list of determinants, how likely is it that a control group can be identified for valid comparison? In fact, in actual research, it is extraordinarily difficult. The access to large numbers of women delivering in maternity hospitals does not obviate this very specific research problem.

CONCLUSION

Researchers all suffer from the diseases of jumping to conclusions regarding cause and effect, failing to recognize confounding variables, and depending excessively on the validity of self-reporting. Researchers have difficulty in obtaining unbiased samples and valid control groups and are more adept at recognizing and differentiating adverse outcomes that are rare, affect overt physical structures, and occur immediately, as opposed to more long-term problems that are not as visible. Solutions include development of new methods of toxicologic testing for long- and short-term biologic markers, funding of longitudinal studies to understand both immediate and long-term effects, and attention to rigorous preparation of medical records. Before credible intervention strategies can be devised, researchers must be able to understand the vagaries of the dose-effect relationship. Therefore, it is necessary to dissect the variations in human biology, biochemistry, physiology, and biophysics and determine their genetic bases.

The fundamental question is, What proximal and distal causes result in proximal and distal effects? In asking this, researchers must remain alert to identifying and factoring mediating and confounding variables, as well as effect modifiers. The conclusion is that no single factor will stand alone as a sufficient cause for either an adverse or a healthy pregnancy outcome.

REFERENCES

Blum, K.; Noble, E.P.; Sheridan; P.J.; Montgomery; A.; Ritchie; T.; Jagadelswaran; P.; Nogami; H.; Briggs; A.H.; and Cohn, J.B. Allelic association of human dopamine D2 receptor gene in alcoholism. *JAMA* 263:2055-2060, 1990.

Buehler, B.A.; Delimont, D.; van Waes, M.; and Finnell, R.H. Prenatal prediction of risk of the fetal hydantoin syndrome. *N Engl J Med* 322:1567-1572, 1990.

Danis, R.P., and Keith, L. Fetal alcohol syndrome: Incurable but preventable. *Contrib Obstet Gynecol* 21:57-68, 1983.

Ernhart, C.B.; Sokol, R.J.; Martier, S.; Moron, P.; Nadler, D.; Ager, J.W.; and Wolf, A. Alcohol teratogenicity in the human: A detailed assessment of specificity, critical period, and threshold. *Am J Obstet Gynecol* 156:33-39, 1987.

Freinkel, N. Of pregnancy and progeny. *Diabetes* 29:1023-1033, 1980.

Frezza, M.; di Padova, C.; Pozzato, G.; Terpin, M.; Bavaona, E.; and Lieber, C.S. High blood alcohol levels in women: The role of decreased gastric alcohol dehydrogenase activity and first-pass metabolism. *N Engl J Med* 322:95-99, 1990.

Kramer, M.S. Determinants of low birth weight: Methodologic assessment and meta-analysis. *Bull World Health Organ* 65:663-737, 1987.

Martier, S.S.; Bottoms, S.F.; Sokol, R.T.; and Ager, J.W. Pregnancy risk drinking: Optimized screening with tolerance. *Soc Gynecol Invest Abst*. No. 126. 167:31, 1990.

Mills, J.L.; Rhoads, G.G.; Simpson, J.L.; Cunningham, G.C.; Conley, M.R.; Lassman, M.R.; Walden, M.E.; Depp, R.O.; and Hoffman, H.S. The absence of a relation between the periconceptional use of vitamins and neural tube defects. *N Engl J Med* 321:430-435, 1989.

Milunsky, A.; Jick, M.; Jick, S.S.; Bruell, C.L.; MacLaughlin, D.S.; Rothman, K.J.; and Willett, W. Multivitamin/folic acid supplementation in early pregnancy reduces the prevalence of neural tube defects. *JAMA* 262:2847-2852, 1989.

Ostrea, E.M.; Asensio, D.; Naluz, A.; Semkowski, K.; Subramanian, M.; and Abel, E.L. The detection of heroin, cocaine and cannabinoid metabolites in the stools of infants of drug dependent mothers. In: Harris, L.S., ed. *Problems of Drug Dependence, 1987: Proceedings of the 49th Annual Scientific Meeting, The Committee on Problems of Drug Dependence, Inc.* National Institute on Drug Abuse Research Monograph 81. DHHS Pub. No. (ADM)88-1564. Washington, DC: Supt. of Docs., U.S. Govt. Print. Off., 1988. p. 262.

Piper, J.M.; Baum, C.; and Kennedy, D.L. Prescription drug use before and during pregnancy in a Medicaid population. *Am J Obstet Gynecol* 157:148-156, 1987.

AUTHOR

Ronald A. Chez, M.D.
Professor
Department of Obstetrics and Gynecology
University of South Florida
Suite 500
Four Columbia Drive
Tampa, FL 33606

What We Can Learn From the Status of the Newborn

T. Berry Brazelton

Although there have been other epidemics of drug abuse (cocaine and alcohol in the late 1930s, alcohol in every recent decade, marijuana and heroin in the 1960s and 1970s), the most serious threat to young adults and their offspring—multiple drug abuse—has been booming since the 1980s, seriously affecting the fetuses of these young adults and threatening the future of approximately one-fifth of neonates born in the United States. New approaches are needed to assess, study, and intervene with the adult and newborn victims of this epidemic.

It has long been known that intrauterine influences affect the DNA and RNA replication of the developing fetus. These effects can be seen in reduced head circumference, linear growth, and birth weight. In turn, these effects influence the neonate's behavioral responses in significant ways. In a study in Guatemala, Brazelton and colleagues (1977) were able to demonstrate that poor intrauterine nutrition significantly affected the behaviors of the neonate in ways that led to poorer maternal nurturing. In addition, postnatal malnutrition became synergistic with prenatal undernutrition. The significantly poorer outcome of these children at ages 6 to 7 years was predicted by their neonatal behavior, because it affected the responses to them by their already undernourished, overstressed mothers. To interrupt this cycle of poverty, which repeats itself from one generation to another, the prenatal and perinatal periods would be the target spots for intervention (figure 1).

The ponderal index (a ratio of weight to length) can be used to indicate fetal malnutrition. Als and colleagues (1976) compared full-term infants underweight for length (below the 10th percentile) and average weight for length at 1, 3, 5, and 10 days of life on the Neonatal Behavioral Assessment Scale (NBAS) (Brazelton 1984a). These normal, healthy, but underweight infants differed from controls along behavioral dimensions that are particularly important for caregiving, such as attractiveness, need for stimulation, and interactive and motor processes. The groups also differed on reflexive behavior. Moreover, in followup by telephone during the first few weeks of life of the underweight

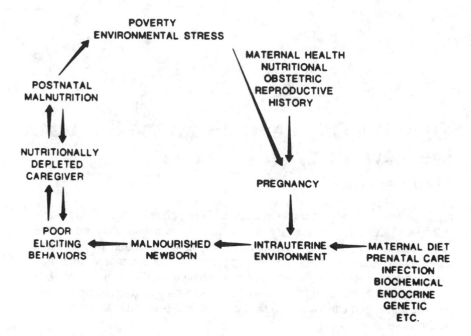

FIGURE 1. *Synergistic model of the effects of prenatal malnutrition*

infants, mothers reported difficulties in temperamental organization and indications of psychosomatic reaction to stress. Neonatal behavior predicted difficulties in state behavior in later infancy (as late as 9 months), such as hypersensitivity to stimuli, rapid and distractible state changes, and increased crying spells of long duration. Difficult newborns remained difficult throughout infancy.

Lester and Zeskind examined infants who were below the third percentile on the ponderal index and showed that these infants exhibited poorer performance across all NBAS behavioral dimensions (Lester et al. 1976; Lester and Zeskind 1978). Correlations between the NBAS dimensions and the acoustic features of babies' cries indicated that poor NBAS scores were related to differences in cry features. The cry of the underweight-for-length babies showed a higher and more variable fundamental frequency and more harmonic distortion, in contrast to the generally flat melody form of the cry of the full-weight infant. Cry features and NBAS scores were highly related. Babies' behavior and cry features can reflect intrauterine stress. In a recent study, the NBAS clusters and supplementary items were found to discriminate infants with atypical patterns of fetal growth from infants with appropriate patterns of fetal growth (Lester et al. 1986).

Lester and Zeskind (1978) used multiple regression to determine the relative contribution of six high-risk variables on factor scores of the NBAS. Low attention scores were associated with low-birth-weight babies who were likely to be the infants of younger mothers. Low Apgar scores were associated with babies who scored lower on a temperament-arousal dimension. The 52 babies of this study also were included in a study of 140 infants of low, average, and high birth weight (Lester et al. 1976). Factor scores representing three dimensions—attention, arousal, and temperament—were compared among the three birth-weight groups with gestational age as a covariant. Both extremes— low and very high birth-weight babies—scored lower on attentional behavior than did infants of average birth weight. Low-birth-weight males and high-birth-weight females scored lower on arousal and temperament than did other sex-by-birth-weight groups. Postmature as well as immature babies may be at risk for attentional deficits and poor state control. There are 20 to 30 such studies using the NBAS that demonstrate the effects on the neonate's behavior of intrauterine deprivation.

These studies point to the importance of assessing as carefully as possible the evidence in the neonate of maturity and of intrauterine deprivation—due to nutrition and addiction as well as to other teratogenic or infectious influences. A careful assessment of maturity (e.g., gestational age) (Dubowitz and Dubowitz 1981), of deprivation (as reflected by a measure such as ponderal index), and of intrauterine insults (a careful assessment of dysgenetic features, e.g., Smith's Atlas) needs to be added to any study of the pediatric and neurological adequacy. Neurological evaluations alone have not been particularly fruitful in demonstrating future developmental dysfunction in high-risk infants. Behavioral assessments are recommended to identify subtler central nervous system (CNS) and autonomic nervous system dysfunction that will affect babies and their environment's response to them.

In particular, alcohol and stress must be considered as significant covariants in any study of the effects of multiple drug abuse on the fetus and on neonatal behavior. A growing number of studies demonstrate these effects. For example, infants born to alcohol-addicted mothers were first studied by Streissguth and colleagues (1983). They examined the effects of intrauterine alcohol exposure in a sample of 417 infants, who were examined once on the NBAS between 9 and 35 hours after delivery. Data on maternal alcohol usage were obtained by self-report during the fifth month of pregnancy. Factor analysis yielded six factors that were entered into a multiple-regression analysis as dependent variables. Maternal alcohol use in midpregnancy was related to poorer habituation and to significantly lower arousal in newborns, even after adjusting for maternal smoking and caffeine use, maternal age, and nutrition during pregnancy; for sex and age of the infant; and for obstetric medication.

Alcohol levels in the mother do seem to affect the baby's CNS, as reflected by the infant's behavior at birth.

The NBAS has been in development for 25 years. Its goal is to attempt to establish the newborn's relative contribution to the parent-infant interaction and to the infant's own future. The original purpose of the NBAS was to attempt to record the dimensions of state—autonomic, motor, sensory-receptive, and responsive—that were seen as integrative and interacting with each other in the normal, healthy, full-term infant. The NBAS was seen not as a set of discrete stimulus-response presentations, but as an interactive assessment in which the adult participant played a major role, facilitating the performance and organizational skills of the infant. The hope was to establish the infant's capacities and limits in contributing to the caregiving environment. The expectation was to gain a deeper understanding of the meaning of infant behavior as it reflected relative contribution to these developmental lines. A single assessment in the neonatal period was seen as only one, brief glimpse into the continuum of the infant's adjustment to labor, delivery, and new environment. As such, it was expected to reflect the baby's inborn characteristics and the behavioral responses that had already been shaped by the intrauterine environment. Repeated exams should demonstrate the infant's coping capacities and capacities for experiencing, integrating, and profiting developmentally from the environment. Indeed, day-to-day change in behaviors can be more predictive of the baby's future functioning than any one set of assessments (Lester et al. 1987). If recovery curves (that is, the infant's pattern of change from day to day) can be seen as evidence for coping with the stress of labor and delivery and for the baby's capacity for integrating new environmental information, perhaps coping patterns in the neonatal period can be seen as predicting future patterns of coping and learning.

CONTENT OF THE NBAS

The NBAS was published 18 years ago (Brazelton 1973). Recently, revisions were made, and the experience of 10 years was summarized in the revision (Brazelton 1984a). Four centers and eight authors contributed to the revised edition. The scale is in use in more than 600 locations all over the world; 6 training centers have been established in the United States, 6 in Europe, and 1 in Israel; more than 125 published studies have appeared within the United States and in crosscultural contexts. In these studies, the characteristics of the NBAS have been explored, evaluated, and criticized.

FUTURE DIRECTIONS

Since it was first published, the NBAS has become the most widely used neonatal behavioral assessment instrument. Its use as a research instrument has been validated by many studies. It is a dynamic assessment, and it has taken time to evaluate its psychometric properties. The scale has been shown to have face validity as well as concurrent validity. Predictive validity seems to depend on the changes seen in repeated tests, and the data so far suggest that when repeated tests are used, predictive validity is achieved (Lester 1984; Nugent and Sepkoski 1984; Lester et al. 1987).

The assessment is a global one rather than a test of any one or two systems in the newborn. Because the scale is so widely used, the next effort will be to collect and collate the data from the many studies in an attempt to establish a normative database against which can be tested the many variables that influence neonatal behavior. A multivariate analysis of prenatal factors is one obvious technique. Understanding its use as a communicative system between parents and a concerned professional, in order to provide intervention and/or an understanding of the baby to enhance the parent-infant interaction, may be the most important future goal for the NBAS. How does one use it best as a communication system?

In working with the NBAS, several issues have become clear. An assessment of the newborn presents an opportunity for looking forward into the baby's future and backward into his or her intrauterine experience. The intrauterine influences that shape newborn behavior are becoming more and more commonly recognized. The newborn's behavior at birth is phenotypic, not genotypic, in that complex behaviors are already shaped by influences *in utero* that probably act in a synergistic fashion.

The NBAS has revealed the baby's impressive capacity to actively seek stimuli in an appropriate range for the level of stimulation the infant can tolerate. This ability in the normal baby fits with Osofsky's thesis (1976) that such a baby is both readable and predictable for the caregiver. Expectable behavior makes it more likely that the parent will nurture the infant appropriately.

EARLY INTERVENTION

The importance of assessing the behavioral repertoire of the infant as early as possible has now been widely accepted (see additional items in Brazelton 1984a). Recognition of neurological difficulties in organizing response systems that make it difficult for an infant to adjust to his or her environment would facilitate an optimal outcome for babies. It has long been recognized that the environment is an influence in improving or reinforcing potential deficits toward optimal development in high-risk infants.

Research in neurophysiology demonstrates the redundancy of neurological pathways in the immature CNS (St. James-Roberts 1979). Some modes for recovery are vicarious functioning, equipotentiality of redundant pathways, behavioral substitution, regrowth and supersensitivity, diaschisis, and recovery from trauma (St. James-Roberts 1979). Unassigned pathways can be captured for substitution of function for damaged or impaired pathways if such pathways are offered experiences from which they are able to learn. Behavioral substitution for impaired sensory or motor areas is possible; for instance, a blind infant uses highly sensitized auditory and tactile cues to replace the usual visual cues. The concept of substitution of these unassigned pathways reinforces the concept of plasticity in the immature nervous system, but these pathways must be provided with information appropriate to them for organizing and learning responses rather than disorganizing responses. For example, an impaired brain is likely to be hypersensitive, and ordinary stimuli may be inappropriate or disorganizing. Hence, a behavioral assessment that can identify individuated stimuli, graded to produce positive responses in a hypersensitive individual, might point to the kind of environmental stimuli that would lead toward organization and learning for that baby's future. The best use of the NBAS might be to identify as early as possible the individual differences in receptivity of such babies and to identify each baby's capacity for receiving and using environmental stimuli.

Standardization data for the NBAS has been difficult to establish because of the subtle influences of different prenatal and perinatal variables that affect neonatal behavior. The large data sets being collected need to be pooled and a database established to explore questions about the effect of these variables on the day-to-day behaviors of the newborn. Prenatal and perinatal variables are likely to act in combination in affecting neonatal behavior; thus, multivariate analytic techniques are appropriate.

One plan for use with multidrug-abused babies would be to collect data from many locations in the United States where the NBAS is being used to study some of the effects of single as well as multiple variables on neonatal behavior and to work toward developing a national database. Because of the changing nature of newborns' behavior as they respond to labor, delivery, and the new environment, patterns of change over repeated NBAS administrations are seen as systematic and part of the developmental process. High test-retest stability from day to day would be unlikely, and a norm is needed for each day with normal, full-term infants within our U.S. culture. These norms would be influenced by the conditions of each newborn nursery, and the variables affecting them would need to be carefully established. In addition, such prenatal influences as malnutrition, addiction, medication, and infection would be synergistic but could be accounted for as interacting variables.

In the second edition of the NBAS (Brazelton 1984b), nine supplementary items were added, for use with the NBAS in the assessment of high-risk infants. It became clear that the NBAS as originally designed was not an appropriate assessment for premature infants before they reached 36 weeks gestational age (Brazelton 1984b). Furthermore, its use with premature infants after 36 weeks necessitated items that could capture the range and quality of the behavior exhibited by such sensitive, fragile infants. This led to the attempt to develop a number of supplementary items for high-risk fragile infants, based on items used in the Assessment of Preterm Infant Behavior (APIB) (Als et al. 1982a, 1982b) and the NBAS, Kansas version (Horowitz and Linn 1978). These items attempt to summarize the quality of the baby's responsiveness, the cost to the baby of such responses, and the amount of input from the examiner necessary to organize them. These items are used to reflect the lowered thresholds and the high cost of responsiveness in fragile and at-risk infants. The NBAS in its present form cannot be used before an infant is 36 weeks of gestational age and/or until a fragile infant is off life supports and in room air. Only examiners trained specifically to work with high-risk infants should use the NBAS with these populations. These items have been successful in delineating the recovery of these infants and provide a window into their current functioning, indicated by the following categories:

1. Quality of alert responsiveness
2. Cost of attention
3. Examiner persistence
4. General irritability
5. Robustness and endurance
6. Regulatory capacities
7. State regulation
8. Balance of motor tone
9. Reinforcement value of the infant's behavior

These items can help in understanding the unique behavioral patterns of the premature or fragile infant (Brazelton 1984a).

In a study of high-risk infants, Tronick and colleagues (1985) found that these additional items added significantly to the prediction of the fragile infant's outcome. These nine items can be revised and used at age 2 years to establish subtle deficits in the quality of performance on such standardized instruments as the Bayley (1969) and Ainsworth and colleagues (1978) assessments.

Trained and reliable examiners need to collaborate after using the present form of the NBAS and its additional items to adapt it to the fragile neonates of multiple drug abusers. Ideally, the trained observers would have established their reliability as NBAS examiners for fragile infants and would have been trained in the sensitive observations of the APIB.

The concept of "best performances" used in the neonatal exam demands training and flexibility in the examiner. It was originally conceived of as a way to overcome subtle, uncontrollable environmental influences and to reproduce parental responses to an infant's best achievements. If it is used by trained examiners to help these babies achieve their best responses and if the maneuvers, the latency, and the cost to examiner and baby are recorded carefully, it will give insight into the techniques needed for intervention with these babies. For example, fragile small-for-gestational-age (SGA) and preterm infants need to be contained carefully. Then a stimulus is introduced from only one modality at a time—visual, auditory, tactile, or kinesthetic. That stimulus needs to be carefully geared to the baby's threshold for responsiveness. Unless it is, the baby's threshold for taking in, processing, and using the usual environmental stimuli is impaired. These babies, who had to adapt to repeated intrauterine stress, are likely to be either very high or very low on such measures as habituation to stimuli, to state changes, and to autonomic demands. Their ability to adapt to internal demands for autonomic compliance is likely to be restricted. Their ability adapted *in utero* to insults by shutting out disturbing stimuli may make them appear either lethargic or hypersensitive and extremely irritable. Their inability to handle state changes may be reflected in extreme lability, switching from unreachable sleep to unreachable crying, unable to respond to environmental stimuli, or difficult to move out of "hooked" states (of sleep, apparent attention, crying). To differentiate the effects of multiple drugs, including alcohol, and malnutrition on the neonate's behavior will be an enormous challenge. To then differentiate effects of withdrawal, of permanent CNS impairment, and of more temporary CNS effects (such as those of neurotransmitter disorders affected by these intrauterine influences acting synergistically) will be the next challenge. These issues need to be addressed to the best of the scientific community's capacity—applying standardized measures and intersite reliability to large, multisite samples.

The real goal for understanding the behavior and the underlying CNS and autonomic functions of the neonate will be to plan early intervention programs based on the knowledge gained from these assessments. To understand the babies and their caregivers, they must be reached with supportive, understanding interventions and followed with sensitive measurement techniques that include and reward their caregivers for any developmental gains, for these are difficult, fragile babies. What is learned about the functioning of the nervous system and its potential for repair will more than repay all the efforts to try to understand them. In addition, if it can be learned how to salvage these mothers from their addiction and poor self-image by using the behaviors of the baby, a whole new system will develop for outreach and cooperative feedback for a besieged population. The cost of salvaging these babies and their parents will be great, but if any can be salvaged, billions of dollars will be saved—money that would be spent in educating and controlling these children, whose fragility in infancy is likely to be predictive of disabled, impulse-ridden adolescents in the future.

The parents of these drug-exposed newborns are usually the products of poverty and hopelessness. Few other countries in the world have created the kind of hopelessness and devastated self-image from being poor that exists in the United States. The victims of this hopelessness and its attendant depression turn to alcohol and polydrug abuse and even to unwanted pregnancies. A punitive response to their addiction will destroy any opportunity to reach them for prenatal care and prevention, for care during delivery, and for care of their fragile offspring. On the other hand, a search for new models of understanding and support for these addicted, depressed, hopeless women might create a new system for outreach. A high goal would be to create fragile-infant centers and fragile-mother centers in parallel and in proximity, so that babies could be stabilized safely and be introduced to their mothers, who had managed to cease their drug abuse under the protection of these centers. Returning these women to their environments will result in a return to their addiction. The environment that an addicted parent will provide for a fragile infant binds them both to failure. Because studies have demonstrated that at-risk infants will have a significantly better chance at outcome if their environments can be flexible and oriented to the child's developmental needs, the most important intervention for these infants' future would be to provide safe and nurturing environments.

What is the role of health professionals? For 20 years at Harvard Medical School, the author has been training pediatricians and, more recently, nurse practitioners and psychologists to work with families and infants as part of the parent-infant system—this is where parental and infant outcome for all families, high and low risk, can be affected (figure 2). Teaching or telling parents how to parent is demeaning and carries with it a negative implication: "I know and you don't." The best influence on parents would be that of nurturing support to find their own best potential as parents. The model to use with addicted parents would be to nurture them toward a solution to their addiction, using successful parent-infant interaction as one of the ways of inducing recovery and as their goal. As their infant's behavior improved and as they went through their own withdrawal and recovery, their potential for caring for their fragile infant would be augmented by caring for them. If all of this could be achieved under the cover of a safe environment, it could be ascertained which parents and which

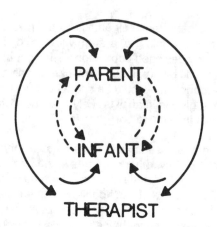

PARENT

INFANT

THERAPIST

SUPPORT, POINTING THEM TOWARD THEIR GOAL

FIGURE 2. *Therapist forms an envelope for the family*

infants would recover. A better future could then be predicted than is likely under present conditions of discharge to their chaotic, addiction-prone environments. The NBAS, a model for assessing the neonate's behavior over time, has been used with a high-risk group of babies (suffering from intrauterine growth retardation) and both middle-class and lower class mothers (Nugent and Brazleton 1989). The babies' behaviors at 40, 42, and 44 weeks of age were shared with their mothers. Lower class women barely participated until the third observation, saying they didn't trust the staff until the third visit. Only the babies' behavior was shared with one group, but mothering was also discussed with the other. Both groups profited (unpublished data) see lists below.

Intervention Effects at 1 Month

IUGR effects on NBAS orientation (p<.02)

IUGR effects on NBAS motor organization (p<.0001)

IUGR effects on NBAS state regulation (p<.06)

Intervention effects on degree of improvement on NBAS habituation over first month (p<.02)

Intervention effects on degree of improvement on NBAS orientation over first month (p<.03)

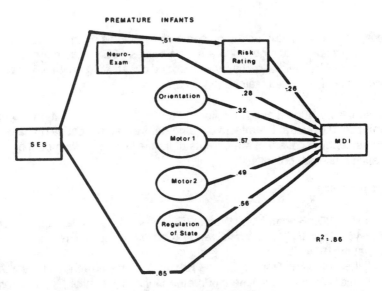

FIGURE 3. *Variables that influenced premature babies' outcome on the Bayley 18-month MDI*

Nutritional status, maternal interest, SES effects on NBAS motor behavior at 1 month (p<.003)

Nutritional status, maternal anxiety, SES effects on NBAS range of state at 1 month (p<.02)

Nutritional status, maternal anxiety, SES effects on NBAS state regulation at 2 months (p<. 03)

Intervention Effects at 4 Months

SES effects on Bayley MDI (p<.02)

Nutritional status, maternal anxiety, SES effects on Bayley PDI (p<.01)

Nutritional status, clinician-mother relationship, SES effects on Bayley MDI (p<.06)

The shared observation did affect both the mothers' and the babies' behavioral outcome. The influence on maternal behavior was to affect their self-image and to reduce maternal depression at 4 months. The babies' behavior improved at 1 month on the NBAS in all parameters across the two groups. It was hoped that the behavioral responsiveness of the neonates would give these depressed young women an anchor toward their own recovery. Indeed, Lester and coworkers (1984) evaluated the outcome at 18 months on the mental aspect of the Bayley scale of 20 high-risk premature babies. SES had an r^2 of .65. When the neonates' behavioral recovery was added over the 40- to 44-week period, a predictive r^2 of .85 was obtained (figure 3).

The studies by Nugent and Brazelton (1989) and others in the literature have been used to evaluate the effects of using behavioral responses of the newborn to enhance the recovery of the parents of fragile infants. This model of outreach has great potential.

REFERENCES

Ainsworth, M.D.; Blehar, M.C.; Waters, E.; and Wall, S. *Patterns of Attachment: A Psychological Study of the Strange Situation.* Hillsdale, NJ: Lawrence Erlbaum, 1978.

Als, H.; Lester, B.M.; Tronick, E.; and Brazelton, T.B. Towards a research instrument for the assessment of preterm infants' behavior. In: Fitzgerald, H.E.; Lester, B.M.; and Yogman, M.W., eds. *Theory and Research in Behavioral Pediatrics.* New York: Plenum Press, 1982a. pp. 35-63.

Als, H.; Lester, B.M.; Tronick, E.; and Brazelton, T.B. Manual for the assessment of preterm infants' behavior (APIB). In: Fitzgerald, H.E.; Lester, B.M.; and Yogman, M.W., eds. *Theory and Research in Behavioral Pediatrics.* New York: Plenum Press, 1982b. pp. 65-132.

Als, H.; Tronick, E.; Adamson, L.; and Brazelton, T.B. The behavior of the full term yet underweight newborn infant. *Dev Med Child Neurol* 18:590-602, 1976.

Bayley, N. Development of mental abilities. In: Mussen, P.H., ed. *Manual of Child Psychology.* 3rd ed. New York: Wiley, 1969. pp. 1163-1209.

Brazelton, T.B. *Neonatal Behavioral Assessment Scale.* Philadelphia: Lippincott, 1973.

Brazelton, T.B. Neonatal behavioral assessment scale. *Monograph.* No. 88 (rev. ed.). Philadelphia: Lippincott, 1984a.

Brazelton, T.B. *Neonatal Behavioral Assessment Scale.* 2d ed. London: Spastics International Medical Publications, 1984b.

Brazelton, T.B.; Tronick, E.; Lichtig, A.; Lasky, R.; and Klein, R. The behavior of the nutritionally deprived Guatemalan infants. *Dev Med Child Neurol* 19:344-372, 1977.

Dubowitz, V., and Dubowitz, L. The neurological assessment of the preterm and full term newborn infant. *Dev Med Child Neurol* 79:10-44, 1981.

Horowitz, F.D., and Linn, P.L. Use of the NBAS in research. In: Brazelton, T.B., ed. *Neonatal Behavorial Assessment Scale.* Philadelphia: Lippincott, 1984. pp. 97-105.

Lester, B.M. Data analysis and prediction. In: Brazelton, T.B., ed. *Neonatal Behavioral Assessment Scale.* Philadelphia: Lippincott, 1984. pp. 85-97.

Lester, B.M.; Boukydis, C.Z.; Hoffman, J.; Censullo, M.; Zahr, L.; and Brazelton, T.B. Behavioral and psychophysiological assessment of the preterm infant. In: Lester, B.M., and Tronick, E., eds. *In Defense of the Premature Infant: The Limits of Plasticity.* New York: Lexington Books, 1987.

Lester, B.M.; Emory, E.K.; Hoffman, S.L.; and Eitzman, D.V. A multivariate study of the effects of high risk factors on performance on the Brazelton Neonatal Assessment Scale. *Child Dev* 47:515-517, 1976.

Lester, B.M.; Garcia-Coll, C.T.; Valcarcel, M.; Hoffman, J.; and Brazelton, T.B. Effects of atypical patterns of fetal growth on newborn (NBAS) behavior. *Child Dev* 57:11, 1986.

Lester, B.M.; Hoffman, J.; and Brazelton, T.B. The rhythmic structure of mother-infant interaction in term- and preterm infants. *Child Dev* 56:15-28, 1984.

Lester, B.M., and Zeskind, P.S. Brazelton scale and physical size correlates of neonatal cry features. *Infant Behav Dev* 1:393, 1978.

Nugent, J.K., and Brazelton, T.B. Preventive intervention with infants and families. The NBAS Model. *Infant Ment Health J* 10:84-99, 1989.

Nugent, J.K., and Sepkoski, C. The training of NBAS examiners. In: Brazelton, T.B., ed. *Neonatal Behavioral Assessment Scale.* 2d ed. London: Blackwell, 1984. p. 324.

Osofsky, J. Neonatal characteristics and mother-infant interaction in two observational studies. *Child Dev* 47:1138-1140, 1976.

St. James-Roberts, I. Neurological plasticity. In: Reese, H., and Lipsett, L., eds. *Advances in Child Development.* New York: Academic Press, 1979. pp. 38-62.

Streissguth, A.D.; Barr, H.M.; and Martin, D.C. Maternal alcohol use and neonatal habituation assessed with the Brazelton scale. *Child Dev* 54(5):1109-1118, 1983.

Tronick, E.; Scanlon, J.; and Scanlon, K. A comparative analysis of the validity of several approaches to the scoring of the behavior of the preterm infant. *Infant Behav Dev* 8:35, 1985.

AUTHOR

T. Berry Brazelton, M.D.
Professor
Department of Pediatrics
Harvard Medical School
23 Hawthorn Street
Cambridge, MA 02138

Neurobehavioral Organization of the Newborn: Opportunity for Assessment and Intervention

Heidelise Als

INTRODUCTION

Infants come into the world equipped with a repertoire of neurobehavioral functional competencies that serve to adaptively regulate their own functioning as well as the behavior of their caregivers—parents or other adults—thus ensuring the input and feedback the infants need to support their own development. When newborn behavior is disturbed by focal insult, difference in neurobiologic substrate, difference in caregiver input, or any combination of these, a disturbance or difference in self-regulatory and other regulatory behavior is to be expected. Altered developmental interactive trajectories and feedback loops may result.

Early assessment of the newborn's neurobehavioral functioning, therefore, is important to identify possible differences and to ameliorate if not prevent subsequent cyclical maladaptations. Intrauterine exposure to drugs of abuse appears to have varying effects on brain function of the fetus. Behavior is seen as the infant's prime expression of brain function and key route of communication. Can the behavioral functioning of the newborn serve as a reliable and accurate yardstick of drug exposure and as an opportunity for appropriate intervention and amelioration?

Als and colleagues have developed methodologies for newborn behavioral assessment to document individual behavioral regulation differences thought to be brain based. So far, these methodologies have been tested on a population of preterm and fullterm infants free of documented medical complications to determine the degree of sensitivity of the instruments to subtle behavioral differences due to presumed difference in neurosensory experience *in utero* compared with *extra utero*. If documentation of the effects of such subtle input differences were successful, clearly this would be promising for the assessment of the effects of prenatal drug exposure and possibly for an approach to functional amelioration of such effects. The following overview and discussion of results are adapted from Als (1989a).

QUESTION 1: DO MEDICALLY HEALTHY PRETERMS SHOW BEHAVIORAL MODULATION DIFFERENCES COMPARED WITH FULLTERMS?

Behavioral Assessment

Two assessment methodologies were designed specifically to assess the behavioral regulation and organizational differences between preterm and fullterm infants. The first is an assessment of newborn behavioral organization called the Assessment of Preterm Infants' Behavior (APIB) (Als et al. 1982a, 1982b); the second is an experimental play paradigm called the Kangaroo-Box Paradigm (Als and Berger 1986). Both were developed to assess the degree of flexibility and modulation of behaviorally identified subsystems of functioning, their interplay with each other, and their joint interplay with the environment. The subsystems observed include the autonomic, motor, state, attentional interactive, and self-regulatory systems, as well as the facilitation necessary to support the infant's regulation. These are assessed as the infant is brought through a systematic sequence of manipulations or is observed in a standard paradigm designed to bring out the infant's current level of regulation.

The APIB was developed in an effort to extend the Brazelton Neonatal Behavioral Assessment Scale (NBAS) (Brazelton 1984) to the behavior of prematurely born infants and to assess the level of differentiation and modulation of functioning. The APIB casts the maneuvers of the NBAS into a graded sequence of increasingly vigorous environmental inputs to systematically assess the infant's threshold from organization to disorganization. The differential cost to infants in handling and responding to the maneuvers of the examination becomes a key feature of analysis. For instance, some newborns may move from sleep state to alert state only with accompanying respiratory irregularity consisting of respiratory pauses, alternating with tachypneic episodes, accompanied by visceral upheaval, color changes, and motoric hyperextension oscillating with flaccidity. Once achieving an alert state, they may appear facially bland or even strained, with acrocyanosis and poor respiratory stability, unable to focus consistently on a stimulus and process the sensory input. After a fleeting episode of strained alerting, they may move quickly to a motorically hyperaroused state accompanied by tachypnea, from which they may be brought to a more balanced level of modulated flexor tone with regular respirations only with great difficulty. Yet they will visually track and follow a target through a 60-degree angle. Other newborns, in contrast, will move easily from sleep to alert state without autonomic instability or motoric disorganization. Once in alertness, they maintain themselves there readily and focus on various stimuli with ease and alacrity while their angle of visual excursion is also 60 degrees. Despite the same visual orientation angle, the second group of infants would be considered more well organized than the first along the differentiation and modulation continuum of subsystems, and their scores on the autonomic, motor, state, attentional, and self-regulatory systems, as well as on examiner facilitation, would be lower, reflecting better behavioral organization and, therewith, a difference in regulation as defined in the framework of the APIB.

The Kangaroo-Box Paradigm (K-Box) was developed to assess the strategies and degree of overall subsystem modulation and differentiation exhibited by infants at 9, 18, and 36 months, with a version available for the 5- to 8-year-old range. By 9 months postterm, the infants' world has expanded considerably. Their mobility allows them to approach and leave situations, objects, and persons in a very different way than they did earlier. They initiate interactions and explorations beyond their immediate reach space, pursue objects and persons locomotively, and structure situations by incorporating much larger space frames and with more temporal flexibility than before. To assess competence along comparable dimensions of subsystem differentiation and modulation analogous to the newborn period as measured by the APIB, Als constructed a paradigm that uses a transparent plexiglass box accessible through a transparent mobile porthole latch door and containing a hopping, windup kangaroo. The box is placed on the floor of a playroom. During the observation, all other distractions (pictures, chair, etc.) are removed, and mother and infant are asked to go into the room and play with the toy so that "they both have a good time." They are observed and videotaped with a two-camera split-screen system through one-way mirror walls for 6 minutes. Then the kangaroo is placed back in the box, the latch door closed, and the mother is asked to sit against the wall of the room looking at the infant but not interacting in any way. The infant is observed in this Stillface situation for 6 minutes. Then a 3-minute reunion is observed when the mother again is asked to play with the infant. The K-Box challenges the infant's cognitive, gross and fine motor, social and affective capacities, and, for some more sensitive infants, even physiological regulation, as the infant attempts to retrieve the kangaroo from the box. It also provides an opportunity to observe the mother's strategies in facilitating and expanding the infant's competence.

Als and Berger (1986) developed a scoring manual to score the infant's capacities during the Play and Stillface episodes along 21 dimensions on a scale from 1 (minimum) to 5 (optimal). These include autonomic organization, gross and fine motor organization, symmetry of tonus, movement and posture, apparent cognitive functioning, language and vocal organization, affective

108

organization, social-interactive organization, competence in play with the object, competence in combining object play and social interaction, degree of self-regulation, degree of facilitation and structure necessary, and degree of pleasure and pride displayed by the infant. Attention is paid to autonomic reactions, movements, tone, vocalizations, and facial expressions. And, as in the APIB, the degree of flexibility, differentiation, and modulation of each subsystem is measured as an index of competence and regulation. The mother's behavior also is scored on parallel scales.

The K-Box for the older children consists of a large plexiglass tower with three tiers and varying degrees of difficulty of access to the windup toy inside two of the plexiglass cubes making up the tower. As an aid to reaching the top level, a footstool and various raking tools are provided. The kangaroo either can be taken out or dropped through a latch door in the floor of the top cube to the second level. Once on the second level, it needs to be pushed via one of the several raking tools provided at the second level opening to fall to the ground level; from there it can be obtained via the door, which opens with a key. The second kangaroo sitting in the ground level cube can be obtained independently of the first. Both can be obtained and incorporated into exploration of the various possibilities of this apparatus.

At each of the different age levels the K-Box apparatus is designed to have built-in, immediate demand characteristics, yet to allow for individual differences in the order, sophistication, and complexity of its manipulation and use. Because the total child is directly involved in the K-Box Paradigm rather than only selected facets of the child's functioning, it is expected to yield useful and systematic information about the integration and modulation of overall behavioral functioning.

Results

So far, Als and coworkers have studied and analyzed the behavior of 160 healthy preterm and fullterm infants who spanned the gestational age (GA) continuum in relatively equal numbers from 26- to 32-week pre-preterm (PPT), 33- to 37-week preterm (PT), and 38- to 41-week fullterm (FT). All infants were selected to be free of known neurological insult, including perinatal asphyxia, neonatal seizures, bronchopulmonary dysplasia, and intraventricular hemorrhage, as well as free of necrotizing enterocolitis and sepsis. All infants were appropriate for age in weight at birth; all were singletons and free of any congenital abnormalities and infections. There were 48 FTs, 48 PTs , and 64 PPTs. All infants were studied with the APIB at 2 weeks after due date. The results indicate that the six system variables (autonomic, motor, state, attentional organization, self-regulation, and examiner facilitation) show strong differences among FTs, PTs, and PPTs, with the strongest differences between

109

FTs and the two preterm groups together, and fewer, yet significant, differences between the PTs and PPTs. The PPTs are consistently the most reactive, hypersensitive, and disorganized. The PTs take a middle position, and the FTs are the most well modulated and well differentiated. Thus, the APIB appears very sensitive in identifying gestational age effects (Als et al., in press). The robustness of the APIB in identifying GA group membership also was shown by successful prospective classification of an earlier sample of 20 FTs and 20 PTs. Ninety-five percent (38 of 40) of the infants were correctly classified as to GA status on the basis of their APIB scores (Als et al. 1988a). Furthermore, three reliable (tested on two independent split-half samples), behaviorally defined clusters of infants were identified (Als et al. 1988b; Als et al., in press), with a preponderance of PPTs in the most reactive group and a preponderance of FTs in the most well-organized group. Brain electrical activity mapping (BEAM) data (Duffy 1989) implicated primarily frontal lobe and right hemispheric functional differences between the behaviorally defined clusters (Als et al. 1989; Duffy 1989; Duffy et al. 1990).

One-hundred forty-eight infants were restudied at 9 months after expected date of confinement (EDC) using the Bayley Scales (Bayley 1969) and the K-Box Paradigm; 73 of the infants were restudied at 3 years post-EDC with a comprehensive neuropsychological battery as well as the K-Box Paradigm. While the Bayley Scale Scores, Mental Development Index (MDI), and Psychomotor Development Index (PDI) did not show GA differences, the K-Box Paradigm elicited consistent differences in autonomic, gross and fine motor, social interactive, affective, and spatial regulation (Als et al., in press). Preliminary analyses of the data at age 3 years again showed few differences on the standardized psychological assessments, yet the K-Box Paradigm showed many highly significant GA group effects (autonomic regulation, gross and fine motor modulation, social interactive and affective regulation, and language functioning) (Als et al. 1990). Furthermore, three clusters of neurobehavioral functioning again emerged on the basis of the K-Box data at each of the age points. Cluster concordance from the newborn period to the later age points was very good (Als et al., in press).

Aside from these findings, K-Box data on 14 healthy preterm (<34 weeks) and 14 healthy fullterm children from the earlier sample of 20 each have been collected and analyzed at 5 years. The results showed striking group differences in this paradigm in the face of only very small differences on standardized cognitive assessments, and BEAM again implicated frontal and right hemispheric functioning (Als et al. 1989; Duffy and Als 1988).

Thus, it appears that there is a profile of regulatory difficulties characteristic of preterm infants reflecting lower GA at birth that can be documented from the newborn period on and that shows consistency to age 3 years and perhaps to age 5 years. It appears to encompass not only greater autonomic reactivity but also poorer modulation of gross and fine motor functioning, poorer affective and attentional regulation, with more static facial expression, narrowed affective range, higher distractibility and perseveration, poorer modulation of transition from one task aspect to another, and poorer articulation and expressive language use in the face of normal overall intellectual capacity. These differences were found in the absence of documented brain injury, indicating a difference in neurobehavioral organization possibly due to difference in sensory experience and consequent brain function.

QUESTION 2: WILL THE COMPREHENSIVE MODIFICATION OF SENSORY INPUT TO THE VERY EARLY BORN PRETERM INFANT (<32 WEEKS) REDUCE DEVELOPMENTAL COMPROMISE?

Als (1986) developed an intervention approach that focuses on reduction of purported stress behaviors and increase of self-regulatory behaviors of the poorly modulated infant by modification of the physical environment in the neonatal intensive care unit (e.g., shielding from overhead lighting and from noise) and the caregiving practices of nurses and other professionals as well as the parents interacting with the infant (e.g., provision of prone or sidelying flexor position support by specially constructed buntings, nonnutritive sucking, containment during medical procedures, sleep state regulation protection). A training program in individualized observation and caregiving is available at various centers (Boston, Tucson, Oakland, Raleigh). Focus is on the behavioral observation of the infant, on designing an individualized care plan, and on comprehensive implementation of developmental support in collaboration with the parents.

This approach has been tested with encouraging results in two studies focusing on very-low-birth-weight infants.

Initial Study

Als and coworkers (1986) studied eight control infants in the course of 1 year, conducting detailed behavioral observations on the infants every 10th day. In the second year of the study, the same observations were applied to infants who, in addition, received carefully designed individualized intervention, based on the observations, from the primary nursing teams and their parents. All infants were initially respirator-dependent and met stringent selection criteria that put them at high risk for the development of bronchopulmonary dysplasia (e.g., birthweight <1,250g; mechanical ventilation within 3 hours of delivery; mechanical ventilation >24 hours in the first 48 hours at ≥.60 FiO_2 for ≥2 hours

111

(Cohen and Taeusch 1983); no chromosomal or other genetic anomalies; no major congenital infections; no major maternal illness, including intrauterine infections; no twins). The control and intervention groups did not differ on any other medical variables up to day 10, when intervention started, nor did they differ on any demographic variables. The results of the study showed the intervention group with a significantly decreased number of days on the respirator, on supplemental oxygen, and on tube feeding (Als et al. 1986). The children were subsequently studied at 4 weeks post-EDC with the APIB; at 3, 6, 9, and 18 months post-EDC with the Bayley Scales (Bayley 1969); at 9, 18, and 36 months post-EDC with the K-Box Paradigm (Als 1984); and at 36 months post-EDC with the McCarthy Scales of Children's Abilities (McCarthy 1972), the Kaufman Assessment Battery for Children (K-ABC) (Kaufman and Kaufman 1983), and the Psychomotor Scale of the Bayley Scores (Bayley 1969). The intervention infants were better modulated, as measured by the APIB systems scores, in terms of motor system and self-regulation ability. Of the five body signal parameters measured, the intervention group showed a significantly lower incidence of motoric extension behavior, such as grimacing or arching. They also showed a higher number of normal reflexes. Furthermore, the MDI and PDI scores for the control and intervention groups at 3, 6, and 9 months consistently showed the intervention infants scoring significantly above the control infants. Thus, the intervention appears to have had a substantial impact on both the mental and motor development of these infants (Als 1989b; Als et al. 1986). The K-Box Paradigm at 9, 18, and 36 months (Als 1989b; Als et al. 1986; Als et al. 1991) showed that the intervention children performed significantly better than the control infants. Furthermore, the initial advantage of the intervention children was well maintained, while the control children deteriorated over time on many of the parameters. All parent-child interaction parameters significantly favored the intervention children and their parents. This advantage also was demonstrated on the McCarthy Scales, the Bayley Psychomotor Scale raw score, and K-ABC performance (Kaufman and Kaufman 1983) at age 3 years. These results demonstrate that behavioral modulation, by modification of sensory input, shows striking continuity in behavioral improvement over time, at least to age 3 years.

Replication Study

Als and colleagues (1988c) replicated and extended this study to a larger sample (18 control and 20 intervention infants) using similar selection criteria. This time, the preterms were randomly assigned to the control and intervention groups, with intervention starting in the first 24 hours after delivery. Intervention infants were cared for by nursing teams trained in special behavior observation. The results, which are currently available through 2 weeks after due date, again showed striking medical improvement of the intervention infants, with significantly reduced respirator stay, oxygen need, tube feeding, and bronchopulmonary dysplasia and marked reduction in the incidence of intraventricular hemorrhage (10 out of 18 controls; 1 out of 20 intervention infants). Furthermore, length of hospital stay was significantly reduced, as was hospital cost. At 2 weeks post-EDC, APIB scores and electrophysiological functioning, as assessed with BEAM, again showed highly significant group differences favoring the intervention infants (Als et al. 1988c). The functional advantage of the intervention infants is expected to last over time, as was seen in the initial intervention study reported above.

SUMMARY

A functional model has been formulated that attempts to specify the behavioral subsystems of functioning that exemplify in their respective interplay an infant's individuality of behavioral functioning in the manner in which they move from stable to disorganized functioning and in the flexibility with which they maintain organized functioning in the face of varied exogenous and endogenous events. Based on this model, Als and colleagues have attempted to develop systematic assessments, the APIB and the K-Box Paradigm, to quantify the degree of differentiation and modulation of these behaviorally defined subsystems of functioning. It is hypothesized that the differences documented via these assessments are brain based (i.e., part of the child's biological makeup, which is influenced by the intrauterine and extrauterine environment, be it sensory and/or drug exposure, and which shows a recognizable pattern along a definable trajectory).

The studies reported to date employing these methodologies show the following:

1. Medically healthy preterm infants show a gradient of modulation differences by GA group, with the earlier born infants showing much greater sensitivity, reactivity, and lower threshold to disorganization. BEAM studies appear to implicate primarily the frontal lobes and secondarily the right hemisphere.

2. Behavioral organizational group membership in the newborn period predicts to neuropsychological functioning at later ages, with the low-threshold-reactive newborns showing greater difficulty in motor and spatial planning, social interactive modulation capacity, and attentional regulation.

3. Behavioral organizational functioning of the newborn, at least the early-born preterm infant, appears to be modified and supported by individualized caregiving based on the the infant's own behavioral cues indicating sensory thresholds to disorganization.

The brain of the newborn is the organ that orchestrates and influences all aspects of functioning. The synactive model of development outlines access

113

avenues for the observation of that brain's function via the behavior displayed by the infant. Autonomic, motoric, state organizational, attentional, and self-regulatory capacities of the infant can be observed to identify succinctly and specifically an individual infant's thresholds to sensory input for self-maintenance and for increasing differentiation. To take the next step in differentiation, previously integrated and synchronized connections open up, necessitating the temporary disorganization and dyssynchronization of subsystems in their interplay. Then the subsystems realign and support each other again at a more differentiated level of functioning. In this model, if stress is too massive, as may be the case in disease and/or intrauterine drug exposure, more differentiated realignment of subsystems may not be possible, and maladaptive, costly realignment may occur at a more rigid, canalized level of functioning. Detailed observation of the behavior of the infant is seen as an opportunity to estimate and infer from the infant's behavior how appropriate comprehensive physical environments and caregiving can be provided to support the rapid brain and behavioral development of the infant, even in the face of insult.

It appears that medical and developmental management must be geared to the individual infant's sensory thresholds to prevent secondary consequences from generalization of defect, akin to deprivation and subsequent active neuronal suppression (Duffy et al. 1984), and to enhance compensatory strategies in overcoming and integrating possible damage and insult into each infant's endogenously fuelled developmental trajectory. Only careful environmental manipulation in controlled studies with sensitive outcome measures will provide the answers.

REFERENCES

Als, H. "Manual and Scoring System for the Assessment of Children's Behavior: Kangaroo-Box Paradigm." Unpublished manuscript, Children's Hospital, Boston, 1984.

Als, H. Synactive model of neonatal behavioral organization: Framework for the assessment and support of the neurobehavioral development of the premature infant and his parents in the environment of the neonatal intensive care unit In: Sweeney, J.K., ed. *The High-Risk Neonate: Developmental Therapy Perspectives.* New York: Hayworth Press, 1986. pp. 3-55.

Als, H. Continuity and consequences of behavior in preterm infants. In: von Euler, C.; Forssberg, H.; and Lagercrantz, H., eds. *Neurobiology of Early Infant Behaviour. Wenner-Gren Center International Symposium Series, Vol. 55.* Hampshire, England: Macmillan Press Ltd., 1989a. pp. 87-106.

Als, H. Self-regulation and motor development in preterm infants. In: Lockman, J., and Hazen, N., eds. *Action in Social Context: Perspectives on Early Development.* New York: Plenum Press, 1989b. pp. 65-97.

Als, H., and Berger, A. "Manual and Scoring System for the Assessment of Infants' Behavior: Kangaroo-Box Paradigm." Unpublished manuscript. Children's Hospital, 1986.

Als, H; Duffy, F.H.; and McAnulty, G.B. Behavioral differences between preterm and fullterm newborns as measured with the A.P.I.B. system scores: I. *IBD* 11:305-318, 1988a.

Als, H.; Duffy, F.H.; and McAnulty, G.B. The A.P.I.B., an assessment of functional competence in preterm and fullterm newborns regardless of gestational age at birth: II. *IBD* 11:319-331, 1988b.

Als, H.; Duffy, F.H.; and McAnulty, G.B. Neurobehavioral regulation disorder of prematurity. *IBD* 13:159, 1990.

Als, H.; Duffy, F.H.; and McAnulty, G.B. Neurobehavioral competence in healthy preterm and fullterm infants: Newborn period to nine months. *Dev Psychol*, in press.

Als, H.; Duffy, F.H.; McAnulty, G.B.; and Badian, N. Continuity of neurobehavioral functioning in preterm and full-term newborns. In: Bornstein, M., and Krasnegor, N., eds. *Stability and Continuity in Mental Development.* Hillsdale, NJ: Lawrence Erlbaum, 1989. pp. 3-28.

Als, H.; Lawhon, G.; Gibes, R.; Duffy, F.H.; McAnulty, G.B.; and Blickman, J.G. Individualized behavioral and environmental care for the very low birth weight preterm infant at high risk for bronchopulmonary dysplasia: Neonatal intensive care unit and developmental outcome. *Pedia* 78:1123-1132, 1986.

Als, H.; Lawhon, G.; Gibes, R.; Duffy, F.H.; McAnulty, G.B.; and Blickman, J.G. "Individualized Behavioral and Developmental Care for the VLBW Preterm Infant at High Risk for Bronchopulmonary Dysplasia and Intraventricular Hemorrhage. Study II NICU Outcome." Paper presented at New England Perinatal Association Annual Meeting, Woodstock, VT, 1988c.

Als, H.; Lawhon, G.; McAnulty, G.B.; Duffy, F.H.; and Gibes, R. "Developmental Outcomes to Age Three Years of Early Behaviorally Based Care in the NICU," unpublished manuscript, 1991.

Als, H.; Lester, B.M.; Tronick, E.; and Brazelton, T.B. Towards a research instrument for the assessment of preterm infants' behavior. In: Fitzgerald, H.E.; Lester, B.M.; and Yogman, M.W., eds. *Theory and Research in Behavioral Pediatrics. Vol. I.* New York: Plenum Press, 1982a. pp. 35-63.

Als, H.; Lester, B.M.; Tronick, E.; and Brazelton, T.B. Manual for the assessment of preterm infants' behavior (APIB). In: Fitzgerald, H.E.; Lester, B.M.; and Yogman, M.W., eds. *Theory and Research in Behavioral Pediatrics. Vol. I.* New York: Plenum Press, 1982b. pp. 65-132.

Bayley, N. *Manual for the Bayley Scales of Infant Development.* New York: Psychological Corporation, 1969.

Brazelton, T.B. *Neonatal Behavioral Assessment Scale. Clinics in Developmental Medicine, No. 88 (rev. ed.).* Philadelphia: Lippincott, 1984.

Catto-Smith, A.G.; Yu, V.Y.H.; Bajuk, B.; Orgill, A.A.; and Astbury, J. Effect of neonatal periventricular hemorrhage on neurodevelopmental outcome. *Arch Dis* 60:8-11, 1985.

Cohen, A., and Taeusch, H.W. Prediction of risk for bronchpulmonary dysplasia. *Am J Perinatol* 1:21-22, 1983.

Duffy, F.H. Electrophysiological evidence for gestational age effects in infants studied at term: A BEAM study. In: von Euler, C.; Forssberg, H.; and Lagercrantz, H., eds. *Neurobiology of Early Infant Behaviour. Wenner-Gren Center International Symposium Series, Vol. 55.* Hampshire, England: Macmillan Press Ltd., 1989. pp. 337-355.

Duffy, F.H., and Als, H. Neural plasticity and the effect of a supportive hospital environment on premature newborns. In: Kavanagh, J.F., ed. *Understanding Mental Retardation. Research Accomplishments and New Frontiers.* Baltimore: Paul H. Brookes Publishing Co., 1988. pp. 179-206.

Duffy, F.H.; Als, H.; and McAnulty, G.B. Behavioral and electrophysiological evidence for gestational age effects in healthy preterm and fullterm infants studied two weeks after expected due date. *Child Dev* 61:1271-1286, 1990.

Duffy, F.H.; Mower, G.D.; Jensen, F.; and Als, H. Neural plasticity: A new frontier for infant development. In: Fitzgerald, H.E.; Lester, B.M.; and Yogman, M.W, eds. *Theory and Research in Behavioral Pediatrics, Vol. II.* New York: Plenum Press, 1984. pp. 67-96.

Kaufman, A.S., and Kaufman, N.L. *Kaufman Assessment Battery for Children, K-ABC.* Circle Pines, MN: American Guidance Service, 1983.

McCarthy, D. *Manual for the McCarthy Scales of Children's Abilities.* New York: Psychological Corporation, 1972.

ACKNOWLEDGMENTS

The work described in this chapter was supported by grants to the author from the National Institute of Child Health and Human Development (RO1 HD-18654, RO1 HD-18761); the National Institute for Disability and Rehabilitation Research (GO-08435063); the H.P. Hood Foundation; the Merck Family Fund; the U.S. Department of Education, Handicapped Children's Early Education Program (H0-24590003); and a Mental Retardation Center Grant (P30 HD-18655) to Joseph J. Volpe, M.D., Chairman, Department of Neurology, Children's Hospital, Boston.

AUTHOR

Heidelise Als, Ph.D.
Associate Professor of Psychology (Psychiatry)
Harvard Medical School
Director
Neurobehavioral Infant and Child Studies
Enders Pediatric Research Building, EN-029
Children's Hospital
320 Longwood Avenue
Boston, MA 02115

Substance Abuse in Pregnancy: Effects on Cardiorespiratory Function in the Infant

Eduardo Bancalari

Substance abuse during pregnancy has become more prevalent in recent years, but little is known about the short- and long-term effects on the infant. Because of a possible increase in the incidence of sudden infant death syndrome (SIDS) in infants born to substance-abusing mothers (ISAM), special emphasis has been placed on the possible consequences of substance abuse on the cardiorespiratory function of the offspring.

EFFECTS ON THE FETUS

Respiratory System

Respiratory activity in the fetus is intermittent and does not contribute to gas exchange; however, many substances used during pregnancy may influence respiratory adaptation and function after birth.

Fetal Breathing. A recent report described a markedly abnormal breathing pattern in human fetuses of cocaine-abusing mothers. The pattern was characterized by persistent rhythmic, hyperpneic, and regular breathing that lasted up to 30 minutes (Gingras et al. 1989). Similar results have been reported in fetal lambs acutely exposed to methadone (Szeto 1983). This hyperactivity may be associated with a significant increase in fetal oxygen consumption. In contrast to these findings, Richardson and colleagues (1984) reported a depressed breathing response to CO_2 in human fetuses of chronic methadone-exposed mothers. The different results may be due to the different subjects and to the fact that the animals were only exposed to an acute dose of methadone.

Maternal smoking during pregnancy is also associated with a reduction in fetal breathing movements (Manning and Feyerabend 1976; Gennser et al. 1975). This effect seems to be secondary to the increased nicotine levels in the fetus and not to the increase in carboxyhemoglobin.

117

Lung Maturation. There is some evidence that substance abuse, especially of opioids, during pregnancy may accelerate lung maturation through enzyme induction and reduce the incidence of respiratory distress syndrome (RDS) (Gluck and Kulovich 1973). On the other hand, substance abuse is associated with an increased risk of premature delivery that offsets any possible beneficial effect on lung maturation and increases the risk of RDS in drug-exposed infants (Ostrea and Chavez 1979).

Meconium Aspiration. Many substances used during pregnancy, such as cocaine and opioids, can interfere with placental gas exchange and may induce fetal distress. They also may cause elimination of meconium into the amniotic fluid, resulting in aspiration of this fluid into the lungs and meconium aspiration syndrome in the newborn (Ostrea and Chavez 1979).

Cardiovascular System

Because most substances abused during pregnancy cross the placenta, the cardiovascular effects on the fetus are similar to those observed in the mother. Many recent studies have focused on the effects of cocaine because of its increasing use and the severe cardiovascular effects it produces.

Experiments done in pregnant ewes (Moore et al. 1986; Woods et al. 1987, 1989) have demonstrated that intravenous injection of cocaine, in doses that produce levels similar to those observed during human use, produce a significant increase in maternal arterial blood pressure, with a decrease in uterine blood flow. This effect lasts at least 15 minutes and is associated with marked increase in catecholamine plasma concentration. The fetus also responds with an increase in arterial blood pressure and heart rate and a decrease in arterial PO_2. When the fetus is injected directly, the change in blood pressure and heart rate is smaller and there is no change in arterial blood gases. This suggests that the latter is due to impaired placental gas exchange secondary to the decreased uterine blood flow. The half-life of the drug (between 12 and 13 minutes) was similar in both mother and fetus.

EFFECTS ON THE NEONATE

Respiratory System

Respiratory Adaptation After Birth. As mentioned earlier, because of its effects on the fetus, abuse of such substances as opioids may increase or decrease the incidence of RDS (Gluck and Kulovich 1973; Ostrea and Chavez 1979). The increased incidence of fetal asphyxia produced by substance abuse also increases the risk of meconium aspiration syndrome in these infants (Chappel 1972; Ostrea and Chavez 1979; Little et al. 1989).

118

Use of any drug that depresses central nervous system (CNS) function increases the risk of neonatal respiratory depression and asphyxia at birth. This is even more important if the substance interferes with placental gas exchange and the infant had become hypoxic before birth (Gerhardt et al. 1977). On the opposite side, infants with signs of withdrawal after prenatal exposure to heroin can show respiratory irritability with hyperventilation and hypocapnia (Glass et al. 1972).

Respiratory Control in Infancy. Several reports have suggested that the incidence of SIDS is higher in ISAM (Chavez et al. 1989; Chasnoff et al. 1989). Because of this, special emphasis has been placed on the possible effect of substance abuse during pregnancy on the respiratory control mechanisms of the infant.

Maternal Substance Abuse and SIDS. The mechanisms for the increased risk of SIDS in ISAM is controversial because of the many confounding factors associated with substance abuse that also may affect the risk of SIDS during pregnancy. For example, Chavez and colleagues (1979) reported a fivefold increased risk of SIDS in infants born to mothers who used different substances during pregnancy. In this study, it is impossible to separate the effect of each of these drugs on the risk of SIDS because of the small number of subjects and the lack of specific information. Moreover, premature infants with birth weights under 1.9 kg, who have an increased risk for SIDS, were excluded from this study. As in other studies, Chavez and colleagues found that ISAM who died from SIDS expired at an earlier age than did the SIDS cases in the control group (9.2 weeks vs. 13.8 weeks). Chasnoff and coworkers (1989) also reported a high incidence of SIDS (15 percent) in infants of mothers who used cocaine during pregnancy. This was a retrospective study without a simultaneous nonexposed control group; the incidence of SIDS in a methadone-exposed group used as control was 4 percent.

More recently, Bauchner and colleagues (1988) found a similar incidence of SIDS (5.6 percent per thousand) in 175 infants exposed to cocaine *in utero* and in 821 controls (4.9 percent per thousand). This study has the limitation of a relatively small sample size and a low death rate (one infant) in the cocaine-exposed group. As discussed by the investigators, to detect an increase in SIDS to 10 percent per thousand with a power of 80 percent would require a population of 680 women who used cocaine.

Other methodological limitations of this study, common to many other reports, were (1) there was no distinction made on the severity of drug use or the period during pregnancy when the fetus was exposed, (2) there was no control for the possible use of other drugs, and (3) there is always a good chance of underreporting of SIDS cases.

In conclusion, although there appears to be an association between maternal substance abuse and an increased risk of SIDS, there is no clear causal relationship; and larger study populations will be required to adjust for the many confounders that may have an influence on SIDS.

Breathing Pattern. Several investigators have reported abnormal respiratory patterns in ISAM. Because similar alterations have been reported in infants with apparent life-threatening events (ALTE), it has been suggested that these abnormalities in respiratory function may predispose these infants to SIDS.

Davidson Ward and coworkers (1986) evaluated the respiratory pattern in 27 ISAM (5 were exposed to opiates, 7 to phencyclidine, 3 to cocaine, and 12 to multiple drugs) and compared the results with 43 nonexposed controls. ISAM had more sleep time, more duration of apnea greater than 6 seconds, more periodic breathing, higher respiratory rates, and lower heart rates than the controls. Pneumograms were considered abnormal in 32 percent of ISAM in contrast to 9.3 percent in the controls. With one exception, all abnormal pneumograms in the ISAM group were detected during the first 2 months, suggesting that the effect of drug exposure disappears with postnatal age. No infant with abnormal pneumograms died of SIDS. This is in agreement with other data in the literature demonstrating that pneumograms do not predict the risk of SIDS in individual patients (Southall et al. 1986). Davidson Ward and coworkers' study (1986) also has the limitation of mixing the results of infants exposed to different substances. Furthermore, the controls were not screened to assure that, in fact, they were not exposed to drugs.

Recently, Chasnoff and colleagues (1989) also reported an increased incidence of apnea density and prolonged apneic episodes in a group of 32 infants exposed to cocaine *in utero* when compared to a group of 18 methadone-exposed infants. Although many confounding variables were equal in both groups, this study did not include a group of normal nonexposed infants. The abnormal respiratory pattern observed in the cocaine-exposed infants was normalized with the administration of aminophylline. This finding stresses the importance of evaluating these infants before they receive any intervention that may influence their respiratory function.

Two studies (Bachman et al. 1990; Gibson et al. 1990) recently reported alterations in respiratory pattern in infants born to mothers who used amphetamines or opiates similar to those described in infants of cocaine-abusing mothers.

Maternal smoking during pregnancy or after delivery increases the risk of central apneas in the offspring (Toubas et al. 1986). The same investigators found that maternal caffeine consumption was associated with an increased risk of central and obstructive apneas in the infant. The mechanism for the caffeine effect is not clear, but it may be related to an increased number of adenosine receptors in the brain stem (Marangos et al. 1984). Smoking during pregnancy interferes with fetal oxygenation, and this may result in impaired CNS function. In these studies, it is difficult to separate the effects of prenatal smoking from those of passive smoking after birth.

Ventilatory Response to Stimuli

One of the characteristics of respiratory control in the neonate is that the ventilatory response to hypoxia is not sustained during the first few postnatal days. In the premature infant, this abnormal response may last for several weeks after birth.

Several publications have reported abnormal arousal and ventilatory responses to hypoxia and hypercapnia in infants with ALTE (Shannon et al. 1977; Hunt 1981; Hunt et al. 1981; Graff 1986). This alteration may be responsible for the severe apneic episodes observed in these infants.

Davidson Ward and colleagues (1989) compared arousal from sleep during exposure to an inspired PO_2 of 80 mm Hg in a group of infants born to cocaine-abusing mothers with a group of nonexposed controls. While control infants were aroused in 89 percent of the trials, infants exposed to cocaine were aroused in only 27 percent of the hypoxic exposures. This observation is important because another study (Rodriguez et al. 1987) also described abnormal hypoxic arousal in a group of infants with apnea of infancy, and elevated serum epinephrine levels were found in these infants. Perrin and coworkers (1984) found a significant increase in the concentration of dopamine and noradrenalin in the carotid bodies of infants who died of SIDS. These findings suggest that the elevated endogenous catecholamine levels may interfere with the function of the carotid bodies and the ventilatory response to hypoxia observed in some of these infants. It is likely that infants exposed to cocaine *in utero* also have increased concentrations of circulating catecholamines (Ritchie and Greene 1987), although no data are available in human neonates. Weese-Mayer and colleagues (1990) also reported an attenuation of the ventilatory response to hypoxia in newborn rabbits chronically exposed to cocaine *in utero*. This study as well as those of Davidson Ward and colleagues (1986, 1989) suggest that chronic prenatal cocaine exposure may alter the central or peripheral mechanisms responsible for a normal ventilatory and arousal response to hypoxia.

Olsen and Lees (1980) also described a depressed ventilatory response to CO_2 in infants born to mothers receiving methadone during pregnancy. This depression persisted for 15 to 31 days, suggesting that the effect was not directly related to the blood methadone levels in the infant. The depression of the response to CO_2 did not influence basal ventilation, alveolar PCO_2, or oxygen consumption.

Chen and coworkers (1989) demonstrated an increased number of respiratory pauses induced by a facial airstream stimulation in infants born to mothers who used cocaine during pregnancy compared to nonexposed controls. However, the ventilatory response to CO_2 was similar in both groups. These results also support the theory that ISAM have an alteration in the integration of the mechanisms that are responsible for a normal respiratory pattern after birth.

Cardiovascular System

Little information is available regarding the effects of substance abuse during pregnancy on neonatal cardiovascular adaptation and function. Because of the marked cardiovascular effects of cocaine in the adult, one study (van de Bor et al. 1990a) evaluated the hemodynamic function during the first 2 postnatal days in 15 full-term infants born to mothers who used cocaine during pregnancy. Cocaine metabolites were present in the urine of all infants. When, on the first postnatal day, the results were compared with a group of 22 normal nonexposed infants (negative urine screen), the cocaine-exposed neonates had lower stroke volume, lower cardiac output, and higher systemic blood pressures than did the controls. These differences disappeared in the second day, suggesting that the effect was due to the circulating cocaine rather than to a more permanent derangement of the cardiovascular control mechanisms. The observed changes were attributed to an increase in circulating catecholamines secondary to the blocking of catecholamine reuptake receptors, but plasma catecholamine levels were not measured.

The same investigators (van de Bor et al. 1990b) found an increased cerebral blood flow velocity in full-term infants of mothers who abused cocaine during pregnancy. This increase in arterial blood pressure and cerebral blood flow may increase the risk of intracranial hemorrhage, especially in preterm infants.

Methodological Considerations

The evaluation of the respiratory pattern and respiratory control mechanisms in infants is subject to a number of methodological difficulties. Some are related to the selection of the subjects included in these studies and to the presence of many confounding variables. Others are related to the instrumentation available for the measurements; and, finally, some are due to errors that occur in the analysis and interpretation of the data.

Subjects. In any evaluation of control of breathing it is crucial to consider the gestational, postnatal, and conceptional age of the infants because the respiratory pattern, reflexes, and the ventilatory response to hypoxia and hypercapnia are markedly influenced by these factors. Also, because abuse of many substances during pregnancy is associated with an increased rate of premature birth and intrauterine growth retardation, it is critical to use control groups with the same distribution of gestational age and weight as in the study population.

The incidence of both perinatal asphyxia and infection also is increased in ISAM, and both are additional confounders that may alter cardiopulmonary function. In considering the effect of a substance used during pregnancy, it is very important to establish as accurately as possible the duration and dose of exposure, as well as the time during pregnancy when the substance was used. It is also extremely difficult to eliminate the possibility of polydrug use and its interactive effect on the variables that are measured.

Poor nutrition, a common problem associated with substance-abusing mothers, is a confounding variable that should not be overlooked because of its possible effects on fetal growth and cardiorespiratory function. The history of previous ALTE is also very important, because these episodes may be responsible for some of the alterations in respiratory pattern observed later in these infants that may otherwise be attributed to the drugs. Finally, one must also keep in mind that substances that are used by the mother postnatally are frequently transferred to the infant through breast-feeding and may have significant effects on the variables being measured.

Methods and Instrumentation. A limitation of many studies that include breathing patterns is that respiration is most commonly monitored by transthoracic impedance. This signal alone cannot differentiate between central and obstructive apneas. To do this, it is necessary also to record airway flow using a nasal thermistor, a pneumotachograph, a capnograph, or other device capable of detecting airway flow. The problem with these devices is that they may irritate the infant or may increase the respiratory deadspace or airway resistance. Inductance plethysmography is a noninvasive method that can provide more information on specific patterns of breathing. Because the electrical properties of the electrodes and the skin changes over time, impedance monitors characteristically change their output and the quality of the respiratory signal within a relatively short period of time.

Among the challenges when evaluating respiratory or cardiovascular function in the neonate or small infant is that the equipment must be noninvasive to eliminate any risk and the need for sedation. Obviously, the infant does not collaborate with the tests, and it is essential to obtain the measurements in an environment that preserves normal physiologic functions as much as possible and that avoids any stressful condition that may influence the measurements. Ambient temperature, sound, light, feeding, tactile stimulation, posture, or any physical activity may have a profound effect on cardiorespiratory function and must be standardized.

Findings in studies of respiratory control are strongly influenced by sleep state. Sleep or awake state or type of sleep is commonly defined only by the respiratory and heart-rate pattern in the pneumogram. This method requires subjective interpretation and may be influenced by equipment artifact. As much as possible, sleep state must be controlled or adequately defined. This requires the use of electroencephalograms, oculograms, and myograms that increase the number of electrodes and instrumentation needed for the studies. In the preterm infant, sleep state is frequently indeterminate and, even with the proper instrumentation, it is difficult or impossible to define.

Analysis and Interpretation of Data

Because of the subjective interpretation of pneumograms or other respiratory tests, it is essential to include a simultaneous control group. The traces must be read blindly by at least two experienced observers using clear, preestablished criteria.

Another problem with cardiorespiratory data is that there is frequently a large individual variability even in the normal population. This results in a wide overlap of the data between normal and abnormal subjects and requires very large populations to detect any differences.

When evaluating any physiologic function, it is important to differentiate alterations that may result from the chronic prenatal exposure to a given substance from the direct effect of the drug that remains in the circulation or in the tissues of the infant for some time after birth. In other situations, the effects of drug withdrawal are the ones that predominate, possibly influencing the results.

REFERENCES

Bachman, K.; Dixon, S.; and Bejar, R. Deficient respiratory control in methamphetamine- and cocaine-exposed neonates. *Pediatr Res* 27:196A, 1990.
Bauchner, H.; Zuckerman, B.; McClain, M.; Frank, D.; Fried, L.E.; and Kayne, H. Risk of sudden infant death syndrome among infants with in utero exposure to cocaine. *J Pediatr* 113:831-834, 1988.

Chappel, J.N. Treatment of morphine-type dependence. *JAMA* 221:1516-1517, 1972.

Chasnoff, I.J.; Hunt, C.E.; Kletter, R.; and Kaplan, D. Prenatal cocaine exposure is associated with respiratory pattern abnormalities. *Am J Dis Child* 143:583-587, 1989.

Chavez, C.J.; Ostrea, E.M.; Stryker, J.C.; and Smialek, Z. Sudden infant death syndrome among infants of drug-dependent mothers. *Pediatrics* 95(3):407-409, 1979.

Chen, C.; Silva-Neto, G.; Tan, S.; Bandstra, E.; Duara, S.; Gerhardt, T.; Hurwitz, B.; and Bancalari, E. Respiratory stability in neonates with prenatal exposure to cocaine. *Pediatr Res* 25:48A, 1989.

Davidson Ward, S.L.; Bautista, D.B.; Schuetz, S.; Wachsman, L.; Bean, X.; and Keens, T.G. Abnormal hypoxic arousal responses in infants of cocaine abusing mothers. *Ann N Y Acad Sci* 562:347-348, 1989.

Davidson Ward, S.L.; Schuetz, S.; Krishna, V.; Bean, X.; Wingert, W.; Wachsman, L.; and Keens, T.G. Abnormal sleeping ventilatory pattern in infants of substance-abusing mothers. *Am J Dis Child* 140:1015-1020, 1986.

Gennser, G.; Marsal, K.; and Brantmark, B. Maternal smoking and fetal breathing movements. *Am J Obstet Gynecol* 123:861-867, 1975.

Gerhardt, T.; Bancalari, E.; Cohen, H.; and Macias-Loza, M. Respiratory depression at birth-value of Apgar score and ventilatory measurements in its detection. *J Pediatr* 90:971-975, 1977.

Gibson, E.; Evans, R.; Finnegan, L.; and Spitzer, A.R. Increased incidence of apnea in infants born to both cocaine and opiate addicted mothers. *Pediatr Res* 27:10A, 1990.

Gingras, J.; Hume, R.; O'Donnell, K.; and Stranger, C. Atypical fetal breathing patterns associated with in utero cocaine exposure. *Pediatr Res* 25(4):310A, 1989.

Glass, L.; Rajegowda, B.K.; Kahn, E.J.; and Floyd, M.V. Effect of heroin withdrawal on respiratory rate and acid-base status in the newborn. *N Engl J Med* 286(14):746-748, 1972.

Gluck, L., and Kulovich, M.V. Lecithin/sphingomyelin ratios in amniotic fluid in normal and abnormal pregnancy. *Am J Obstet Gynecol* 115:539-546, 1973.

Graff, M.A.; Novo, R.P.; Smith, C.; Zapanta, V.; Diaz, M.; Hiatt, I.M.; and Hegyi, T. Ventilatory responses to carbon dioxide in infants at risk for sudden infant death syndrome. *Crit Care Med* 14:873-877, 1986.

Hunt, C.E. Abnormal hypercarbic and hypoxic sleep arousal responses in near-miss SIDS infants. *Pediatr Res* 15:1462-1464, 1981.

Hunt, C.E.; McCulloch, K.; and Brouillete, R.T. Diminished hypoxic ventilatory responses in near-miss sudden infant death syndrome. *J Appl Physiol* 50(6):1313-1317, 1981.

Little, B.B.; Snell, L.M.; Klein, V.R.; and Gilstrap III, L.C. Cocaine abuse during pregnancy: Maternal and fetal implications. *Obstet Gynecol* 73:157-160, 1989.

Manning, F.A., and Feyerabend, C. Cigarette smoking and fetal breathing movements. *Br J Obstet Gynaecol* 83:262-270, 1976.

Marangos, P.J.; Boulenger, J.P.; and Patel, J. Effects of chronic caffeine on brain adenosine receptors: Regional and ontogenetic studies. *Life Sci* 34:899-907, 1984.

Moore, T.R.; Sorg, J.; Miller, L.; Key, T.C.; and Resnik, R. Hemodynamic effects of intravenous cocaine on the pregnant ewe and fetus. *Am J Obstet Gynecol* 155:833-888, 1986.

Olsen, G.D., and Lees, M.H. Ventilatory response to carbon dioxide of infants following chronic prenatal methadone exposure. *J Pediatr* 96(6):983-989, 1980.

Ostrea, E.M., and Chavez, C.J. Perinatal problems (excluding neonatal withdrawal) in maternal drug addiction: A study of 830 cases. *J Pediatr* 94:292-295, 1979.

Perrin, D.G.; Becker, L.E.; Madapalliamatum, A.; Cutz, E.; Bryan, A.C.; and Sole, M.J. Sudden infant death syndrome: Increased carotid-body dopamine and noradrenalin content. *Lancet* 2(8402):535-537, 1984.

Richardson, B.S.; O'Grady, J.P.; and Olsen, G.D. Fetal breathing movements and the response to carbon dioxide in patients on methadone maintenance. *Am J Obstet Gynecol* 150:400-405, 1984.

Richie, J.M., and Green, N.M. Local anesthetics. In: Gilman, A.; Goodman, L.S.; Rall, T.W.; and Murad, F., eds. *Goodman and Gilman's The Pharmacological Basis of Therapeutics.* New York: Macmillan, 1987. pp. 311-331.

Rodriguez, A.M.; Warburton, D.; and Keens, T.G. Elevated catecholamine levels and abnormal hypoxic arousal in apnea of infancy. *Pediatrics* 79:269-274, 1987.

Shannon, D.C.; Kelly, D.H.; and O'Connell, K. Abnormal regulation of ventilation in infants at risk for sudden-infant-death-syndrome. *N Engl J Med* 297:747-750, 1977.

Southall, D.P.; Richards, J.M.; Stebbens, V.; Wilson, A.J.; Taylor, V.; and Alexander, J.R. Cardiorespiratory function in 16 full-term infants with sudden infant death syndrome. *Pediatrics* 78:787-796, 1986.

Szeto, H.H. Effects of narcotic drugs on fetal behavioral activity: Acute methadone exposure. *Am J Obstet Gynecol* 146:211-216, 1983.

Toubas, P.L.; Duke, J.C.; McCaffree, M.A.; Mattice, C.D.; Bendell, D.; and Orr, W.C. Effects of maternal smoking and caffeine habits on infantile apnea: A retrospective study. *Pediatrics* 78:159-163, 1986.

Van de Bor, M.; Walther, F.J.; and Ebrahimi, M. Decreased cardiac output in infants of mothers who abused cocaine. *Pediatrics* 85(1):30-32, 1990a.

Van de Bor, M.; Walther, F.J.; and Sims, M.E. Increased cerebral blood flow velocity in infants of mothers who abuse cocaine. *Pediatrics* 85(5):733-736, 1990b.

Weese-Mayer, D.; Klemka-Walden, L.; and Gingras, J. Effect of chronic in utero cocaine administration on the hypoxic ventilatory response in the rabbit pup. *Pediatr Res* 27:56A, 1990.

Woods, J.R.; Plessinger, M.A.; and Clark, K.E. Effect of cocaine on uterine blood flow and fetal oxygenation. *JAMA* 257:957-961, 1987.

Woods, J.R., Jr.; Plessinger, M.A.; Kimberly, S.; and Miller, R.K. Prenatal cocaine exposure to the fetus: A sheep model for cardiovascular evaluation. *Ann N Y Acad Sci* 562:267-279, 1989.

AUTHOR

Eduardo Bancalari, M.D.
Professor
Department of Pediatrics, Obstetrics, and Gynecology
Director
Division of Neonatology
Department of Pediatrics
University of Miami
P.O. Box 016960
Miami, FL 33101

The Effect of Cocaine on Developing Human Brain

Barry E. Kosofsky

INTRODUCTION

Central nervous system (CNS) development requires a complex orchestration of genetic factors and environmental forces that direct brain maturation and shape infant development in a reproducible yet individualized manner. There are eight major stages in the development of each part of the brain: neural plate induction, cell proliferation (neurons and glia), cell migration, cell aggregation, neuronal maturation, neuronal connectivity (including synaptogenesis), cell death, and process elimination (Cowan 1979). Volpe (1987) divides human brain development into a proliferative phase (for neurons 2 to 4 months gestation and for glia 5 months gestation to 1 year postnatal), a migratory phase (peak time 3 to 5 months gestation), and an organizational phase (peak time 6 months gestation to several years postnatal). The protracted timetable of CNS maturation affords a continuum of biologic vulnerability to developing brain. Moreover, the developmental consequences of a toxic CNS insult relate critically to the gestational timing of the exposure. Evrard and colleagues (1989) distinguish two classes of CNS developmental disorders: those occurring in the first half of gestation that affect cytogenesis and histogenesis and those occurring during the second half of gestation that affect brain growth and differentiation (figure 1). During the organizational phase in the second half of gestation, progressive events (neuronal maturation, connection formation, and synaptogenesis) and regressive events (cell death and selective elimination of processes) critically shape the maturation of brain circuitry. Toxic influences during this period may dramatically alter brain development but may also alter the regressive events that underlie the capacity of developing brain to compensate for injury. A pattern of metabolic maturation must parallel normal brain development and may impose regional stage-specific metabolic requirements and vulnerabilities.

Within this context of brain development, one must consider potential modes of toxicity of cocaine on developing brain. The action of cocaine is mediated by blocking the reuptake of the catecholamine neurotransmitters norepinephrine

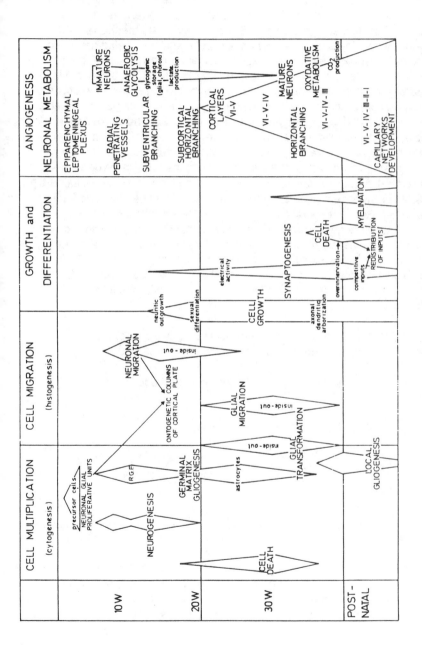

FIGURE 1. *Schematic representation of the chronology of the main neocortical developmental events*

SOURCE: Evrard et al. 1989, copyright 1989, Paul H. Brookes Publishing Company

129

and dopamine and the indoleamine serotonin at nerve terminals (Gold et al. 1985). The peripheral effects of cocaine are a catecholamine-induced increase in sympathetic drive leading to vasoconstriction, hypertension, and tachycardia. The central effects of cocaine derive from increased central aminergic drive leading to CNS stimulation (Ritchie and Greene 1985). The mechanisms by which maternal cocaine exposure may compromise fetal well-being have been suggested by physiologic studies in pregnant sheep. In the model of the fetal ewe, injection of cocaine into the pregnant mother leads to fetal blood levels approximately one-eighth that of the mother, within 5 to 7 minutes of injection (Woods et al. 1989). After single intravenous injections of cocaine comparable to commonly abused doses (1 mg/kg), maternal heart rate and oxygenation were stable, but maternal mean arterial pressure increased. Concomitant with maternal hypertension was a 34-percent decrease in uterine blood flow from catecholamine-mediated vasoconstriction of the uterine arteries (Woods et al. 1987). The fetal consequences of decreased uterine blood flow are reduced oxygen delivery (hypoxemia), fetal hypertension, and tachycardia. The fetal response to hypoxemia is release of endogenous catecholamines (Phillippe 1983). The fetal catecholamines and maternal catecholamines, which are transmitted to fetus via the placenta, are circulating in high quantities in the fetus because cocaine, which diffuses to the fetal circulation, prevents their reuptake. These animal studies point to the following classes of potential mechanisms whereby maternal cocaine abuse can compromise fetal brain development:

1.   Indirect (maternal) via catecholamine-mediated placental vascular compromise with consequent fetal hypoxemia and/or ischemic injury

2.   Direct (fetal) peripheral via catecholamine-mediated effects on fetal vasculature

3.   Direct (fetal) central via aminergic mechanisms

     (a) Altering the integrity of aminergic transmitter systems secondary to developmental perturbation of amine concentration and distribution in fetal brain

     (b) Altering the fidelity of aminergic signals, which may subserve a trophic role in CNS maturation (Lauder 1988)

One central question is to establish whether cocaine is a behavioral teratogen (Vorhees 1989), a drug capable of generating a reproducible alteration in behavior consequent to fetal exposure. Grimm (1987) outlines four levels of research at which one should consider a behavioral teratogen:

- Cognitive level—define the behavioral and cognitive deficit

- Systems level—specify the brain structures and neurochemical systems that subserve the behavioral or cognitive deficit

- Developmental level—specify the time course of brain vulnerability to the insult

- Pharmacologic-physiologic level—specify the mechanism of action of the teratogen

Part of the difficulty in establishing cocaine as a behavioral teratogen is that the behavioral consequences of prenatal exposure to cocaine may not be evident at birth but may appear as the behavioral repertoire of the developing child matures. Therefore, one strives to identify antecedents of the behavioral abnormality. One also strives to identify predictive markers (clinical, anatomic, physiologic, or chemical) of the subsequent expression of the behavioral anomaly. Implicit in this approach is a consideration of the role of genetic and environmental factors that may alter the susceptibility to or expression of a teratogenic effect.

This chapter reviews the clinical studies that consider the toxic effects of cocaine on developing brain. These studies focus on perinatal growth parameters, infant behavior and development, and neuroanatomic and neurophysiologic assessments.

CLINICAL STUDIES: PERINATAL OUTCOME

Bingol and colleagues (1987) compared pregnancy outcome in 50 women and their offspring who were exposed only to cocaine during gestation (as defined by maternal history and newborn urine screening) and 50 non-drug-exposed mother-infant pairs. Stillbirth rate was higher in mothers who abused cocaine during gestation (8 percent, all related to *abruptio placentae*, occurring shortly after cocaine administration in all four mothers, $p \leq 0.001$), but no differences were found in the rate of spontaneous abortions. In infants with gestations of 37 weeks or longer who were exposed to cocaine *in utero*, birth weight, length, and head circumference were decreased ($p \leq 0.001$). An increased incidence of major congenital malformations was reported in infants exposed to cocaine *in utero* (10-percent incidence in cocaine-exposed infants vs. 2-percent incidence in controls, $p \leq 0.01$). The study did not evaluate the contribution of other maternal characteristics and habits related to cocaine use that may adversely influence pregnancy outcome.

Analysis of 1,776 consecutive deliveries in an urban labor and delivery unit by Neerhof and colleagues (1989) compared perinatal outcome in 114 newborns exposed only to cocaine *in utero* (documented by positive maternal urine screening and confirmed by history) with 88 randomly chosen unexposed newborns (negative maternal history and urine screening). Cocaine-exposed infants demonstrated shorter gestational age (GA) (mean GA=37.5 weeks in cocaine-exposed vs. GA=39.0 weeks in controls), increased incidence of preterm (less than 37 weeks) delivery (25 percent of cocaine-exposed infants vs. 9 percent of controls), and an increased incidence of small-for-gestational age infants (28 percent of cocaine-exposed infants vs. 7 percent of controls were less than the 10th percentile for weight). Of note is the rapid increase in incidence of mothers who had cocaine detected in their urine at delivery during the time of the study: from 4 percent of mothers delivering between September 1, 1986, and March 1, 1987, to 12 percent of mothers delivering between February 1, 1988 and August 1, 1988. Statistical comparisons between infants exposed only to cocaine and controls were not made, and the independent role of cocaine in influencing developmental outcome was not assessed.

Zuckerman and colleagues (1989) reported a prospective study of 1,226 inner-city mothers who were followed by interview and urine screening for cocaine and marijuana use during pregnancy. The large number of study participants and careful study design allowed a multivariate regression analysis, which clearly established the independent effect of cocaine exposure on fetal growth. Infants of women who had a positive urine assay for cocaine weighed 93 grams less (p≤0.07), were 0.7 cm shorter (p=0.01), and had a 0.43 smaller head circumference (p=0.01) compared with infants born to women who were otherwise identical for age; prepregnancy weight and weight gain during pregnancy; parity; prenatal visits; sexually transmitted diseases; and marijuana, cigarette, alcohol, and opiate use. Additionally, these investigators established that (1) there was no independent association of cocaine exposure with shorter duration of gestation; (2) cocaine may have an additional indirect effect on fetal growth mediated by maternal undernourishment (see below); (3) 25 percent of women who used cocaine during pregnancy denied use when interviewed (they were identified by the urine assay alone); and (4) multiple regression analyses recalculated based on reporting alone showed no statistically significant difference in fetal growth between infants born to mothers who reported cocaine use compared with those who did not report use. The finding of dramatic reduction in head circumference (.43 cm decrement) of newborns because of the additional burden of maternal cocaine abuse during pregnancy is in sharp contrast with their finding of "head sparing" in infants born to gestational marijuana abusers and with the established principle regarding relative sparing of head size with nutritional compromise during gestation (Ballabriga 1989). Attention is thereby focused on the specific toxicity of cocaine exposure in compromising fetal brain growth.

The interpretation of studies that relate maternal cocaine habits with neonatal outcome requires consideration of confounding biologic, methodologic, and epidemiologic variables. As Neerhof and coworkers (1989) point out, drug history alone identified fewer than 50 percent of the women who had positive urine toxicologic screens at delivery. Conversely, urine screening at delivery only identifies mothers who have abused cocaine in the 3 to 5 days prior to delivery, despite slower cocaine metabolism because of lower plasma and liver cholinesterase activity evident in pregnant women (and in newborns, especially infants born prematurely) (Ecobichon and Stephens 1973). Errors in proper identification of exposed as well as control infants yield erroneous conclusions, as discussed above in the Zuckerman study (1989). Attempts to provide more complete fetal drug-exposure profiles include serial, prospective historic, and toxicologic screening. Other screening methods being developed include analysis of neonatal meconium, from which cocaine metabolites (benzoylecgonine) were isolated in higher concentration than in paired urine samples (Ostrea et al. 1989). Because meconium is accumulated by a fetus during gestation, such analysis may serve as an adjunct in providing an expanded temporal profile of maternal drug intake during the second half of gestation. Another approach evolving in toxicology is the determination of cocaine use by analysis of deposition of cocaine metabolites in hair. Graham and colleagues (1989) reported a study of 21 adults wherein self-reported drug histories correlated with amount of cocaine metabolite contained in samples of hair (when concurrent urine screening was negative). Hair samples from seven neonates, four infants (2.5 to 3.5 months of age) and three toddlers (1 to 3 years), exposed to cocaine *in utero* (documented by maternal history) were analyzed. All seven neonates, two out of four infants, and none of the toddlers had evidence of benzoylecgonine in samples of hair, documenting the potential usefulness of hair analysis in screening neonates (though loss of neonatal hair renders the assay less sensitive as the infant develops). Because hair analysis provides data on long-term rather than recent drug exposure, this technique may supplement urine screening (and extend toxic analyses, should the method provide semiquantitative results). The better defined the prenatal cocaine exposure can be (amount of cocaine the fetus is exposed to, the gestational timing of that exposure, and the route, frequency, and duration of drug exposure), the more informative the perinatal and postnatal characterization of the effect of drug exposure can be.

Whether cocaine exposure is a risk factor for development of congenital malformations has been controversial. It has been speculated that such a teratogenic effect of cocaine is a consequence of fetal vascular disruption during organogenesis (Hoyme et al. 1990). However, to establish a causal role for cocaine in producing a low-incidence event such as a particular major congenital anomaly requires a well-designed statistical analysis of a large cohort. This was accomplished by Chavez and colleagues (1989), who analyzed data from the population-based Atlanta Birth Defects Case-Control Study and established an increased risk of all urinary tract anomalies in mothers who reported cocaine use during the time from 1 month before the pregnancy began through the first 3 months of pregnancy when compared with population controls (adjusted odds ratio=4.81, 95-percent confidence interval 1.15-20.14). The adjusted risk estimate includes consideration of potential confounding variables (maternal age and education, cigarette smoking, alcohol intake, and use of other illicit drugs) through a multiple logistic analysis. Clarification of whether *in utero* cocaine exposure imparts an increased risk for other low-incidence outcomes (such as intestinal atresia, neural tube defects, necrotizing enterocolitis, or sudden infant death syndrome) awaits large-scale epidemiologic analysis.

One of the advantages of well-designed, large-scale, case-controlled or prospective studies is the ability to perform statistical analyses to assess the independent contribution imparted by exposure to cocaine *in utero* on a particular outcome. The developmental outcome of children exposed to cocaine prenatally also may be influenced by maternal characteristics (race, age, gravity, parity, history of sexually transmitted diseases, socioeconomic status), maternal habits during gestation (prenatal care, nutrition and weight gain, cigarette smoking, alcohol consumption, other drug habits), and additional factors that influence maternal-infant interactions (maternal education, maternal depression/isolation/ stress, home life, including marital status and social supports, continued drug habits).

The Boston City Hospital study (Zuckerman et al. 1989) helps to clarify the roles such individual factors play in fetal growth, thereby extending the findings of previous prenatal analyses. These investigators emphasized this point by contrasting bivariate comparisons with findings of their multiple regression analyses on the same data. Bivariate analysis suggested that maternal cocaine use (vs. nonuse, as defined by maternal urine screening) caused a statistically significant (p<0.05) decrease in GA and increase in congenital anomalies (three minor or one major). After controlling for potentially confounding variables, the results of regression analysis revealed no independent statistical association of maternal cocaine use with shorter duration of gestation or with an increase in congenital malformation (p=.10 for three minor anomalies or one major anomaly). These investigators noted that women in their study with urine assays positive for cocaine weighed less and gained less weight during pregnancy than women with assays negative for cocaine. By repeating the regression analysis of infant birth weight without independent consideration of maternal pregnancy weight and pregnancy weight gain, the magnitude of the effect of cocaine on lowering birth weight increased (from 93 grams to 137 grams). The implication is that cocaine has a direct effect on decreasing fetal

134

weight, as well as an indirect effect via maternal undernutrition. In summary, studies that relate maternal cocaine habits to fetal outcome must incorporate toxicologic screens to supplement self-reported drug histories, must consider the contribution of potentially confounding variables associated with maternal cocaine abuse, and must strive to identify markers that will predict subsequent developmental compromise.

CENTRAL NERVOUS SYSTEM

Studies on newborns and infants that focus on markers for CNS insult can be divided into clinical studies (behavioral, neurologic, and developmental assessments), electrophysiologic studies (analysis of electroencephalograms [EEGs], and evoked potentials), and imaging studies (employing head ultrasounds [HUSs], and computerized axial tomography [CAT] scans). The lack of long-term studies of neurologic, developmental, behavioral, and growth outcome in children exposed to cocaine *in utero* reflects the recent emergence and appreciation of the problem and emphasizes the additional difficulties involved in longitudinal followup of this disenfranchised population.

NEUROBEHAVIORAL OUTCOME

Chasnoff and colleagues (1989) showed that a group of women who abused cocaine solely during the first trimester did not have the increased risk of preterm delivery, risk of having low-birth-weight infants, or increased rates of intrauterine growth retardation (IUGR) that were seen in a group of mothers who abused cocaine throughout pregnancy. These investigators employed the Brazelton Neonatal Behavioral Assessment Scale (NBAS), a standardized assessment of the pattern of an infant's state change in response to external and internal stimuli. Infant performance on 28 standard items is reduced to cluster scores reflecting global function, including habituation, orientation, motor performance, range of state, regulation of state, autonomic regulation, and reflexes. In Chasnoff and colleagues' study, 7 out of 16 infants born to mothers who abused cocaine solely during the first trimester as well as 8 out of 36 infants whose mothers abused cocaine throughout gestation were unable to reach alert states and were thereby unable to attend to visual or auditory stimuli. Cluster-score comparisons between cocaine-exposed infants and a control population demonstrated significant impairment of orientation, motor ability, state regulation, and a number of abnormal reflexes when tested between 12 and 72 hours of life. The implication of altered NBASs in infants exposed to cocaine solely during the first trimester is that the window of biologic vulnerability of developing brain to cocaine for subsequent behavioral effects may be very early in gestation. This first-trimester insult may be independent of second- and third-trimester effects of cocaine on fetal growth.

Neurologic and developmental followup of infants exposed to cocaine was reported by Rosen and Johnson (1988). They followed three groups of pregnant women prenatally: Multidrug abusers (70 percent were using cocaine with marijuana and/or mild to moderate intake of alcohol, and 30 percent were using marijuana with or without alcohol); mothers on methadone maintenance; and mothers free of substance abuse (during the second and third trimesters, screened by history, and with serial urine evaluations in a prenatal clinic setting). At birth each infant had a neurologic evaluation. Neurologic evaluation and administration of the Bayley Scales of Infant Development were repeated at 6 months and at 12 months. At birth, infants of polysubstance abusers (70 percent of whom abused cocaine) had a 10-percent incidence of abnormalities on neurologic exam. Neurologic exam was suspect to abnormal in 21 percent of these infants at 6 months (compared with 16 percent of controls) and in 6 percent of these infants at 12 months (vs. 4 percent of controls), with normal Bayley scores, both mental development index (MDI) and psychomotor development index (PDI) reported at both time points.

Chasnoff and Griffith (1989) published in abstract form a 2-year followup of developmental scores (Bayley) and growth parameters in 125 infants exposed to cocaine during gestation compared with 40 infants born to drug-free women. Cocaine-exposed infants displayed a statistically significant decrease in weight through 12 months of age ($p < 0.05$), with normalization thereafter, but demonstrated smaller head circumferences at all time points evaluated (through 24 months). There were no differences in the Bayley Scales (MDI or PDI) at any of the time points assessed.

Dixon (1989), in reviewing a population of infants born to mothers who abused stimulants during pregnancy (cocaine and/or methamphetamine), noted that three-fourths of exposed infants had development quotients of less than 100 during the first year, with areas of fine motor and visual motor coordination showing the greatest delays, with age-related decremental performance. Dixon has observed that infants exposed to cocaine may go through a secondary "withdrawal phase of neurobehavioral disturbance" at 2 to 8 weeks, characterized by irritability, hypertonia, diaphoresis, mild hyperthermia, hyperphagia, and hyposomnia. The most severely impaired of the stimulant-exposed children had overt neurologic deficits, including spastic quadriparesis, hemiplegia, microcephaly, global delay, and seizures. More prevalent were developmental problems, including altered adaptive behaviors during the first year of life and delayed acquisition of language skills during the second year of life.

In a review of infants exposed to multiple drugs *in utero* (the majority exposed to a combination that included cocaine), Howard (1989) emphasized the deviant psychologic behavior evident in the mood states and ability to experience pleasure during the first 2 years of life. She studied the emotional response of 20 18-month-olds when separated from their parent figures and described that three-fourths of these infants "remained unsettlingly neutral in their emotional response throughout the period of observation."

ELECTROPHYSIOLOGIC STUDIES

Doberczak and coworkers (1988) prospectively studied serial EEGs in 39 neonates born to mothers abusing only cocaine (as confirmed by maternal history and urine screening of both mothers and newborn infants). Initial EEGs during the first week of life were abnormal in 17 infants, characterized by bursts of sharp waves and spikes, which were multifocal in 14 of 17 tracings. All initial EEGs showed features of background discontinuity. Abnormal tracings did not correlate with historical data on route or quantity of maternal cocaine use or with severity of neurologic signs (34 out of 39 infants displayed greater muscle tone, brisk deep tendon reflexes, irritability, or tremors, most evident on day 3). Of the 17 initially abnormal EEGs, 5 were normal at 8 to 19 days, and no infant tested had an abnormal EEG at 3 to 12 months. Of note, clinical seizures were not observed in any of these infants.

Kramer and coworkers (1990) reported on 16 infants exposed only to cocaine *in utero* (documented historically and confirmed by urine testing of both mothers and newborn infants). All infants examined within hours of birth demonstrated multiple stereotypic events considered to be seizures, in addition to excessive startle, irritability, and tremulousness. Clinical classification of seizures were subtle in 10 out of 16, tonic in 2 out of 16, clonic in 3 out of 16, and focal in 1 out of 16 subjects (the only infant to demonstrate focal lesions on computerized tomography [CT] consisting of recent bihemispheric middle cerebral artery [MCA] infarcts). Seven of 16 had ictal EEGs, confirming the diagnosis. Seizures were poorly responsive to therapeutic levels of phenobarbital and phenytoin, alone and in combination. Five out of 16 infants continued to have seizures (generalized, tonic, or tonic-clonic) after 6 months of age. Although only 2 infants had extensive developmental testing, the investigators' impression, based on clinical examination, suggested that all 16 children revealed delayed motor milestones, which improved with age.

Shih and colleagues (1988) performed brain stem auditory evoked responses (BAERs) in 18 newborns (within 6 days of delivery) who were exposed to cocaine *in utero* (documented by history and by maternal and neonatal urine screening) and in 18 newborns whose mothers were drug free (documented by history and confirmed in a few cases with urine screening). Infants exposed to cocaine *in utero* were somewhat younger (GA=37 weeks vs. 38 weeks in controls) and smaller (birth weight [BW]=2,600 g vs. 3,400 g in controls). They showed that wave V was prolonged, as was the I-V interpeak latency in the 80dB condition in the cocaine-exposed infants. Prolongation of the III-V interpeak latency for the cocaine-exposed infants was evident in the 40dB and 80dB testing conditions. Since that report, data generated by other investigators, presented in abstract form (Salamy et al. 1990) have confirmed these findings of delayed brain stem transmission time in cocaine-exposed infants (as determined by positive infant or maternal toxicology reports). However, when cocaine-exposed infants were evaluated 52 to 65 weeks postconception (3 to 6 months of age), they were no longer statistically distinguishable from control values. Of note, two abstracts (Carzoli et al. 1990; Schwartz et al. 1990) described studies where BAERs were not affected by cocaine exposure *in utero*.

Anday and coworkers (1989) examined the effect of *in utero* cocaine exposure (by history and by maternal and fetal urine screening demonstrating cocaine only) on auditory augmentation of the glabellar eyeblink (startle) days to weeks postdelivery. Nineteen cocaine-exposed infants were compared with 19 control infants matched for GA and BW (GA=35.0 in cocaine-exposed infants, 34.8 in controls; BW=2,139 g in cocaine-exposed infants, 2,222 g in controls). Cocaine-exposed infants demonstrated a higher amplitude glabellar eyeblink and a statistically significant increased augmentation of eyeblink when the glabellar tap was accompanied by a tone (startle).

Dixon and colleagues (1987) reported alterations in visual evoked responses (VERs) in 12 term neonates exposed to cocaine *in utero* (neonatal urine screens positive at birth). Flash VERs were abnormal in 11 out of 12 infants studied, including gross hemispheric asynchrony with major positive wave component delays (n=1), abnormal latency of major wave forms (n=1), and no interpretable response (n=5). Of note, 11 out of 12 infants demonstrated abnormalities in EEGs described as disturbances in state organization, excess sharp wave activity, and bursts of theta activity. Cranial ultrasounds were normal in all infants.

NEUROIMAGING STUDIES

Chasnoff and coworkers (1986) reported a perinatal cerebral infarct in a full-term, average for gestational age (AGA) infant born to a mother who used cocaine intranasally during the first 5 weeks of pregnancy, then abstained throughout the rest of her pregnancy until 3 days before delivery (5 grams) and on the day of delivery (1 gram, 15 hours prior to delivery) with maternal and fetal urine positive for cocaine only (and nicotine in the mother). The infant displayed mildly decreased right upper extremity muscle tone at birth, and at 16 hours of life demonstrated multiple right focal motor seizures (right leg and right arm). CT scan done at 24 hours of life revealed a wedge-shaped left MCA distribution acute infarction. Followup CT scan at 3 1/2 months showed extensive cortical tissue loss in the left frontoparietal region (MCA territory distribution). Chasnoff and coworkers (1989) reported a perinatal infarction in an infant born to a mother who abused cocaine in the 2 to 3 days before delivery. Kramer and colleagues (1990) published the case of a full-term 2-day-old infant exposed to crack *in utero* (documented by history and by urine screening of mother and infant) with the onset of tonic left-upper-extremity seizures associated with variable eye deviation and irregular breathing pattern on day two of life. CT scan revealed recent large bihemispheric MCA distribution cortical infarctions. Dixon and coworkers (1989) reported two infants exposed to cocaine *in utero* (documented on infant urine screening) who sustained perinatal cerebral infarctions confirmed by CT.

Dixon and Bejar (1989) reported HUS findings on or before day 3 of life in 32 full-term, "well" neonates prenatally exposed only to cocaine (defined by infant urine screening). Forty-one percent (13 out of 32) of cocaine-exposed infants had abnormal HUS studies, including white-matter cavitation (15.6 percent), white-matter densities (12.5 percent), acute infarction (6.3 percent), intraventricular hemorrhage (12.5 percent), subarachnoid hemorrhage (12.5 percent), subependymal hemorrhage (12.5 percent), and ventricular enlargement (12.5 percent). The white-matter cavities, 3-10 mm cystic lesions, were in the frontal lobes and in the basal ganglion. These lesions are suggestive of prior hemorrhagic or ischemic injury, with secondary white-matter cavitation, whereas white-matter densities are suggestive of acute hemorrhage or infarction. Forty-one percent of "well" neonates exposed to cocaine prenatally had HUS lesions, suggesting prior or acute CNS structural injury. These infants with ultrasonographically definable CNS lesions could not be differentiated from infants with normal studies on clinical grounds (no alteration in anthropometric measures or specific neurobehavioral markers such as the NBAS). Dixon is employing additional imaging modalities to follow this population to assess degree of cerebral atrophy (on CT scans) and maturation of myelination (on magnetic resonance imaging scans) to confirm and extend the HUS findings.

SYNTHESIS

The data reviewed suggest the following:

1. Infants born to mothers who abuse cocaine during gestation demonstrate impaired fetal growth. This appears to be mediated through an indirect effect of poor maternal nutrition and a direct effect of cocaine. The independent contribution of cocaine is a .43 cm decrement in head circumference of the newborn.

139

2. Newborns of mothers who abuse cocaine during gestation (including women who limit their cocaine habits to the first trimester) demonstrate altered behavior, as evidenced by abnormalities in state control (abnormalities on the NBAS), with difficulties in orientation/alertness being the most affected.

3. Electrophysiologic studies suggest that newborns exposed to cocaine *in utero* evidence CNS dysmaturation; that is, they characterize the cocaine-exposed infant as being younger than chronologic age by demonstration of more immature patterns of electrophysiologic activity.

4. Normalization of electrophysiologic testing and of neurologic testing occurs during the first year, except in a minority of patients who sustain significant structural insults (large vessel distribution infarction) or perinatal asphyxia (related to acute dramatic placental insufficiency as in *abruptio placentae*).

5. A significant fraction of children exposed to cocaine *in utero* show evidence of focal structural CNS damage. Most of this group identified with abnormal cranial imaging is otherwise indistinguishable on clinical grounds.

6. A persistent deficit may be evident in delayed language acquisition, cognitive impairment, and/or behavioral abnormalities in some children exposed to cocaine during gestation as they get older. A clearer characterization of the deficits evident in these children and the extent and role that *in utero* cocaine exposure contributes to these deficits remain to be determined.

In considering some future directions, clinical questions can be formulated at the four levels of analysis previously discussed (Grimm 1987):

1. Pharmacologic/physiologic—what are the mechanisms by which cocaine can exert a toxic effect on developing brain (chronic-placental insufficiency, nutritional compromise, acute-focal vascular injury, perinatal asphyxia, recurrent-hypoxic ischemic injury, disruption of aminergic systems and signals)?

2. Developmental level—what are the factors that influence the individual susceptibility (e.g., maternal and fetal genetic factors) and window of biologic vulnerability (drug dose, frequency, quantity, duration, timing with respect to gestational age) of developing brain to the toxic effects of cocaine?

3. Systems level—what are the brain structures and neurochemical systems that subserve the behavioral or cognitive deficit?

Clinicoanatomic and clinicobiochemical correlations await the application of more sensitive anatomic methods, such as magnetic resonance imaging, and dynamic imaging methods, such as positron emission tomography scanning, which allow *in vivo* assessment of individuals at multiple developmental timepoints to assess anatomic, metabolic, and chemical integrity of specific neuronal systems and structures.

4. Behavior/cognitive level—what behavioral and cognitive deficits are evident in children exposed to cocaine *in utero*? When do these deficits become evident? What tests are available (or can be developed) to assess these deficits and to identify their antecedents? What role do postnatal factors (e.g., environment) play in the expression of these deficits?

The challenge for the next phase of clinical research on the effects of cocaine on developing brain is to design studies that will provide meaningful answers to these questions at each level of analysis.

REFERENCES

Anday, E.K.; Cohen, M.E.; Kelley, N.E.; and Leitner, D.S. Effect of in utero cocaine exposure on startle and its modification. *Dev Pharmacol Ther* 12:137-145, 1989.

Ballabriga, A. Some aspects of clinical and biochemical changes related to nutrition during brain development in humans. *Dev Neurobiol* 12:271-286, 1989.

Bingol, N.; Fuchs, N.; Diaz, V.; Stone, R.K.; and Gromisch, D.S. Teratogenicity of cocaine in humans. *J Pediatr* 100(1):93-96, 1987.

Carzoli, R.P.; Hammer-Knisel, J.; and Houy, J. Evaluation of auditory evoked response in infants of cocaine abusing mothers. *Pediatr Res* 27(4):240A, 1990.

Chasnoff, I.J.; Bussey, M.E.; Savich, R.; and Stack, C.M. Perinatal cerebral infarction and maternal cocaine use. *J Pediatr* 108(3):456-459, 1986.

Chasnoff, I.J., and Griffith, D.R. Cocaine-exposed infants: Two year follow-up. *Pediatr Res* 25(4):249A, 1989.

Chasnoff, I.J.; Griffith, D.R.; MacGregor, S.; Dirkes, K.; and Burns, K.A. Temporal patterns of cocaine use in pregnancy. *JAMA* 261(12):1741-1744, 1989.

Chavez, G.F.; Mulinare, J.; and Cordero, J.F. Maternal cocaine use during early pregnancy as a risk factor for congenital urogenital anomalies. *JAMA* 262(6):795-798, 1989.

Cowan, W.M. The development of the brain. *Sci Am* 241(3):112-134, 1979.

Dixon, S.D. Effects of transplacental exposure to cocaine and methamphetamine on the neonate (specialty conference). *West J Med* 150(4):436-442, 1989.

Dixon, S.D., and Bejar, R. Echoencephalographic findings in neonates associated with maternal cocaine and methamphetamine use: Incidence and clinical correlates. *J Pediatr* 115(5):770-778, 1989.

Dixon, S.D.; Coen R.W.; and Crutchfield, S. Visual dysfunction in cocaine-exposed infants. *Pediatr Res* 21(4):359A, 1987.

Doberczak, T.M.; Shanzer, S.; Senie, R.T.; and Kandall, S.R. Neonatal neurologic and electroencephalographic effects of intrauterine cocaine exposure. *J Pediatr* 113(2):354-358, 1988.

Ecobichon, D.J., and Stephens, D.S. Perinatal development of human blood esterases. *Clin Pharmacol Ther* 14(1):41-47, 1973.

Evrard, P.; de Saint-Georges, P.; Kadhim, H.J.; and Gadisseux, J.F. Pathology of prenatal encephalopathies. In: *Child Neurology and Developmental Disabilities*. Baltimore, MD: Paul H. Brookes Publishing Co., 1989. pp. 153-176.

Gold, M.S.; Washton, A.M.; and Dackis, C.A. Cocaine abuse: Neurochemistry, phenomenology, and treatment. In: Kozel, N.J., and Adams, E.H., eds. *Cocaine Use in America: Epidemiologic and Clinical Perspectives*. National Institute on Drug Abuse Research Monograph 61. DHHS Pub. No. (ADM)87-1414. Washington, DC: Supt. of Docs., U.S. Govt. Print. Off., 1985. pp. 130-150.

Graham, K.; Koren, G.; Klein, J.; Schneiderman, J.; and Greenwald, M. Determination of gestational cocaine exposure by hair analysis. *JAMA* 262(23):3328-3330, 1989.

Grimm, V.E. Effect of teratogenic exposure on the developing brain: Research strategies and possible mechanisms. *Dev Pharmacol Ther* 10:328-345, 1987.

Howard, J. Cocaine and its effects on the newborn. *Dev Med Child Neurol* 31:255-263, 1989.

Hoyme, H.E.; Jones, K.L.; Dixon, S.D.; Jewett, T.; Hanson, J.W.; Robinson, L.K.; Msall, M.E.; and Allanson, J.E. Prenatal cocaine exposure and fetal vascular disruption. *Pediatrics* 85(5):743-747, 1990.

Kramer, L.D.; Locke, G.E.; Ogunyemi, A.; and Nelson, L. Neonatal cocaine-related seizures. *J Child Neurol* 5(1):60-64, 1990.

Lauder, J.M. Neurotransmitters as morphogens. *Prog Brain Res* 73:365-387, 1988.

Neerhof, M.G.; MacGregor, S.N.; Retzky, S.S.; and Sullivan, T.P. Cocaine abuse during pregnancy: Peripartum prevalence and perinatal outcome. *Am J Obstet Gynecol* 161(3):633-638, 1989.

Ostrea, E.M.; Brady, M.J.; Parks, P.M.; Asensio, D.C.; and Naluz, A. Drug screening of meconium in infants of drug-dependent mothers: An alternative to urine testing. *J Pediatr* 115(3):474-477, 1989.

Phillippe, M. Fetal catecholamines. *Am J Obstet Gynecol* 146(7):840-855, 1983.

Ritchie, J.M., and Greene, N.M. Cocaine. In: Gilman, A.G.; Goodman, L.S.; Rall, T.W.; and Murad, F., eds. *The Pharmacologic Basis of Therapeutics.* 7th ed. New York: Macmillan, 1985. pp. 309-310.

Rosen, T.S., and Johnson, H.L. Drug-addicted mothers, their infants, and SIDS. *Ann N Y Acad Sci* 89-95, 1988.

Salamy A.; Eldredge L.; and Anderson, J. Effects of cocaine on brainstem transmission time in early life. *Pediatr Res* 27(4):254A, 1990.

Schwartz, D.; Morris, M.; Civitello, B.; Spydell, J.; and Anday E. Lack of effect of in utero on auditory brainstem evoked potential. *Pediatr Res* 25:348A, 1990.

Shih, L.; Cone-Wesson, B.; and Reddix, B. Effects of maternal cocaine abuse on the neonatal auditory system. *Int J Pediatr Otorhinolaryngol* 15:245-251,1988.

Volpe, J.J. *Neurology of the Newborn.* Philadelphia, PA: W.B. Saunders Company, 1987.

Vorhees, C.V. Concepts in teratology and developmental toxicology derived from animal research. *Ann N Y Acad Sci* 562:31-41, 1989.

Woods, J.R.; Plessinger, M.A.; and Clark, K.E. Effect of cocaine on uterine blood flow and fetal oxygenation. *JAMA* 257(7): 957-961, 1987.

Woods, J.R.; Plessinger, M.A.; Scott, K.; and Miller, R.K. Prenatal cocaine exposure to the fetus: A sheep model for cardiovascular evaluation. *Ann N Y Acad Sci* 562:267-279, 1989.

Zuckerman, B.; Frank, D.A.; Hingson, R.; Amaro, H.; Levenson, S.M.; Kayne, H.; Parker, S.; Vinci, R.; Aboagye, K.; Fried, L.E.; Cabral, H.; Timperi, R.; and Bauchner, H. Effects of maternal marijuana and cocaine use on fetal growth. *N Engl J Med* 320(12):762-768, 1989.

AUTHOR

Barry E. Kosofsky, M.D., Ph.D.
Research and Clinical Fellow
Department of Neurology
Massachusetts General Hospital
Harvard Medical School
Fruit Street
Boston, MA 02114

Discussion: Assessing Status of the Newborn

Edward Z. Tronlck

In their presentation at the technical review, Als and Duffy combined neurophysiologic and neurobehavioral assessments into a single paradigm (Als, this volume). This approach provides critical information on the effects of lesions on particular neurophysiologic systems and on the functional pathology resulting from these lesions. Much of the work in this area lacks the latter type of information. As a consequence, little is known about the functional implications of lesions on the functional status of the newborn and child. If the scientific and human implications of drug exposure are to be understood, it is critical that their lead be followed. This means that future work with humans must utilize the most sophisticated physiologic, neurologic, and behavioral measures available.

Two of the best standardized assessments of newborn functioning are the Assessment of Preterm Infants' Behavior (APIB) (Als et al. 1982) and its parent, the Neonatal Behavioral Assessment Scale (NBAS) (Brazelton 1984). These scales evaluate the infant's capacities in a number of domains such as orientation, self-regulation, habituation, motor control, and autonomic regulation. Both scales are useful in providing a first picture of the effects of substances of abuse on these areas of functioning. These assessments, however, need to be followed up with more sensitive and sophisticated tests to examine in detail areas of potential compromise. For example, motor dysfunction as found on the NBAS can be followed up with computerized forms of kinematic analysis (Fetters and Todd 1987), and autonomic dysfunction can be followed up with an analysis of vagal tone (Lester 1983; Porges and Greenspan, this volume). Such techniques are more objective and sensitive than omnibus assessments. In addition, they overcome the problems of the halo effects of an observer coding an entire behavioral assessment.

The assessment of infant functioning must take three forms. Examiners should elicit the infant's optimal and typical performances as well as his or her coping responses to stress. Each of these approaches reveals something different about the organization of the infant's behavior, and taken together, they are far

144

more informative than any one technique. Eliciting optimal performance, as demanded by the NBAS, uncovers the infant's underlying capacities when the infant is given as much support as possible by the examiner. This approach may be most useful in understanding whether there is underlying residual brain damage. For example, this approach helps determine whether a drug-exposed infant can follow an object with smooth movements when the examiner has minimized other interfering factors and has brought the infant into his or her best state of consciousness. Tests eliciting the infant's typical performance, on the other hand, assess the infant's capacities under normal handling conditions. This method may be particularly relevant for understanding the effects that the infant has on his or her caregivers, who, after all, are not necessarily experienced handlers of newborns. Stressful evaluations—sometimes called provocative tests—examine the infant's regulatory capacities for dealing with disruptive events. These tests often bring out underlying problems that are not evident during either optimal or typical assessment techniques. However, these tests are not as specific as the other two approaches. Stressful evaluations disrupt the infant's capacity to maintain homeostasis and behavioral state, which, in turn, may disrupt the infant's other functional capacities.

As emphasized by Kosofsky (this volume), the assessment of infant functioning must be carried out serially. Serial assessment is required because, first of all, in a rapidly developing organism, such as the human infant, both the organism's capacities and its progressive change—the capacity to develop—must be assessed to evaluate the infant's status. Second, as in all developing organisms, exposure to drugs at different times during prenatal development has different effects. A critical study—in full recognition of the difficulties inherent in conducting such a study—would mimic a dose-related animal study. Such a study would evaluate the effects of drug exposure by examining subgroups of women who have used only cocaine only at certain periods (e.g., women who used cocaine during the first trimester only, the first and second trimesters, and so on with different drugs and periods of use).

Obviously, from all the research presented in this monograph, the human populations studied are not groups of infants exposed to only one drug but groups of infants that have been exposed to multiple toxic factors. This, as Zuckerman (this volume) notes, makes simply labeling a group as cocaine-exposed a misnomer at the very least. More than likely, this labeling for drug of preference from a drug history or for drug of record from a toxicologic assessment is deceptive and serves to distort understanding. Many steps need to be taken to correct this. One possibility is to carry out a study that examines the effects of cocaine exposure in a population in which other risk factors are minimized. It should be possible to identify and study a group of newborns whose mothers have middle to high incomes, good medical care, and good

145

prenatal care, and are well educated but who have used cocaine prior to pregnancy, in the first weeks of pregnancy before pregnancy was identified and then stopped its use, in the first trimester, and so on. The work by Striessguth and colleagues (Streissguth and Giunta 1990) is a start in this direction.

Whatever the nature of the effects of intrauterine exposure on the newborn, it must be understood that the infant is an active participant and creator of his or her own development. As argued elsewhere (Tronick 1987), infants have a developmental agenda of engaging the inanimate and social environments with increasingly sophisticated forms of behavior. Successful engagement requires normal brain functioning and a capacity to regulate homeostatic and behavioral states. When the infant is unable to regulate homeostatic or behavioral states, his or her ability to maintain engagement is disrupted. Similarly, disruptions of a specific function will compromise the infant's state and preclude engagement. For example, if a drug-exposed infant's visual capacities are compromised, then visual stimuli will stress the infant and disrupt other aspects of his or her behavioral organization. The assessment task, then, is not only to uncover dysfunctions but also to evaluate how these dysfunctions will lead the infant to further compromise his or her own development.

Drug exposure *in utero* is not a one-time insult. Rather, it is likely to lead to significant compromises in the developmental capacity of the infant that go well beyond the initial insult. To the extent that these problems can be uncovered, appropriate regulation from the environment can facilitate the infant's capacities to self-correct and achieve normal development.

REFERENCES

Als, H.; Lester, B.M.; Tronick, E.Z; and Brazelton, T.B. Manual for the assessment of preterm infants' behavior (APIB). In: Fitzgerald, H.E.; Lester, B.M.; and Yogman, M.W., eds. *Theory and Research in Behavioral Pediatrics*. Vol. 1. New York: Plenum, 1982.

Brazelton, T.B. *Neonatal Behavioral Assessment Scale*. 2d ed. London: Spastics International Medical Publications, 1984.

Fetters, L., and Todd, J. Quantitative assessment of infant reaching movements. *J Mot Behav* 19:147-166, 1987.

Lester, B.M. A method for study of change in neonatal behavior. In: Brazelton, T.B., and Lester, B.M., eds. *Infants at Risk: Assessment and Intervention*. New York: Elsevier, 1983.

Streissguth, A., and Giunta, C. "Subject Recruitment and Retention With Special Reference to Population-Based Prospective Studies of Pregnant Women and Their Offspring: A Nonintervention Model." Paper presented at the NIDA Technical Review Meeting on "Methodological Issues in Epidemiological, Prevention, and Treatment Research on Drug-Exposed Women and Their Children," Baltimore, MD, June 25-26, 1990.

Tronick, E.Z. The Neonatal Behavioral Assessment Scale as a biomarker of the effects of environmental agents on the newborn. *Environ Health Perspect* 74:185-189, 1987.

AUTHOR

Edward Z. Tronick, Ph.D.
Associate Professor of Pediatrics
Harvard Medical School
Chief
Child Development Unit
The Children's Hospital
300 Longwood Avenue
Boston, MA 02115

Measurement of Drug-Induced Physical and Behavioral Delays and Abnormalities in Animal Studies: A General Framework

Sheldon B. Sparber

INTRODUCTION

A technical review centered around methodological issues related to experimental design and interpretation of data derived from studies on the developmental effects of exposure of infrahuman species to drugs might seem out of place in 1990. After all, one might imagine that there have been clear and unambiguous demonstrations that drug exposure during development (i.e., *in utero*, during the postnatal developmental period, and perhaps exposure of the gamete prior to fertilization) adversely affects physical and/or behavioral parameters (and occasionally their underlying biological substrates) often enough to accept such phenomena without question. Unfortunately, great ambiguity exists. The key word is "exposure." Accepting the notion that *any* behavioral teratogenic or dysfunctional effect in offspring of pregnant subjects administered a drug is the consequence of the drug acting directly on the developing organism can be misleading. Most drugs have the potential to cause indirect effects by virtue of their capacity to:

- Cause hypoxic, ischemic, and possibly metabolic hypoxia or hypercapnia by suppressing respiration, causing severe vasoconstriction, or interfering with metabolic processes.

- Induce malnutrition or undernutrition by suppressing food intake or altering metabolic activity in pregnant dams (or during postnatal development).

- Cause severe distress due to pain or inflammation at the site of injection because of intrinsic properties (e.g., vasoconstriction) or physical-chemical properties of the drug or its vehicle (e.g., pH, insolubility).

- Induce dependence, which itself may not compromise normal developmental processes. However, consequences of withdrawal *in utero* or postnatally may be more responsible for potential dysfunction than exposure *per se*.

It may not matter whether a dysfunction outcome of exposure of the fetus or neonate is direct or indirect, if the agent of use or abuse is used by the pregnant woman in a similar manner and route, and with relative doses similar to those chosen by animal experimenters for their subjects. A cerebrovascular accident (CVA), premature delivery with major complications, obvious dysmorphia, or severe dysfunction in the child is no less important if caused by an indirect rather than a direct drug effect. If these clinical outcomes can be mimicked in the animal laboratory, such studies may offer insight into the prognosis for such children and may help researchers understand the cause of the affliction so that prevention or effective intervention strategies could be tried experimentally or used in the clinic. However, as discussed below, by observations, it is illogical to conclude that, in the absence of dysmorphia or obvious pathophysiological consequences, there must be more subtle and insidious consequences of exposure (direct or indirect) to much lower doses. Vorhees (1986) almost argues such a case and, in his otherwise very good historical treatment of the field of behavioral teratology, points to the leads derived from studies on the dysmorphic effects of excessive vitamin A, salicylates, or other drugs, which may produce behavioral teratogenic effects at doses that do not cause anatomical changes or gross neurological symptoms. It is obvious that in the case of salicylates or other drugs, pregnant women (or fetuses) need not be exposed, if not absolutely necessary. However, it obviously is imprudent to suggest that vitamin A, or even oxygen, which at excessive exposure levels are toxic or potentially teratogenic, be eliminated from the pregnant woman's diet or environment.

In the case of most of the drugs of abuse that have been studied in animals, the incidence of physical deformities (i.e., dysmorphia) attributable to drug exposure is low. This is probably consistent with the clinical consensus. Nevertheless, experimental protocols in behavioral teratology too often have assumed that exposure should be only, or mainly, during periods of specific organ developmental spurts (i.e., organogenesis). Thus, x-irradiation, large doses of vitamin A, glucocorticoids, or other substantial insults are able to induce structural deformities within organ systems that are undergoing cell division and growth at their greatest rate during time of the insult. This design may be inappropriate for functional teratology studies, and limiting exposure to a specific stage in developing subjects could result in inappropriate interpretations of data. Multiple factors should dictate experimental designs of animal studies, the most reasonable and logical ones being related to the probable manner in which the human fetus and/or developing child will be exposed. Several of these factors are discussed below.

There are many ways to compromise behavioral pharmacology/toxicology animal studies. These include the use of purchased, timed-pregnant subjects, instead of attempting to breed four to five times as many females as are ultimately needed, so that reasonably equal numbers of drug-exposed litters are delivered at the same time. Not only is there a chance that excessive stress during shipment of pregnant subjects may be responsible (entirely or in part) for postnatal effects of interest to the investigator (Peters 1990), but it is also possible that drug-inducible subtle dysfunctional effects may be masked by a potentially greater effect of the stress that may attend shipping pregnant dams under noncontrollable conditions. An associated problem is that of having to start drug treatment some time after receiving pregnant subjects because they were not bred in the laboratory—thereby missing an opportunity to expose experimental embryos even prior to implantation (if not prior to fertilization of the egg), which also may be more consistent with "modeling" human exposure.

Another reason why an experimenter may choose to start treatment of pregnant subjects after implantation, even if laboratory bred, is because treatment of dams earlier during pregnancy with the dose(s) chosen may not be compatible with ovulation, normal implantation rates, and/or the successful outcome of pregnancies that result in 90 to 100 deliveries of viable offspring. Such a success rate is necessary if one wishes to determine if a drug insult is potentially able to cause, directly or indirectly, long-lasting or permanent so-called dysfunctional effects in offspring exposed during development. In utero or neonatal death, runting, or dysmorphia are sufficient indices to conclude that the dose, route, time, or the interactive effects of all three are incompatible with the normal growth and survival of offspring, but viable offspring are necessary to study potential subtle dysfunction. It is the responsibility of the animal experimenter to design and carry out prospective studies that approximate as closely as possible the conditions and dosing schema that mimic human drug abuse patterns, with the many identifiable variables that must be controlled. Thus, data can be correctly interpreted and can be used for meaningful medical, social, and regulatory policy decisions.

Basically, animal experiments using a drug as an independent variable can be classified broadly into two categories. The first category asks questions about whether exposure to illicit drugs in utero modifies developmental processes. The second asks questions about the mechanisms that cause such modifications. However, it would be premature to focus on the issue of whether a sensitive period (Bateson 1987) exists for a drug-induced structural or functional abnormality or to search for a mechanism—biobehavioral, biochemical, or otherwise—before establishing that there is an unequivocal reason to do so. For example, if an investigator wished to determine the importance of GABAergic neurotransmission on the development of sleep-wake cycles, or so-called state regulation, perhaps barbiturates or benzodiazepines could be incorporated into the experimental protocol, along with agents that "selectively" alter GABA synthesis, alter metabolism, or act as antagonists or inverse agonists at one or more of the GABA receptors, if such drugs were available. It also would be necessary to determine if the biochemical and physiological "machinery" were present and functional during the particular stage of development of interest, because most drugs suppress or amplify function that already exists. It would not be a well-designed study if cocaine, phencyclidine, methadone, or a host of other drugs were used because these drugs do not have sufficiently selective GABAergic actions to be used as tools to ask the experimental questions posed.

On the other hand, if it can be established that something related to cocaine exposure during development interferes with normal sleep-wake cycles or state regulation *in utero* or during the neonatal period, it may be of interest to determine the importance of GABAergic neurotransmission for such observations, if it were previously established that this transmitter is pivotal in regulating such phenomena. However, if there were no evidence that state regulation shifts associated with cocaine exposure are acutely dangerous (e.g., are associated with sleep apnea or sudden infant death syndrome [SIDS]) or may be long-term markers for or potential causes of long-lasting dysfunction after exposure to cocaine during development, investing significant resources (intellectual, financial, or otherwise) to study cocaine in this manner may be wasteful, even though the technological feasibility can be demonstrated or is the forte of a particular laboratory.

The material introduced above can be summarized and extended in the following way.

PURPOSES OF THE EXPERIMENTAL PROGRAM

An experimental program should ask fundamental questions about developmental processes that can be modified *selectively* by drugs. In these cases drugs are used, first, as tools to alter biochemical variables, such as general metabolic processes (e.g., streptozocin to selectively destroy pancreatic b cells, thereby causing hypoinsulinemic diabetes mellitus). Second, drugs are used to alter nervous system communication by interfering with a specific class of neurotransmitters (e.g., alpha-methyl-p-tyrosine to inhibit syntheses of catecholamines or 6-OH-dopamine to selectively destroy one or more subtypes of catecholamine cells). In instances where 6-OH-dopamine type neurotoxins are to be used, it is important to know about the species differences in the rate of development of the blood-brain barrier to such agents. This in turn will dictate the route of administration and/or the need to use selective reuptake blockers in conjunction with 6-OH-dopamine. Third, drugs are used to determine if so-called critical or sensitive periods exist during development when a selective insult may or may not cause (directly or indirectly) developmental delays or functional abnormalities.

An experimental program also should ask if administration of drugs to pregnant animals, developing animals postnatally, or *in ova* (for oviviparous species) directly or indirectly causes developmental delays or functional abnormalities. In these cases, the animal subjects and their various biochemical, physiological, and/or behavioral processes should be used as tools to determine if therapeutic doses of drugs (e.g., maintenance doses of methadone or treatment of infectious diseases with antiviral or antibiotic agents) are potentially toxic or teratogenic and to determine if and to what extent nonmedical use of or detoxification from (i.e., withdrawal) prescribed or self-administered drugs is potentially toxic or teratogenic. The subjects also should be used to search for effective intervention strategies for alternative pharmacotherapy as substitutes for drugs that are legally administered or illicit (e.g., contaminated with other potentially toxic agents or of unknown concentration and, therefore, potency). Under some circumstances, in the future it may be necessary to maintain a pregnant woman on a drug to treat a pathophysiological condition and coadminister another drug (agonist or antagonist) to the fetus to prevent or reverse effects of the mother's therapeutic agent. The obverse possibility also may be a goal. Animal research may be directed at establishing the efficacy and safety of such procedures.

Another purpose of the experimental program may depend on the goals of the investigator, the physical and financial resources available, the nature of the database on which the program is built, and the availability of appropriate technology. These factors usually do not operate to influence such programs individually but often operate in concert. Before questions relating to fundamental mechanisms underlying desirable or undesirable developmental effects of drugs are asked, it should be ascertained if such effects in an animal model have been observed under conditions that appropriately model actual or projected human exposure and if enough is known about the pharmacological and/or toxicological properties of the experimental drug(s) in terms of its action in mature subjects. For example, a drug class that causes severe respiratory depression and/or vasoconstriction may affect a developing subject indirectly by causing dangerous degrees of ischemia, hypertension, hypoxia, and/or hypercapnia. Such knowledge is important and should be appropriately considered. Pregnant women may self-administer toxic doses of cocaine,

152

which in turn can cause severe vasoconstriction, leading to hypertension and fetal hypoxia, thereby affecting development indirectly. It therefore would be valid to use such high doses of cocaine in experimental animals and/or to study effects of similar degrees of fetal hypoxia, hypercapnia, and/or hypertension.

However, to use high doses of cocaine to induce fetal hypoxia, or in other ways cause placental or fetal vasoconstriction to study the potential effects of low doses of cocaine, may be as inappropriate as using low doses of cocaine to study potential consequences of fetal hypoxia, hypertension, and vasoconstriction or maternal hypertension and placental vasoconstriction. Just as cocaine may have proconvulsant as well as anticonvulsant properties, depending on the dose and situation (Russell and Stripling 1985), different doses may produce different effects, including no noteworthy effect, and animal developmental experiments should be designed to evaluate this range of outcomes. It is obvious that doses of cocaine that produce CVAs and/or convulsions in animals or humans threaten survival and are detrimental to normal development and function. Fortunately, most cocaine-exposed infants do not seem to have had a CVA and are not hemiplegic or epileptic. They may or may not suffer long-term functional impairment directly attributable to passive cocaine exposure. Polydrug abuse on the part of the mother, poor nutritional status, lack of appropriate parenting, or other early experience factors may be more important determinants of the social and cognitive development and function of most "crack babies" than drug exposure per se. Large-scale, well-designed, retrospective clinical studies employing sophisticated multivariate and multiple-regression analyses, combined with well-designed prospective human and animal studies in which a few variables are manipulated and/or adequately controlled for, will be needed to determine the extent of damage suffered by these children and its long-term consequence.

Questions have been raised about the safety of methadone treatment for pregnant women and their offspring. However, the toxicologic effects of methadone in animals have resulted from the use of high doses. Such doses, often given only once a day (in spite of the fact that its duration of action and plasma t1/2 are not sufficient to induce and maintain a stable degree of dependence in a rat given the drug so infrequently), cause respiratory depression, often leading to death in a significant number of pregnant experimental subjects. Studies using these dosing regimens have not taken into account fundamental principles of pharmacology and specific knowledge already available to the investigator about the nature of methadone's relatively short duration of action in rats (i.e., relative to humans) and its acute toxicity, and their findings are not applicable to women in methadone treatment programs. Women enrolled in maintenance programs who become pregnant are already tolerant to many of methadone's acutely toxic or potentially teratogenic effects, such as its effects upon the endocrinium. Such tolerance of the endocrinium may have allowed them to ovulate and become pregnant to begin with, after stabilization on methadone.

At a time of limited resources, which include financial restrictions, inadequate numbers of trained individuals, and pressures of inadequate time, investigators and funding agencies must choose whether to study a particular agent in great detail or to study several agents in lesser detail for safety and efficacy. Each philosophy has its merits and drawbacks. If the goal of the funding agency or investigator is to determine safety, at otherwise efficacious doses, it is counterproductive to study the molecular, cellular, or behavioral mechanisms of developmental toxicity of excessively large doses. Too little attention has been paid to questions relating to *why* treatment of pregnant or developing subjects has led to the many published reports of developmental delays and/or behavioral abnormalities. In other words, it should be determined if it is necessary to administer what often turns out to be overtly toxic doses of drugs (i.e., lethal or capable of inducing severe morbidity) in order to observe more subtle (i.e., behavioral teratogenic) effects. Also to be determined is whether such observations are sufficient to conclude that, if it were possible to study the appropriate numbers of subjects or if sufficiently sensitive measures were used, behavioral consequences of insult during development also would have been observed after lower doses. Such a philosophy is not embraced often enough and denies the existence of threshold doses or concentrations of drugs, below which there might be pharmacological efficacy with little or no toxicity.

Investigators are generally unaware of the number and quality of experiments or clinical observations that do not result in noteworthy (i.e., published) results. Such information would be extremely helpful in interpreting the reliability and frequency of congenital anomalies in relation to the number of women and children exposed to drugs. A recent report in the December 16, 1989, issue of *Lancet* titled "Bias Against the Null Hypothesis: The Reproductive Hazards of Cocaine" (Koren et al. 1989) is enlightening. These authors reviewed all the abstracts submitted for presentation at the meeting of the Society of Pediatric Research during a 10-year period (1980-1989). Only 1 of 9 (11 percent) was accepted from those reporting no adverse effects of exposure to cocaine, whereas 28 of 49 (57 percent) abstracts reporting adverse effects were accepted for presentation. The studies that were "negative" and not accepted for presentation verified cocaine use more often and generally had larger sample sizes. Koren and colleagues argue convincingly that such a bias, in the face of perceived teratogenic potential, may be responsible for excessive numbers of women who have used cocaine sparingly during pregnancy requesting termination by abortion. The authors go on to suggest that "it is the duty of editorial boards, scientific committees, and funding agencies to

154

acknowledge this serious bias and to indicate clearly that research results are not more important if they are positive." They also suggest that such "bias by journals, scientific societies, and funding agencies against negative results may have far-reaching detrimental effects. . . . This bias may lead scientists to massage or misrepresent data to obtain positive results."

The question of whether to study one or relatively few agents in greater detail, compared with studying more agents in lesser detail, deserves some discussion. One could easily be misled into believing that it is valid to generalize between agents of the same class, if a few are studied in great detail. This would be axiomatic if it could be agreed that all drugs of a class differed only in their potency, for example, and not in their selectivity. Unfortunately, the real world of pharmacology is not so ideal. Some drugs that are classified broadly, based on therapeutic or illicit use, are structurally dissimilar and/or have different actions or affinities for receptors other than those to which they owe their therapeutic (or illicit) use. Amphetamine and cocaine, for example, may owe their abuse liability to similar actions on a specific central nervous system (CNS) function, but they also do not share many properties (e.g., the ability to inhibit monoamine oxidase), nor are they metabolized the same way, to the same products. Furthermore, amphetamine is not metabolized by rats and humans in the same way, and if a metabolite rather than a parent compound is responsible for one or more developmental effects, generalizing from cocaine to amphetamine vis-a-vis developmental effects in rats may be just as inappropriate as generalizing about amphetamine's developmental effects in rats to its effects in humans without taking such factors into account.

METHODOLOGICAL ISSUES

The material above raises some philosophical issues that should be considered by experimentalists prior to carrying out developmental drug studies with animals. Following is a discussion of some methodological issues that speak specifically to some of the concerns raised and to identify some ways to control for identifiable and unidentifiable sources of variation that can contribute to or be responsible for postnatal effects associated with drug exposure. In some instances, identification of a secondary or tertiary effect may be important for entirely different reasons. For example, significant anorexia coupled with behavioral activation associated with cocaine or amphetamine administration may lead to *in utero* and/or postnatal undernutrition. The undernutrition in turn may be responsible for one or more structural (e.g., neuroanatomical) or functional perturbations in "exposed" offspring. If similar nutritional deficiencies attend human abuse of these drugs by pregnant women, the observation of such an effect in experimental animals is consistent with the protocol approximating human use of cocaine and its consequences.

It also may be the case that an undernourished dam or fetus is more or less vulnerable to other actions of the drug that caused the undernutrition. For these and other reasons it would be important to control for the compromised nutritional status by inducing a similar degree of undernutrition via a nondrug procedure. A dose of drug given to the undernourished drug-experiencing dam and the undernourished drug-naive dam should result in the same drug concentrations in fetuses (and/or pregnant dams). Either pharmacokinetic experiments can be used to this end or a sufficiently wide range of doses can be given to pregnant dams fully nourished (i.e., *ad lib* fed) and to undernourished dams, the assumption being that similar pharmacokinetic factors would hold, for example, in a dam on free food given a higher dose of drug and a dam on a drug-induced restricted diet given a lower dose of drug. The null hypothesis being tested experimentally in this case would be that undernourished pregnant dams and/or their offspring are more (or less) vulnerable to an acutely toxic or congenital effect.

One of the major problems with such a drug study is that protective mechanisms are available to the fetus and, whereas a pregnant dam may gain considerably less weight as a result of drug treatment or restricted access to food, the neonate may be born of normal weight in a normal-size litter. Even when prenatal drug exposure is not a factor, the relationship between short- and long-term structural consequences and between structural and functional consequences is not clear. (See, for example, Bedi [1987] and the discussion that follows Bedi's presentation.)

The issue becomes even more complicated when treatment with drugs (or spontaneous withdrawal) postnatally is accompanied by retarded growth or undernutrition. This dilemma is faced by practically every experimentalist studying the *in utero* developmental effects of opiates (and drugs administered via milk or via injection of neonates). Because a considerable degree of CNS development continues into the first few years of human postnatal life, it is sometimes necessary to manipulate rodents for 1 to a few weeks postnatally in order to "model" the human condition. In the literature, different stages of development of various parts of the CNS of different species are compared. For example, the cerebellum (and to some extent parts of the limbic system) shows substantial development postnatally in the rat. Therefore, the CNS effects of drug treatment during development, which also is somehow associated with retarded somatic growth of the neonate, should be interpreted with caution. There also should be an attempt to determine experimentally if the undernutrition (and/or associated stresses) may be responsible for the presumed direct drug effect, especially if children exposed passively to the experimental drug when it is used by their pregnant mothers or while they are nursing do not experience protracted undernutrition or experience any undernutrition at all. One to several weeks of undernutrition in the rat represents a considerably greater fraction of their lifespan than several weeks of drug-induced or withdrawal-induced undernutrition in the human neonate. Besides, lower maintenance doses of methadone, swaddling, and supplemental parenteral feeding, if necessary, can be used to prevent or attenuate withdrawal-induced effects in the human neonate. Nevertheless, practically every animal study in which opiates are administered to pregnant rodents has reported significant postnatal runtings of exposes pups. A critical review of the literature (Lichtblau and Sparber 1984) as well as our own experiments have led me to believe that most effects on growth are secondary to neonatal withdrawal (or toxicity of milk-borne opiates). Moreover, Sparber and Lichtblau (1983) have demonstrated that it is not necessary for neonatal rats to be exposed to opiates and opiate withdrawal during development for them to be differentially sensitive to opiates later in life, an effect that has been interpreted by others to be proof of a selective, direct opiate action. It is sufficient for nondrug subjects to experience very similar degrees of neonatal undernutrition, which include reductions in brain weight and protein and nucleic acid concentrations similar to those reported to be associated with perinatal opiate exposure (Sparber and Lichtblau 1983). The juxtaposition of my discussion about the need to control for such a source of variation in studies with drugs and the difficulties encountered by experimentalists interested in developmental effects of undernutrition per se on later CNS function is amply demonstrated by a recent study from my laboratory in which Tonkiss and colleagues (1988) found dramatically different changes in the brain parameters mentioned above in two cohorts that were rendered "undernourished" via two different postnatal manipulations. In both cases, body weight and length on postnatal day 10, at the time nutritional rehabilitation was started, were identically reduced, about 35 percent and 17 percent, respectively. However, the manipulation that restricted access to milk by forming excessively large litters (i.e., 20/litter) relatively spared effects on the CNS. The other procedure (i.e., intermittent starvation by giving the litters to nonlactating foster "aunts") caused dramatically greater CNS effects than did the large litter procedure (Tonkiss et al. 1988). Indeed, when these groups were tested in adulthood for their ability to express acute dependence on morphine, a divergence of effects again emerged (Cohen et al., in press).

There also is available a means by which the potential deleterious, long-term consequences of opiate withdrawal can be studied without having to expose the developing subject to opiates. Several drugs, including isobutylmethylxanthine (IBMX), are capable of inducing a withdrawal syndrome in animals that is virtually indistinguishable from true opioid-type withdrawal. This quasi-morphine withdrawal syndrome (QMWS) can be prevented by opiates, worsened by the opioid antagonist naloxone, and attenuated by clonidine, which also attenuates opiate withdrawal in humans and rats (Collier et al. 1981; Gold et al. 1978; Kleven and Sparber 1989; Meyer and Sparber 1976). By administering IBMX to rat pups, one should be able to study consequences of postnatal withdrawal without the "confounding" effect of exposure to opiates. The same can be said of exposure to withdrawal *in utero*, which we have reported to be more detrimental than continued exposure to otherwise nontoxic maintenance doses of the long-acting opiate l-α-acetylmethadol (for review see Sparber et al. 1986). Neal and Sparber (1991) and Neal and coworkers (1991) have found evidence that mild QMWS during the neonatal period can cause significant retardation in learning or performing autoshaped operant behavior and can attenuate the expression of acute morphine withdrawal in adulthood. The dose of IBMX administered over a few days during the neonatal period did not cause significant weight loss compared with controls. This means that it is not necessary to experience undernutrition similar to that often experienced by opiate-dependent pups undergoing severe withdrawal. It is sufficient to experience the stress of withdrawal and its attending biological consequences, whatever they may be, to show long-lasting behavioral changes and differential responsiveness to opiates in adulthood.

The results of these studies do not demonstrate that opiates cannot cause similar or different behavioral or functional teratogenic effects, but they do demonstrate ways in which one can design studies with appropriate methods to control for secondary effects and/or uncover, at one or another level of analysis, the mechanism of action whereby exposure to drugs during development can affect function later in life.

I have chosen not to review the many arguments regarding when and when not to use fostering and cross-fostering procedures, when it may be appropriate to use more than one male and one female offspring from each outbred litter of treated subjects, and why the litter should be used as the experimental unit for statistical analyses of birth weight, eye opening, and other such variables that are highly correlated within a litter. There have been adequate discussions and reviews on these issues (e.g., see Abbey and Howard 1973), and I would counsel investigators developing expertise in developmental biology and behavioral teratology to seek advice and collaborations with knowledgeable scientists and statisticians in planning studies. It is a pity when several person-years are spent only to discover that the data are useless because of poor planning and wrong assumptions.

The question of which sex of the offspring to study for congenital effects of exposure to drugs (or any other insult) is not now as important a problem as it has been. It is now known that many of the effects (direct or indirect) of drugs on transmitters, trophic factors, sex, and glucocorticoid or mineralocorticoid steroids can modify organizational processes (Lauder 1983), leading to sex-related or -dependent structural and functional congenital effects. Sexual dimorphic outcomes of stress, drug manipulations, or other manipulations of pregnant subjects (Sparber 1974; McGivern et al. 1984; Meyerson et al. 1988) make it mandatory that offspring of *both* sexes be studied. It is possible to miss or misinterpret functional teratogenic actions of such manipulations if, as has been the case in the past, only one sex (usually males, because of their propensity for generating less variable data) is studied. There may be opposite effects of drug treatment or stress during development on function or responsiveness to drug challenge in adult male and female offspring (Kinsley et al. 1988).

The recent interest in cocaine-exposed or so-called "crack babies" has resulted in comparisons of routes of administration in nonpregnant and/or pregnant experimental subjects, usually rats. It is a given that pregnant rats should not be injected intraperitoneally with drugs because of multiple potentially confounding effects, including the possibility of direct intrauterine injection, locally large concentrations leading to great visceral vasoconstriction and diffusion of drug unevenly across uterine walls, and so forth. Subcutaneous administration of cocaine can lead to severe necrotic lesions and ulcerations at the injection site (Bruckner et al. 1982; Dow-Edwards et al. 1989). It may be difficult to induce identical lesions, systemic hypertension in the dam, and/or vasoconstriction of placental vessels with other "control" agents such as epinephrine and norepinephrine. However, if the subcutaneous route is to be chosen for developmental drug studies, such controls are mandatory for determining if the cocaine is producing any functional teratogenic effects directly on the fetus or if stress of pain or other indirect actions of the cocaine are responsible. Cocaine generally is self-administered intranasally, intravenously, by smoking it, or by chewing leaves. It is reasonably well absorbed after oral gavage. Inducing and achieving comparable fetal and/or maternal blood or brain levels of cocaine and its major metabolites should lead to comparable behavioral effects in the pregnant dam and/or her offspring if caused by cocaine and not an epiphenomenon because of factors that are not clinically relevant. Establishing equivalence of exposure by the least stressful means for the large numbers of subjects required for developmental studies should be the initial goal of every program studying cocaine's action. If it is not plausible to have pregnant dams self-administer cocaine intravenously, dosing schedules of cocaine, using other routes, should attempt to bracket the dose and duration of self-administration data available from the literature.

For example, Pickens and Thompson (1968) reported that rats would self-administer about 6 mg/kg/hr intravenously over a 14-hour period of access to 0.25-3.00 mg/kg/infusion. By administering oral doses of 15 mg/kg/3.5 hr, three times daily as a low dose and 45 mg/kg/3.5 hr, three times daily as a high dose, Sparber and Kubak (1989) posited that such bracketing of the self-administered doses reported by Pickens and Thompson would be a reasonable schedule for treatment of pregnant rats with doses that approximated what they would have self-administered over 12± hours. Nonpregnant female rats treated in this way showed operant behavioral suppression 1/2 hour after treatment with a second daily high dose, after a few days, no effect after the low dose, and no effect 3 hours after the high dose, before their next oral gavage. Sparber and Kubak (1989) demonstrated that the cocaine had a behavioral effect in nonpregnant females shortly after several days of oral administration of the high dose (i.e., there was some evidence of cumulative toxic effects when spaced about 3 hours apart over a 4- to 5-day period). Cocaine was administered orally to pregnant rats that had been habituated to oral gavage with water prior to mating (to reduce or eliminate stress of the procedure) during the last trimester of pregnancy. A 12-percent reduction in weight gain by the last day of treatment (gestation day 20) was the only obvious drug-induced effect observed in the pregnant dams given the high dose (i.e., 145 mg/kg/day over 9 to 12 hours). Seven days of treatment with the low dose (45 mg/kg/day) did not affect this measure. No maternal mortality or fetal mortality was evident prior to or at birth. Such a cohort, therefore, satisfies some of the requirements set forth previously in this chapter for examining the possibility that exposure to cocaine during late *in utero* life can cause congenital dysfunction of the CNS manifested as long-lasting behavioral or neurochemical changes, relative to control offspring.

Because of the potential for indirect effects being responsible for treatment outcome, or because placental, uterine, and other physiological and anatomical differences of great magnitude exist between the rodent and human species, it is important to carry out comparative studies with more than one infrahuman species to assess the potential generalities of observations. The cost of procuring and maintaining adequate numbers of primates for such studies seems impractical and prohibitively high. My laboratory has been using the developing domestic chicken embryo, fetus, and chicken for comparative, parallel functional teratogenic studies. They are inexpensive, come with an enormous database from experimental embryologists and poultry scientists, are a renewable domesticated resource, and offer the advantage of being able to study, even *in ova*, biochemical and behavioral variables associated with exposure to drugs and other chemicals. Direct injection into the yolk, near the embryo (chorioallantois) or via other routes can be easily accomplished, depending on age of exposure, solubility of agent, and other factors (Seran and Sparber 1988). Developmental pharmacologists and functional teratologists might consider this species, along with a suitable rodent species, for comparative experiments. Their phylogenetic diversity would support the notion that drug effects observed in the altricial mammalian (rodent), as well as in the precocial avian (chick), if fundamentally similar, should generalize to most other vertebrates, including humans (see Sparber et al. 1986 for a more extensive review of such comparative studies).

Last, I would like to touch on the issue of when to study exposed offspring and how long they should be studied. I have no difficulty with the premise that behavioral development and drug effects on behavioral development are important experimental topics. Developmental psychobiology has a long tradition, and much can be learned much from its practitioners about experimental design, statistical analyses, and early experience factors that might interact with drug treatment to produce apparent behavioral teratogenic effects. I am most concerned with the idea that demonstrating early postnatal behavioral differences between drug-exposed and appropriate control offspring is sufficient to conclude that such effects predict permanent dysfunction. To accept this is to assume that there are no residual drug or withdrawal effects of a *transient* nature or that plasticity, rehabilitation, and other forms of "catch-up" cannot be expected. I also believe that it is mandatory that lifespan, or at least long-term (i.e., to 1- to 2-year) studies be carried out with rats and comparative long-term studies with other special species before one can conclude that there is no functional teratogenic effect of exposure to a particular insult during development. The aging process itself may unmask heretofore unrecognized or delayed effects (Kolta et al. 1990; Meaney et al. 1988; Robbins et al. 1978).

REFERENCES

Abbey, H., and Howard E. Statistical procedure in developmental studies on species with multiple offspring. *Dev Psychobiol* 6:329-335, 1973.

Bateson, P. Biological approaches to the study of behavioral development. *Intl J Behav Dev* 10:1-22, 1987.

Bedi, K.S. Lasting neuroanatomical changes following undernutrition during early life. In: Dobbing, J., ed. *Early Nutrition and Later Achievement*. London: Academic Press, 1987. pp. 1-49.

Bruckner, J.V.; Jiang, W.D.; Ho, B.T.; and Levy, B.M. Histopathological evaluation of cocaine-induced brain lesions in the rat. *J Cutan Pathol* 9:83-95, 1982.

Cohen, C.A.; Tonkiss, J.; and Sparber, S.B. Acute opiate withdrawal in rats undernourished during infancy: Impact of undernutrition method. *Pharmacol Biochem Behav*, in press.

Collier, H.O.J; Cuthbert, N.J.; and Francis, D.L. Character and meaning of quasi-morphine withdrawal phenomena elicited by methylxanthines. *Fed Proc* 40:1513-1518, 1981.

Dow-Edwards, D.; Fico, T.A.; Osman, M.; Gamaris, Z.; and Hutchings, D.E. Comparison of oral and subcutaneous routes of cocaine administration on behavior, plasma drug concentration and toxicity in female rats. *Pharmacol Biochem Behav* 33:167-173, 1989.

Gold, M.S.; Redmond, D.E.; and Kleber, H.D. Clonidine blocks acute opiate withdrawal symptoms. *Lancet* 1:599-602, 1978.

Kinsley, C.H.; Mann, P.E.; and Bridges, R.S. Prenatal stress alters morphine- and stress-induced analgesia in male and female rats. *Pharmacol Biochem Behav* 30:123-128, 1988.

Kleven, M.S., and Sparber, S.B. Morphine blocks and naloxone enhances suppression of operant behavioral by low doses of 3-isobutyl-1-methylxanthine. *J Pharmacol Exp Ther* 248:273-277, 1989.

Kolta, M.G.; Scalzo, F.M.; Ali, S.F.; and Holson, R.R. Ontogeny of the enhanced behavioral response to amphetamine in amphetamine-pretreated rats. *Psychopharmacology* 100:377-382, 1990.

Koren, G.; Shear, H.; Graham, K.; and Einarson, T. Bias against the null hypothesis: The reproductive hazards of cocaine. *Lancet* 8677:1440-1442, 1989.

Lauder, J.M. Hormonal and humoral influences on brain development. *Psychoneuroendocrinology* 8:121-155, 1983.

Lichtblau, L., and Sparber, S.B. Opioids and development: A perspective on experimental models and methods. *Neurobehav Toxicol Teratol* 6:3-8, 1984.

McGivern, R.F.; Clancy, A.N.; Hill, M.A.; and Noble, E.P. Prenatal alcohol exposure alters adult expression of sexually dimorphic behavior in the rat. *Science* 224:896-898, 1984.

Meaney, M.J.; Aitken, D.H.; van Berkel, C.; Bhatnagar, S.; and Sapolsky, R.M. Effect of neonatal handling on age-related impairments associated with the hippocampus. *Science* 239:766-768, 1988.

Meyer, D.R., and Sparber, S.B. Clonidine antagonizes body weight loss and other symptoms used to measure withdrawal in morphine pelleted rats given naloxone. *Pharmacologist* 18:236, 1976.

Meyerson, B.J.; Berg, M.; and Johansson, B. Neonatal naltrexone treatment: Effects on sexual and exploratory behavior in male and female rats. *Pharmacol Biochem Behav* 31:63-67, 1988.

Neal, B.S., and Sparber, S.B. Long-term effects on neonatal exposure to isobutylmethylxanthine: I. Retardation of learning with antagonism by mianserin. *Psychopharmacology* 103:388-397, 1991.

Neal, B.S.; Messing, R.B.; and Sparber, S.B. Long-term effects of neonatal exposure to isobutylmethylxanthine: II. Attenuation of acute morphine withdrawal in mature rats. *Psychopharmacology* 103:398-406, 1991.

Peters, D.A.V. Maternal stress increases fetal brain and neonatal cerebral cortex 5-HT synthesis in rats: A possible mechanism by which stress influences brain development. *Pharmacol Biochem Behav* 35:943-947, 1990.

Pickens, R., and Thompson, T. Cocaine-reinforced behavior in rats: Effects of reinforcement magnitude and fixed ratio size. *J Pharmacol Exp Ther* 161:122-129, 1968.

Robbins, M.S.; Hughes, J.A.; Sparber, S.B.; and Mannering, G.J. Delayed teratogenic effect of methylmercury on hepatic cytochrome p-450-dependent mono-oxygenase system of rats. *Life Sci* 22:287-294, 1978.

Russell, R.D., and Stripling, J.S. Monoaminergic and local anesthetic components of cocaine's effects on kindled seizure expression. *Pharmacol Biochem Behav* 22(3):427-434, 1985.

Seran, G.F., and Sparber, S.B. Metabolism of methadone by chicken embryos prevents induction of opioid-type dependence after single injection: Use of osmotic pumps for continuous infusion. *Pharmacol Biochem Behav* 30:357-363, 1988.

Sparber, S.B. Postnatal behavioral effects of in utero exposure to drugs which modify catecholamines and/or serotonin. In: Vernadakis, A., and Weiner, N., eds. *Drugs and the Developing Brain*. New York: Plenum Press, 1974. pp. 81-102.

Sparber, S.B., and Kubak, M. Behavioral toxicity of orally administered cocaine is greater in male, compared with female S.-D. rats. *Neurosci Soc Abstr* 15:634, 1989.

Sparber, S.B., and Lichtblau, L. Neonatal undernutrition alters responsiveness to morphine in mature rats: A possible source of epiphenomena in developmental drug studies. *J Pharmacol Exp Ther* 225:1-7, 1983.

Sparber, S.B., Lichtblau, L.; and Kuwahara, M.D. Experimental separation of direct and indirect effects of drugs on neurobehavioral development. In: Krasnegor, N.; Gray, D.; and Thompson, T., eds. *Developmental Behavioral Pharmacology*. Hillsdale, NJ: Lawrence Erlbaum Assoc., 1986. pp. 225-263.

Tonkiss, J.; Cohen, C.A.; and Sparber, S.B. Different methods for producing neonatal undernutrition in rats cause different brain changes in the face of equivalent somatic growth parameters. *Dev Neurosci* 10:141-151, 1988.

Vorhees, C.B. Origins of behavioral teratology. In: Riley, E.P., and Voorhees, C.V., eds. *Handbook of Behavioral Teratology*. New York: Plenum Press, 1986. pp. 3-22.

ACKNOWLEDGMENT

The preparation of this document and the research carried out in the author's laboratory described herein were supported in part by U.S. Public Health Service grants DA-01880, DA-04979, T32DA-07097, and HD-20111.

AUTHOR

Sheldon B. Sparber, Ph.D.
Professor
Department of Pharmacology, Psychiatry, and Psychology
University of Minnesota
435 Delaware Street, S.E.
Minneapolis, MN 55455

Regulatory Disorders I: Clinical Perspectives

Stanley I. Greenspan

There is growing evidence that the effects of maternal prenatal substance abuse on the developing fetus and the newborn infant are often indirect. Rather than causing a specific physical or behavioral deficit, in many instances the infant's capacity for using sensory, motor, language, cognitive, or affective systems for healthy adaptation is compromised. Depending on the type of drug, pattern of usage (including pattern during various phases of pregnancy), physical status of the mother (including her overall health and underlying susceptibilities), as well as clinical conditions, one may see different types of compromises in various aspects of the infant's adaptive capacity and potential.

To understand the impact of prenatal substance abuse, this chapter presents a new construct that focuses on the infant's adaptive capacities. To be useful, however, this construct must be highly specific in the way it organizes understanding of these indirect compromises to the adaptation of the central nervous system. In the context of behaviors and interactions between the infant and his or her caregivers, the proposed construct will have certain advantages over existing constructs that attempt to look at the infant's innate capacities or interactive behaviors.

For example, although an important and valuable literature exists on "temperament" as a way of capturing the infant's innate tendencies, most such research relies on parental reports of the infant's capacities, rather than on "hands-on" assessment of the infant. In addition, most temperament constructs tend to assume a general tendency within the infant toward such global behaviors as introversion, extraversion, shyness, inhibition, outgoingness, and so forth. These global behavioral tendencies may be secondary to highly specific, hands-on, verifiable infant tendencies such as tactile or auditory sensitivity or motor tone and motor planning difficulties.

As another example, there is a growing literature on attachment (e.g., Ainsworth et al. 1974) and types of attachment difficulties using an experimental paradigm that focuses on the infant's reaction to a "strange situation." While this important body of work relates problems in later childhood to qualities of the infant-caregiver attachment pattern in infancy, it ignores the infant's individual differences in terms of physical and maturational differences as an important component of the infant's adaptive capacities.

The model suggested in this chapter focuses on three important parameters of the infant's behavior: (1) the infant's individual sensory, motor, cognitive (including language), and affective differences; (2) infant-caregiver interaction patterns; and (3) the caregiver-family and related cultural patterns. To look at these variables in a highly specific manner, it has been useful to develope a construct of regulatory disorders (Greenspan 1989, 1991). While the caregiver-infant relationship and family patterns are certainly not new ways of thinking about infant and child behavior, this construct is a potentially useful clinical and research model. It looks at the back-and-forth influence of highly specific, verifiable constitutional and maturational factors on interactive and family patterns (and vice versa). It also looks at the influence of these factors and each of six developmental phases in relationship to later developmental and psychopathologic disorders.

A regulatory disorder is a disturbance in the expected processes of regulation that enable an infant to adapt to his or her own physical individual differences and to the environment, including caregivers. The infant's regulatory processes that may be compromised include:

1. The ability to take in, modulate, discriminate, and comprehend impersonal sensory and sensory affective experience. This ability is in evidence as part of the infant's capacity to attend to the world.

2. The ability to employ his or her developing motor system, language capacities, and affective gestures to adaptively influence his or her impersonal and interpersonal world.

3. The ability to accomplish 1 and 2 above as part of a calm, regulated state, compared with states of hypoarousal or hyperarousal or excitability.

4. The ability to accomplish 1, 2, and 3 above in the context of increasingly complex levels of organization, each of which adds demands and new adaptive or coping capacities to the infant's functional abilities. These increasingly complex levels of organization include:

    a. The ability to attend to multisensory affective experience and at the same time organize a calm, regulated state and experience pleasure.

    b. The ability to engage a caregiver with pleasure and evidence affective preference for a caregiver.

c. The ability to initiate and respond to two-way presymbolic gestural communication.

d. The ability to organize chains of two-way communication (opening and closing many circles of communication in a row), maintain communication across space, integrate affective polarities, and synthesize an emerging behavioral prerepresentational organization of self and other.

e. The ability to represent (symbolize) affective experience (e.g., pretend play, functional use of language). It should be noted that this ability calls for higher level auditory and verbal sequencing ability.

f. The ability to create representational (symbolic) categories and gradually build conceptual bridges between these categories. This ability creates the foundation for such basic personality functions as reality testing, impulse control, self/other representational differentiation, affect labeling and discrimination, stable mood, and a sense of time and space that allows for logical planning. It should be noted that this ability rests not only on complex auditory and verbal processing abilities but also on visual-spatial abstracting capacities.

It is important to note that each of these new organizational levels puts demand on the infant to organize new types of experience. For example, engaging the animate world or caregivers and becoming emotionally involved and dependent on human relationships demand that the infant adjust to the unpredictable behaviors, mood shifts, and frustrations of a real person. While infants can bang a block on the floor and reliably hear a sound, they may not get back a vocalization or receive a hug every time they vocalize or reach out invitingly with their arms. When infants learn to use words and can form an internal picture of their mother, they rely on the word and the picture to convey certain internal feeling states such as security. The language and symbolic mechanisms underlying this representational ability initially may not be as reliable as mother's continuing physical (and tactile) presence. Auditory or verbal sequencing difficulties or sensory hyperreactivity or hyporeactivity in any modality can easily compromise such emerging symbolic capacities. Yet, at the same time, the ability to engage as well as the ability to represent or symbolize experience provide great flexibility and new adaptive range for the growing infant. In this respect, each new level of organization is, indeed, a "double-edged sword."

In considering the infant's capacity for regulation and the various ways it can be compromised, it is important to look at the processes that influence regulation.

On one side of the equation are the infant's constitutional and maturational patterns. On the other side is the infant's environment, including caregivers, family, community, and culture. These influences, however, are mediated through the caregiver-infant relationship, which is the learning ground for the infant. Here the infant either does or does not learn how to negotiate each of the six levels of organization outlined in point 4 above. To picture this, maturational and constitutional characteristics would be on the left; caregiver, family, and cultural patterns on the right; the caregiver-infant relationship in the middle; and the six levels of organization that the relationship attempts to negotiate would be under the caregiver-infant relationship. For each of these six levels, it is critical to understand the role of specific constitutional and maturational characteristics and specific caregiver, family, and cultural patterns.

To specify the constitutional and maturational characteristics that should be observed, the following list may prove helpful:

- Sensory reactivity, including hyporeactivity and hyperreactivity in each sensory modality (tactile, auditory, visual, vestibular, olfactory)

- Sensory processing in each sensory modality (e.g., the capacity to decode sequences, configurations, or abstract patterns)

- Sensory-affective reactivity and processing in each modality (e.g., the ability to process and react to degrees of affective intensity in a stable manner)

- Motor tone

- Motor planning

A new instrument to clinically assess aspects of sensory functions in a reliable manner has been developed and is available (DeGangi and Greenspan 1988, 1989; DeGangi et al. 1988). At the same time, the characteristics of the environment that relate to these constitutional and maturational characteristics also can be systematized, as can characteristics of the parent-infant or caregiver-infant relationship as it relates to the six levels of organization. A discussion of these issues can be found elsewhere (Greenspan 1989).

BRIEF CASE ILLUSTRATION

The mother of an infant 7 1/2 months old worried that "he cries any time I try to leave him, even for a second. If I'm not standing right next to him when he is sitting on the floor, he cries and I have to pick him up. He's a tyrant. He's waking up four times a night and is a fussy eater. He eats for short bursts [breastfeeding] and then stops eating. I'm feeding him all the time."

The mother was feeling cornered, controlled, manipulated, and bossed around. Her baby was like [my term] a "fearful dictator." She said, "That's the perfect way to describe him." The father was impatient with the mother; he felt that she indulged the baby too much. He was getting "fed up," because she had no time for him.

The mother was frightened of aggression and was dependent on her own mother. She wanted her baby to be happy (meaning no crying or discomfort), and it made her "shake" to think that he could be uncomfortable. The father, an angry sort of person, took the opposite approach—a "John Wayne," tough-it-out strategy. In interactions with the baby, each showed his or her characteristic pattern.

The infant was very interactive and sensitive to every emotional nuance. As he came into the room, he immediately caught my eye. We exchanged smiles and motor gestures. He interacted with his parents with smiles, coos, and motor movements. Father intruded somewhat. He would roughhouse until the baby would cry, put the baby down, and then roughhouse again. Mother, in contrast, was ever so gentle, but she had long silences between her vocalizations. During her long silences, the baby would rev up, get more irritable, and start whining. He whined with the mother and cried fearfully with the father. Even before he could finish his motor gestures or vocalizations, his mother moved in and picked him up, gave him a rattle, or spoke for him. In this way, she undermined his initiative. Even while whining, however, he was interactive.

Physical examination showed this baby to be sensitive to loud noises, as well as to light touch on the arms, legs, abdomen, and back. He had a mild degree of low motor tone and was posturally insecure. He was not yet ready to crawl.

From a regulatory perspective, babies who are constitutionally most worrisome are those who are oversensitive to the normal sounds and sensations of the environment yet have poor control over their motor systems. Because of their motor immaturity, they cannot do much to correct their sensitivities themselves. They are passive victims of their own sensory and motor systems.

Mother, terribly frightened of her own and her infant's potential assertiveness, was not able to help her baby learn assertive coping because she was so overprotective. At the same time, however, she was undernurturing, evidenced most notably in the empty spaces in the rhythm of her speech. She was not silent consciously. She wanted to do everything possible for her baby, but her own depression and anxiety kept her from having a securing or soothing vocal or gestural rhythm. The spaces in her vocal pattern conveyed a sense of emotional emptiness. At the same time, father was impatient and moved in too quickly. The baby was being challenged from all sides.

Related to the mother's patterns were worrisome fantasies that her baby would be sick and not survive. These were related to anger at her own very ambivalent mother. Behind father's John Wayne approach was his relationship to his own austere, tough-guy father. Father had been taught to "control" his needs and longings very early in life.

In terms of mastering the first developmental challenge of shared attention and engagement, the infant's constitutional and maturational patterns did not compromise development. This was an attentive, engaged baby. But at the second developmental stage, intentional communication and assertiveness, this baby was a passive reactor. He was not learning to initiate two-way communication, to be assertive, and to take charge of his interactions. His low motor tone was compromising his ability to control his motor movements. His sensory hyperreactivity was compromising his ability to regulate sensation. He was frequently overloaded by the basic sensations of touch and sound. At the same time, he was not receiving support from his mother through nurturing and rhythmic, self-initiating, fostering caretaking. Father obviously was not supporting assertive communication either. The maturational patterns and the family patterns played themselves out through the caregiver-infant interactions.

This family required therapeutic work on a number of fronts at once. The infant's special constitutional maturational patterns was discussed. Hands-on practice helped the parents help their baby be attentive and calm. Also addressed were how to play with the baby; how to get in front of him and help him to take more initiative; how to help mother be more patient, waiting for him to finish what he started; and how to support initiative (e.g., to put something in front of the baby while the baby was on his tummy in order to motivate him to crawl and reach). The mother was assisted in putting more affect into her voice and to increase the rhythm and speed of her vocalizations; we worked on getting the father to be more gentle. Other matters explored were the parents' own feelings about the interactions—the father's background, the mother's fear of her own assertiveness and of her baby being injured, and their own associated family patterns.

Gradually, the baby began to sleep through the night and became more assertive and less clinging and fearful. He also became happier. Because he was slow to reach his motor milestones, an occupational therapist began to work with him and to give the parents advice on motor development and normalizing his sensory overreactivity. In 4 months, this infant was functioning in an age-appropriate manner with a tendency toward a cautious but happy and assertive approach to life's developmental challenges.

CHILDREN WITH SEVERE REGULATORY PROBLEMS

Some children who come in for treatment present with severe communication problems, sensory underreactivity and overreactivity and processing difficulties, motor delays, and "autistic features," with the diagnosis of pervasive developmental disorder or atypical development. Such children often have problems at all the developmental levels described earlier—attention, engagement, two-way gestural communication, and the symbolization of emotions.

At each developmental level there are problems on all fronts—family, maturation, and interaction. The constitutional problems with sensory reactivity and processing (of a severe nature, especially auditory-verbal processing), motor tone and motor planning, family system problems, parent-child interaction problems, and the parents' own reactions and fantasies about the child undermine attending, forming relationships, being intentional, and using words or complex symbols and gestures to convey needs or desires. Treatment involves a comprehensive approach. Often, with these children, however, professionals may try to work with splinter skills at the symbolic level and not enough with the regulatory difficulties and the early levels of engagement, shared attention, and gestural interactions. Play therapy four times a week that focuses on all developmental levels, occupational therapy twice a week (for some children), speech therapy twice a week, parent counseling once or twice a week, and a psychoeducational program half days, five times a week are elements of a comprehensive program.

With such a program, many children who have been treated in the past few years have done remarkably well, better than one would have expected at the start. Within 6 months, for example, withdrawn preschoolers are comfortable with dependency and closeness, seeking out their parents, and learning to be intentional. Within 1 year, they are beginning to symbolize affect and to become comfortable with peers. Over time, specific severe learning disabilities become the focus of treatment as the pervasive emotional difficulties improve compared with children where the focus is on controlling behavior and splinter skills. Working comprehensively on the underlying regulatory difficulties and their associated emotional patterns leads to children having greater warmth and spontaneity.

For each case, one must pinpoint the family system dynamics, the parents' fantasies, the baby's constitutional-maturational contributions, and the caregiver-child interactions for each developmental level: attention and engagement, two-way communication, shared meanings, and emotional thinking.

CONCLUSION

The infant and child's ability for "regulation" can be viewed in the context of the infant's sensory, motor, interactive, and family patterns. Each of these variables in turn, can, be viewed in the context of several developmental-emotional levels of functioning. The model of regulation and regulatory disorders provides a construct that is sensitive to an infant's individual differences, family, and environmental patterns, on the one hand, and his or her emerging adaptive and psychopathological patterns on the other hand. It provides a bridging construct between genetic, prenatal, perinatal, or early developmental variables and later developmental outcomes. This type of construct may be particularly useful for understanding the developmental course of conditions where multiple etiological factors interact with one another or where the impact of certain etiological factors is part of a dynamic system. In this respect, the model suggested here may prove especially valuable for conceptualizing the impact of substance abuse on development. It also has implications for constructing a comprehensive treatment approach that can work with the multiple intervening variables that influence the course of development.

REFERENCES

Ainsworth, M.; Bell, S.M.; and Stayton, D. Infant-mother attachment and social development: Socialization as a product of reciprocal responsiveness to signals. In: Richards, M., ed. *The Integration of the Child into a Social World*. Cambridge, England: Cambridge University Press, 1974.

DeGangi, G.A., Berk, R.A.; and Greenspan, S.I. The clinical measurement of sensory functioning in infants. A preliminary study. *Phys Occupat Ther Pediatr* 8(2/3): 1-23, 1988.

DeGangi, G.A., and Greenspan, S.I. The development of sensory functions in infants. *Phys Occupat Ther Pediatr* 8(4):21-33, 1988.

DeGangi, G., and Greenspan, S.I. *Test of Sensory Functions in Infants*. Los Angeles: Western Psychology Services, 1989.

Greenspan, S.I. *The Development of the Ego: Implications for Personality Theory, Psychopathology, and the Psychotherapeutic Process*. Madison, CT: International Universities Press, 1989.

Greenspan, S.I. *The Psychology of Infant and Early Childhood Disorders: Clinical Assessment, Treatment, and Prevention*. Madison, CT: International Universities Press, 1991.

AUTHOR

Stanley I. Greenspan, M.D.
7201 Glenbrook Road
Bethesda, MD 20814

Regulatory Disorders II: Psychophysiologic Perspectives

Stephen W. Porges and Stanley I. Greenspan*

INTRODUCTION

Many infants exposed to drugs *in utero* have characteristics similar to a subset of non-drug-exposed infants who have difficulty regulating their behavior. These infants exhibit significant impairments in their ability to regulate internal homeostatic processes (e.g., sleep patterns, digestion, general arousal) and in organizing behavioral and physiological systems in response to environmental challenges. This chapter discusses the behavioral and physiological characteristics of the regulatory-disordered infant and how the construct of regulatory disorders might be useful in the study of infants exposed to drugs *in utero*.

The impact of prenatal drug exposure on the developing fetus and infant is difficult to evaluate. The inability to control variables, either through selection or manipulation, makes human research very different from animal studies and highlights the methodological problems. For example, with human research, it is not possible to control drug exposure or to remove all the confounding variables related to outcome.

Drugs that increase the frequency of spontaneous abortions or massive morphological abnormalities have been most easily detected. Prenatal exposure to lead, alcohol, and thalidomide are historical examples. Yet, even with these potent causal agents, the link between prenatal exposure and outcome was not readily made. If the outcome characteristics are more subtle related to neurophysiological, neurobehavioral, or socioemotional systems), it is extremely difficult to develop causal links via traditional clinical observations.

Animal preparations have generally focused on the direct toxic effects of drugs. However, toxicity may not be the major problem in dealing with the complex (system that characterizes the human fetus within the intrauterine environment, the drug-abusing pregnant woman within society, or the compromised

173

caregiving capabilities of a drug abuser. It is possible that indirect and interactive effects may contribute more to neurobehavioral debilitation than do direct toxic effects.

Drug exposure can indirectly influence the fetus. For example, various drugs, such as cocaine, have direct cardiovascular effects and can reduce the uterine blood flood and, thus, indirectly compromise the fetus (van de Bor et al. 1990). These indirect effects and interactions create problems in developing research strategies and paradigms that will enable us to dissect the factors that are related to prenatal drug exposure from the myriad social and health conditions that, in themselves, are risk factors for developmental outcome.

Drug abuse does not exist independent of many other sociobiological factors influencing the lives of pregnant women. Risks associated with drug abuse are confounded, especially if the embryo-lethal or neurotoxic effects of the drugs are minimal. For example, low birth weight is a risk factor whether it is or is not associated with prenatal drug exposure. Causal arguments may be difficult to make because many infants born of substance-abusing mothers experience a variety of risk factors, including poorly managed pregnancies, teenage pregnancies, highly stressed environments, and poor nutrition. In contrast to these varied and interactive risk factors of pregnancy associated with prenatal drug exposure, it *is* known that the offspring of these women are at extremely high risk for problems associated both with adaptation to the extrauterine environment and with normal neurophysiological regulation.

Similar to many high-risk infant populations, including premature and hypoxic infants, infants exposed to drugs *in utero* exhibit significant impairment in their ability to regulate internal homeostatic processes (i.e., sleep patterns, digestion, general arousal) and to organize behavioral and physiological response systems. These infants have deficient interactive abilities, emotional regulation, motor maturity, and attentional and organizational responses to environmental demands (e.g., see Chasnoff et al. 1985).

Before becoming too pessimistic regarding human research, let us deal with a few issues. First, methods are improving that will allow the duration of exposure to various drugs to be evaluated. For example, such sophisticated techniques as meconium evaluations and radioimmunoassay of the hair may provide more accurate detection and a potential evaluation of a time line of prenatal drug exposure (Graham et al. 1989). Second, many of the interactive effects can be statistically controlled. Third, methods of assessing neurobehavioral outcome of these infants have improved. Methods using sophisticated techniques have been developed to assess newborns, including acoustic evaluation of the infant cry (Lester and Dreher 1989), extraction of a vagal tone index from the heart rate pattern (Porges 1988), neurobehavioral assessment of brain insult (Gardner et al. 1990), and detailed quantification of behavioral patterns (Brazelton 1973). Thus, researchers are becoming more successful in describing the drug-exposed infant, even if the infant does *not* exhibit gross abnormalities at birth.

To study the developmental sequelae of prenatal drug exposure, it is necessary to have an appropriate model. In developing this model, the focus is on the infant for two reasons: First, we are interested in assessing risk for these infants and in developing appropriate interventions; second, it is the infant and not the complex sociobiological context of the pregnancy that is most frequently observed in clinical and research programs.

Regardless of the interaction with and confounding by other variables, the neurobehavioral organization of many prenatal drug-exposed infants may be described by two clusters of behavioral characteristics: hyperreactivity and hyporeactivity. Hyperreactivity is associated with irritability, tremors, jitteriness, and hypertonicity during early infancy. Hyporeactivity is associated with low activity levels and hypotonicity. Both groups may have poor attention control systems, state regulation, and digestive problems. Drug withdrawal may exacerbate these symptoms.

The adaptive competence of the hyperreactive or hyporeactive infant provides the basis for discussing regulatory disorders as a construct related to the developmental outcome of infants prenatally exposed to drugs. The defining characteristics of the regulatory-disordered infant and the theoretical relevance of regulatory processes to cognitive and affective development have been elaborated by Greenspan (1989). From a clinical research perspective, Greenspan (this volume) describes observations of the behavioral, affective, and cognitive characteristics of these regulatory-disordered infants.

The early regulation of arousal and physiological state is essential for successful adaptation to the complex extrauterine environment. Infants must accommodate to varying sensory challenges and maintain homeostatic processes. The infant must be able to regulate sleep states, to digest food effectively, to self-soothe in response to changing sensory stimuli, and to be capable of contingent and appropriate responses to social stimuli.

In research with term and high-risk neonates, Porges (1988) identified a physiological response system that seems to parallel many of the neurobehavioral systems responsible for regulatory disorders. This system is modulated by the vagus, a major component of the parasympathetic nervous system. The vagus is a cranial nerve that conveys information from the brain stem to many of the peripheral autonomic organs.

In general, the vagal system is continuously functioning to maintain physiological homeostasis. However, central nervous system responses associated with perception or emotion may elicit immediate autonomic reactivity via selective inhibition or excitation of vagal activity. Unlike its antagonistic partner, the sympathetic nervous system, the vagus can respond rapidly to foster the expression and regulation of autonomic reactivity. Moreover, excursions from autonomic homeostasis arising from excitation may be rapidly ameliorated by reflexive vagal activation. Thus, a well- functioning vagal system should be associated with greater autonomic reactivity and more rapid return to homeostatic level.

Vagal tone can be assessed by evaluating the amplitude of heart rate oscillations mediated by the respiratory system. Usually, heart rate increases during inhalation and decreases during exhalation. This component of heart rate variability is often called respiratory sinus arrhythmia. In our research, it is labeled $\hat{V}$ to emphasize that it is an estimate of vagal tone and is quantified with a specific patented time-series-analysis technique (Porges 1985).

In investigations of the heart rate patterns of risk populations, differences in the amplitude of respiratory sinus arrhythmia can be easily observed. In the study of high-risk infants, Porges (1988) found that high-risk neonates have, in general, lower vagal tone than do full-term infants. Moreover, within the high-risk sample, the developmental sequelae of the low-vagal-tone infant is different than that of the higher vagal-tone infant. High-risk infants with low vagal tone are more likely to suffer from apnea and to have poor long-term outcome.

With full-term neonates, the vagal-tone measure was associated with greater irritability at birth (DiPietro et al. 1987) and higher Bayley scores at 15 months (Larson et al. 1990). With 5-month-old infants, higher vagal tone was associated with greater facial expressivity (Stifter et al. 1989). Thus, it appears that vagal tone modulates behavioral, affective, and autonomic reactivity and that many risk factors are associated with low vagal tone.

The vagal system is responsive to the changing needs of the organism. Often, the vagal system will respond by selectively increasing or decreasing its influence on the periphery. This might be observed as a withdrawal of vagal tone to increase heart rate to support metabolic demands or an increase in vagal tone to regulate polypeptides and gastric motility.

The adaptive success of the infant is not based merely on the tonic level of the autonomic nervous system but also on the ability of the autonomic nervous system to appropriately respond to environmental and internal challenges. For example, we have studied vagal reactivity in preterms in response to gavage feeding. Vagal responsivity to orogastric stimulation is necessary for the regulation of gastrointestinal hormones and motility. Thus, the clinical status of the preterm infant might be related to vagal responsivity during gavage feeding. However, infants whose vagal tone increased during feeding and decreased following feeding had significantly shorter hospitalizations. This effect was independent of the gestational age, birth weight, baseline vagal tone, and the occurrence and magnitude of transient bradycardias elicited by tube insertion. In summary, independent of tonic basal levels, vagal responsivity to gavage feeding can provide a measurable index of risk status (DiPietro and Porges 1991).

In other contexts, such as attention to the external environment or stress associated with pain, the vagal system immediately reduces its influence on periphery. For example, during circumcision there is a systematic reduction of vagal tone during the invasive procedures, the degree of reduction being related to basal levels (Porter et al. 1988).

Thus, we may hypothesize based on a large number of studies conducted in our laboratory and in others that neonatal vagal tone is related to reactivity and that low vagal tone is associated with clinical risk. Our research has identified a second risk dimension related to vagal reactivity. We propose that inappropriate and unreliable vagal responsivity is a physiological substrate of regulatory disorders. Based on our previous studies relating high basal vagal tone to irritability, we have approached the clinical problem of studying infants with regulatory disorders. Therefore, in the study of hyperreactive regulatory-disordered infants, we would expect to identify a subset of infants who would exhibit problems of vagal regulation in response to stimulation.

In our first study, we selected normal and regulatory-disordered 8-month-old infants. We recorded vagal tone during a baseline condition and during the administration of the Bayley Scales of Mental Development. In the normal sample, the higher the baseline vagal tone, the greater the vagal withdrawal during the task. This pattern also has been observed in normal adults when evaluating the relationship between baseline vagal tone and changes during sustained attention. For the regulatory-disordered infants, there was no systematic relationship between baseline and vagal reactivity, although the infants tended to have higher vagal tone during the baseline (DeGangi et al. 1991).

These infants were retested at 4 years on the McCarthy Scales of Children's Abilities. When the Bates dimension of fussy-difficult at 9 months was plotted against the child's score on general cognition, a very interesting relationship emerged. Within the normal sample, the higher the level of cognitive

177

performance, the greater the infant fussiness. These data are consistent with other studies that have identified early irritability as a positive attribute (e.g., DiPietro et al. 1987). However, if we selected subjects with extreme irritability and other regulatory problems (note that fussiness is merely one of the dimensions required for the regulatory diagnosis), the relationship changed. With this select sample, the greater the fussiness, the poorer the cognitive performance. Moreover, as a sample, the regulatory-disordered infants had a significantly lower level of cognitive performance. In a replication with an independent sample, the relationship between baseline vagal tone and changes in vagal tone was evaluated during both the Bayley test and the Fagan Test of Infant Intelligence (Doussard-Roosevelt et al. 1990). The findings were convergent. The regulatory-disordered infants had higher vagal tone and did not exhibit a relationship between baseline vagal tone and suppression of vagal tone during the attention-demanding tasks.

At 20 months, 42 infants from the second study were retested with a variety of infant and maternal assessments. There was a striking stability of the fussiness dimension, with a correlation of .72 and stability of the vagal-tone measure during the Bayley test, r=.76. Moreover, important causal paths related the difficult dimension, and not mental or motor development, to parenting stress and to parenting self-esteem and marital satisfaction. Maternal mood state, which was influenced by social support, contributed directly to marital satisfaction and to parenting stress (Portales et al. 1990).

The identified causal paths relating infant difficultness to the family presents a model that might be useful in studying infants and young children in a substance-abusing environment. Substance abuse can affect the child and family on a number of levels. Prenatal exposure might directly compromise the young infant's capacity to self-regulate. Maternal addiction might contribute to maternal mood-state problems that would lead to parenting and family problems. Also, the weak social-support system of the substance abuser might contribute to these observed problems.

It is the authors' belief that the regulatory problems of prenatal drug-exposed infants, like those of most infants who exhibit regulatory problems, are manifested in dysfunctional vagal regulation of autonomic processes. This dysfunction would be manifested in attentional, emotional, sleep, and digestive processes—all of which are dependent on vagal regulation.

The vagal system has been linked to drug exposure. In *Science*, a report (April 13, 1990) from the Federation of American Societies for Experimental Biology described a study by Stephen W. Hull in which vagal reactivity was inhibited and disorganized by cocaine. Moreover, current research at the National

178

Insititute on Drug Abuse Addiction Research Center, under the direction of Dr. David Newlin, is demonstrating that marijuana and cocaine have massive and rapid influences on vagal tone. Moreover, Newlin and colleagues (1990) have demonstrated that low doses of alcohol block the normal vagal reflexes associated with digestive processes.

It is possible that, via direct neurotoxic effects, various drugs such as cocaine can influence the central cholinergic regulation and the parallel regulation of the vagus. This might produce the behavioral characteristics of irritability and emotional lability and the autonomic characteristics of sleep, arousal, and eating disorders observed in infants who have been prenatally exposed to drugs. Alternatively, reduced intrauterine blood flow may result in hypoxia or growth retardation. These factors also may be causal in influencing the central cholinergic system, which also influences vagal regulation. Thus, the regulatory-disordered infant might exhibit autonomic hyperirritability caused by defective central neural programs and mediated via neurotransmitters through the vagus (for elaboration of this theory, see Porges 1991).

Measures of spontaneous vagal tone and changes in vagal tone during a variety of psychological processes might identify the regulatory-disordered infant. The results of our research on two independent samples provide preliminary support for the *vagotonic* hypothesis. Our research has demonstrated that the regulatory-disordered infant exhibits (1) atypical spontaneous levels of vagal tone and (2) atypical changes in vagal tone during sensory and cognitive challenges. These differences may reflect the difficulty that the regulatory-disordered infant has in modulating the autonomic nervous system to support the behavioral state required for attention and information processing during cognitive activities (for a model relating vagal-tone suppression to sustained attention, see Porges 1984).

CONCLUSION

The regulatory-disorder model is an important starting point in the study of the neurobehavioral outcome of infants prenatally exposed to drugs. Many of the behaviors observed in drug-exposed infants appear to be consistent with those observed in regulatory-disordered infants. At the core of the regulatory disorder appears to be the inability to appropriately inhibit both behavioral and physiological reactivity in response to environmental demands. We have speculated that similar inhibitory processes are required for a child to attend to relevant stimuli. We believe that the successful accomplishment of many adaptive processes, including sustained attention, requires systematic modulation of vagal tone. The observed inability of the regulatory-disordered infants to systematically regulate vagal tone may evolve into subsequent developmental problems associated with attention skills and emotional control.

Deficits in these processes would lead to general learning and emotional problems. Followup evaluations of regulatory-disordered infants confirm these speculations. Thus, the possibility exists that prenatal exposure to drugs and postnatal stress associated with substance abuse environments may compromise the infant's ability to develop the regulatory processes necessary to deal with the complex environment.

REFERENCES

Brazelton, T.B. *Neonatal Behavioral Assessment Scale.* Philadelphia: Lippincott, 1973.

Chasnoff, I.J.; Burns, W.J.; Schnool, S.H.; and Burns, K.A. Cocaine use in pregnancy. *N Engl J Med* 313(11):666-669, 1985.

DeGangi, G.A.; DiPietro, J.A.; Greenspan, S.I.; and Porges, S.W. Psychophysiological characteristics of the regulatory disordered infant. *Inf Behav Dev* 14:37-50, 1991.

DiPietro, J.A.; Larson, S.K.; and Porges, S.W. Behavioral and heart-rate pattern differences between breast-fed and bottle-fed neonates. *Dev Psychol* 23:467-474, 1987.

DiPietro, J.A., and Porges, S.W. Vagal responsiveness to gavage feeding as an index of preterm status. *Pediatr Res* 29:231-236, 1991.

Doussard-Roosevelt, J.A.; Walker, P.S.; Portales, A.L.; Greenspan, S.I.; and Porges, S.W. Vagal tone and the fussy infant: Atypical vagal reactivity in the difficult infant. (Abstract.) *Inf Behav Dev* 13:352, 1990.

Gardner, J.M.; Karmel, B.Z.; Magnano, C.; Norton, K.I.; and Brown, E.G. Neurobehavioral indicators of early brain insult in high-risk neonates. *Dev Psychol* 26(4):563-575, 1990.

Graham, K.; Koren, G.; Klein, J.; Schneiderman, J.; and Greenwald, M. Determination of gestational cocaine exposure by hair analysis. *JAMA* 262:3328-3330, 1989.

Greenspan, S.I. *The Development of the Ego: Implications for Personality Theory, Psychopathology, and the Psychotherapeutic Process.* Madison, CT: International Universities Press, 1989.

Larson, S.K.; Porges, S.W.; and DiPietro, J.A. "Neonatal Psychophysiological Assessment and 15-Month Developmental Outcome of Healthy Full-term Infants." Unpublished manuscript, 1990.

Lester, B.M., and Dreher, M. Effects of marijuana use during pregnancy on newborn cry. *Child Dev* 60(4):765-771, 1989.

Newlin, D.B.; Byrne, E.A.; and Porges, S.W. Vagal mediation of the effect of alcohol on heart rate. *Alcohol Clin Exp Res* 14:421-424, 1990.

Porges, S.W. Physiological correlates of attention: Core process underlying learning disorders. *Pediatr Clin N Am: Symp Learn Disord* 31:371-385, 1984.

Porges, S.W. "Method and Apparatus for Evaluating Rhythmic Oscillations in Aperiodic Physiological Response Systems." U.S. Patent 4,510,944. 16 Apr. 1985.

Porges, S.W. Neonatal vagal tone: Diagnostic and prognostic implications. In: Vietze, P.N., and Vaughn, H.G., eds. *Early Identification of Infants with Developmental Disabilities.* Philadelphia, PA: Grune and Stratton, 1988. pp. 147-159.

Porges, S.W. Vagal tone: An autonomic mediator of affect. In: Garber, J.A., and Dodge, K.A., eds. *The Development of Affect Regulation and Dysregulation.* New York: Cambridge University Press, 1991.

Portales, A.L.; Porges, S.W.; and Greenspan, S.I. Parenthood and the difficult child. (Abstract.) *Inf Behav Dev* 13:573, 1990.

Porter, F.L.; Porges, S.W.; and Marshall, R.E. Newborn pain cries and vagal tone: Parallel changes in response to circumcision. *Child Dev* 59:495-505, 1988.

Stifter, C.A.; Fox, N.A.; and Porges, S.W. Facial expressivity and vagal tone in five- and ten-month old infants. *Inf Behav Dev* 12:127-137, 1989.

van de Bor, M.; Walther, F.J.; and Ebrahimi, M. Decreased cardiac output in infants of mothers who abused cocaine. *Pediatrics* 85(1):30-32, 1990.

ACKNOWLEDGMENT

The research described in this chapter was supported in part by National Institutes of Health grant HD-22628.

AUTHOR

Stephen W. Porges, Ph.D.
Professor
Department of Human Development
University of Maryland
College Park, MD 20742

Stanley I. Greenspan, M.D.
7201 Glenbrook Road
Bethesda, MD 20814

Discussion: Measurement of Drug-Induced Physical and Behavioral Delays and Abnormalities—A General Framework

Joseph L. Jacobson

This chapter discusses the chapters of Sparber, Greenspan, and Porges and Greenspan (this volume), then comments briefly on an important topic raised by several authors in this volume, namely, the assessment of confounding influences in drug studies.

Sparber makes an important and very helpful distinction between laboratory animal studies that focus on whether a drug causes functional abnormalities and those that ask fundamental questions about how drugs modify developmental processes. In the former type of study, there is an emphasis on degree of toxicity at different doses, thresholds below which no deficits are observed, and on pharmacological agents that might protect the fetus from adverse effects of the drug. These studies are more analogous to human drug studies, where the focus is usually on whether and at what doses developmental exposure impairs function. In both human and animal toxicity studies, a range of developmental outcomes must be tested to evaluate the safety of an exposure. Sparber's second class of studies, which focus on mechanism of action, are appropriate only after detrimental effects have been demonstrated in either humans or laboratory animals. As noted in Jacobson and Jacobson (this volume), although it is difficult to investigate neuroanatomical and neurochemical mechanisms in human subjects, human studies can contribute to the understanding of such mechanisms by incorporating assessment procedures that are domain specific. Evidence of lowered IQ scores provides little indication regarding which aspects of central nervous system (CNS) function may be impaired, but a test indicating a specific deficit in, for example, spatial memory would suggest possible damage to hippocampus and related structures.

Several authors in this volume emphasize the accumulating evidence that effects of developmental exposures to drugs are often indirect. This contrasts

182

with the classical teratogenic model, based on studies of x-irradiation, thalidomide, and other substances, in which exposure during a critical period of organogenesis causes a structural deformity with long-term implications for function. Sparber emphasizes that deleterious effects of developmental exposures to drugs are often indirect consequences of hypoxia, reduced blood flow, malnutrition, or stress associated with withdrawal. At a different level of analysis, Porges and Greenspan also point to indirect effects mediated by environmental stress and lack of social support. An important working hypothesis from classical behavioral teratology, which has influenced the work of many in the field today, is that agents that produce gross CNS damage at high doses are likely to be associated with subtle behavioral changes when exposure occurs at lower levels (Hutchings 1978; Vorhees 1986). Whereas this hypothesis remains plausible for agents that disrupt cell differentiation during critical periods, it may not hold for substances that affect function indirectly. Where hypoxia or malnutrition is the mechanism of action, deficits may be more transitory or may occur only at very high exposure levels where fetal deprivation is severe.

Sparber points out that one important goal of drug studies is to determine at what dose levels a pharmacological agent may be "safe." Citing data from an important recent *Lancet* study (Koren et al. 1989), also noted by Zuckerman (this volume), he suggests that bias by journals and funding agencies against negative results and pressure from society to demonstrate deleterious effects from illegal drugs have led to an overrepresentation of positive research results in the cocaine literature. Although the concerns articulated are serious, it is important to note that the scientific bias against negative findings has a sound basis in research methodology. Inadequate sample size, insensitive measures, and lack of research skill and/or precision all can lead to Type II error, that is, failure to detect real effects. Therefore, the fact that pediatric journals may publish more articles with negative effects is not, in itself, necessarily cause for concern. On the other hand, evidence that the studies not accepted for publication were more valid in the sense that they verified cocaine use more often or had larger sample sizes does suggest that journal editors need to give more serious consideration to the publication of negative results. Sound research design always should be required in peer review journals. However, due to the increased risk of Type II error, it may be advisable to subject studies reporting negative effects to somewhat more stringent criteria in terms of sample size, verification of exposure levels, and validity and sensitivity of the outcome measures used.

Greenspan and Porges outline an important hypothesis suggesting that long-term effects of prenatal drug exposures on attention and learning may be mediated by regulatory disorders, including sleep disturbances, difficulties in self-consoling, and hypersensitivity to stimulation. This hypothesis focuses attention on a dimension of human function first emphasized in Brazelton's pioneering work on newborns, which has received relatively little attention from psychometricians. In addition, Porges has developed psychophysiological measures involving vagal tone, which could facilitate identification of regulatory disorders in drug-exposed children.

Porges and Greenspan point to evidence that infants exposed prenatally to cocaine, alcohol, and other drugs appear to be at risk for regulatory disorders, which they suggest may interfere with the attentional skills and emotional control needed for learning during childhood. However, to date most of the evidence of regulatory disorders in drug-exposed children comes from early infancy when such disorders may be transitory and have little impact on subsequent function. In their research on 4- and 7-year-old children exposed prenatally to alcohol, Streissguth and associates (1984, 1986) reported deficits in one aspect of self-regulation, sustained attention, which could be responsible in part for the cognitive deficits observed in these children. Although there is evidence that prenatal alcohol exposure also can have a direct impact on neuronal development, the role of regulatory disorders clearly warrants further investigation.

It has been noted that the failure of prenatal narcotics exposure to have a negative impact on the Bayley Scales may be due to the limited sensitivity of that instrument and does not necessarily indicate that no true differences exist. This criticism points to the need for investigators to consider a broader range of endpoints, including physiological and neuroendocrine, and potentially more sensitive measures of cognitive function. It also underscores the importance of focusing more attention on the sensitivity and validity of the measures used. Inadequate measurement can substantially increase the risk of Type II error, which is especially serious in teratological studies where, despite all caveats to the contrary, a null finding is likely to be interpreted as evidence that a drug is safe. Indeed, the only indication that a chemical may be safe is the failure of a competent, comprehensive investigation to detect harmful effects. Therefore, it is especially important to use highly sensitive and valid measures in this type of study and to include sufficient numbers of highly exposed individuals so that, if an effect exists, it will be detected.

Several authors in this volume allude to the difficulties associated with controlling for confounding influences in human studies. For some confounders, elegant experimental animal studies, such as those described by Sparber for controlling for nutrition and drug withdrawal, can be very helpful. Other confounders can be controlled by sampling subjects selectively to reduce collinearity. More attention also needs to be paid to the reliability and validity of the control variables used. Confounding influences are typically controlled statistically by removing any variance attributable to the control variables before entering drug exposure in a multivariate analysis. If exposure or outcome is not adequately measured, there is an increased risk of Type II error. But, if control variables are not measured adequately, the underestimation of their impact can artificially inflate the variance attributed to exposure, increasing the risk of attributing to the drug an effect that really is due to a confounder. An example of this problem would be a study in which alcohol consumption and/or smoking during pregnancy were assessed in a single dichotomous measure: Did the mother smoke or drink alcohol? Unless smoking and drinking have the same impact on development, neither exposure can be adequately assessed in a single composite measure. Moreover, most effects of pregnancy drinking are at high levels of exposure, yet most pregnant women drink at low levels. A dichotomous measure may not be sufficiently powerful to detect the effects of high-level drinking since most of those coded as drinkers will have consumed very little alcohol.

More effort also needs to be devoted to identifying control variables that not only are reliable and valid but also can be administered relatively quickly and efficiently. Efficiency is important because there are so many potential confounding influences that must be considered even though the confounders are not the focus of the investigation. In some domains, such as socioeconomic status (SES) and quality of intellectual stimulation by the parent, valid and efficient measures have been developed. Thus, the Hollingshead Scale has been shown to be a reliable predictor of early childhood cognitive function (Gottfried 1985), and the HOME Inventory (Caldwell and Bradley 1984), which assesses parental input more directly, has been found to explain variance in child performance over and above that attributable to SES (Brumitt and Jacobson 1989; Gottfried and Gottfried 1984; Siegel 1984). Jacobson and Jacobson (in press) have found that the Peabody Picture Vocabulatory Test-Revised provides a quick, yet valid assessment of maternal cognitive function. For other domains, however, such as familial stress or quality of maternal support, more work is needed to develop measures that are both valid and efficient to administer.

REFERENCES

Brumitt, G.A., and Jacobson, J.L. The influence of home environment and socio-economic status on cognitive performance at 4 years. *Abst Soc Res Child Dev* 6:203, 1989.
Caldwell, B.M., and Bradley, R.H. *Home Observation for Measurement of the Environment*. Little Rock, AR: University of Arkansas Press, 1984.

Gottfried, A.W.   Measures of socioeconomic status in child development research: Data and recommendations. *Merrill-Palmer Q* 31:85-92, 1985.

Gottfried, A.W., and Gottfried, A.E.   Home environment and cognitive development in young children of middle-socioeconomic-status families. In: Gottfried, A.W., ed. *Home Environment and Early Cognitive Development: Longitudinal Research.* Orlando, FL: Academic Press, 1984.

Hutchings, D.E.   Behavioral teratology: Embryopathic and behavioral effects of drugs during pregnancy. In: Gottlieb, G., ed. *Studies on the Development of Behavior and the Nervous System.* Vol. 4. New York: Academic Press, 1978.

Jacobson, S.W., and Jacobson, J.L.   Early exposure to PCBs and other suspected teratogens: Assessment of confounding. In: Greenbaum, C., and Auerbach, J., eds. *Longitudinal Studies of Infants Born at Psychological Risk.* Norwood, NJ: Ablex, in press.

Koren, G.; Shear, H.; Graham, K.; and Einarson, T.   Bias against the null hypothesis: The reproductive hazards of cocaine. *Lancet* 8677:1440-1442, 1989.

Siegel, L.   Home environmental influences on cognitive development in preterm and full-term children during the first 5 years. In: Gottfried, A.W., ed. *Home Environment and Early Cognitive Development: Longitudinal Research.* Orlando, FL: Academic Press, 1984.

Streissguth, A.P.; Barr, H.M.; Sampson, P.D.; Parrish-Johnson, J.C.; Kirchner, G.L.; and Martin, D.C.   Attention, distraction, and reaction time at age 7 years and prenatal alcohol exposure. *Neurobehav Toxicol Teratol* 8:717-725, 1986.

Streissguth, A.P.; Martin, D.C.; Barr, H.M.; Sandman, B.M.; Kirchner, G.L.; and Darby, B.L.   Intrauterine alcohol and nicotine exposure: Attention and reaction time in 4-year-old children. *Dev Psychol* 20:533-541, 1984.

Vorhees, C.V.   Origins of behavioral teratology. In: Riley, E.P., and Vorhees, C.V., eds. *Handbook of Behavioral Teratology.* New York: Plenum, 1986.

AUTHOR

Joseph L. Jacobson, Ph.D.
Associate Professor
Psychology Department
Wayne State University
71 West Warren Avenue
Detroit, MI 48202

Postnatal Development of Cardiac and Respiratory Control Following Prenatal Drug Exposure

Ronald M. Harper

INTRODUCTION

Evidence of the effects of prenatal drug exposure on subsequent postnatal cardiac and respiratory control is sparse. However, prenatal exposure to particular agents results in the disturbance of several physiologic characteristics in the newborn, particularly altered motor and sensory control systems and the ways in which these systems interact. The activation of these systems is closely allied with mechanisms underlying cardiac and respiratory control. The integration of these physiologic systems with cardiorespiratory control mechanisms during development raises several theoretical and methodological issues.

The disturbed physiologic and structural characteristics following prenatal drug exposure include growth retardation (Ryan et al. 1987; Chasnoff et al. 1987; Zuckerman et al. 1989); disturbed sleep states (Dinges et al. 1980); disturbed motor behavior, including tremors and extensor rigidity (Oro and Dixon 1987); disruptions of normal breathing patterns, particularly during sleep (Chasnoff et al. 1989; Ward et al. 1989a); evidence of exposure to extreme vasoconstriction or hypoxia during fetal life (Telsey et al. 1988); and disruptions in the integrity of sensory pathways or central processing of afferent activity (Church 1987; Church and Gerkin 1988). At least some of the symptomatology associated with prenatal drug exposure also may be characteristic of premature infants because, at least superficially, particular characteristics such as retarded growth and altered breathing patterns are shared in these populations. It is the objective of this chapter to demonstrate the interaction of physiologic mechanisms contributing to some of these signs that may be manifested in these groups.

GROWTH AND DEVELOPMENT

Prenatal exposure to agents such as cocaine or marijuana results in adverse growth effects, with infants exposed prenatally to cocaine exhibiting reduced head circumference and diminished body weight (Ryan et al. 1987; Chasnoff et al. 1987; Zuckerman et al. 1989), characteristics similar to those observed in premature infants. The growth retardation may result from poor nutrition associated with maternal self-neglect, from repetitive exposure to hypoxic events induced by extreme vasoconstriction in the fetus and reduced blood flow through the uterine artery (see below), or from other as yet undescribed cocaine effects. Although prenatal opiate exposure exerts state organization changes remarkably different from those of nonopiate substance exposure (see below), certain aspects of birth weight and gross dimensions appear to be a function of the amount of drug exposure, rather than whether the drug is an opiate or a nonopiate (Dinges et al. 1980).

Normal respiratory patterning is dependent on age-appropriate development of respiratory muscle and upper airway structures. Disproportionate growth or retardation of structures within the upper airway might alter greatly the normal sequence of respiratory patterning, particularly in certain sleep states, and the potential for alteration of such development by prenatal drug exposure is substantial (Lauder, this volume). Disturbances in upper airway structural components are known to cause respiratory patterning difficulties, especially in sleep; hypertrophy of the tongue musculature or enlarged tissue of the soft palate, particularly when combined with micrognathia, leads to obstructive sleep apnea (Harper 1988) (figure 1). Some animal models with recessed facial structures, such as the English bulldog, are particularly prone to obstructive apnea and early death (Hendricks et al. 1987). Thus, specific drug effects on the development of craniofacial structures are particularly important because of the potential influence of these structures on later respiratory function.

CARDIOVASCULAR SIGNS

The clinical cardiovascular dysfunction exhibited by infants who have been exposed prenatally to drugs includes signs of ischemia or hypoxia suggestive of repetitive exposure to extreme vasoconstriction. There is evidence that vessels supplying the bowel have been affected, causing ischemia to that area (Telsey et al. 1988). In addition, the incidence of cerebral vasculature abnormalities, including ventricular bleeding, is excessive (Dixon and Bejar 1989), and there is evidence of cerebral infarction (Chasnoff et al. 1986). Extreme vasoconstriction should be expected from maternal use of cocaine because cocaine acts directly to produce that effect when administered in animal models in which both the mother and the fetus show transient hypertension following cocaine

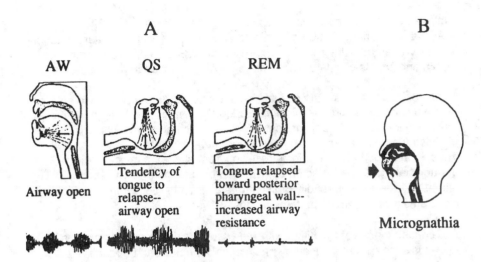

FIGURE 1. *Developmental disturbances in mandibular morphology, particularly micrognathia, can profoundly alter respiratory patterning during sleep. Normal integrity of airflow is dependent on respiratory cycling action of upper airway muscles, such as the genioglossal fibers that move the tongue forward and dilate the airway with each breath (A). REM sleep causes a relative loss of tone in the tongue musculature, which enhances the possibility for narrowing the airway; any additional condition, such as micrognathia (B), would cause the mass of the tongue to approach even further the posterior pharyngeal wall and heighten the possibility for airway occlusion following negative pressure generated by a descending diaphragm.*

KEY: AW=waking; QS=quiet sleep; REM=rapid eye movement

SOURCE: Harper and Sauerland 1978, copyright 1978, Wiley-Liss

administration (Woods et al. 1989). Somewhat paradoxically, cocaine-exposed neonates exhibit vasodilatory signs of abnormally dilated and "tortuous" iris vessels (Isenberg et al. 1987). Isenberg and colleagues suggest that the vasodilation may be a rebound phenomenon or that cocaine's vasoconstrictive effect acts on vessels downstream from the eyes.

Additional cardiovascular signs of prenatal exposure to cocaine include elevated heart rate during quiet sleep. Heart rates are elevated over those of controls both in normoxia and in hypoxic conditions (Woo et al. 1990); the elevated rates during sleep are reminiscent of findings with premature infants, infants who are at risk for sudden infant death syndrome (SIDS) (Harper et al. 1982), and infants who later succumb to SIDS (Schechtman et al. 1988).

Strong evidence exists that cocaine administered to the pregnant ewe enters the fetal circulation, directly raises fetal blood pressure, and increases fetal heart rate in addition to any indirect effects from maternal vasoconstriction and diminished uterine artery blood flow (Moore et al. 1986; Woods et al. 1989). Thus, fetal blood pressure effects resulting from exposure to cocaine are greater than could be expected by hypoxia from uterine artery vasoconstriction alone. In rats, cocaine readily passes to fetal brain tissue, where it particularly stimulates metabolism in the female (Dow-Edwards 1989).

The consequences of repetitive extreme vasoconstriction and hypoxemia in the fetus such as that induced by habitual cocaine use can be manifested postnatally as local ischemia, as in the case of local bowel lesions described earlier (Telsey et al. 1988). Repetitive exposure to hypoxia from vasoconstriction also has the potential to alter overall growth and development of particular regions and to modify development of neurotransmitter release or receptor responsivity. Major questions exist for the relative importance of effects exerted by vasoconstriction on neural and other structural systems.

The cardiovascular sequelae of acute cocaine administration in animals are well known and include tachycardia, greatly reduced heart rate variability, and elicitation of a variety of conductive arrhythmias. Some of the arrhythmias observed following cocaine administration follow patterns of extreme order intermixed with other patterns; the patterning of cardiac R-R intervals (the time between R waves of successive cardiac cycles) also follows an organization of extreme order. Nonlinear dynamic procedures are of particular use in assessing both the R-R interval and these moment-to-moment arrhythmia patterns (Harper et al. 1989; Raetz et al., in press).

SLEEP STATES

Of all the considerations in assessing drug action on physiologic activity during postnatal development, sleep state is of primary importance. Sleep state can affect heart and respiratory rate and variability by a factor of two or more in normal infants (Harper et al. 1983a). Differences between risk groups for SIDS on measures of cardiac and respiratory control can disappear unless state is controlled (Schechtman et al. 1988). Significant sources of cardiac variability, such as respiratory contributions, emerge primarily in particular states (Trelease et al. 1986). Adding to the complications of state are developmental changes:

The effect of state on physiology markedly changes with development, exerting massive effects at some ages and minimal effects at others (Harper et al. 1976, 1983a). The temporal organization of state is useful in assessing neurologic development in the infant, because abnormal numbers of arousals, prolonged state durations, erratic circadian appearances of state, or abnormal "clustering" of physiologic variables during particular states all may be indicative of abnormal development (Monod and Pajot 1965; Monod et al. 1967; Harper et al. 1983b).

The normal development of sleep state in the infant consists of 50- to 60-minute epochs alternating between quiet and active sleep, modulated early in life by a 3- to 4-hour feeding rhythm and later (about 3 months) by single sleep periods of 7 to 8 hours usually at night (figure 2). Premature infant sleep states are more difficult to differentiate. Active and quiet periods can be differentiated at a gestational age of from 3 to 6 weeks using several parameters and by single measures several weeks earlier (Parmelee 1974). The normal development of sleep state is characterized by increasing amounts of quiet sleep and decreasing amounts of REM sleep, with the amount of quiet sleep doubling at 3 months over the newborn period. Because the relative proportion of REM sleep to quiet sleep states changes so markedly at a time of peak risk for SIDS, considerable attention has focused on the relationship between arousability from each of these states and SIDS. Infants at risk for SIDS (Harper et al. 1981a) and infants who later succumb to SIDS (Schechtman et al. 1991) exhibit alterations in organization of state, particularly at certain times of the night (figure 3). Further examination of state organization in the prenatally drug-exposed infant might contribute substantially to knowledge of mechanisms for switching to an aroused condition to overcome potentially fatal challenges in these infants.

Prenatal drug exposure can markedly affect the organization of sleep states. Newborn infants who have been exposed chronically in utero to low-dose methadone with or without heroin exhibit less quiet sleep and more REM sleep than controls; infants fetally exposed to both opiates and nonopiates show disturbed organization of sleep states (Dinges et al. 1980). Other investigators describe a diminution in low-voltage, irregular state patterns and an increase in "mixed" state patterns independent of the withdrawal syndrome even after phenobarbital treatment (Stefanini et al. 1984).

Sleep state, arousal, and respiratory patterning are closely interrelated. Disturbances in sleep state organization can interact with respiratory patterning and greatly disturb the normal sequencing of breathing. The disorganization of sleep states observed in prenatally cocaine-exposed infants can interact with other physiologic activity such as respiratory patterning. The disorganization

191

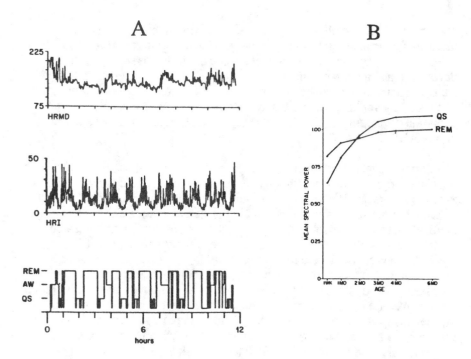

FIGURE 2. *(A) These traces illustrate the temporal organization of observer-scored sleep states in a 1-month-old infant, together with the corresponding changes in median heart rate (HRMD) and heart rate variability (HRI, interquartile range) that accompany state changes. Note that the REM states occur at approximately hourly intervals and that heart rate undergoes a 3- to 4-hour modulation (e.g., between 3.5 and 7 hours). (B) Spectral estimates of the hourly organization of quiet and REM sleep development over the first few months of life. The figure illustrates that multiple temporal "organizers" operate on state timing, that this organization matures, and that substantial physiological variation accompanies each state.*

KEY: AW=waking; QS=quiet sleep; REM=rapid eye movement

SOURCES: Harper et al. 1981a, copyright 1981, Academic Press; Harper 1985, copyright 1985, Academic Press

3 months, waking

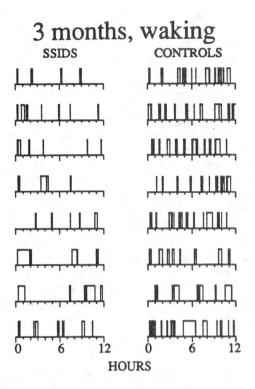

FIGURE 3. *Binary plots of occurrence of waking across a 12-hour nighttime recording period in eight infants who were siblings of SIDS victims (SSIDS) and eight controls at 3 months of age. Note that the SSIDS infants exhibited long interwaking periods and an absence of short waking epochs. These findings suggest that these infants at risk for SIDS tend to remain asleep and that they may exhibit a relative "failure to arouse" from sleep when confronted with challenges.*

SOURCE: Harper et al. 1981b, copyright 1981, American Association for the Advancement of Science

often consists of frequent arousals from sleeping states. Arousal events often are associated with apnea in animal models (Baker and McGinty 1979). Apneic occurrences may be concomitant with the transient hypertension associated with an arousal episode, because a momentary rise in pressure accompanies arousal events and momentary increases in pressure cause suppression of diaphragmatic and upper airway activity, particularly if the pressure rise occurs within a sleep state (Trelease et al. 1985). The increased number of apneas observed in cocaine-exposed infants thus may reflect the increased numbers of arousal events observed in these infants.

TEMPERATURE CONTROL: MOTOR AND RESPIRATORY INTERACTIONS

Both respiratory and cardiovascular patterning in infants depend heavily on core temperature, although no descriptive data are available on temperature regulation during sleep following prenatal drug exposure. Assessment of temperature during different states is important because rostral brain temperature control mechanisms dissociate during REM sleep; that is, normal mechanisms for controlling temperature are not operative during that state (Parmeggiani 1980). Acute intravenous or intraventricular cocaine exposure in adult cats leads to marked rises in temperature and tachypnea (figure 4) (Harper et al. 1991). In rats the thermal response is apparently dependent on ambient temperature, with hyperthermia accompanying high ambient temperature (Lomax and Daniel 1990). Prenatal cocaine exposure has the potential to greatly modify temperature-regulating mechanisms by interfering with development of rostral brain regions, modifying neurotransmitters of descending neural pathways, or altering receptors at the peripheral level.

Integrated Diaphragmatic Activity

Control

Cocaine

FIGURE 4. *Integrated diaphragmatic electromyographic activity from a cat before and 5 minutes following 5 mg/kg intravenous cocaine administration. Intraventricular and intravenous cocaine administration will raise respiratory rates rapidly in a cat, approaching a fourfold to fivefold increase from baseline levels. Time bar=1 second.*

Prenatal cocaine exposure alters neural systems regulating motor control in a significant fashion, since affected infants exhibit tremors postnatally; this finding has been almost universal in the published literature (e.g., Chasnoff et al. 1987) and anecdotal reports (M. Regalado, personal communication, February 1991). Detailed characteristics of these tremors (e.g., frequency, amplitude, and muscle distribution) have not been described, but it should be noted that a major mechanism of many mammalian species for raising core temperature is to produce high-frequency tremors, that is, shivering (Gordon 1990). One could speculate that tremors associated with prenatal exposure to cocaine thus might incidentally raise core temperature in the infant or the tremors may become a learned response, to raise core temperature, in an infant for whom temperature regulation is disturbed. The possibility of deficits in temperature regulation existing in infants prenatally subjected to drugs should be considered when questions related to swaddling of infants arise.

Motor Control

The tremors observed in infants exposed prenatally to cocaine may result from a disturbance of motor control structures, perhaps by neurotransmitter excess or depletion or supersensitivity of receptors. Tremors frequently are concomitant with motor system neurotransmitter disturbance as evidenced by the oscillatory motor activity observed in tardive dyskinesia of adults, a syndrome specifically resulting from chronic use of benzodiazepine agents and other neuroleptics (See and Ellison 1990). Chronic prenatal cocaine exposure modifies benzodiazepine receptor densities in the rat model (McAllister et al. 1988); similar receptor modifications may take place in the human fetal brain after long-term maternal cocaine use.

An additional postnatal motor pattern associated with prenatal cocaine exposure is extensor hypertonicity, characterized by excessive activation of the extensor musculature, at least during the waking state. Acute administration of cocaine to adult ewes (Woods et al. 1989) or cats (Harper et al. 1991) results in extreme extensor rigidity reminiscent of decerebrate rigidity. The extensor rigidity observed in human infants prenatally exposed to cocaine is milder and frequently described with reference to reactivity to stimulation. The excessive muscle tone occurring in this condition most likely would generate heat beyond normal values and may have the incidental effect of raising overall core temperature (although that possibility has not been directly examined). If core temperature is raised in these infants, tachypnea and fixed respiratory patterns most likely would result, because respiratory pattern timing is heavily dependent on core temperature (figure 5).

The relationships between core temperature and respiratory patterning are of interest because of the supranormal temperatures found at autopsy in SIDS victims (Stanton 1984). It is also of interest that one respiratory characteristic of infants who later succumb to SIDS is a diminution of pauses in breathing of

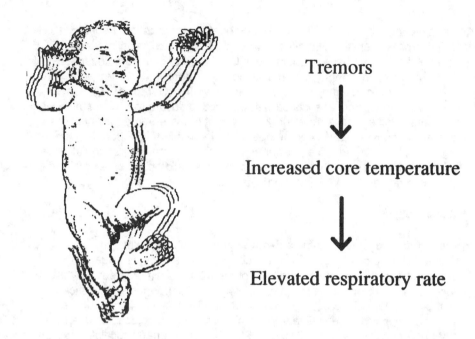

Tremors

↓

Increased core temperature

↓

Elevated respiratory rate

FIGURE 5. *This figure illustrates the possibility that motor activity, core temperature, and respiratory rate are inextricably related. Increased muscle activity leads to increased core temperature; respiratory rate is heavily dependent on temperature.*

from 4 to 30 seconds (Schechtman et al. 1991), suggesting a more fixed respiratory patterning and perhaps a more "brittle" breathing pattern (i.e., these infants are less able to cope with influences that lead to pauses in respiratory cycling than normal infants). Siblings of SIDS victims also exhibit higher respiratory rates and fewer apneas than controls (Hoppenbrouwers et al. 1980). The relationship between SIDS and core temperature is speculative. However, the interdependence of physiologic systems illustrates the potential for failure if these interactions are altered. Thus, overall muscle tone, core temperature, and respiratory patterning are inextricably related, and the effect of prenatal drug exposure on neurotransmitters that regulate motor control or temperature control inevitably also affects respiratory patterning.

Respiratory Control

Data on alterations of respiratory patterning following prenatal exposure to drugs are much more sparse than reports of cardiovascular sequelae. The data from infants exposed to prenatal cocaine suggest a variety of respiratory patterning consequences, including enhanced periods of periodic breathing and apnea of more than 6 seconds (Chasnoff et al. 1989). Infants of cocaine-abusing mothers have abnormal arousal responses to hypoxia (Ward et al. 1989a), a finding that stresses the importance of potential drug effects on organization of state as well as direct effects on respiratory control. In this latter study, infants exposed to cocaine prenatally failed to make the transition from quiet sleep to waking when subjected to hypoxia; two infants displayed extreme periodic breathing and O_2 desaturation. The diminished hypoxic arousal responses are similar to responses observed in infants who exhibit "apnea of infancy." Cocaine-exposed infants also exhibit elevated catecholamines; mean plasma norepinephrine levels in these infants show more than a twofold increase from normal levels (Ward et al. 1989b).

The relationships among tremors, extensor motor hypertonicity, temperature, respiratory patterning, and state organization may have some bearing on the relationship of cocaine to SIDS. As mentioned earlier, SIDS victims have a higher-than-normal core temperature following death (Stanton 1984). High core temperatures could lead to tachypnea and to particular problems of breathing control during REM sleep, when temperature control by rostral brain regions appears to be greatly diminished or abolished (Parameggiani 1980). If core temperatures of infants exposed *in utero* to cocaine are excessively high, resulting from late-developing tremors and hypertonicity, the respiratory consequences could be severe.

Acute cocaine administration results in extreme extensor rigidity in sheep and adult cats. Cocaine is not alone in this characteristic; however, high-dose opiate administration also results in extreme muscle hypertonicity and respiratory depression (Lowenstein 1969). The respiratory depression may result from direct action of opiates on brain stem respiratory regions. However, because opiates cause extreme hypertonicity, respiratory cycling may be masked by hyperactivity of breathing musculature, resulting in loss of airflow. The consequences of the opiate-induced extreme hypertonicity may be similar to those observed with cocaine; however, such muscle activation is followed by rises in core temperature, which in turn may further alter "drives" to respiratory patterning.

The possibility exists that *in utero* drug exposure can dramatically raise core temperature in the human fetus, which then could alter spontaneous fetal "respiratory" movements or subsequently alter responsivity of neural systems that mediate respiratory or other motor patterning. Peripheral vasoconstriction in the mother from cocaine use would raise maternal core temperature and fetal temperature as well. Animal studies that manipulate temperature in fetal life, through a uterine-implanted cooling apparatus or by cold fluid perfusion of the fetal lamb (Gluckman et al. 1984), demonstrate significant temperature-related breathing movement effects, including initiation of continuous respiratory movements from respiratory muscle silence that are maintained for 15 minutes after cooling ceases (Gluckman et al. 1984). It would be especially valuable to assess the hyperthermic effects of prenatal cocaine on fetal breathing movements.

In examining the influence of temperature on respiration, temperature effects may be exerted differentially on upper airway musculature over the diaphragm and thoracoabdominal musculature; some of these effects may be particularly exerted on expiratory rather than inspiratory aspects of the respiratory cycle. For example, Johnson (1988) demonstrated the necessity for laryngeal constrictors to maintain thoracic volume in young lambs, a mechanism familiar to every neonatologist who has listened to newborn "grunting," a mechanism used frequently to "rest" the diaphragm under conditions of excessive load. The laryngeal constrictors are under separate control from the phrenic motoneurons controlling the diaphragm, and control of these output neurons to the larynx is mediated by separate central neural pathways, including the periaqueductal gray projections to laryngeal motoneurons (Holstege 1989). These descending projections may use very different neurotransmitters than neural mechanisms mediating cyclic diaphragmatic action. Such neural transmitters may be affected differentially by drugs of exposure during fetal development.

SENSORY INTEGRATION

A major concern in examining the function of any complex integrative system such as that involved in respiratory patterning or cardiovascular control is the integrity of afferent systems. These systems determine the sensory properties of chemical, chest wall expansion, irritant, and airflow stimulation (in the case of respiration) and baroreceptor, temperature, and chemical stimulation, among other sensory sources, for the cardiovascular system. Thus, if prenatal drug exposure alters thresholds in afferent systems that sense CO_2 or hypoxia, respiratory pattern control systems dependent on such chemical senses obviously would be affected. Similarly, respiratory timing is heavily determined by afferent activity from lung and chest wall stretch receptors to switch respiratory phases; similarly, alterations in this sensory system would greatly affect respiratory patterning.

Although prenatal drug exposure may alter these sensory systems, little information is available on prenatal drug exposure effects on these sensory processing systems; however, the available clinical data suggest that prenatal drug exposure can cause substantial damage to primary visual and auditory sensory systems. Prenatal cocaine exposure alters visual evoked potentials (Dixon et al. 1987), is associated with dilated vessels in the iris (as described earlier), and has been implicated in subsequent microphthalmia, persistent hyperplastic primary vitreous, and retinopathy of prematurity (Teske and Trese 1987). Infants with a diagnosis of fetal alcohol syndrome have a greater probability of exhibiting a variety of visual system abnormalities (Stromland 1985). Similarly, the auditory sensory system can be damaged severely with early alcohol or cocaine exposure, with altered auditory evoked potentials in infants and animals, and a variety of structural signs in animals, including cochlear damage (Church 1987; Church and Overbeck 1989). These alterations in specific sensory systems of vision and audition suggest that other sensory systems directly related to cardiac and respiratory patterning might be affected as well. Dopamine receptors in the carotid body likely would be affected by prenatal cocaine exposure, for example, and the excessive levels of catecholamines found in drug-exposed infants might well interact with these sensors. Although the information on drug effects on such sensory systems is meager, a chemical sensory process closely allied to the afferent system used to assess CO_2, namely the olfactory system, appears to be altered in behavioral tasks in rat pups exposed to cocaine (Spear et al. 1989). This may be an integrative task deficit rather than a specific sensory deficit; cocaine preferentially concentrates in olfactory mucosa of fetal mice (Brittebo 1988). The olfactory system shares many neuroanatomical projections with the respiratory chemosensory system and may provide an important source of "drive" to respiration by sensing nasal airflow; disturbance to the olfactory system not only might directly alter respiratory patterning but also suggests that the chemosensory system may be similarly damaged by prenatal drug exposure.

EEG

The first few months of life in normal full-term infants are accompanied by characteristic electroencephalogram (EEG) changes as measured by spectral procedures or by raw traces (Schulte and Bell 1973; Parmelee 1974; Sterman et al. 1977). Preterm infants exhibit EEG traces markedly different from those of full-term infants; in particular, the traces of preterm infants exhibit significantly lower amplitude spectral values at different bands and lower amplitude photic-evoked responses than those of full-term infants (Duffy et al. 1990). The premature infant quiet sleep EEG pattern (until 40 weeks conceptional age) typically consists of a "burst and flat" pattern (tracé alternant); at 3 to 8 months, the most prominent pattern is slow waves with 11-14 Hz spindles (Parmelee 1974). In REM sleep, the premature infant EEG consists of occasional slow waves occurring in conjunction with low-amplitude faster activity; after 40 weeks conceptional age, 4-6 Hz activity appears. The characteristics of any one state merge with those of other states in the very young infant.

199

There are limited data available on modification of infant EEG characteristics by early drug exposure. Any assessment of such data must be interpreted in the context of sleep states and must recognize the frequent arousals or transitions from different states observed in these infants. Acceleration in development of particular EEG spectral bands has been noted in infants at risk for SIDS (Sterman et al. 1982). Development of "coupling" or interpendencies between bilaterally recorded EEG signals may be of assistance in quantifying EEG development postnatally.

Assessment of EEG should be constrained by a realization of what the underlying signals represent, the differential distribution of EEG signals on the skull, the multiplicity of influences on cortical EEG, and the relatively scant knowledge of effects of neurotransmitter depletion/excess on such activities. Multiple "arousal" systems may activate the EEG, operating through the classic thalamic systems (Steriade et al. 1982) and through ascending ventral systems rising through the basal forebrain, which can elicit arousal even in the absence of the thalamus (Vanderwolf and Stewart 1988). "Arousal" here is defined as a desynchronization of the EEG, or a reduction in slow waves. Considerable evidence exists that EEG "arousal" can be dissociated from behavioral arousal; high-amplitude slow waves can occur in an atropinized animal, for example, although the animal can be extremely alert (Wikler 1952). It also now appears that at least two major neurotransmitters, a cholinergic system and a serotonergic system, may underlie these EEG arousal systems (Vanderwolf and Baker 1986). The serotonergic system may be of particular interest in this context because of the role this neurotransmitter plays in modulating temperature and motor activity as well as the possibility for interaction with other agents to cause structural deficits in prenatal life (Lauder, this volume). Prenatal drug effects on the serotonergic system thus may have profound indirect effects on respiratory control, particularly within the context of state.

SUMMARY

Of primary importance in the consideration of animal models of prenatal drug exposure is the recognition of interdependence among physiologic systems, the pervading influence of sleep and waking states, and the potential interaction between drug-induced structural changes and physiologic function. It is difficult for a drug effect on the cardiovascular system not to modify respiratory pattern; any change in blood pressure, systemic perfusion, or heart rate is immediately reflected in breathing; respiratory pattern, in turn, through negative thoracic pressure and other sensory activity, can alter cardiac patterning. The respiratory system itself is one component of a somatic motor system, and neural motor control structures undergo substantial modification by drug action.

Enhancing or diminishing any aspect of interaction is the influence of sleep states, which nonlinearly can alter relationships between physiologic systems, occasionally dissociating systems, as in the case of temperature effects on breathing during REM sleep. Finally, drug-induced structural changes that alter morphology of the upper airway can result in obstructive respiratory events, leading to pronounced cardiovascular sequelae.

REFERENCES

Baker, T.L., and McGinty, D.J. Sleep apnea in hypoxic and normal kittens. *Dev Psychobiol* 12:577-594, 1979.

Brittebo, E.B. Binding of cocaine in the liver, olfactory mucosa, eye, and fur of pigmented mice. *Toxicol Applied Pharmacol* 96:315-323, 1988.

Chasnoff, I.J.; Burns, K.A.; and Burns, W.J. Cocaine use in pregnancy: Perinatal morbidity and mortality. *Neurotoxicol Teratol* 9:291-293, 1987.

Chasnoff, I.J.; Bussey, M.E.; Bussey, C.A.; Stack, C.A.; and Savitch, R. Maternal cocaine use and perinatal cerebral infarction. *J Pediatr* 108:456-459, 1986.

Chasnoff, I.J.; Hunt, C.E.; Kletter, R.; and Kaplan, D. Prenatal cocaine exposure is associated with respiratory pattern abnormalities. *Am J Dis Child* 143:583-587, 1989.

Church, M.W. Chronic in utero alcohol exposure affects auditory function in rats and in humans. *Alcohol* 4:231-239, 1987.

Church, M.W., and Gerkin, K.P. Hearing disorders in children with fetal alcohol syndrome: Findings from case reports. *Pediatrics* 82:147-154, 1988.

Church, M.W., and Overbeck, G.W. Prenatal cocaine exposure: Sensorineural hearing loss as evidenced by the brainstem auditory evoked potential. *Soc Neurosci Abstr* 15:253, 1989.

Dinges, D.F.; Davis, M.M.; and Glass, P. Fetal exposure to narcotics: Neonatal sleep as a measure of nervous system distrubance. *Science* 209:619-621, 1980.

Dixon, S.D., and Bejar, R. Echoencephalographic findings in neonates associated with maternal cocaine and methamphetamine use: Incidence and clinical correlates. *J Pediatr* 115:770-778, 1989.

Dixon, S.D.; Coen, R.W.; and Crutchfield, S. Visual dysfunction in cocaine-exposed infants. *Pediatr Res* 21:359A, 1987.

Dow-Edwards, D.L. Long-term neurochemical and neurobehavioral consequences of cocaine use during pregnancy. *Ann N Y Acad Sci* 562:280-289, 1989.

Duffy, F.H.; Als, H.; and McAnulty, G.B. Behavioral and electrophysiological evidence for gestational age effects in healthy preterm and fullterm infants studied two weeks after expected due date. *Child Dev* 61:1271-1286, 1990.

Gluckman, P.D.; Gunn, T.R.; Johnston, B.M.; and Quinn, J.P. Manipulation of the temperature of the fetal lamb in utero. In: Nathanielsz, P.W., ed. *Animal Models in Fetal Medicine.* Vol. III. Ithaca, NY: Perinatology Press, 1984. pp. 38-56.

Gordon, C.J. Thermal biology of the laboratory rat. *Physiol Behav* 47:963-991, 1990.

Harper, R.M. Cardiovascular development in normal infants and infants at risk. In: Jones, C.T., and Nathanielsz, P.W., eds. *The Physiological Development of the Fetus and Newborn.* New York: Academic Press, 1985. pp. 571-580.

Harper, R.M. OSA mechanisms. *Calif Dental Assoc J* 16(10):35-39, 1988.

Harper, R.M.; Frostig, Z.; and Taube, D. Infant sleep development. In: Mayes, A., ed. *Sleep Functions and Mechanisms: An Evolutionary Perspective.* New York: Van Nostrand Reinhold, 1983a. pp. 107-125.

Harper, R.M.; Frostig, Z.; Taube, D.; Hoppenbrouwers, T.; and Hodgman, J.E. Development of sleep-waking temporal sequencing in infants at risk for the sudden infant death syndrome. *Exp Neurol* 79:821-829, 1983b.

Harper, R.K.; Frysinger, R.C.; Terreberry, R.R.; Garfinkel, A.; Richard, C.A.; and Harper, R.M. Nonlinear dynamic analysis of cardiac R-R interval variation following cocaine administration. *Soc Neurosci Abstr* 15:335, 1989.

Harper, R.M.; Harper, R.K.; Terreberry, R.R.; Richard, C.A.; and Trelease, R.B. The effect of acute cocaine administration on cardiac and respiratory patterning in the freely moving cat. In: Thadani, P.V., ed. *Cardiovascular Toxicity of Cocaine: Underlying Mechanisms.* National Institute on Drug Abuse Research Monograph 108. Washington, DC: Supt. of Docs., U.S. Govt. Print. Off., in press.

Harper, R.M.; Hoppenbrouwers, T.; Sterman, M.B.; McGinty, D.J.; and Hodgman, J. Polygraphic studies of normal infants during the first six months of life: I. Heart rate and variability as a function of state. *Pediatr Res* 10:945-951, 1976.

Harper, R.M.; Leake, B.; Hodgman, J.E.: and Hoppenbrouwers, T. Developmental patterns of heart rate and heart rate variability during sleep and waking in normal infants and infants at risk for the sudden infant death syndrome. *Sleep* 5:28-38, 1982.

Harper, R.M.; Leake, B.; Hoffman, H.; Walter, D.O.; Hoppenbrouwers, T.; Hodgman, J.; and Sterman, M.B. Periodicity of sleep states is altered in infants at risk for the sudden infant death syndrome. *Science* 213:1030-1032, 1981b.

Harper, R.M.; Leake, B.; Miyahara, L.; Mason, J.; Hoppenbrouwers, T.; Sterman, M.B.; and Hodgman, J. Temporal sequencing in sleep and waking states during the first 6 months of life. *Exp Neurol* 72:294-307, 1981a.

Harper, R.M., and Sauerland, E.K. The role of the tongue in sleep apnea. In: Guilleminault, C., and Dement, W.C., eds. *Sleep Apnea Syndromes.* New York: Alan R. Liss, 1978. pp. 219-234.

202

Harper, R.M.; Terrebery, R.R.; Richard, C.A.; and Harker, R.K. Upper airway and diaphragmatic muscle activity following acute cocaine administration. *Pharmcol Biochem Behav* 39:137-142, 1991.

Hendricks, J.C.; Kline, L.R.; Kovalski, R.J.; O'Brien, J.A.; Morrison, A.R.; and Pack, A.I. The English bulldog: A natural model of sleep-disordered breathing. *J Appl Physiol* 63:1344-1350, 1987.

Holstege, G. Anatomical study of the final common pathway for vocalization in the cat. *J Comp Neurol* 284:242-252, 1989.

Hoppenbrouwers, T.; Hodgman, J.E.; McGinty, D.; Harper, R.M.; and Sterman, M.B. Sudden infant death syndrome: Sleep apnea and respiration in subsequent siblings. *Pediatrics* 66:205-214, 1980.

Isenberg, S.J.; Spierer, A.; and Inkelis, S.H. Ocular signs of cocaine intoxication in neonates. *Am J Ophthalmol* 103:211-214, 1987.

Johnson, P. Environmental temperature and the development of breathing. In: Harper, R.M., and Hoffman, H.J., eds. *Sudden Infant Death Syndrome: Risk Factors and Basic Mechanisms.* New York: PMA Publishing, 1988. pp. 233-248.

Lomax, P., and Daniel, K.A. Cocaine and body temperature in the rat: Effects of ambient temperature. *Pharmacology* 40:103-109, 1990.

Lowenstein, E. Cardiovascular response to large doses of intravenous morphine in man. *N Engl J Med* 281:1389-1393, 1969.

McAllister, K.; Goeders, N.; and Dworkin, S. Chronic cocaine modifies brain benzodiazepine receptor densities. In: Harris, L.S., ed. *Problems of Drug Dependence, 1987: Proceedings of the 49th Annual Scientific Meeting, The Committee on Problems of Drug Dependence.* National Institute on Drug Abuse Research Monograph 81. DHHS Pub. No. (ADM)88-1564. Washington, DC: Supt. of Docs., U.S. Govt. Print. Off., 1988. pp. 101-108.

Monod, N.; Eliet-Flescher, J.; and Dreyfus-Brisac, C. Le sommeil du nouveau-né et du prématuré. III. Les troubles de l'organisation du sommeil chez le nouveau-né pathologique: Analyse des études polygraphiques. *Biol Neonat* 11:216-247, 1967.

Monod, N., and Pajot, N. Le sommeil du nouveau-né et du prématuré. I. Analyse des études polygraphiques. *Biol Neonat* 8:281-307, 1965.

Moore, T.R.; Sorg, J.; Miller, L.; Key, T.C.; and Resnik, R. Hemodynamic effects of intravenous cocaine on the pregnant ewe and fetus. *Am J Obstet Gynecol* 155:883-888, 1986.

Oro, A.S., and Dixon, S.D. Perinatal cocaine and methamphetamine exposure: Maternal and neonatal correlates. *J Pediatr* 111:571-578, 1987.

Parmeggiani, P.L. Temperature regulation during sleep: A study in homeostasis. In: Orem, J., and Barnes, C.D., eds. *Physiology in Sleep.* New York: Academic Press, 1980. pp. 97-143.

Parmelee, A.H., Jr. Ontogeny of sleep patterns and associated periodicities in infants. *Mod Probl Paediatr* 13:298-311, 1974.

Raetz, S.L.; Richard, C.A.; Garfinkel, A.; and Harper, R.M. Dynamic characteristics of cardiac R-R intervals during sleep and waking states. *Sleep*, in press.

Ryan, L.; Ehrlich, S.; and Finnegan, L. Cocaine abuse in pregnancy: Effects on the fetus and newborn. *Neurotoxicol Teratol* 9:295-299, 1987.

Schechtman, V.L.; Harper, R.M.; Kluge, K.A.; Wilson, A.J.; Hoffman, H.J.; and Southall, D.P. Cardiac and respiratory patterns in normal infants and victims of the sudden infant death syndrome. *Sleep* 11:413-424, 1988.

Schechtman, V.L.; Harper, R.M.; Wilson, A.J.; and Southall, D.P. Sleep apnea in infants who succumb to the sudden infant death syndrome. *Pediatrics* 87(6):841-846, 1991.

Schulte, F.J., and Bell, E.F. Bioelectric brain development: An atlas of EEG power spectra in infants and young children. *Neuropediatrics* 4:3-45, 1973.

See, R.E., and Ellison, G. Intermittent and continuous haloperidol regimens produce different types of oral dyskinesias in rats. *Psychopharmacology* 100:404-412, 1990.

Spear, L.P.; Kirstein, C.L.; and Frambes, N.A. Cocaine effects on the developing central nervous system: Behavioral, psychopharmacological, and neurochemical studies. *Ann N Y Acad Sci* 562:290-307, 1989.

Stanton, A.N. Overheating and cot death. *Lancet* 2(8413):1199-1201, 1984.

Stefanini, M.C.; Torrioli, M.G.; Mariotti, P.; Pitolli, M.V.; Salvaggio, E.; and Tempesta, E. The modifications of sleep in babies born from opiate addicted mothers. *Sleep Res* 13:69, 1984.

Steriade, M.; Oakson, G.; and Ropert, N. Firing rates and patterns of midbrain reticular neurons during steady and transitional states of the sleep-waking cycle. *Exp Brain Res* 46:37-51, 1982.

Sterman, M.B.; Harper, R.M.; Havens, B.; Hoppenbrouwers, T.; McGinty, D.J.; and Hodgman, J.E. Quantitative analysis of infant EEG development during quiet sleep. *Electroencephalogr Clin Neurophysiol* 43:371-385, 1977.

Sterman, M.B.; McGinty, D.J.; Harper, R.M.; Hoppenbrouwers, T.; and Hodgman, J.E. Developmental comparison of sleep EEG power spectral patterns in infants at low and high risk for sudden death. *Electroencephalogr Clin Neurophysiol* 53:166-181, 1982.

Stromland, K. Ocular abnormalities in the fetal alcohol syndrome. *Acta Ophthalmol* 63[Suppl 171]:1-50, 1985.

Telsey, A.M.; Merrit, T.A.; and Dixon, S.D. Cocaine exposure in a term neonate: Necrotizing enterocolitis as a complication. *Clin Pediatr* 27:547-550, 1988.

Teske, M.P., and Trese, M.T. Retinopathy of prematurity-like fundus and persistent hyperplastic primary vitreous associated with maternal cocaine use. *Am J Ophthalmol* 103:719-720, 1987.

Trelease, R.B.; Harper, R.M.; Arand, D.L.; and Zimmermann, E.G. Use of heart rate analysis for differentiation of sleep disorders. *Proc 8th Annu Conf IEEE Eng Med Biol Soc* 2:1203-1206, 1986.

Trelease, R.B.; Sieck, G.C.; Marks, J.D.; and Harper, R.M. Respiratory inhibition induced by transient hypertension during sleep in unrestrained cats. *Exp Neurol* 90:173-186, 1985.

Vanderwolf, C.H., and Baker, G.B. Evidence that serotonin mediates non-cholinergic neocortical low voltage fast activity, non-cholinergic hippocampal rhythmical slow activity and contributes to intelligent behavior. *Brain Res* 374:342-356, 1986.

Vanderwolf, C.H., and Stewart, D.J. Thalamic control of neocortical activation: A critical re-evaluation. *Brain Res Bull* 20:529-538, 1988.

Ward, S.L.D.; Bautista, D.B.; Buckley, S.; Schuetz, S.; Wachsman, L.; Bean, X.; and Warburton, D. Circulating catecholamines and adrenoreceptors in infants of cocaine-abusing mothers. *Ann N Y Acad Sci* 562:349-351, 1989b.

Ward, S.L.D.; Bautista, D.B.; Schuetz, S.; Wachsman, L.; Bean, X.; and Keens, T.G. Abnormal hypoxic arousal responses in infants of cocaine-abusing mothers. *Ann N Y Acad Sci* 562:347-348, 1989a.

Wikler, A. Pharmacologic dissociation of behaviour and EEG "sleep patterns" in dogs: Morphine, N-allylnormorphine and atropine. *Proc Soc Exp Biol Med* 79:261-265, 1952.

Woo, M.S.; Chang, M.Y.; Bautista, D.B.; Keens, T.G.; and Ward, S.L.D. Elevated heart rates in infants of cocaine abusing mothers during normoxia and hypoxia. *Am Rev Respir Dis* 141:908a, 1990.

Woods, J.R.; Plessinger, M.A.; Scott, K.; and Miller, R.K. Prenatal cocaine exposure to the fetus: A sheep model for cardiovascular evaluation. *Ann N Y Acad Sci* 562:267-279, 1989.

Zuckerman, B.; Frank, D.A.; Hingson, R.; Amaro, H.; Levenson, S.M.; Kayne, H.; Parker, S.; Vinci, R.; Aboagye, K.; Fried, L.E.; Cabral, H.; Timperi, R.; and Bauchner, H. Effects of maternal marijuana and cocaine use on fetal growth. *N Engl J Med* 320:762-768, 1989.

ACKNOWLEDGMENT

This research was supported by National Institute on Drug Abuse grant DA-04913.

AUTHOR

Ronald M. Harper, Ph.D.
Professor
Department of Anatomy and Cell Biology
University of California at Los Angeles
Los Angeles, CA 90024-1763

Endocrine Function as a Target of Perinatal Drug Effects: Methodologic Issues

Cynthia Kuhn, Diane Ignar, and Rolf Windh

INTRODUCTION

Gestational exposure to many drugs of abuse, including ethanol, marijuana, cocaine, and heroin, causes a general impairment of somatic growth and physical development in addition to many agent-specific effects on particular developmental events (Hollister 1986; Zagon and McLaughlin 1984; Rosett and Weiner 1984). The physiologic mechanisms mediating this growth suppression are not well understood and probably involve many factors, including placental insufficiency, inadequate nutrition, and direct impairment of protein or nucleic acid synthesis. Because both maternal and fetal endocrine function are known to contribute substantially to regulation of growth, there is a growing appreciation of the possible role that drug-induced changes in endocrine function might play in somatic growth and development. Endocrine factors play an additional and perhaps more important role after birth, when growth regulation becomes independent of maternal factors and is governed entirely by metabolic and endocrine functions within the offspring. Therefore, evaluation of drug effects on maternal, fetal, and neonatal endocrine function may prove important in understanding the physiologic consequences of drug exposure during development. Furthermore, endocrine function provides a model system for studying the impact of drugs on specific central nervous system (CNS) systems.

Unfortunately, the few studies of endocrine function in human infants exposed to drugs *in utero* have used diverse and often inappropriate methodologies for evaluating endocrine function. However, several laboratories working in animal models have demonstrated convincingly that, when function is evaluated appropriately, marked perturbations of development can be detected. The purposes of this chapter are to (1) briefly describe endocrine functions in the parent or offspring that play a role in regulation of growth and development, (2) summarize current information available about drug effects on these systems,

(3) discuss the use of animal models of endocrine function to elucidate drug effects, and (4) discuss methodologic issues in appropriate evaluation of drug effects on endocrine function.

ENDOCRINE FACTORS IN DEVELOPMENT

In the developing fetus, endocrine function is both a modulator of growth and a rapidly developing organ system that represents a target of drug action. Endocrine regulation of fetal and postnatal growth and development differ dramatically from each other. In the developing fetus, fetal, placental, and maternal factors all integrate to modulate growth and development. Most fetal endocrine systems are functional in many mammals by midgestation, and fetal hormone secretion is critical to normal growth and development. The fetal thyroid is vital for growth (Fisher et al. 1977), and the fetal gonad plays a well-described, vital role in sexual differentiation of both the gonad and the brain (Gorski 1984; Winter et al. 1981). Finally, the activity of the fetal adrenal cortex is vital for physiologic homeostasis, normal differentiation of metabolic enzymes, and pulmonary surfactant production. In addition, fetal secretion of insulin is thought to regulate growth (Casey et al. 1985). Therefore, fetal endocrine function plays an important role in specific developmental events. Although placental transfer of physiologically active glucocorticoid, thyroid hormone, or growth hormone is minimal (Nathienelsz 1976), fetal endocrine function can be affected indirectly through perturbations of maternal metabolic state (e.g., hyperglycemia evoking insulin secretion in the fetus). Placental factors also play a role in growth regulation. Placental lactogen assumes the role of growth hormone in the fetus during gestation, when pituitary growth hormone plays little role in growth regulation.

Postnatally, neonate hormone secretion becomes almost completely autonomous, although maternal hormones in milk may play a modulatory role in endocrine function in the offspring. Thyroid and adrenocortical function continue to be critical to normal growth and development. In addition, pituitary secretion of growth hormone becomes a major regulator of somatic growth. Finally, sexual differentiation continues postnatally and remains critically dependent upon appropriate hypothalamic regulation of luteinizing hormone (LH) and follicle-stimulating hormone (FSH) secretion (McEwen 1987).

MECHANISM OF DRUG ACTION IN THE FETUS

The endocrine functions described above are potential targets of drug action. The mechanisms through which drugs might act are shown in figure 1. Most drugs of abuse act primarily within the CNS on the afferent input to the releasing factor neurons in the hypothalamus. However, additional direct

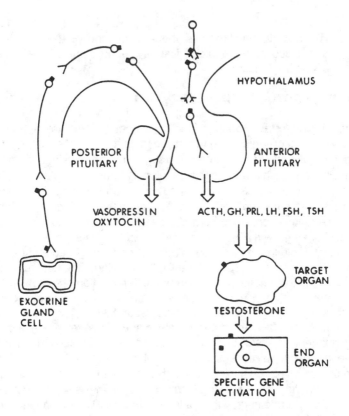

FIGURE 1. *Schematic indicating potential sites of psychoactive drug action on endocrine function*

actions on peripheral neurons and/or the target glands themselves have been described. In the developing animal, the various elements of this axis are being assembled, and there are additional potential sites of drug action, as shown in figure 2. Drugs can inhibit protein synthesis, specific gene expression, or some aspect of initial embryogenesis. For example, oral contraceptives can influence the developing gonad, and alcohol influences protein synthesis in general. Drugs also can act through inhibition of fetal endocrine functions. For example, some antithyroid drugs cross the placenta, inhibit thyroid hormone production in the fetus, and produce fetal hypothyroidism (Cooper 1984). Similarly, opioids and ethanol can directly inhibit testosterone production from the developing testes in some situations (Singh et al. 1980; Anderson et al. 1987, 1989). Also, agents that act through specific neurotransmitter systems can influence hormone production through actions on the hypothalamus. This probably represents a major site of opiate, cocaine, tetrahydrocannabinol (THC), and

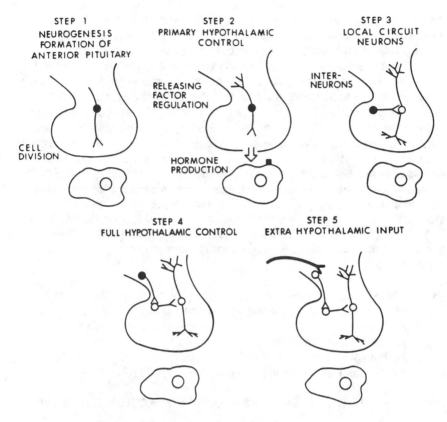

STEP 1
NEUROGENESIS
FORMATION OF
ANTERIOR PITUITARY

STEP 2
PRIMARY HYPOTHALAMIC
CONTROL

STEP 3
LOCAL CIRCUIT
NEURONS

RELEASING
FACTOR
REGULATION

INTER-
NEURONS

CELL
DIVISION

HORMONE
PRODUCTION

STEP 4
FULL HYPOTHALAMIC CONTROL

STEP 5
EXTRA HYPOTHALAMIC INPUT

FIGURE 2. *Schematic indicating potential sites of psychoactive drug action on endocrine function during development*

ethanol action. Finally, the potential interruption of hormone action at the receptor or postreceptor level represents an unexplored area.

ENDOCRINE CONSEQUENCES OF DRUGS OF ABUSE IN ADULTS

The major rationale for concern about potential drug effects on endocrine function is the broad literature demonstrating effects of almost all drugs of abuse on endocrine systems in adults. These are summarized briefly below. Opiates stimulate receptors for endogenous opioids, which play a role in regulation of every major endocrine system. Acute opiate administration affects LH, FSH, prolactin (PRL), growth hormone (GH), adrenocorticotrophic hormone (ACTH), vasopressin, oxytocin, and insulin. These effects are robust enough that chronic opiate exposure suppresses thyroid and gonadal function and alters glucose homeostasis in adults (Kuhn and Windh 1991). Marijuana, through actions on hypothalamic neurotransmitter systems, decreases LH secretion, and suppresses ovulation during chronic administration in the female and in males decreases testosterone synthesis and sperm production (Tyrey 1984; Smith and Asch 1987). Ethanol has direct effects on the testes in humans and animals that impair testosterone production and cause abnormal sperm production (Smith and Asch 1987; Gavaler and Van Thiel 1987). In addition, ethanol inhibits vasopressin secretion and has been reported to elicit changes in GH, PRL, and possibly adrenocortical function (Anderson 1981; Anderson et al. 1989). While there is little information available yet about neuroendocrine effects of cocaine in humans, preliminary studies in rodents and nonhuman primates suggest that cocaine, through actions on central monoamine systems, influences LH, PRL, and ACTH secretion (Borowsky and Kuhn 1991a; Mendelson et al. 1989; Moldow and Fischman 1987). These effects in rodents are robust enough to disrupt estrous cyclicity during chronic administration.

Most of these endocrine effects occur through actions on specific receptor mechanisms at anatomically defined sites within the hypothalamus. Opioid inhibition of LH secretion in females provides a well-described example (Kalra and Kalra 1984). Opiates inhibit LH secretion through actions on opiate receptors that impair transmission in the afferent noradrenergic control that is stimulatory to luteinizing hormone releasing hormone (LH-RH) secretion.

DRUG EFFECTS ON OFFSPRING ENDOCRINE FUNCTION IN HUMANS

Despite the overwhelming evidence that many drugs of abuse have marked effects on endocrine function, the literature on endocrine function in offspring of drug-using women is sparse. A series of studies in offspring of opiate-addicted women revealed only a transient elevation of thyroxine, renin, and sympathetic nervous system activity, with normal levels of other major hormones (Jhaveri et al. 1980; Rosenfeld et al. 1981; Dube et al. 1981; Glass 1982). There are no extant studies published on endocrine function in offspring of THC- or cocaine-exposed infants. However, pubertal arrest has been reported in older children chronically exposed to THC (Copeland et al. 1980).

Studies in humans are highly compromised by methodologic problems, including poor maternal nutrition that could directly influence hormone secretion, polydrug use; maternal illness, including human immunodeficiency virus (HIV) infection in intravenous drug users; and the difficulty of long-term followup in the patient population. However, there are three issues of experimental design that are more important reasons that endocrine effects have not been detected in offspring of drug-using women: (1) the timing of the assessment relative to cessation of drug exposure (usually at birth) or the ontogeny of the endocrine system under investigation, (2) the index used for evaluation, and (3) the failure of most studies to focus on the most likely targets (e.g., opiate receptors after perinatal opiates, catecholamine mechanisms after cocaine).

Most of the few extant studies of drug effects on offspring endocrine function employed single assessments of hormone concentration in the circulation at an arbitrary time point, usually during the first postnatal weeks. There are many serious limitations to the use of single assessments. First, infants during this period of time are experiencing drug abstinence, which is often accompanied by a marked endocrine response that can bear little resemblance to the initial action of the drug (Eisenberg and Sparber 1978; Kuhn and Bartolome 1985). The second and major issue relates to the timing of such assessments relative to the endocrine function under consideration. One example of the importance of sampling time is shown in figure 3, which summarizes work on the ontogeny of growth hormone secretion in the rat. Obviously, a single sample taken near birth might not detect significant changes in the ontogenetic pattern of secretion, particularly if changes were mediated by effects on systems that matured later. Therefore, a single sampling minimizes the chance of detecting physiologically significant changes. Third, because most evaluations must be conducted postnatally, changes that occurred in the fetus before drug was withdrawn can be drastically underestimated. For example, chronic exposure to opiates *in utero* could produce a prolonged suppression of thyroxine or testosterone production, which would never be detected. Finally, many studies neglect the most likely target of drug action: the neural mechanisms that mediate the actions of the drugs to which the fetus was exposed. Assessing the effects of some drugs, such as ethanol and THC, is difficult, because specific mechanisms are not well understood. However, many physiologic and pharmacologic tools are available to assess the effects of other drugs. For example, figure 4 contrasts the corticosterone response of morphine-tolerant rats to a test dose of morphine and to the classic "stressor," ether. While opiate-dependent mechanisms are markedly unresponsive, other aspects of adrenocortical regulation are quite normal. Therefore, single arbitrary measures might not detect substantial physiologic changes.

USE OF ANIMAL MODELS TO ASSESS ENDOCRINE FUNCTION

Given the difficulties cited above, it is likely that effects of drugs of abuse on endocrine maturation are markedly underestimated by the typical assessments conducted in humans. Animal models offer the obvious benefits of experimental control of drug dose, duration and timing of exposure, as well as

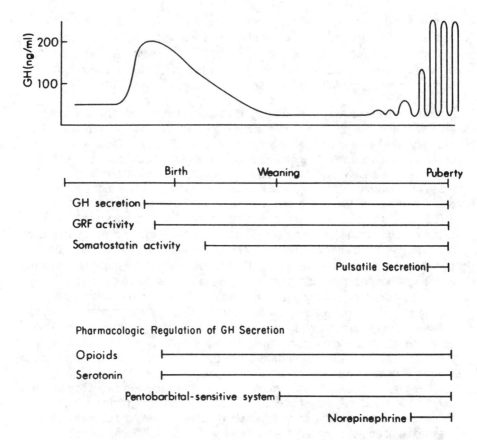

FIGURE 3. *Schematic showing the ontogeny of growth hormone secretion in the rat*

SOURCES: Blazquez et al. 1974; Khorram et al. 1983; Kuhn and Schanberg 1981; Rieutort and Jost 1976; Rieutort 1981; Walker et al. 1977

the option to conduct more invasive studies than in humans. Therefore, endocrine development can be studied across ontogeny and sampled at appropriate times, and more thorough methodologies can be used to evaluate function. In addition, most animal models mature more quickly than humans, so that ontogeny can be studied through puberty within a short period. However, an animal model also must fulfill two other criteria. First, the mechanism of drug action must be similar in the animal model and in the human. For most of

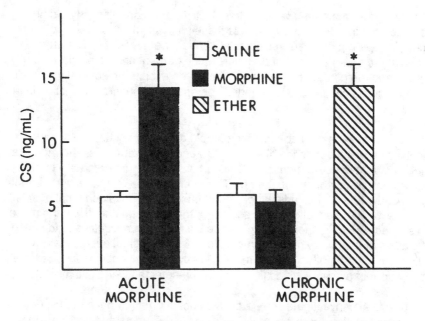

FIGURE 4. *Serum corticosterone levels in neonatal rats treated chronically with saline or morphine (increasing doses from 20 mg/kg, increasing 5 mg/kg/day starting on day 2 for 5 days to 40 mg/kg bid) and treated acutely with morphine (10 mg/kg) or exposed to ether for 30 seconds 45 minutes before blood collection (n=8-10/ group)*

*Indicates p<.05 or better relative to saline-treated control

the drugs under consideration (stimulants, THC, opiates, and ethanol), the fundamental mechanisms of drug action are similar across most mammalian species. Second, the drug action on the specific endocrine system under study must be similar.

Fortunately, an appropriate experimental animal model exists for each of the major endocrine systems that are important in growth and differentiation. Rats, primates, and sheep all show major similarities to humans in the general maturation of gonads and hypothalamic control of gonadal function (Gluckman 1982; Nathienelsz 1976). Similarly, prolactin secretion, particularly the important dopaminergic control, is similar in humans, primates, rodents, and sheep (Gluckman et al. 1980; Gluckman 1982; McMillian and Deayton 1989).

The basic hypothalamo-pituitary-adrenal (HPA) axis controlling thyroid hormone secretion again is fairly similar across these species, although specific neural controls have not been so well delineated (Fisher et al. 1977). Therefore, in terms of the pharmacology of drug action, the general neurobiologic sites of action, and the general scheme of endocrine development, several mammalian animal models can adequately model drug effects on endocrine function in the human.

The rodent provides the advantages of rapid development, low cost, and similarity in many endocrine systems. The only disadvantage of the rat is that a major amount of neuroendocrine development that occurs prenatally in the human occurs postnatally in the rat. This characteristic can be either a benefit or a disadvantage. The advantage is that the specific developmental events (e.g., sexual differentiation of LH secretion) that occur postnatally in the rat can be studied directly in the offspring. While this provides a significant advantage in studies of the mechanism of drug action, developmental events that are influenced by drug effects on maternal physiology (e.g., cocaine-induced impairment of placental blood flow) will not be detected using this model.

It is possible to investigate separately the impact on maternal and offspring endocrine function using the fetal sheep, as many events that occur postnatally in the rat occur prenatally in the sheep. The additional strength of this model is that both maternal and fetal circulations can be sampled, and *in vivo* physiologic studies can be conducted. The elegant work of Grumbach and colleagues has demonstrated the value of this model (Gluckman et al. 1980; Clark et al. 1989; Cuttler et al. 1985).

Finally, the primate obviously provides the closest model in terms of development. Many endocrine functions can be assessed carefully in the developing primate, which has proved particularly useful in studies of puberty (Ojeda et al. 1980; Resko and Ellinwood 1984). The disadvantages are clear: expense, slow development, and ethical issues involved in experimentation.

In summary, there are several excellent animal models for studying drug effects on endocrine development. Overall, the rodent has been used most widely and represents a valuable model with the one limitation discussed above. Other small mammals (mice, dogs, cats, rabbits, hamsters) have been studied much less extensively because assay techniques for pituitary hormones are more limited, and they have not been so widely exploited in the pharmacology literature.

METHODOLOGIC ISSUES IN EVALUATING ENDOCRINE FUNCTION IN DEVELOPING ANIMALS

Dose, Duration, and Timing

The first group of methodologic considerations are not unique to endocrine systems: the issues of dose, duration, and timing of drug exposure. Regarding dose, two approaches are generally used in animal studies. The first is to attempt to approximate human dose regimens. The disadvantage of this strategy is that such treatment paradigms will not detect deficits that occur at low frequency. This has been a particularly sensitive issue in the area of ethanol-induced deficits, in which deficits seem to be clearly dose-related. An alternative approach has been to give doses exceeding those commonly used in humans. The benefit of this strategy is that no potential adverse effects go undetected. The disadvantage is that physiologic compromise of the mother is maximal using such a strategy, and deficits might be described that never occur at typical dose levels. Nutritional compromise of the mother or offspring can be a major issue with high-dose regimens, which is particularly problematic for studying endocrine functions such as thyroid function that are sensitive to nutrition. Obviously, the optimal strategy is to conduct dose-response studies, modeling different levels of drug exposure. Unfortunately, this approach is expensive, time-consuming, and animal-intensive. A compromise strategy that has proved productive is to bracket high- and low-dose regimens with a restricted dose-response approach in combination with careful utilization of nutritional controls.

The second issue in evaluating endocrine effects of perinatal drug exposure is the timing of exposure. The expected effect of a drug obviously is determined by the physiologic process that it disrupts. Therefore, the timing must take into account the ontogeny of the system under study. For most endocrine systems, the first trimester is the time of rapid organogenesis and differentiation. During the end of the first and the beginning of the second trimester, many of the neurotransmitter systems through which these drugs act are developing, while during the end of gestation and the first postnatal weeks, the major events are active synaptogenesis, sexual differentiation, and overall growth. Therefore, drugs that inhibit testosterone production, for example, would be particularly effective during later phases of development, when testosterone production is critical. Similarly, cocaine should be most effective within the fetal brain *after* catecholamine synapses have formed. However, effects on placental blood flow would affect development throughout.

Sexual differentiation provides the best example of the impact of timing on endocrine consequences. For example, opioid control of LH secretion provides a useful example. Opioid inhibition of LH secretion can be demonstrated in female rats immediately after birth, while in males opioid inhibition cannot be demonstrated until near puberty (Cicero et al. 1986; Blank et al. 1979). Early studies of vaginal opening in females treated chronically with opiates did not report uniform, dramatic inhibition of sexual development (Blank et al. 1979; Litto et al. 1983; Sonderegger et al. 1979; Vathy et al. 1983; Zimmerman et al. 1974), an effect that seemed inconsistent with the early opioid inhibition that had been demonstrated. However, more careful examination demonstrated that opioid inhibition of LH secretion diminished markedly near puberty, an effect that is thought to contribute to the onset of cyclic LH secretion in many mammalian species, including humans (Bhanot and Wilkinson 1983). Early studies involved gestational and postnatal studies, during periods of time when endogenous opioid inhibition of LH secretion was already maximal. When opiate effects on reproductive function were studied in males, preceding the time of puberty, when endogenous opioid influences are minimal, a much more dramatic effect was observed. However, a marked inhibition of LH secretion, decreased secretion of testosterone, and impaired morphologic development of the gonads occurred when animals were treated during the sensitive period (Cicero et al. 1989).

The other major timing issue pertains to the development of tolerance. If drug treatments are conducted throughout development, without regard to possible critical periods, it is possible that tolerance to the primary endocrine action of the drug develops before the critical period is reached. The effects of THC on pubertal development provide a good example of this problem. In the adult, THC inhibits LH production (Tyrey 1984). Acute THC administration to the developing rat also has this action (Field and Tyrey 1986). Therefore, suppression of LH secretion should delay pubertal development in females, which is dependent on pulsatile secretion of LH. However, chronic THC administration through development does not achieve this goal, while limited chronic treatment during the peripubertal period does so (Field and Tyrey 1984, 1986; Wenger et al. 1988) because tolerance develops to the ability of THC to inhibit LH production in neonates (Field and Tyrey 1986).

Phasic Nature of Hormone Secretion

The second major methodologic issue specific to evaluating endocrine function in development is the phasic nature of hormone secretion. This basic characteristic determines the nature of assessments that must be conducted. For example, in the human, basal growth hormone secretion is very low and a poor indicator of pituitary secretory capacity. Most endocrinologists instead measure the growth hormone response to a pharmacologic challenge. Furthermore, diurnal rhythms in hormone secretion (cortisol, for example) are important considerations in timing.

216

Similarly, effects of drugs of abuse on neuroendocrine function can best be detected by evaluating evoked changes in hormone secretion. As described above, the HPA axis provides a representative example of this issue. First, HPA activation can be triggered by several stimuli that act through distinct neural mechanisms. Therefore, multiple mechanisms can be evaluated by comparing the response of various evocative stimuli. As shown in figure 5, stresses as well as neurotransmitters evoke marked secretion of corticosterone even in neonatal rats. Furthermore, using this strategy, the particular neural mechanism that is the target of drug action (opiate receptors, etc.), can be tested in comparison with independent mechanisms that might not be affected. Furthermore, drug-induced changes can be characterized even more thoroughly by evaluating the time course of the response.

The adaptations involved in tolerance and abstinence superimpose additional phasic endocrine responses. For example, following chronic administration of morphine, animals or humans show daily cycles of corticosterone secretion that are entrained to the daily dose. As seen in figure 6, rats show abstinence-induced elevations between doses. When drug is administered, a marked fall occurs, followed by a surge of drug-induced secretion. After the drug-induced

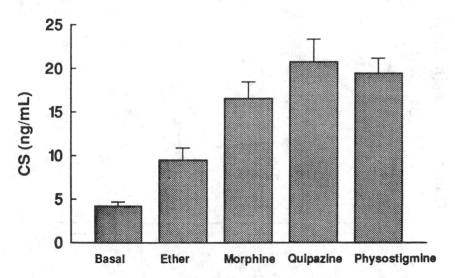

FIGURE 5. *Serum corticosterone levels in 10-day-old neonatal rats after administration of morphine (5 mg/kg), physostigmine (0.25 mg/ kg), quipazine (5 mg/kg), or exposure to ether (30 seconds) or immobilization (30 min) (n=8-10/group)*

surge diminishes, levels begin to rise again with abstinence. When drug is withdrawn for several days, basal levels are completely normal. If animals were sampled at a specific, single time point, widely different conclusions would be reached about the state of adrenocortical stimulation caused by morphine.

Furthermore, impose upon this cyclic change in hormone secretion during repeated injections the typical ontogenetic pattern of HPA axis function. As shown in figure 7, the capacity of the axis to respond to morphine is markedly suppressed during the first 2 weeks of life. However, morphine is still capable of eliciting changes in secretion, which if anything are more prolonged.

In summary, when developing animals are treated chronically with morphine, a single arbitrary blood sample could give very different pictures of HPA function, depending on when blood is sampled. As shown in figure 8, if animals are sampled at the end of a chronic regimen, corticosterone levels are enhanced during abstinence. If animals are sampled several days later, basal levels are normal. However, if animals are sampled after a challenge injection of

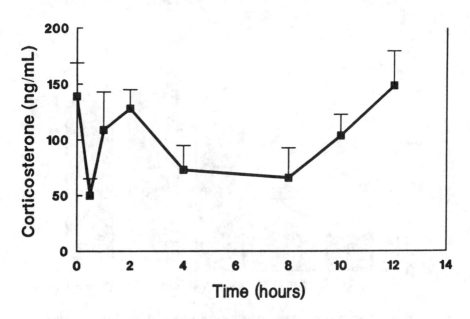

FIGURE 6.   *Serum corticosterone in opiate-tolerant adult rats at various times after the last injection on day 5 of an increasing dose morphine treatment regimen (see figure 4 legend)*

218

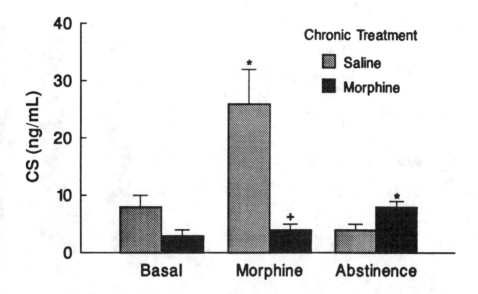

FIGURE 7. *Ontogeny of endocrine response to morphine (5 mg/kg). Rat pups were treated with saline or morphine (10 mg/kg) and killed 30 minutes later, and serum hormone levels determined by radioimmunoassay (n=8-10/group).*

morphine, markedly suppressed responses are observed, reflecting tolerance. Therefore, one could conclude levels were either (1) enhanced, (2) normal, or (3) suppressed. These findings demonstrate the importance of sampling basal levels, changes evoked by normal stimuli for this pathway, as well as changes evoked by the drug itself.

The vulnerability of endocrine function, like other CNS functions, is determined by the combination of the ontogeny of the system, the dose and timing of drug exposure, and the methods used to evaluate endocrine function. The extensive work of Cicero's laboratory on opiate actions on reproductive development provides a good demonstration of the interaction of all these factors (Cicero et al. 1975, 1976, 1977). A single injection of morphine suppresses LH and testosterone production, which become more exaggerated with chronic treatment until tolerance develops. However, there are marked developmental changes in the function of the axis in general and in its response to morphine. Analogous treatment regimens have no effect in the male immediately after birth but markedly inhibit testosterone later, after opioid regulation of LH secretion has been established. Furthermore, Cicero and colleagues (1989)

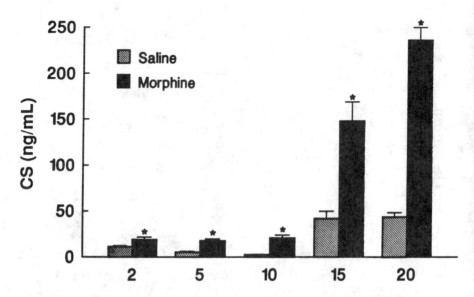

FIGURE 8. *Serum corticosterone levels in 10-day-old rats following a 5-day morphine treatment regimen (5 mg/kg bid increasing 5 mg/kg/day to 25 mg/kg bid). Abstinent pups were killed 12 hours after the last injection. Basal pups were killed 48 hours after the last injection following a single saline injection, and morphine pups were killed 48 hours after the last injection following a single treatment with morphine (20 mg/kg) (n=8-10/group).*

have shown that prepubertal male rats show a diminished ability to become tolerant to morphine effects on gonadal function. Therefore, the magnitude of evoked changes in hormone secretion is even greater in the developing animal than in the adult. These findings demonstrate that exposure to opiates in development might cause more severe outcome than in adult animals, because the developing receptor systems lack the capacity to downregulate their function as efficiently as the adult. Therefore, the opiate-addicted female can self-administer doses of opiates to which she is highly tolerant but to which her fetus will respond dramatically. Finally, like many developing systems, the impact of drug exposure during development on endocrine function can appear long after exposure has ended. Pubertal development is a prime example of the "delayed" effects of perinatal drug exposure. It is well known that exposure of the developing rat to steroid during the "critical period" around the time of birth can prevent the eventual development of cyclic LH secretion (McEwen 1987). Therefore, many drugs that influence gonadal steroid production during early development could have consequences not detected until much later. It has been reported that gestational exposure to THC has such effects (Kumar et al. 1986).

STRESS AND ENDOCRINE CHANGES IN DEVELOPMENT

The contribution of stress on either the dam or the offspring to endocrine function in development has probably been underestimated. Stress elicits marked changes in almost every endocrine function. Therefore, drug administration to either dam or offspring could cause endocrine changes that were secondary to the primary site of drug action and more related to the "stress" imposed by the drug. For example, it has been demonstrated clearly in several animal models that intense stress to pregnant dams alters adrenal gland function in the offspring (Cadet et al. 1986). Therefore, it is possible that the physiologic and/or psychologic stresses of the drug-using lifestyle, including malnutrition, periodic abstinence, and disturbed sleep, contribute significantly to the endocrine state of the pregnant woman. Such changes cannot be detected in endocrine studies conducted postnatally and must be considered in experimental design of animal models.

The "stress" of periodic drug abstinence is experienced by the offspring as well as the pregnant woman. It has been suggested that opiate abstinence at birth plays an important role in the neurobehavioral sequelae of perinatal opiate addiction (Lichtblau and Sparber 1984). Furthermore, even neonatal rats show abstinence-related endocrine responses (figure 8). The endocrine impact of THC, alcohol, or stimulant abstinence is unknown even in adults and is totally unexplored in developing animals.

The development of normal reproductive function is another endocrine function in which maternal stress has been reported to influence normal development (Herrenkohl 1986; Ward 1984). This function provides an example of how a drug might elicit a response indirectly. It has been shown in animal models that gestational stress influences neonate sexual differentiation and that this response appears mediated by activation of opioid systems in the dam or offspring.

Finally, drug effects on maternal behavior can have a major impact on hormone secretion in the offspring. Many aspects of neonate physiology are affected by maternal behavior. In rats inappropriate maternal behavior is capable of eliciting dramatic changes in growth hormone and corticosterone secretion (Pauk et al. 1986). Similar findings have been reported in monkeys denied appropriate maternal care (Coe et al. 1978). Therefore, maternal impairment associated with the drug-taking lifestyle can have an impact on offspring endocrine function through behavioral mechanisms.

MATERNAL ENDOCRINE FUNCTION AS A TARGET OF DRUG ACTION

The previous paragraph raises another important issue: the relative contribution of drug-induced changes in maternal vs. neonate physiology. Drug-induced changes in maternal endocrine function represent one possible mediator of such effects. There are several mechanisms by which this can happen.

This first is mediated by changes in the physiology of the pregnant animal. It has been shown recently that ethanol administration to pregnant rats elicits changes in the dam's adrenocortical function (Weinberg and Bezio 1987). These effects do not necessarily cease at birth, nor are they simplistically mediated by maternal hormones influencing offspring endocrine organs directly. For example, maternal hyperglycemia is transmitted to the developing fetus, which responds by hypersecreting insulin, as described previously. Both the elevated glucose and the insulin have been implicated in disrupted growth in the fetus. As most drugs that influence autonomic function have measurable effects on blood glucose (including cocaine, amphetamine, alcohol, and opiates), this is another maternal physiologic response that can mediate physiologic change in the offspring.

Finally, a growing literature has demonstrated that most maternal hormones are present in milk and cross into the offspring circulation intact. These hormones include PRL, thyroid-stimulating hormone (TSH), LH-RH, and gonadotropin-releasing hormone (Gn-RH) (Grosvenor and Whitworth 1983; Kacsoh et al. 1989; Koldovsky et al. 1989; Mosinger and Placer 1959; Werner et al. 1986). These maternally derived hormones play an important role in offspring endocrine regulation during the immediate postnatal period when many endocrine functions in the neonate are immature. For example, maternal PRL crosses into the offspring through the milk in amounts sufficient to produce direct PRL effects on developing dopamine neurons (Grosvenor and Whitworth 1983; Shyr et al. 1986). This finding is potentially important in consideration of drug effects on development, given the recent demonstration by Mendelsohn and colleagues (1989) and Borowsky and Kuhn (1991b) that cocaine inhibits PRL secretion in rodents and primates.

In summary, there are at least three described mechanisms by which changes in maternal endocrine status can influence fetal development: direct transfer of maternal hormone, indirect offspring responses to altered maternal physiology, and altered transfer of milk-borne hormones. As outlined in the beginning of this chapter, most drugs of abuse influence adult endocrine function. Therefore, these indirect offspring adaptations represent a likely target of drug action on maternal physiology.

ANIMAL STUDIES OF DRUG EFFECTS ON OFFSPRING ENDOCRINE FUNCTION

No one study can address all potential drug effects. Furthermore, many of the endocrine responses described above represent fairly subtle abnormalities that are dwarfed by the major neurologic and physiologic damage experienced by the offspring. Nevertheless, a growing animal literature has shown that exposure to psychoactive drugs during ontogeny affects endocrine development. These are summarized below as a demonstration of the multiple abnormalities that can be detected if appropriate evaluation of endocrine function is conducted. These studies employ a variety of treatment paradigms and endocrine indices, but each demonstrates a substantial consequence on fetal development.

The important role that endogenous opioids play in normal endocrine regulation is translated into multiple potential actions of opiates in the developing fetus. The major impact of opiates during development is on reproductive function. Cicero and colleagues (1989) have demonstrated that exposure of male rats to opiates tonically inhibits LH production, decreases testosterone production by the developing testes, and retards morphologic maturation of the testes. Two studies (Bakke et al. 1973; Litto et al. 1983) reported that gestational opiate exposure delayed pubertal development in both males and females and diminished feedback sensitivity of the hypothalamus to gonadal steroids. Other studies (Sonderegger et al. 1979; Zimmerman et al. 1974) reported little or no alteration in pubertal development but did report impaired glucocorticoid responses to stress in adults exposed to morphine during development. These conflicting results reflect in part the variable vulnerability of different opiate receptor systems and different endocrine responses to perinatal opiate treatment. Kuhn and Bartolome (1984) have shown that marked attenuation of hypothalamo-pituitary adrenal can result from perinatal opiate treatment, while other endocrine functions, including PRL and GH secretion, are fairly resistant to perturbation.

Disruption of reproductive development results from THC exposure either during gestation or during puberty (Chakravarty et al. 1979; Field and Tyrey 1984, 1986; Gupta and Elbracht 1983; Kumar et al. 1986). However, the endocrine effects of THC are not well understood even in adults, and conflicting results of THC effects on maternal endocrine function during pregnancy have been reported (Blaunstein et al. 1983; Asch and Smith 1986).

In contrast to studies on THC, there are numerous reports of gestational alcohol effects on endocrine functions. Furthermore, some of the effects reported possibly play a role in the developmental effects of ethanol. The most important of these are several reports of decreased circulating thyroid hormone levels in developing rats or sheep exposed to ethanol during gestation (Castro et al. 1986; Kornguth et al. 1979; Portoles et al. 1988). In addition, significant effects on maternal endocrine function, including decreases in GH, PRL, estriol, and thyroid hormones, have been reported (Lee and Wakabayashi 1986; Guerri et al. 1984). A single report in humans that decreased estriol production is correlated with the severity of fetal alcohol syndrome is a particularly intriguing suggestion that maternal endocrine factors might play a role in the developmental effects of opiate exposure (Halmesmaki et al. 1987). Furthermore, placental as well as maternal endocrine function may be affected by ethanol: Altered somatomedin binding in placenta has also been reported (Kennedy 1984). Finally, several long-lasting effects of perinatal ethanol exposure have been reported in rats exposed to ethanol during gestation, including altered glucoregulatory responses and marked perturbation of adrenocortical function (Angelogianni and Gianoulakis 1989; McGivern et al. 1986; Lopez-Tejero et al. 1989; Singh et al. 1984; Taylor et al. 1981, 1984, 1986; Weinberg 1988, 1989).

ENDOCRINE FUNCTION AS A MODEL SYSTEM FOR STUDYING DEVELOPMENTAL EFFECTS OF DRUGS

This last section addresses a different approach to the investigation of endocrine function: its utility as a model system for studying drug effects on specific neural systems rather than as a mediator of growth disruption. As well as being an important factor for growth, hormone secretion provides an easily measured function of the nervous system that can be quantitated across development. Unlike many physiologic and behavioral responses to drugs, hormone secretion changes only quantitatively across development; most responses remain qualitatively similar. Furthermore, endocrine responses can be quantitated with some accuracy, in contrast to other drug effects such as euphoria and sedation. For these reasons, endocrine function can provide an extremely useful model system for evaluating the impact of drugs on specific neural systems.

This fact has been used to develop endocrine responses to agonist challenge as markers of opiate receptor function through development. Studies of opiate effects on the HPA axis provide an example of the power of this approach. Acute opiate administration to rats elicits a marked rise in ACTH and corticosterone secretion (Kokka et al. 1973). This response reflects actions on at least two opiate receptors (Pfeiffer et al. 1985; Eisenberg 1985; Iyengar et al. 1986). When adult rats are treated chronically with receptor-specific agonists, specific tolerance develops at the appropriate receptor. Therefore, this endocrine response can be used as an indicator of the sensitivity of the two receptors. Furthermore, as shown in figure 4, HPA responses to opiate agonists can be contrasted with responses to agents acting through different neural mechanisms to identify the extent of the adaptations in HPA function. This strategy of using evoked changes in hormone secretion can reveal adaptations in function that are highly specific for both the receptor type and the timeframe of exposure. This strategy has provided an extremely powerful tool in evaluating the neural consequences of perinatal drug exposure.

SUMMARY

The goal of this chapter is to indicate potential endocrine targets of perinatal drug exposure, to describe the methodologic issues involved in detecting changes in hormone secretion, and to provide examples of several endocrine systems in which exposure to drugs during development significantly impaired normal endocrine development. Finally, we attempted to show that endocrine function is both a target and useful marker for detecting effects of drug of abuse on development that provides the advantages of accurate quantitation and relative response stability across ontogeny.

REFERENCES

Anderson, R.A. Endocrine balance as a factor in the etiology of the fetal alcohol syndrome. *Neurobehav Toxicol Teratol* 3:89-104, 1981.

Anderson, R.A.; Berryman, S.H.; Phillips, J.F.; Feathergill, K.A.; Zaneveld, L.J.D.; and Russell, L.D. Biochemical and structural evidence for ethanol-induced impairment of testicular development: Apparent lack of leydig cell involvement. *Toxicol Appl Pharmacol* 100:62-85, 1989.

Anderson, R.A.; Willis, B.R.; Phillips, J.F.; Oswald, C.; and Zaneveld, L.J.D. Delayed pubertal development of the male reproductive tract associated with chronic ethanol ingestion. *Biochem Pharmacol* 36:2157-2167, 1987.

Angelogianni, P., and Gianoulakis, C. Prenatal exposure to ethanol alters the ontogeny of the beta endorphin response to stress. *Alcoholism* 13:564-571, 1989.

Asch, R.H., and Smith, C.G. Effects of delta 9 THC, the principal psychoactive component of marijuana, during pregnancy in the rhesus monkey. *J Reprod Med* 31:1071-1081, 1986.

Bakke, J.L.; Lawrence, N.L.; and Bennett, J. Late effects of perinatal morphine administration on pituitary-thyroidal and gonadal function. *Biol Neonate* 23:59-77, 1973.

Bhanot, R., and Wilkinson, M. Opiatergic control of gonadotropin secretion during puberty in the rat: A neurochemical basis for the hypothalamic gonadostat? *Endocrinology* 113:596-602, 1983.

Blank, M.S.; Panerai, A.E.; and Friesen, H.G. Opioid peptides modulate luteinizing hormone secretion during sexual maturation. *Science* 203:1129-1130, 1979.

Blaunstein, G.D.; Buster, J.E.; Soares, J.R.; and Gross, S.J. Pregnancy hormone concentrations in marijuana users. *Life Sci* 33:195-199, 1983.

Blazquez, E.; Simon, F.A.; Blazquez, M.; and Foa, P.P. Changes in serum growth hormone levels from fetal to adult age in the rat. *Proc Soc Exp Biol Med* 147:780-783, 1974.

Borowsky, B., and Kuhn C. Monoamine mediation of cocaine-induced HPA activation. *J Pharmacol Exp Ther* 256:204-210, 1991a.

Borowsky, B., and Kuhn, C. Monoamine mediation of cocaine-induced HPA activation. *J Pharmacol Exp Ther* 256:204-210, 1991a.

Borowsky, B., and Kuhn, C. Chronic cocaine sensitizes behavior but not neuroendocrine responses. *Brain Res* 543:301-306, 1991b.

Cadet, R.; Pradier, P.; Dalle, M.; and Delost, P. Effects of prenatal maternal stress on the pituitary adrenocortical reactivity in guinea pig pups. *J Dev Physiol* 87:467-475, 1986.

Casey, M.L.; Madonald, P.C.; and Simpson, E.R. Endocrinological changes of pregnancy. In: Wilson, J.D., and Foster, D.W., eds. *Williams Textbook of Endocrinology*. Philadelphia: W.B. Saunders, 1985. pp. 422-451.

Castro, M.I.; Koritnik, D.R.; and Rose, J.C. Fetal plasma insulin and thyroid hormone levels during acute in utero ethanol exposure in a maternal-fetal sheep model. *Endocrinology* 118:1735-1742, 1986.

Chakravarty, I.; Shah, P.G.; Sheth, A.R.; and Ghosh, J.J. Mode of action of delta-9-tetrahydrocannabinol on hypothalamo-pituitary function in adult female rats. *J Reprod Fertil* 57:113-115, 1979.

Cicero, T.J.; Bell, R.D.; Meyer, E.R.; and Koch, G.A. Narcotics and the hypothalamic-pituitary-gonadal axis: Acute effects on luteinizing hormone, testosterone, and androgen-dependent systems. *J Pharmacol Exp Ther* 200:76-83, 1977.

Cicero, T.J.; Meyer, E.R.; Bell, R.D.; and Koch, G.A. Effects of morphine and methadone on serum testosterone and luteinizing hormone levels and on the secondary sex organs of the male rat. *Endocrinology* 98:367-372, 1976.

Cicero, T.J.; Meyer, E.R.; Wiest, W.G.; Olney, J.W.; and Bell, R.D. Effects of chronic morphine administration on the reproductive system of the male rat. *J Pharmacol Exp Ther* 192:542-548, 1975.

Cicero, T.J.; O'Connor, L.; Nock, B.; Adams, M.L.; Miller, B.T.; Bell, R.D.; and Meyer, E.R. Age-related differences in the sensitivity to opiate-induced perturbations in reproductive endocrinology in the developing and adult rat. *J Pharmacol Exp Ther* 248:256-261, 1989.

Cicero, T.J.; Schmoeker, P.F.; Meyer, E.R.; Miller, B.T.; Bell, R.D.; Cytron, S.M.; and Brown, C.C. Ontogeny of the opioid-mediated control of reproductive endocrinology in the male and female rat. *J Pharmacol Exp Ther* 236:627-633, 1986.

Clark, S.J.; Hauffa, B.P.; Rodens, K.P.; Styne, D.L.; Kaplan, S.L.; and Grumbach, M.M. Hormone ontogeny in the ovine fetus, XIX: The effect of a potent luteinizing hormone releasing factor agonist on gonadotropin and testosterone release in the fetus and neonate. *Pediatr Res* 25:347-352, 1989.

Coe, C.L.; Mendoza, S.P.; Smotherman, W.P.; and Levine, S. Mother-infant attachment in the squirrel monkey: Adrenal response to separation. *Behav Biol* 22:256-263, 1978.

Cooper, D.S. Antithyroid drugs. *N Engl J Med* 311:1353-1362, 1984.

Copeland, K.C.; Underwood, L.F.; and Van Wyk, J.J. Marijuana smoking and pubertal arrest. *J Pediatr* 96:1079-1080, 1980.

Cuttler, L.; Egli, C.A.; Styne, D.M.; Kaplan, S.L.; and Grumbach, M.M. Hormone ontogeny in the ovine fetus, XVIII. The effect of an opioid antagonist on luteinzing hormone secretion. *Endocrinology* 116:1997-2002, 1985.

Dube, S.K.; Jhaveri, R.C.; Rosenfeld, W.; Evans, H.E.; Khan, F.; and Spergel, G. Urinary catecholamines, plasma renin activity and blood pressure in newborns: Effects of narcotic withdrawal. *Dev Pharmacol Ther* 3:83-87, 1981.

Eisenberg, R.M. Plasma corticosterone changes in response to central or peripheral administration of kappa and sigma opiate agonists. *J Pharmacol Exp Ther* 233:863-869, 1985.

Eisenberg, R.M., and Sparber, S.B. Changes in plasma corticosterone levels as a measure of acute dependence upon levorphanol in rats. *J Pharmacol Exp Ther* 211:364-374, 1978.

Field, E., and Tyrey, L. Delayed sexual maturation in the female rat during chronic exposure to delta-9-tetrahydrocannabinol. *Life Sci* 35:1725-1730, 1984.

Field, E., and Tyrey, L. Tolerance to the luteinizing hormone and prolactin suppressive effects of delta-9-tetrahydrocannabinol develops during chronic prepubertal treatment of female rat. *J Pharmacol Exp Ther* 238:1034-1038, 1986.

Fisher, D.A.; Dussault, J.H.; Sack, J.; and Chopra, I.J. Ontogenesis of hypothalamic-pituitary-thyroid function and metabolism in man, sheep and rat. *Recent Prog Horm Res* 33:59-116, 1977.

Gavaler, J.S., and Van Thiel, D.H. Reproductive consequences of alcohol abuse: Males and females compared and contrasted. *Mutation Res* 186:269-277, 1987.

Glass, L. Effects of narcotics on perinatal endocrine function. *Semin Perinatol* 6:190-194, 1982.

Gluckman, P.D. The hypothalamic-pituitary unit: The maturation of the neuroendocrine system in the fetus. In: Besser, G.M., and Martini, L., eds. *Clinical Neuroendocrinology Vol 11.* New York: Academic Press, 1982. pp. 31-66.

Gluckman, P.D.; Marti-Henneberg, C.; Kaplan, S.L.; Li, C.H.; and Grumbach, M.M. Hormone ontogeny in the ovine fetus X. The effects of beta endorphin and naloxone on circulating growth hormone, prolactin and chorionic somatomammotropin. *Endocrinology* 107:76-80, 1980.

Gorski, R.A. Sexual differentiation of brain structure in rodents. In: Serio, M.; Motta, M.; Zanisi, M.; and Martini, L., eds. *Sexual Differentiation: Basic and Clinical Aspects.* New York: Raven Press, 1984. pp. 65-72.

Grosvenor, C.E., and Whitworth, N.S. Accumulation of prolactin by maternal milk and its transfer to circulation of neonatal rat: A review. *Endocrinol Exp* 17:271-282, 1983.

Guerri, C.; Esquifino, A.; Sanchis, R.; and Grisolia, S. Growth, enzymes and hormonal changes in offspring of alcohol-fed rat. In: Porter, R.; O'Connor, M.; and Whelan, J., eds. *CIBA Foundation Symposium. Mechanisms of Alcohol Damage In Utero.* CIBA Foundation Symposium. London: Pitman Press, 1984. pp. 85-102.

Gupta, D., and Elbracht, C. Effect of tetrahydrocannabinols on pubertal body weight spurt and sex hormones in developing rats. *Res Exp Med* 182:95-104, 1983.

Halmesmaki, E.; Auttim, I.; Granstrom, M.L.; Stenman, U.H.; and Ylikorkala, O. Estradiol, estriol, progesterone, prolactin and human chorionic gonadotropin in pregnant women with alcohol abuse. *J Clin Endocrinol Metab* 64:153-156, 1987.

Herrenkohl, L.R. Prenatal stress disrupts reproductive physiology and behavior in offspring. *Ann N Y Acad Sci* 474:120-128, 1986.

Hollister, L.E. Health aspects of cannabis. *Pharmacol Rev* 38:1-20, 1986.

Iyengar, S.; Kim, H.S.; and Wood, P.L. Kappa opiate agonists modulate the hypothalamic-pituitary-adrenocortical axis in the rat. *J Pharmacol Exp Ther* 238:429-436, 1986.

Jhaveri, R.C.; Glass, L.; Evans, H.E.; Dube, S.K.; Rosenfeld, W.; Khan, F.; Salazar, J.D.; and Chandavasu, O. Effects of methadone on thyroid function in mother, fetus and newborn. *Pediatrics* 65:557-561, 1980.

Kacsoh, B.; Terry, L.C.; Meyers, J.S.; Crowley, W.R.; and Grosvenor, C.E. Maternal modulation of growth hormone secretion in the neonatal rat. I. Involvement of milk factors. *Endocrinology* 125:1326-1336, 1989.

Kalra, S.P., and Kalra, P.S. Opioid-adrenergic steroid connection in regulation of luteinizing hormone secretion in the rat. *Prog Neuroendocrinol* 38:418-426, 1984.

Kennedy, L.A. Changes in the term mouse placenta associated with maternal alcohol consumption and fetal growth deficits. *Am J Obstet Gynecol* 149:518-522, 1984.

Khorram, O.; DePalatis, R.; and McCann, S.M. Development of hypothalamic control of growth hormone secretion in the rat. *Endocrinology* 113:720-728, 1983.

Kokka, N.; Garcia, J.F.; and Elliott, H.W. Effects of acute and chronic administration of narcotic analgesics on growth hormone and corticotrophin (ACTH) secetion in rats. *Prog Brain Res* 39:347-360, 1973.

Koldovsky, O.; Bedrick A.; and Rao, R.K. Physiological functions of human milk hormones. *Acta Paediatr Scand Suppl* 351:94-96, 1989.

Kornguth, S.E.; Rutledge, J.J.; Sunderland, E.; Siegel, F.; Carlson, I.; Smollens, J.; Juhl, U.; and Young, B. Impeded cerebellar development and reduced serum thyroxine levels associated with fetal alchol intoxication. *Brain Res* 177:347-360, 1979.

Kuhn, C.M., and Bartolome, M. Effect of chronic methadone administration on neuroendocrine function in developing rats. *Dev Pharmacol Ther* 7:384-397, 1984.

Kuhn, C., and Bartolome, M. Effect of chronic methadone administration on neuroendocrine function in young adult rats. *J Pharmacol Exp Ther* 234:204-210, 1985.

Kuhn, C.M., and Schanberg, S.M. Maturation of CNS control of growth hormone secretion in the rat. *J Pharmacol Exp Ther* 217:152-156, 1981.

Kuhn, C.M., and Windh, R. Endocrine effects of opiates. In: Watson, R.R., ed. *Biochemistry and Physiology of Substance Abuse Vol. III*. Boca Raton, FL: CRC Press, 1991. pp. 247-278.

Kumar, A.; Solomon, J.; Patel, V.; Kream, R.M.; Driez, J.M.; and Millard, W.J. Early exposure to delta 9 tetrahydrocannabinol influences neuroendocrine and reproductive functions in female rats. *Neuroendocrinology* 44:260-264, 1986.

Lee, M., and Wakabayashi, K. Pituitary and thyroid hormones in pregnant alcohol-fed rats and their fetuses. *Alcohol Clin Exp Res* 10:428-431, 1986.

Lichtblau, L., and Sparber, S.B. Opioids and development: A perspective on experimental models and methods. *Neurobehav Toxicol Teratol* 6:3-8, 1984.

Litto, W.J.; Griffin, J.P.; and Rabii, J. Influence of morphine during pregnancy on neuroendocrine regulation of pituitary hormone secretion. *J Endocrinol* 98:289-295, 1983.

Lopez-Tejero, D.; Llobera, M.; and Herrera, E. Permanent abnormal response to a glucose load after prenatal ethanol exposure in rats. *Alcohol* 6:469-473, 1989.

McEwen, B.S. Steroid hormones and brain development: Some guidelines for understanding the actions of pseudohormones and other toxic agents. *Environ Health Perspect* 74:177-184, 1987.

McGivern, R.F.; Poland, R.E.; Noble, E.P.; and Lane, L.A. Influence of prenatal ethanol exposure on hormonal responses to clonidine and naloxone in prepubescent male and female rats. *Psychoneuroendocrinology* 11:105-110, 1986.

McMillian, I.C., and Deayton, J.M. Effect of morphine and naloxone on plasma prolactin concentrations in the fetal sheep and pregnant ewe during late gestation. *Neuroendocrinology* 49:286-290, 1989.

Mendelson, J.H.; Mello, N.K.; Teoh, S.K.; Ellingboe, J.; and Cochin, J. Cocaine effects on pulsatile secretion of anterior pituitary, gonadal and adrenal hormones. *J Clin Endocrinol Metab* 69:1256-1260, 1989.

Moldow, R.L., and Fischman, A.J. Cocaine-induced secretion of ACTH, beta endorphin and corticosterone. *Peptides* 8:819-822, 1987.

Mosinger, B., and Placer, Z. Passage of insulin through the wall of the gastro-intestinal tract of the infant rat. *Nature* 184:1245-1246, 1959.

Nathienelsz, P.W. *Fetal Endocrinology.* New York: North Holland, 1976.

Ojeda, S.R.; Andrews, W.W.; Advis, J.P.; and Smith White, S. Recent advances in the endocrinology of puberty. *Endocrinol Rev* 1:228-257, 1980.

Pauk, J.; Kuhn, C.M.; Field, T.M.; and Schanberg, S.M. Positive effects of tactile versus kinesthetic or vestibular stimulation on neuroendocrine and ODC activity in maternally-deprived rat pups. *Life Sci* 39:2081-2087, 1986.

Pfeiffer, A.; Herz, A.; Loriaux, D.L.; and Pfeiffer, D.G. Central kappa- and mu-opiate receptors mediate ACTH-release in rats. *Endocrinology* 116:2688-2690, 1985.

Portoles, M.; Sanchis, R.; and Guerri, C. Thyroid hormone levels in rats exposed to alcohol during development. *Horm Metab Res* 20:267-270, 1988.

Resko, J.A., and Ellinwood, W.E. Sexual differentiation of the brain of primates. In: Serio, M.; Motta, M.; Zanisi, M.; and Martini, L. *Sexual Differentiation: Basic and Clinical Aspects.* New York: Raven Press, 1984. pp. 169-181.

Rieutort, M. Ontogenetic development of the inhibition of growth hormone release by somatostatin in the rat: In vivo and in vitro (perifusion) study. *J Endocrinol* 89:355-363, 1981.

Rieutort, M., and Jost, A. Growth hormone in encephalectomized rat fetuses with comments on the effects of anesthetics. *Endocrinology* 98:1123-1129, 1976.

Rosenfeld, W.; Jhaveri, R.C.; Schaeffer, H.A.; Dube, S.K.; Glass, L.; Evans, H.E.; and Khan, F. Relationship of thyroid hormone levels to the severity of the narcotic withdrawal syndrome. *Dev Pharmacol Ther* 3:197-200, 1981.

Rosett, H.L., and Weiner, L. *Alcohol and the Fetus.* New York: Oxford University Press, 1984.

Shyr, S.W.; Crowley, W.R.; and Grosvenor, C.E. Effect of neonatal prolactin deficiency on prepubertal tuberoinfundibular and tuberohypophyseal dopaminergic neuronal activity. *Endocrinology* 119:1217-1221, 1986.

Singh, H.; Purohit, V.; and Ahluwalia, B.S. Effect of methadone treatment during pregnancy on the fetal testes and hypothalamus in rats. *Biol Reprod* 22:480-485, 1980.

Singh, S.P.; Snyder, A.K.; and Singh, S.L. Effects of ethanol ingestion on maternal and fetal glucose homeostasis. *J Lab Clin Med* 104:176-184, 1984.

Smith, C.G., and Asch, R.H. Drug abuse and reproduction. *Fertil Steril* 48:355-373, 1987.

Sonderegger, T.; O'Shea, S.; and Zimmerman, E. Consequences in adult female rats of neonatal morphine pellet implantation. *Neurobehav Toxicol* 1:161-167, 1979.

Taylor, A.N.; Branch, B.J.; Liu, S.H.; Wiechmann, A.F.; Hill, M.A.; and Kokka, N. Fetal exposure to ethanol enhanced pituitary adrenal and temperature responses to ethanol in adult rats. *Exp Res* 5:237-246, 1981.

Taylor, A.N.; Branch, B.J.; Nelson, L.R.; Lane, L.A.; and Poland, R.E. Prenatal ethanol and morphine. *Alcohol* 3:255-259, 1986.

Taylor, A.N.; Nelson, L.R.; Branch, B.J.; Kokka, N.; and Poland, R.E. Altered stress responsiveness in adult rats exposed to ethanol in utero: Neuroendocrine mechanisms. In: Porter, R.; O'Connor, M.; and Whelan, J., eds. *CIBA Foundation Symposium. Mechanisms of Alcohol Damage In Utero.* London: Pitman Press, 1984. pp. 47-65.

Tyrey, L. Endocrine aspects of cannabinoid action in female subprimates: Search for sites of action. In: Braud, M.C., and Ludford, J.P., eds. *Marijuana Effects on the Endocrine and Reproductive Systems.* National Institute on Drug Abuse Research Monograph 44. DHHS Pub. No. (ADM)84-1278. Washington, DC: Supt. of Docs., U.S. Govt. Print. Off., 1984. pp. 65-81.

Vathy, I.U.; Etgen, A.M.; and Barfield, A.R.J. Effects of prenatal exposure to morphine sulfate on reproductive function of female rats. *Pharmacol Biochem Behav* 19:777-780, 1983.

Walker, P.; Dussault, J.H.; Alvarado-Urbina, G.; and Dupont, A. Development of the hypothalmo-pituitary axis in the neonatal rat: Hypothalamic somatostatin and pituitary and serum growth hormone concentrations. *Endocrinology* 101:782-787, 1977.

Ward, I.L. The prenatal stress syndrome: Current status. *Psychoneuroendocrinology* 9:3-11, 1984.

Weinberg, J. Hyperresponsiveness to stress: Differential effects of prenatal ethanol on males and females. *Alcoholism* 12:647-652, 1988.

Weinberg, J. Prenatal ethanol exposure alters adrenocortical development of offspring. *Alcoholism* 13:73-83, 1989.

Weinberg, J., and Bezio, S. Alcohol-induced changes in pituitary-adrenal activity during pregnancy. *Alcohol Clin Exp Res* 11:274-280, 1987.

Wenger, T.; Croix, D.; and Tramu, G. The effect of chronic prepubertal administration of marijuana (delta-9-tetrahydrocannabinol) on the onset of puberty and the postpubertal reproductive functions in female rats. *Biol Reprod* 39:540-545, 1988.

Werner, H.; Amarant, T.; Fridkin, M.; and Koch, Y. Growth hormone releasing factor-like immunoreactivity in human milk. *Biochem Biophys Res Comm* 135:1084-1089, 1986.

Winter, J.S.D.; Faiman, C.; and Reyes, F. Sexual endocrinology of fetal and perinatal life. In: Austin, C.R., and Edwards, R.G., eds. *Mechanisms of Sex Differentiation in Animals and Man.* New York: Academic Press, 1981. pp. 205-253.

Zagon, I.S., and McLaughlin, P.J. An overview of the neurobehavioral sequelae of perinatal opioid exposure. In: Yanai, J., ed. *Neurobehavioral Toxicology.* New York: Elsevier Press, 1984. pp. 197-234.

Zimmerman, E.; Branch, B.; Taylor, A.N.; Young, J.; and Pang, C.N. Long lasting effects of prepubertal administration of morphine in rats. In: Zimmerman, E., and George, R., eds. *Narcotics and the Hypothalamus.* New York: Raven Press, 1974. pp. 183-194.

AUTHORS

Cynthia Kuhn, Ph.D.
Associate Professor of Pharmacology

Rolf Windh, B.A.

Department of Pharmacology
Duke University Medical Center, Box 3813
Durham, NC 27710

Diane Ignar, Ph.D.
Fellow
National Institute of Environmental Health Sciences
P.O. Box 12233
Research Triangle Park, NC 27709

Discussion: Neuroteratology of Cocaine—Relationship to Developing Monoamine Systems

Jean M. Lauder

DEVELOPMENTAL EFFECTS OF COCAINE

The epidemic of cocaine abuse across all sectors of the human population, including women in various stages of pregnancy, has led to concern about effects on embryonic, fetal, and postnatal development of their offspring. Clinical studies suggest that this now popular drug of abuse may indeed be the cause of a number of developmental defects as well as an important factor in the outcome of pregnancy.

Human Studies

Increases in spontaneous abortions, *abruptio placentae*, preterm labor, fetal deaths, still births, low birth weights, decreased head circumference, skull defects, microcephaly, intracerebral hemorrhage, cardiovascular abnormalities, and hypertension in fetuses and newborns have been reported in clinical studies of cocaine-abusing mothers (Bingol et al. 1987; Chasnoff et al. 1987; Chasnoff, this volume; Hadeed and Siegel 1989; Isenberg et al. 1987; Little et al. 1989; Ryan et al. 1987; Zuckerman et al. 1989).

A number of behavioral disturbances have been noted in children of cocaine-abusing women that suggest abnormal functional development of the nervous system. These include disturbed interactive behavior and motor function (including tremors and hyperactivity), increased irritability, depressed organizational response to environmental stimuli, visual disturbances, altered visual evoked potentials, disturbed sleep states, abnormal arousal responses to hypoxia, disruption of normal breathing patterns during sleep, and increased sudden infant death syndrome (SIDS) (Chasnoff et al. 1987, 1989; Davidson Ward et al. 1989a, 1989b; Dixon et al. 1987; Oro and Dixon 1987).

Animal Studies

In the human population of substance abusers, who often use multiple drugs, it is difficult to ascertain the exact drug-related etiology of developmental defects. Animal studies have the advantage of providing an opportunity to observe effects of one suspected agent at a time on a variety of parameters of structural and functional development. Data obtained from such studies are useful in understanding the effects of drugs on the developing human, provided possible species-related differences are kept in mind.

Animal studies have provided information on the effects of cocaine administered during different periods of prenatal and postnatal development. In general, the findings of these studies are similar to those in humans in terms of behavioral defects, growth retardation and disturbances of pregnancy, including *abruptio placentae*, spontaneous abortions, and fetal deaths (Church et al. 1988; Dow Edwards 1988, 1989; Fantel and MacPhail 1982; Henderson and McMillan 1990).

Many of these studies have provided valuable information regarding specific changes in behavior and the function of neurotransmitter systems, which clearly implicate the developing nervous system in the teratology of cocaine. Recent studies by Dow Edwards (1988, 1989; Dow Edwards et al. 1988) in rats using the 2-deoxyglucose method indicate specific brain regions affected by neonatal exposure to cocaine. Interestingly, neonatal treatment only produced significant effects in females, with the greatest changes occurring in structures related to the limbic system where metabolic activity was increased. These changes were accompanied by hyperactive behavior following pharmacologic challenge with amphetamine. In prenatal studies, however, males also were affected (D.L. Dow Edwards, personal communication, April 1990). Together with the observed effects on the limbic system, a known projection area of dopamine neurons (Kalivas and Nemeroff 1988), the effects of amphetamine suggest alterations in the developing dopaminergic system (Buelke-Sam 1986; Woolverton 1986).

Other studies have reported delayed development of the righting reflex, decreased learning and memory and shock-elicited wall climbing, as well as increased locomotor activity, following subcutaneous cocaine injection throughout pregnancy (Henderson and McMillan 1990) or gestational days 8 to 20 (Spear et al. 1989a, 1989b). Spear and colleagues (1989b) have related changes in wall-climbing behavior to developing catecholamine systems, based on previous studies with 6-hydroxydopamine (Emerich et al. 1985). Suckling, a serotonin (5-HT)-related behavior, was not affected by cocaine in the same study (Spear et al. 1989b). Accelerated development of the righting reflex, cliff avoidance, startle response, and decreased activity in response to amphetamine, have been reported following injection of cocaine during the last trimester of pregnancy (Sobrian et al. 1990). All these studies suggest the importance of critical developmental periods in the functional changes observed following cocaine use in pregnancy, as well as the involvement of developing catecholamine systems.

Microcephaly and small head circumference have been reported in clinical studies of cocaine abuse during pregnancy. Of interest in this regard is a recent report of changes in ornithine decarboxylase levels in developing rat cortex following prenatal exposure to cocaine (Bondy et al. 1990), since this enzyme is known to be active in proliferating cells. Of particular importance is the finding that levels of this enzyme first decreased and then increased during the postnatal period in treated animals, suggesting first an inhibition of cell proliferation, followed by a rebound. Such an effect could have severe consequences for cortical development where correct timing of separate developmental events is critical (Rakic 1988) and might explain some of the features of microcephaly found in humans following prenatal cocaine abuse (Hadeed and Siegel 1989).

EFFECTS OF COCAINE ON ADULT MONOAMINERGIC NEURONS

Evidence for cocaine effects on monoaminergic neurons is unequivocal. Cocaine is a potent inhibitor of the reuptake of dopamine (DA), norepinephrine (NE), and 5-HT into presynaptic nerve terminals in the rat (Koe 1976; Lakoski and Cunningham 1988; Taylor and Ho 1978; Randrup and Braestrup 1977), and cocaine binding sites have been associated with DA and 5-HT nerve terminals in the striatum (Kennedy and Hanbauer 1983) and cerebral cortex (Reith et al. 1983; Reith 1988). Cocaine receptors are thought to be directly linked to the uptake transporters for DA and 5-HT (Reith et al. 1983, 1986), and those on the striatal DA transporter mediate the reinforcing (addictive) qualities of cocaine (Ritz et al. 1987). DA receptors of the D2 subtype are thought to mediate the self-adminstration of cocaine in monkeys (Woolverton et al. 1984; Woolverton 1986), and D1 receptors also have been reported to do so in the rat (Koob et al. 1987). Both D1 and NE receptors appear to be involved in the discriminative stimulus properties of cocaine, based on the effects of d-amphetamine in monkeys (Woolverton and Kleven 1988). D2 receptors are also involved in the locomotor stmulatory properties of cocaine, with D1 receptors apparently playing an ancillary role (Bhattacharyya et al. 1979; Heikkila et al. 1979; Scheel-Kruger et al. 1977).

Cocaine alters the functioning of brain monoamines by blocking their reuptake into presynaptic terminals as well as by affecting their turnover, synthesis, and the firing of the neurons that contain them. For example, cocaine increases striatal DA levels and turnover (Church et al. 1987; Patrick and Barchas 1977) but decreases the levels of NE and 5-HT in the diencephalon, midbrain, and brain stem (Bhattacharyya et al. 1979; Pradhan et al. 1978), probably by inhibiting the enzymes responsible for their synthesis (Trulson et al. 1986). In addition, systemic cocaine administration inhibits the firing of brain stem NE neurons (Pitts and Marwah 1986a, 1986b, 1987a) and DA neurons in the midbrain (Einhorn et al. 1988; Pitts and Marwah 1987b). Cocaine clearly inhibits the functioning of 5-HT neuronal systems in the central nervous system (CNS) (Blackburn et al. 1967; Friedman et al. 1975; Ross and Renyi 1967, 1969; Taylor and Ho 1978), both by inhibiting reuptake into nerve terminals and by inhibiting 5-HT synthesis (Knapp and Mandell 1972). Systemic cocaine administration also inhibits the spontaneous activity of brain stem 5-HT neurons (Cunningham and Lakoski 1986; Pitts and Marwah 1986a). In addition, inhibition of 5-HT synthesis and receptor blockade potentiate the ability of cocaine to increase locomotor activity (Scheel-Kruger et al. 1977).

COCAINE AND DEVELOPING MONOAMINERGIC SYSTEMS

The effects of cocaine on monoamine uptake, synthesis, and receptors in the adult brain as well as developmental effects on such behaviors as shock-elicited wall climbing and amphetamine-induced locomotor activity (discussed above) make it reasonable to speculate that developing monoaminergic systems may be important substrates for the neuroteratologic effects of cocaine, especially given the precocious development and trophic influences they exert on the ontogeny of other brain cells, including their synaptic partners.

Monoamines may have evolved to their roles in chemical neurotransmission from more general humoral functions in primitive organisms (Buznikov 1984; McMahon 1974; Roth et al. 1982; Tompkins 1975). These phylogenetically old functions appear to be reiterated in the embryo (Harris 1981) where these same substances influence a variety of developmental events including cell proliferation, neurite outgrowth, and synaptogenesis (Lauder 1988; Mattson 1988). Cocaine, by affecting the ontogeny of monoaminergic systems, also may exert influences on other components of developing brain circuitry due to the trophic actions of these neurotransmitters on other cells.

CNS monoamine neurons are early developing neurotransmitter systems, beginning their differentiation prior to most of their target cells. In the rat, the NE neurons of the locus coeruleus, DA neurons of the substantia nigra, and 5-HT neurons of the raphe nuclei are formed during the second week of gestation and begin to synthesize transmitter immediately after their last cell division (Lauder and Bloom 1974). In the human brain, both 5-HT and

236

catecholamine neurons can be detected by the end of the second month of gestation (Olsen et al. 1973; Pickel et al. 1980). In both animals and humans, monoamine neurons rapidly elaborate axons that innervate forebrain regions within a short time (Lidov and Molliver 1982a, 1982b; Olsen et al. 1973; Pickel et al. 1980; Olsen and Seiger 1972; Specht et al. 1981; Wallace and Lauder 1983). The neurotransmitters contained in these neurons appear to influence the ontogeny of cells with which they interact during their growth and differentiation, making the developing brain particularly vulnerable to insult by psychoactive drugs (Lauder 1983; Lauder and Krebs 1984).

Studies with the catecholamine neurotoxin 6-hydroxydopamine (6-HODA) in the rat suggest that depletion of brain catecholamines during the early postnatal period produces a variety of changes in developing brain regions innervated by NE or DA nerve terminals. These effects include alterations in cerebellar development (Lovell 1982), reduced cortical thickness (Kalsbeek et al. 1987), decreased cortical cell density (Onteniente et al. 1980), increased synaptic density in the subcortical plate region (Blue and Parnevalis 1982), sprouting of cortical and striatal 5-HT axons (Berger et al. 1985; Blue and Molliver 1987; Luthman et al. 1987; Towle et al. 1987), changes in the dendritic arrangement in somatosensory barrel fields (Loeb et al. 1987), and altered plasticity of the visual cortex (Kasamatsu and Pettigrew 1979; Shirokawa et al. 1989). Depletion of DA in the developing rat or rabbit by reserpine or α-methyl-p-tyrosine reduces the amount of neuropil in the striatum and alters motor activity (Tennyson et al. 1982, 1983). These effects are relevant to in vitro studies where DA has been shown to inhibit neurite outgrowth in specific target cells (Lankford et al. 1987; McCobb et al. 1988), an effect that appears to be mediated by DA receptors (Lankford et al. 1988). It might be expected that exposure to cocaine during different critical periods could exert a variety of region-specific changes in brain development by increasing or decreasing the levels of catecholamines due to blockade of their reuptake into developing nerve terminals and/or inhibiting their synthesis in cell bodies.

5-HT also exerts trophic influences on neural development. Since cocaine inhibits 5-HT reuptake and biosynthesis in the adult brain, it also may affect these processes in developing 5-HT neurons. Inhibition of 5-HT synthesis in embryonic rat brain and raphe neurons (Lauder et al. 1981, 1985) leads to delayed differentiation of cells spatio-temporally associated with developing 5-HT axons (Lauder and Krebs 1978; Lauder et al. 1982). Such effects may lead to mistimed neurogenesis between affected and unaffected brain regions, thereby altering the development of their synaptic connections.

In culture, 5-HT neurons and their target cells respond to direct application of this transmitter by an inhibition of growth cone activity and a retraction of

237

affected neurites, as well as by alterations in synapse formation (Haydon et al. 1984; McCobb et al. 1988). Snail embryos treated with the 5-HT neurotoxin 5,7-dihydroxytryptamine, and raised to adulthood, exhibit alterations in the dendritic morphology of specific 5-HT target cells (Goldberg and Kater 1989). In complex (organotypic) cultures of rat brain regions such as cerebral cortex and hippocampus, stimulation of neurite outgrowth, glial proliferation, and synaptogenesis occurs when 5-HT is added to the culture medium (Chubakov et al. 1986; Gromova et al. 1983).

In dissociated cell cultures from embryonic rat brain, 5-HT or 5-HT$_1$ agonists influence the morphological and biochemical differentiation of 5-HT neurons (Azmitia and Whitaker-Azmitia 1987; Jonakait et al. 1988; Whitaker-Azmitia and Azmitia 1986) but not catecholamine neurons (Liu and Lauder 1991; Liu et al. 1990). These effects appear to involve activation of receptors on 5-HT neurons (autoreceptors) (Whitaker-Azmitia and Azmitia 1986), target neurons (Azmitia and Whitaker-Azmitia 1987), and glia (Whitaker-Azmitia and Azmitia 1989). With regard to glial 5-HT receptors, treatment of neonatal astrocytes (Whitaker-Azmitia and Azmitia 1989) or embryonic radial glia and astrocytes (Liu et al. 1990) with 5-HT, or 5-HT$_{1A}$ agonists, stimulates the release of factors that affect the survival and growth of 5-HT neurons. The factor(s) released from embryonic glia following stimulation by 5-HT (and nialamide) (Liu et al. 1990) does not significantly affect catecholamine neurons, suggesting possible specificity for the serotonergic phenotype. A 5-HT growth factor released from neonatal astrocytes following activation of 5-HT$_{1A}$ receptors has been reported to be the protein S100 (Whitaker-Azmitia et al. 1990).

Recently, cocaine has been reported to inhibit survival, development of 5-HT uptake, and neurite outgrowth in cultured embryonic 5-HT neurons (Azmitia et al. 1989; DeGeorge et al. 1989). This inhibition represents the first evidence that cocaine can alter the morphological and biochemical differentiation of embryonic 5-HT neurons and suggests that investigation of the effects of cocaine on the developing serotonergic system may be fruitful.

The vulnerability of neurotransmitter receptors to developmental insult has been demonstrated repeatedly in studies of postnatal receptor expression following prenatal exposure to psychoactive drugs (Kellogg 1988; Miller and Friedhoff 1988; Schwaab et al. 1988). For example, prenatal exposure to the monoamine uptake inhibitor and tricyclic antidepressant imipramine leads to alterations in the numbers of B-adrenergic receptors expressed postnatally in the rat brain (Ali et al. 1986; Jason et al. 1981). Likewise, treatment of pregnant rats with neuroleptics such as haloperidol, butaclamol, or α-methyl-p-tyrosine (an inhibitor of catecholamine biosynthesis) reduces the number of D2 receptors present in offspring and the ability of such receptors to be upregulated in the adult (Miller and Friedhoff 1986, 1988; Rosengarten and Friedhoff 1979). Moreover, days 15 to 18 of gestation in the rat appear to be a critical period for such effects, since later treatment with the same agents produces opposite effects, similar to the adult pattern of response. This period may represent the time when DA receptors are developing into their mature state (Miller and Friedhoff 1988). Since cocaine exerts some of its behavioral effects via D2 receptors, these components of the DA system may be prime candidates for studying developmental effects of cocaine.

As with catecholamine receptors, treatment of pregnant rats with pharmacologic agents affecting 5-HT synthesis (p-chlorophenylalanine) or receptors (5-methoxytryptamine) leads to changes in the number of 5-HT receptors expressed in offspring (Whitaker-Azmitia et al. 1987), suggesting that the expression or maturation of these receptors may be modulated by 5-HT during embryogenesis. Since cocaine inhibits the development of 5-HT uptake as well as the survival and growth of cultured 5-HT neurons, as discussed above, it is possible that this drug could indirectly alter embryonic 5-HT receptors during the critical period of expression and/or maturation.

SUMMARY

The effects of cocaine on monoaminergic systems in the adult brain and in tissue culture, coupled with the behavioral profiles of animals and humans exposed in utero, suggest that catecholamine and 5-HT neurons and their receptors may be especially vulnerable to this drug during critical periods of their development. Future studies designed to examine the effects of cocaine on specific features of developing monoaminergic systems, such as the expression of reuptake mechanisms and receptors, neurite outgrowth, and synaptogenesis, will be important in further elucidating potential neuroteratologic effects of cocaine abuse in pregnancy.

REFERENCES

Ali, S.F.; Buelke-Sam, J.; Newport, G.D.; and Slikker, Jr., W. Early neurobehavioral and neurochemical alterations in rats prenatally exposed to imipramine. Neurotoxicology 7:365-380, 1986.
Azmitia, E.C.; Hou, X.P.; Whitaker-Azmitia, P.M.; Hochberg, S.A.; and Murphy, R.M. MDMA, cocaine, and fenfluramine but not methamphetamine produce neuropathology of cultured 5-HT neurons. Soc Neurosci Abstr 15:418, 1989.
Azmitia, E.C., and Whitaker-Azmitia, P.M. Target cell stimulation of dissociated serotonergic neurons in culture. Neuroscience 20:47-63, 1987.

Berger, T.W.; Kaul, S.; Stricker, E.M.; and Zigmond, M.J. Hyperinnervation of the striatum by dorsal raphe afferents after dopamine-depleting brain lesions in neonatal rats. *Brain Res* 336:354-358, 1985.

Bhattacharyya, A.K.; Aulakh, C.S.; Pradhan,S.; Ghosh, P.; and Pradhan, S.N. Modification of behavioral and neurochemical effects of cocaine by haloperidol. *Arch Int Pharmacodyn Ther* 238:71-80, 1979.

Bingol, N.; Fuchs, M.; Diaz, V.; Stone, R.K.; and Gromisch, D.S. Teratogenicity of cocaine in humans. *J Pediatr* 110:93-96, 1987.

Blackburn, K.J.; French, P.C.; and Merrills, R.J. 5-Hydroxytryptamine uptake in rat brain in vitro. *Life Sci* 6:1653-1663, 1967.

Blue, M.E., and Molliver, M.E. 6-Hydroxydopamine induces serotonergic axon sprouting in cerebral cortex of newborn rat. *Dev Brain Res* 32:255-269, 1987.

Blue, M.E., and Parnevalis, J.G. The effect of neonatal 6-hydroxydopamine treatment on synaptogenesis in the visual cortex of the rat. *J Comp Neurol* 205:199-205, 1982.

Bondy, S.C.; Nakla, M.; Ali, S.F.; and Ahmad, G. Cerebral ornithine decarboxylase levels following gestational exposure to cocaine. *Int J Dev Neurosci* 8:337-341, 1990.

Buelke-Sam, J. Postnatal functional assessment following central nervous system stimulant exposure. Amphetamine and caffeine. In: Riley, E.A., and Vorhees, C.V., eds. *Handbook of Behavioral Teratology*. New York: Plenum, 1986. pp. 161-172.

Buznikov, G.A. The action of neurotransmitters and related substances on early embryogenesis. *Pharmacol Ther* 25:23-59, 1984.

Chasnoff, I.J.; Burns, K.A.; and Burns, W.J. Cocaine use in pregnancy: Perinatal morbidity and mortality. *Neurotoxicol Teratol* 9:291-293, 1987.

Chasnoff, I.J.; Hunt, C.E.; Kletter, R.; and Kaplan, D. Prenatal cocaine exposure is associated with respiratory pattern abnormalities. *Am J Dis Child* 143:583-587, 1989.

Chubakov, A.R.; Gromova, E.A.; Konovalov, G.V.; Sarkisova, E.F.; and Chumasov, E.I. The effects of serotonin on the morphofunctional development of rat cerebral neocortex in tissue culture. *Brain Res* 369:285-297, 1986.

Church, M.; Dintcheff, B.A.; and Gessner, P.K. Dose-dependent consequences of cocaine on pregnancy outcome in the Long-Evans rat. *Neurotoxicol Teratol* 10:51-58, 1988.

Church, W.H.; Justice, J.B., Jr.; and Byrd, L.D. Extracellular dopamine in rat striatum following uptake inhibition by cocaine, nomifensine and benzotropine. *Eur J Pharmacol* 139:345-348, 1987.

Cunningham, K.A., and Lakoski, J.M. Cocaine: Inhibition of serotonergic cell firing in the dorsal raphe serotonin nucleus (DRN). *Fed Proc* 45:1060, 1986.

Davidson Ward, S.L.; Bautista, D.B.; Buckley, S.; Schuetz, S.; Wachsman, L.; Bean, X.; and Warbuton, D. Circulating catecholamines and adrenoreceptors in infants of cocaine-abusing mothers. *Ann N Y Acad Sci* 562:349-351, 1989a.

Davidson Ward, S.L.; Bautista, D.B.; Scheutz, S.; Wachsman, L.; Bean, X.; and Keens, T.G. Abnormal hypoxic arousal responses in infants of cocaine-abusing mothers. *Ann N Y Acad Sci* 562:347-348, 1989b.

DeGeorge, G.; Hochberg, S.A.; Murphy, R.; and Azmitia, E.C. Serotonin neurons may be a major target for the action of cocaine: Evidence from in vitro and tissue culture studies. *Soc Neurosci Abstr* 15:418, 1989.

Dixon, S.D.; Coen, R.W.; and Crutchfield, S. Visual dysfunction in cocaine-exposed infants. *Pediatr Res* 21:359A, 1987.

Dow Edwards, D.L. Developmental effects of cocaine. In: Clouet, D.; Asghar, K.; and Brown, R., eds. *Mechanisms of Cocaine Abuse and Toxicity.* National Institute on Drug Abuse Research Monograph 88. DHHS Pub. No. (ADM)89-1585. Washington, DC: Supt. of Docs., U.S. Govt. Print. Off., 1988. pp. 290-303.

Dow Edwards, D.L. Long-term neurochemical and neurobehavioral consequences of cocaine use during pregnancy. *Ann N Y Acad Sci* 562:280-289, 1989.

Dow Edwards, D.L.; Freed, L.A.; and Milhorat, T.H. Stimulation of brain metabolism by perinatal cocaine exposure. *Dev Brain Res* 42:137-141, 1988.

Einhorn, L.C.; Johansen, P.A.; and White, F.J. Electrophysiological effects of cocaine in the mesoaccumbens dopamine system: Studies in the ventral tegmental area. *J Neurosci* 8:100-112, 1988.

Emerich, D.F.; Scalzo, F.M.; Enters, E.K.; Spear, N.E.; and Spear, L.P. Effects of 6-hydroxydopamine-induced catecholamine depletion on shock-precipitated wall climbing of infant rat pups. *Dev Psychobiol* 18:215-227, 1985.

Fantel, A.G., and MacPhail, B.J. The teratogenicity of cocaine. *Teratology* 26:17-19, 1982.

Friedman, E.; Gershon, S.; and Rotrosen, J. Effects of acute cocaine treatment on turnover of 5-hydroxytryptamine in the rat brain. *Br J Pharmacol* 54:61-64, 1975.

Goldberg, J.I., and Kater, S.B. Expression and function of the neurotransmitter serotonin during development of Helisoma nervous system. *Dev Biol* 131:483-495, 1989.

Gromova, H.A.; Chubakov, A.R.; Chumasov, E.I.; and Konovalov, H.V. Serotonin as a stimulator of hippocampal cell differentiation in tissue culture. *Int J Dev Neurosci* 1:339-349, 1983.

Hadeed, A.J., and Siegel, S.R. Maternal cocaine use during pregnancy: Effect on the newborn infant. *Pediatrics* 84:205-212, 1989.

Harris, W.A. Neural activity and development. *Ann Rev Physiol* 43:689-710, 1981.

Haydon, P.G.; McCobb, D.P.; and Kater, S.B. Serotonin selectively inhibits growth cone motility and synaptogenesis of specific identified neurons. *Science* 226:561-564, 1984.

Heikkila, R.E.; Cabbat, F.S.; Manzino, L.; and Duvoisin, R.C. Rotational behavior induced by cocaine analogs in rats with unilateral 6-hydroxydopamine lesions of the substantia nigra: Dependence upon dopamine uptake inhibition. *J Pharmacol Exp Ther* 211:189-194, 1979.

Henderson, M.G., and McMillan, B.A. Effects of prenatal exposure to cocaine or related drugs on rat developmental and neurological indices. *Brain Res Bull* 24:207-212, 1990.

Isenberg, S.J.; Spierer, A.; and Inkelis, S.H. Ocular signs of cocaine intoxication in neonates. *Am J Opthalmol* 103:211-214, 1987.

Jason, K.M.; Cooper, T.B.; and Friedman, E. Prenatal exposure to imipramine alters early behavioral development and beta adrenergic receptors in rats. *J Pharmacol Exp Ther* 217:461-466, 1981.

Jonakait, G.M.; Schotland, S.; and Ni, L. Development of serotonin, substance P and thyrotrophin-releasing hormone in mouse medullary raphe grown in organotypic tissue culture: Developmental regulation by serotonin. *Brain Res* 473:336-343, 1988.

Kalivas, P.W., and Nemeroff, C.B., eds. The mesolimbic dopamine system. *Ann N Y Acad Sci* 537:1-50, 1988.

Kalsbeek, A.; Buijs, R.M.; Hofman, M.A.; Matthijssen, M.A.H.; Pool, C.W.; and Uylings, H.B.M. Effects of neonatal thermal lesioning of the mesocortical dopaminergic projection on the development of the rat prefrontal cortex. *Dev Brain Res* 32:123-132, 1987.

Kasamatsu, T., and Pettigrew, J.D. Preservation of binocularity after monocular deprivation in the striate cortex of kittens treated with 6-hydroxydopamine. *J Comp Neurol* 185:139-162, 1979.

Kellogg, C.K. Benzodiazepines: Influence on the developing brain. *Prog Brain Res* 73:207-228, 1988.

Kennedy, L.T., and Hanbauer, I. Sodium-sensitive cocaine binding to rat striatal membrane: Possible relationship to dopamine uptake sites. *J Neurochem* 41:172-178, 1983.

Knapp, S., and Mandell, A.J. Narcotic drugs: Effects on the serotonin biosynthesis systems of the brain. *Science* 177:1209-1211, 1972.

Koe, B.K. Molecular geometry of inhibitors of the uptake of catecholamines and serotonin in synaptosomal preparations of rat brain. *J Pharmacol Exp Ther* 199:649-661, 1976.

Koob, G.F.; Le, H.T.; and Creese, I. The D-1 dopamine receptor anatgonist SCH 23390. *Neurosci Lett* 79:315-320, 1987.

Lakoski, J.M., and Cunningham, K.A. The interaction of cocaine with central serotonergic neuronal systems: Cellular electrophysiologic approaches. In: Clouet, D.; Asghar, K.; and Brown, R., eds. *Mechanisms of Cocaine Abuse and Toxicity.* National Institute on Drug Abuse Research Monograph 88. DHHS Pub. No. (ADM)89-1585. Washington, DC: Supt. of Docs., U.S. Govt. Print. Off., 1988. pp. 78-91.

Lankford, K.L.; DeMello, F.; and Klein, W.L. A transient embryonic dopamine receptor inhibits growth cone motility and neurite outgrowth in a subset of avian retina neurons. *Neurosci Lett* 75:169-174, 1987.

Lankford, K.L.; DeMello, F.; and Klein, W.L. DMDSD1-type dopamine receptors inhibit growth cone motility in cultured retina neurons: Evidence that neurotransmitters act as morphogenic growth regulators in the developing central nervous system. *Proc Natl Acad Sci U S A* 85:2839-2843, 1988.

Lauder, J.M. Hormonal and humoral influences on brain development. *Psychoneuroendocrinology* 8:121-155, 1983.

Lauder, J.M. Neurotransmitters as morphogens. *Prog Brain Res* 73:365-387, 1988.

Lauder, J.M., and Bloom, F.E. Ontogeny of monoamine neurons in the locus coeruleus, raphe nuclei, and substantia nigra of the rat. I. Cell differentiation. *J Comp Neurol* 155:469-481, 1974.

Lauder, J.M., and Krebs, H. Serotonin as a differentiation signal in early embryogenesis. *Dev Neurosci* 1:15-30, 1978.

Lauder, J.M., and Krebs, H. Neurotransmitters in development as possible substrates for drugs of use and abuse. In: Yanai, J., ed. *Neurobehavioral Teratology.* Amsterdam: Elsevier, 1984. pp. 289-314.

Lauder, J.M.; Towle, A.C.; Patrick, K.; Henderson, P.; and Krebs, H. Decreased serotonin content of embryonic raphe neurons following maternal administration of p-chlorophenylalanine: A quantitative immunocytochemical study. *Dev Brain Res* 20:107-114, 1985.

Lauder, J.M.; Sze, P.Y.; and Krebs, H. Maternal influences on tryptophan hydroxylase activity in embryonic rat brain. *Dev Neurosci* 4:291-295, 1981.

Lauder, J.M.; Wallace, J.A.; Krebs, H.; Petrusz, J.; and McCarthy, K. In vivo and in vitro development of serotonergic neurons. *Brain Res Bull* 9:605-625, 1982.

Lidov, H.G.W., and Molliver, M.E. Immunohistochemical study of the development of serotonergic neurons in the rat CNS. *Brain Res Bull* 9:559-604, 1982a.

Lidov, H.G.W., and Molliver, M.E. An immunohistochemical study of serotonin neuron development in the rat: Ascending pathways and terminal fields. *Brain Res Bull* 8:389-430, 1982b.

Little, B.S.; Snell, L.M.; Klein, V.R.; and Gilstrap, L.C. Cocaine abuse during pregnancy: Maternal and fetal implications. *Obstet Gynecol* 73:157-160, 1989.

Liu, J., and Lauder, J.M. Serotonin and nialamide differentially regulate survival and growth of cultured serotonin and catecholamine neurons. *Dev Brain Res* 60: 59-67, 1991.

Liu, J.; Wilkie, M.B.; and Lauder, J.M. Glial-mediated effects of 5-HT and nialamide on in vitro development of raphe and substantia nigra neurons. *Soc Neurosci Abstr* 16:818, 1990.

Loeb, E.P.; Chang, F-L.F.; and Greenough, W.T. Effects of neonatal 6-hydroxydopamine treatment upon morphological organization of the posteromedial barrel subfield in mouse somatosensory cortex. *Brain Res* 403:113-120, 1987.

Lovell, K.L. Effects of 6-hydroxydopamine-induced norepinephrine depletion on cerebellar development. *Dev Neurosci* 5:359-368, 1982.

Luthman, J.; Bolioli, B.; Tsutsumi, T.; Verhofstad, A.; and Jonsson, G. Sprouting of striatal serotonin nerve terminals following selective lesions of nigro-striatal dopamine neurons in neonatal rat. *Brain Res Bull* 19:269-274, 1987.

Mattson, M.P. Neurotransmitters in the regulation of neuronal cytoarchitecture. *Brain Res Rev* 13:179-212, 1988.

McCobb, D.P.; Haydon, P.G.; and Kater, S.B. Dopamine and serotonin inhibition of neurite elongation of different identified neurons. *J Neurosci Res* 19:19-26, 1988.

McMahon, D. Chemical messengers in development: A hypothesis. *Science* 185:1012-1021, 1974.

Miller, J.C., and Friedhoff, A.J. Prenatal neuroleptic exposure alters postnatal striatal cholinergic activity in the rat. *Dev Neurosci* 8:111-116, 1986.

Miller, J.C., and Friedhoff, A.J. Prenatal neurotransmitter programming of postnatal receptor function. *Prog Brain Res* 73:509-523, 1988.

Olsen, L.; Boreus, L.O.; and Seiger, A. Histochemical demonstration and mapping of 5-hydroxytryptamine- and catecholamine-containing neuron systems in the human fetal brain. *Z Anat Entwickl-Gesch* 139:259-282, 1973.

Olsen, L., and Seiger, A. Early prenatal ontogeny of central monoamine neurons in the rat: Fluorescence histochemical observations. *Z Anat Entwickl-Gesch* 137:301-316, 1972.

Onteniente, B.N.; Konig, N.; Sievers, J.; Jenner, S.; Klemm, H.P.; and Marty, R. Structural and biochemical changes in rat cerebral cortex after neonatal 6-hydroxydopamine administration. *Anat Embryol* 159:245-255, 1980.

Oro, A.S., and Dixon, S.D. Perinatal cocaine and methamphetamine exposure: Maternal and neonatal correlates. *J Pediatr* 111:571-578, 1987.

Patrick, R.L., and Barchas, J.D. Potentiation by cocaine of the stimulus-induced increase in dopamine synthesis in rat brain striatal synaptosomes. *Neuropharmacology* 16:327-332, 1977.

Pickel, V.M.; Specht, L.A.; Sumal, K.K.; Joh, T.H.; and Reis, D.J. Immunocytochemical localization of tyrosine hydroxylase in the human fetal nervous system. *J Comp Neurol* 194:465-474, 1980.

Pitts, D.K., and Marwah, J. Effects of cocaine on the electrical activity of single noradrenergic neurons from locus coeruleus. *Life Sci* 33:1229-1234, 1986a.

Pitts, D.K., and Marwah, J. Electrophysiological effects of cocaine on central monoaminergic neurons. *Eur J Pharmacol* 131:95-98, 1986b.

Pitts, D.K., and Marwah, J. Electrophysiological actions of cocaine on noradrenergic neurons in rat locus coeruleus. *J Pharmacol Exp Ther* 240:345-351, 1987a.

Pitts, D.K., and Marwah, J. Cocaine modulation of central monoaminergic neurotransmission. *Pharmacol Biochem Behav* 26:453-461, 1987b.

Pradhan, S.N.; Bhattacharyya, A.K.; and Pradhan, S. Serotonergic manipulation of the behavioral effects of cocaine in rats. *Commun Psychopharmacol* 2:481-486, 1978.

Rakic, P. Defects of neuronal migration and the pathogenesis of cortical malformations. *Prog Brain Res* 73:15-38, 1988.

Randrup, A., and Braestrup, C. Uptake inhibition of biogenic amines by newer antidepressant drugs: Relevance to the dopamine hypothesis of depression. *Psychopharmacology (Berlin)* 53:309-314, 1977.

Reith, M.E.A. Cocaine receptors on monoamine transporters and sodium channels. In: Clouet, D.; Asghar, K.; and Brown, R., eds. *Mechanisms of Cocaine Abuse and Toxicity.* National Institute on Drug Abuse Research Monograph 88. DHHS Pub. No. (ADM)89-1585. Washington, DC: Supt. of Docs., U.S. Govt. Print. Off., 1988. pp. 23-42.

Reith, M.E.A.; Meisler, B.E.; Sershen, H.; and Lajtha, A. Structural requirements for cocaine congeners to interact with dopamine and serotonin uptake sites in mouse brain and to induce stereotyped behavior. *Biochem Pharmacol* 35:1123-1129, 1986.

Reith, M.E.A.; Sershen, H.; Allen, D.L.; and Lajtha, A. A portion of ^{3}H cocaine binding in brain is associated with serotonergic neurons. *Mol Pharmacol* 23:600-603, 1983.

Ritz, M.C.; Lamb, R.J.; Goldberg, S.R.; and Kuhar, M.J. Cocaine receptors on dopamine transporters are related to self administration of cocaine. *Science* 237:1219-1223, 1987.

Rosengarten, H., and Friedhoff, A.J. Enduring changes in dopamine receptor cells of pups from drug administration to pregnant and nursing rats. *Science* 203:1133-1135, 1979.

Ross, S.B., and Renyi, A.L. Inhibition of the uptake of tritiated catecholamines by antidepressants and related agents. *Eur J Pharmacol* 2:181-186, 1967.

Ross, S.B., and Renyi, A.L. Inhibition of the uptake of tritiated 5-hydroxytryptamine in brain tissue. *Eur J Pharmacol* 7:270-277, 1969.

Roth, J.; Le Roith, D.; Shiloach, J.; Rosenzweig, J.L.; Lesniak, M.A.; and Havrankova, J. The evolutionary origins of hormones, neurotransmitters, biology. *N Engl J Med* 306:523-527, 1982.

Ryan, L.; Ehrlich, S.; and Finnegan, L. Cocaine abuse in pregnancy. *Neurotoxicol Teratol* 9:295-299, 1987.

Scheel-Kruger, J.; Braestrup, C.; Nielson, M.; Golembiowska, K.; and Mogilnicka, E. Cocaine: Discussion on the role of dopamine in the

245

biochemical mechanism of action. In: Ellinwood, E.H., Jr., and Kilbey, M.M., eds. *Cocaine and Other Stimulants.* New York: Plenum Press, 1977. pp. 373-407.

Schwaab, D.F.; Boer, G.J.; and Feenstra, M.G.P. Concept of functional teratology and the importance of neurochemistry. *Prog Brain Res* 73:3-14, 1988.

Shirokawa, T.; Kasamatsu, T.; Kupperman, B.D.; and Ramachandran, V.S. Noradrenergic control of ocular dominance plasticity in the visual cortex of dark-reared cats. *Dev Brain Res* 47:303-308, 1989.

Sobrian, S.K.; Burton, L.E.; Robinson, N.L.; Ashe, W.K.; Hutchinson, J.; Stokes, D.L.; and Turner, L.M. Neurobehavioral and immunological effects of prenatal cocaine exposure in rat. *Pharmacol Biochem Behav* 35:617-629, 1990.

Spear, L.P.; Kirstein, C.L.; Bell, J.; Yoottanasumpun, V.; Greensbaum, R.; O'Shea, J.; Hoffmann, H.; and Spear, N.E. Effects of prenatal cocaine exposure on behavior during the early postnatal period. *Neurotoxicol Teratol* 11:57-63, 1989b.

Spear, L.P.; Kirstein, C.L.; and Frambes, N.A. Cocaine effects on the developing central nervous system: Behavioral, psychopharmacological, and neurochemical studies. *Ann N Y Acad Sci* 562:290-307, 1989a.

Specht, L.P.; Pickel, V.M.; Joh, T.H.; and Reis, D.J. Light-microscopic immunocytochemical localization of tyrosine hydroxylase in prenatal rat brain. I. Early ontogeny. *J Comp Neurol* 199:233-253, 1981.

Taylor, D., and Ho, B.T. Comparison of inhibition of monoamine uptake by cocaine, methylphenidate and amphetamine. *Res Commun Chem Pathol Pharmacol* 21:67-75, 1978.

Tennyson, V.M.; Budininkas-Schoenebeck, M.; and Gershon, P. Effects of chronic reserpine treatment on development of maturity of the putamen in fetal rabbits. *Brain Res Bull* 9:651-662, 1982.

Tennyson, V.M.; Gershon, P.; Budininkas-Schoeneback, M.; and Rothman, T.P. Effects of extended periods of reserpine and a-methyl-p-tyrosine treatment on the development of the putamen in fetal rabbits. *Int J Dev Neurosci* 1:305-318, 1983.

Tompkins, G. The metabolic code. *Science* 189:760-763, 1975.

Towle, A.C.; Criswell, H.E.; Maynard, E.H.; Lauder, J.M.; Joh, T.H.; Mueller, R.A.; and Breese, G.R. Serotonin innervation of the rat caudate following a neonatal 6-hydroxydopamine lesion: An anatomical, biochemical and pharmacological study. *Pharmacol Biochem Behav* 34:367-374, 1987.

Trulson, M.E.; Babb, S.; Joe, J.C.; and Raese, J.D. Chronic cocaine administration depletes tyrosine hydroxylase immunoreactivity in the rat brain nigral striatal system: Quantitative light microscopic studies. *Exp Neurol* 94:744-756, 1986.

Wallace, J.A., and Lauder, J.M. Development of the serotonergic system in the rat embryo: An immunocytochemical study. *Brain Res Bull* 10:459-479, 1983.

Whitaker-Azmitia, P.M., and Azmitia, E.C. Autoregulation of fetal serotonergic neuronal development: Role of high affinity serotonin receptors. *Neurosci Lett* 67:307-312, 1986.

Whitaker-Azmitia, P.M., and Azmitia, E.C. Stimulation of astroglial serotonin receptors produces culture media which regulates growth of serotonergic neurons. *Brain Res* 497:80-85, 1989.

Whitaker-Azmitia, P.M.; Lauder, J.M.; Shemmer, A.; and Azmitia, E.C. Postnatal changes in serotonin$_1$ receptors following prenatal alterations in serotonin levels: Further evidence for functional fetal serotonin$_1$ receptors. *Dev Brain Res* 33:285-289, 1987.

Whitaker-Azmitia, P.M.; Murphy, R.; and Azmitia, E.C. Stimulation of astroglial 5-HT$_{1A}$ receptors releases the serotonergic growth factor, protein S-100, and alters astroglial morphology. *Brain Res* 528:155-160, 1990.

Woolverton, W.L. Effects of a D$_1$ and D$_2$ dopamine antagonist on the self-administration of cocaine and piribedil by rhesus monkeys. *Pharmacol Biochem Behav* 24:531-535, 1986.

Woolverton, W.L.; Goldberg, L.I.; and Ginos, J.Z. Intravenous self-administration of dopamine receptor agonists by rhesus monkeys. *J Pharmacol Exp Ther* 230:678-683, 1984.

Woolverton, W.L., and Kleven, M.S. Multiple dopamine receptors and the behavioral effects of cocaine. In: Clout, D.; Asghar, K.; Brown, R., eds. *Mechanisms of Cocaine Abuse and Toxicity.* National Institute on Drug Abuse Research Monograph 88. DHHS Pub. No. (ADM)89-1585. Washington, DC: Supt. of Docs., U.S. Govt. Print. Off., 1988. pp. 160-184.

Zuckerman, B.; Frank, D.A.; Hingson, R.; Amaro, H.; Levenson, S.M.; Kayne, H.; Parker, S.; Vinci, R.; Aboagye, K.; Fried, L.E.; Cabral, H.; Timperi, R.; and Bauchner, H. Effects of maternal marijuana and cocaine use on fetal growth. *N Engl J Med* 320:762-768, 1989.

AUTHOR

Jean M. Lauder, Ph.D.
Professor
Department of Cell Biology and Anatomy
University of North Carolina School of Medicine
CB 37090
Chapel Hill, NC 27599-7090

Assessment of Teratogenic Effects on Cognitive and Behavioral Development in Infancy and Childhood

Joseph L. Jacobson and Sandra W. Jacobson

INTRODUCTION

This chapter focuses on the assessment of developmental delays and abnormalities in cognitive functioning associated with *in utero* exposure to drugs and other toxic substances. First, procedures for assessing cognitive performance in infancy are reviewed, particularly two: the Bayley Scales of Infant Development, the most widely used standardized infant test, and the Fagan Visual Recognition Memory paradigm, the most popular of a newer generation of tests using an information-processing approach to infant assessment. Next is a discussion of which ages may be optimal for developmental assessment. Infant assessment procedures are differentially sensitive at different ages, and performance at certain ages may be more predictive of long-term developmental outcome. Children also differ in their willingness or ability to cooperate with particular testing paradigms at different ages. Finally, the chapter presents three approaches for assessing cognitive functioning in childhood: standardized IQ tests, newer reaction-time tests designed to evaluate cognitive-processing efficiency, and procedures for assessing sustained attention and activity levels.

INFANT ASSESSMENT

The Bayley Scales of Infant Development, which has been standardized for use with infants between the ages of 1 and 30 months (Bayley 1969), provides two standardized scores: the Mental Development Index and the Psychomotor Development Index. The Bayley has been the most extensively used instrument for assessing the effects of prenatal exposure to suspected teratogens. Bayley performance has been found to be affected by *in utero* exposure to alcohol (Streissguth et al. 1980; O'Connor et al. 1986), lead (Bellinger et al. 1987; Dietrich et al. 1987), methadone (Hans, in press), and polychlorinated biphenyl, an environmental toxin (Gladen et al. 1988).

Despite these findings, the Bayley has been extensively criticized in recent years. Inspired by the Gesell (1928) Development Schedule, it grew out of a maturationist tradition that regarded infant development as a series of milestones programmed to emerge over time. The primary purpose of the assessment was to determine where in the normal sequence of development a particular infant fell at the time of testing. Figure 1 shows an excerpt from the scoring sheet for the Mental Development Index. Behaviors are arranged in order of the median age at which they were passed in the standardization sample and reflect a broad range of skills. Items 74 and 75 are primarily attentional; items 78, 80, and 82 require fine motor coordination; and item 79 is a precursor of language.

Figure 1 illustrates one of the principal weaknesses of the Bayley for the study of developmental neurotoxicity: It was not designed to evaluate functioning within specific domains. Items assessing cognitive processing typically require fine motor manipulation, as in item 80, where the infant must pull a string to show his or her understanding of the means-ends relationship between it and the ring. A failure on this item may be due to either a cognitive or fine motor impairment or to a lack of motivation to perform the manipulation. Because the test was not designed to evaluate specific domains of functioning, many important domains are represented by very few items. This raises at least two problems for the assessment drug-related developmental abnormalities. First, there is a risk of Type II error, that is, failure to detect deficits in specific aspects of cognitive functioning not adequately represented among the items tested. Second, where a perinatal exposure is found to be associated with a poorer overall Bayley score, the test provides little information regarding which specific aspects of functioning are impaired. Data on specific deficits can provide important clues for investigating the neurochemical and/or neuroanatomical mechanisms responsible for drug-related central nervous system (CNS) effects.

When administered during the first year of life, the Bayley has very poor predictive validity for later cognitive functioning, except for those infants who are grossly mentally impaired (McCall et al. 1972). Because the drug researcher is interested primarily in effects on longer term functioning, this limited predictive validity may be problematic. It should be noted, however, that most teratogenic exposures found to be associated with poorer Bayley scores also are associated with poorer cognitive performance in the school-age child. Thus, the Bayley appears to be sufficiently sensitive to detect group differences associated with teratogenic exposure, even if it is not sufficiently reliable to predict childhood test scores for individual infants.

Two explanations have been advanced for the Bayley's poor predictive validity. McCall has argued from the perspective of developmental stage theory that

To score: Check P (Pass) or F (Fail). If "Other," mark O (Omit), R (Refused), or RPT (Reported by mother).

Item No.	Age Placement and Range (Months)	Situation	Item Title	Score P	F	Other	Notes
74	5.8 (4-10)	M	Attends to scribbling				
75	6.0 (5-10)	I	Looks for fallen spoon				
76	6.2 (4-12)	K	Playful response to mirror				
77	6.3 (4-10)	H	Retains 2 of 3 cubes offered				
78	6.5 (5-10)	A¹	Manipulates bell: interest in detail				
79	7.0 (5-12)	G³	Vocalizes 4 different syllables				
80	7.1 (5-10)	D²	Pulls string adaptively: secures ring				
81	7.6 (5-12)	E¹	Cooperates in games				Note skill at pat-a-cake for Motor Scale item 44
82	7.6 (5-14)	H	Attempts to secure 3 cubes				

FIGURE 1. *Excerpt from scoring sheet for the Bayley Mental Development Index*

SOURCE: Bayley 1969, copyright 1969, The Psychological Corporation, reproduced by permission, all rights reserved

250

predictive validity from infancy to childhood is not to be expected, because intelligent behavior undergoes significant qualitative transformations as the child matures (McCall et al. 1977). The infant who advances rapidly during an early stage of development will not necessarily be more advanced at later stages when different aspects of functioning may become more focal. On the other hand, Bornstein and others have argued that the Bayley's emphasis on reaching, grasping, and orienting bears little conceptual relation to the encoding and information-processing skills that provide the basis of cognitive functioning in childhood and adulthood (Bornstein and Sigman 1986; Zelazo 1979). They suggest that direct tests of infant information-processing skill should be more valid and, therefore, more predictive.

The Fagan Visual Recognition Memory Test (Fagan and Singer 1983) is designed to assess infant information processing more directly. The infant is seated on the mother's lap in front of an observation chamber containing two stimulus plaques. An observer watches through a peephole in the back of the stage and records the infant's gaze direction on an electronic event recorder. The infant initially is shown two identical target photos, which appear simultaneously in the right and left positions until he or she has looked at them for a total of 20 seconds. The familiar target then is paired with a novel target for two 5-second recognition periods, reversing left-right positions from one period to the next. Because the normative response at this age is to spend more time looking at the novel stimulus, infants who recognize the original target will spend more time looking at the new one. Looking longer at the unfamiliar stimulus, therefore, indicates the ability to recall the original target and to discriminate it from the new one. Although this task requires relatively complex information processing involving stimulus discrimination and memory storage and retrieval, the motoric response—a shift in gaze direction—is minimal.

The Fagan has been found to be sensitive to prenatal exposure to polychlorinated biphenyls in human infants (Jacobson et al. 1985) and to methylmercury in laboratory monkeys (Gunderson et al. 1986). Moderate predictive validity has been reported from performance at 6 to 7 months of age to cognitive functioning at 4 to 7 years (Fagan and McGrath 1981; Rose et al. 1989). In addition to novelty preference, several attentional measures can be derived from this paradigm, including average duration of visual fixation and time off task (Colombo et al. 1988; Rose and Feldman 1987; Jacobson et al. 1989).

OPTIMAL AGES FOR DEVELOPMENTAL ASSESSMENT

McCall and colleagues (1977) investigated discontinuities in mental performance in a principal-components analysis of data from the Berkeley

Growth Study, in which a cohort of infants was assessed monthly on the Bayley Scales. This analysis yielded five empirically derived stages of cognitive development (summarized in table 1), which are remarkably similar to the stages described by Piaget on the basis of clinical observation of his three children and by researchers who have investigated attentional and play development during infancy (e.g., Kagan 1970; Fenson et al. 1976). If McCall and colleagues are correct that mental functioning undergoes fundamental reorganization as the infant progresses through these stages, then assessment procedures that are sensitive or predictive at one age may be less so at others. Thus, the Fagan test may provide a "window" into the infant's information-processing capacity at 6 or 7 months but by 12 months may be cognitively less challenging and, therefore, less indicative of mental competence. Similarly, the Bayley may be less sensitive to teratogenic effects at 18 to 20 months when some, but not all, normally developing children are making an important transition to spoken language. During the preschool period, 4 to 5 years appears to be the best age for cognitive assessment. It is often difficult for younger preschool children to lend themselves to structured tasks, a difficulty that is likely to be compounded for the teratogenically exposed child. For example, we found that polychlorinated biphenyl-exposed preschoolers were less likely to complete the McCarthy Scale testing procedure (Jacobson and Jacobson, in press). The period between 5 and 7 years is one of relatively rapid developmental change in cognitive functioning. Sometimes referred to as the "5 to 7 shift," this period is marked by an improved understanding of the

TABLE 1. *Stages of infant cognitive development*

Stage	Age (months)	Name	Characterization	Piagetian Stage
I	0-2	Newborn	Exercise of endogenous behavioral dispositions	Reflex
II	2-7	Complete subjectivity	World known only through infant's own actions	Primary and secondary circular reactions
III	7-13	Means-ends	Separate cause and effect	Coordination of secondary schemes
IV	13-21	Objectification of environmental entities	Objects have an independent existence	Tertiary circular reactions
V	21+	Symbolic relations	Relations can exist independent of actions and specific entities	Beginning of thought

nature of reality, as indicated by mastery of the Piagetian conservation tasks, as well as an increased ability by the child to monitor his or her behavior, which makes it possible to begin formal schooling. During this period of rapid growth, much of the variance in cognitive performance may be due to individual differences in rate of cognitive maturation and/or exposure to formal educational settings. Given these competing sources of variance, it may be especially difficult to detect effects associated with teratogenic exposure during this period.

At this point, given the assessment paradigms currently available, 6 to 12 months, 4 to 5 years, and 7 to 10 years appear to be the best ages for developmental neurotoxicity testing. Most effects of teratogenic exposure found on the Bayley are from the 6- to 12-month period, and evidence for the predictive validity of the Fagan is strongest at 6 to 7 months. Preschool assessments can be administered most effectively at 4 to 5 years, and by age 7 the child has made the transition to formal schooling and is ready for more structured testing paradigms.

CHILDHOOD ASSESSMENTS

The most popular cognitive assessments for the preschool-age child are the McCarthy Scales of Children's Abilities and the Stanford-Binet IQ Test. Each comprises a series of subtests focusing on specific domains, such as block building, pictorial memory, draw-a-design, and counting and sorting. Most children find these assessments enjoyable and, if the examiner develops the appropriate rapport, they can be administered in a game-like manner. The McCarthy provides standardized test scores in five domains: verbal, perceptual-performance, quantitative, memory, and motor. The General Cognitive Index, computed by summing raw scores from three of these domains, is standardized to a mean of 100 and standard deviation of 15 (like an IQ score) and is highly correlated with IQ as assessed on the Stanford-Binet. The newest version of the Stanford-Binet also provides standardized scores in specific domains: verbal, abstract/visual, quantitative, and short-term memory. As noted earlier, domain-specific data are important for the drug researcher, because a teratogenic exposure may affect only certain aspects of cognitive function and because evidence of a deficit in a particular domain may provide important clues regarding underlying neurochemical or neuroanatomical mechanisms.

In addition to IQ testing, some behavioral teratologists have begun to use newer, more experimental paradigms that are designed to assess specific aspects of cognitive function more directly and could be more sensitive to subtle effects. In our research on polychlorinated biphenyls, we have begun to use reaction-time paradigms from the field of information-processing psychology to assess cognitive-processing efficiency within specific domains. This approach

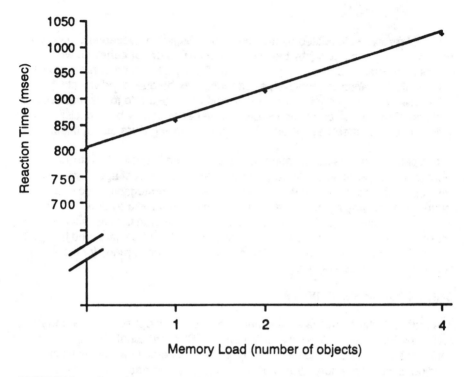

FIGURE 2. *Sternberg recognition memory paradigm: Reaction time by memory load*

is exemplified by the Sternberg (1969) visual search and recognition memory task. The child is shown a stimulus array of one, two, or four objects, which he or she is asked to remember. A series of test stimuli then appear individually on the screen. The child is instructed to press a red button when shown an object that appeared in the original array and a black button if the object was not in the original array. Performance is analyzed by computing the slope and intercept of a line connecting the child's mean reaction times for the different memory loads. Figure 2, based on data we collected in a pilot study in Israel, shows mean reaction times for the children's responses to the red button. As expected, it took the children somewhat longer to process the information when the memory load was larger. Figure 3 compares the reaction times of children with higher or lower performance IQ scores on the Wechsler Intelligence Scales for Children-Revised. The flatter slope for the higher IQ children indicates more efficient short-term memory, because it did not take these children appreciably longer to process the larger memory load than the smaller load. Other aspects of short-term memory processing, including encoding, decision, and response time, are assessed in terms of the intercept, which measures reaction time irrespective of

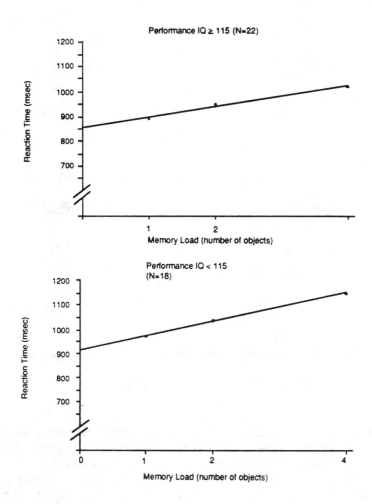

FIGURE 3. *Sternberg recognition memory paradigm performance by performance IQ score*

memory load. Looking at the intercept, the higher IQ children's response times are again faster, indicating more efficient processing.

This type of paradigm also can be used to assess cognitive-processing efficiency in contexts not involving short-term memory. In Kail's (1986) mental-rotation task, the child is shown one of eight alphanumeric characters presented upright, together with the same character or its mirror image, rotated at an angle clockwise from the vertical (figure 4). The child must decide whether the pairs of stimuli are identical or mirror images and respond as quickly as possible without making errors. Performance is analyzed by computing the slope and

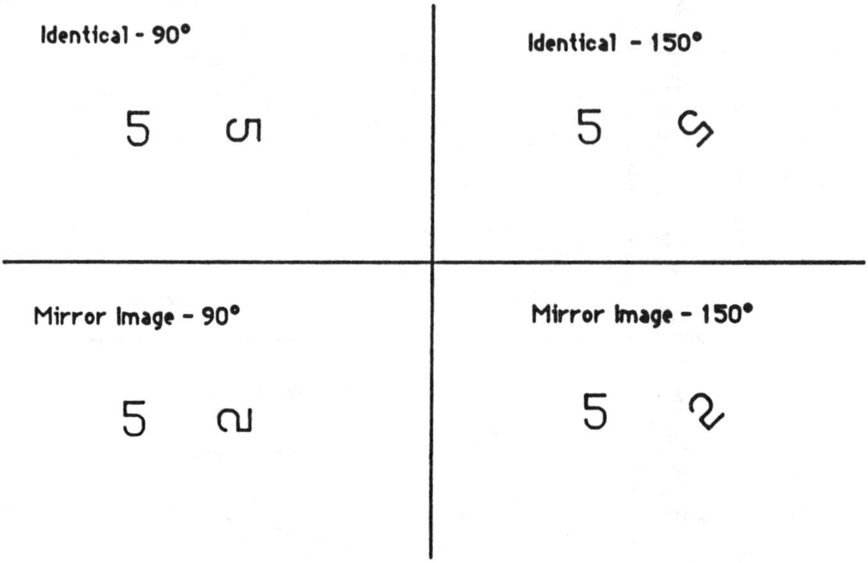

FIGURE 4. *Sample problems from the Kail mental-rotation paradigm*

SOURCE: Kail et al. 1980, copyright 1980, Academic Press

intercept of a line connecting the child's mean reaction times at the different degrees of rotation (figure 5). A flatter slope is assumed to indicate more efficient spatial reasoning because processing time for objects rotated at more extreme angles is not appreciably longer than for those closer to upright. Reaction times on both the short-term memory and mental-rotation tasks become markedly faster as children grow older. Comparisons of performance across several of these tasks can indicate the degree to which observed deficits are domain specific or reflect impairment in aspects of cognitive processing that affect multiple domains.

Two outcomes that have been of considerable interest to investigators of teratogenic exposures are sustained attention and activity level. Sustained attention can be assessed in a vigilance or continuous performance paradigm. In the task we have used, the child sits in front of a video monitor that displays a picture of a house. Any of three stimuli—an apple, a butterfly, or a cat—can appear in any of the three windows of the house, but the child is told to press the red button only when the cat comes to the window. The cat appears 42 times over a 12-minute period at random intervals ranging from 4.5 to 52.0 seconds. Three measures are tabulated: reaction time to the criterion stimulus,

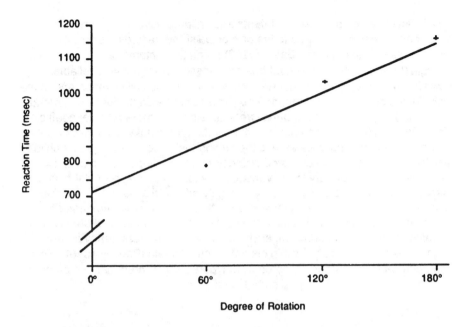

FIGURE 5. *Kail mental-rotation paradigm: Reaction time by degree of rotation (male eighth graders)*

SOURCE: Keating et al. 1985

errors of omission (failing to press the button in response to the criterion stimulus), and errors of commission (pressing in the absence of the criterion, which is a measure of impulsivity). Streissguth and associates (1984, 1986) have found relationships between prenatal alcohol exposure and poorer sustained attention on this type of paradigm at both 4 and 7 years.

Needleman and associates (1979) found sustained attention deficits in low-level lead-exposed children using rating scales completed by classroom teachers. Exposed children were more likely to be rated as easily distracted during school work, were less able to persist with a task for a reasonable amount of time, were overexcitable and impulsive, and were unable to follow a sequence of directions. Both the continuous-performance and rating-scale approaches for assessing sustained attention have their limitations. Whereas the child's score on a 12-minute laboratory paradigm may be affected by his or her mood or level of fatigue on the day of testing, rating scales are less objective and less subject to halo effects. For this reason, multiple measures are recommended, particularly for outcomes considered focal to the study.

Activity level can be assessed in infants and children using an actometer—a mechanical device strapped to the arm or waist that records number of movements per unit of time. Eaton (1983) found that actometer readings from a single 20-minute nursery school free-play session were not very reliable, however, presumably due to day-to-day variability in the child's mood and in the activities he or she chose to engage in. Data from 20-minute sessions spread over 4 or 5 days, on the other hand, were considerably more reliable; coefficient alphas were in the .70s, compared with only .33 for a single-day assessment. Perhaps even more impressive was the finding that parental ratings of a child's activity level were highly correlated with actometer readings totaled over 14 sessions (r=.78). Contrary to conventional wisdom regarding parental bias, parents apparently were able to provide highly accurate assessments of their children's activity levels. Another approach that has been recommended for assessing activity level and sustained attention is direct behavioral observation in which certain target behaviors, such as fidgeting or off-task behavior, are coded as present or absent within discrete time intervals (Barkley 1988). This approach, which has been validated with hyperactive children, has not been used extensively in teratological studies to date.

CONCLUSION

It should be emphasized that, despite a plethora of available alternatives, the Bayley and childhood IQ tests remain the most widely used procedures for assessing the developmental effects of *in utero* toxic exposure. Although the Bayley has been criticized for confounding assessment of cognitive competence with sensorimotor dexterity, the breadth of domains it taps may enhance its sensitivity to teratogenic insult. Due to dissatisfaction with the Bayley's poor predictive validity, many ongoing studies have added the Fagan recognition memory paradigm; whether the Fagan will prove as sensitive to teratogenic exposure has yet to be determined. IQ tests have been used extensively with young children because they are valid predictors of school performance. Despite controversy regarding their interpretation, there is a broad consensus that IQ scores reflect at least some important aspects of intelligence. Problems arise in teratological studies when low-level exposures are found to be associated with small decrements in IQ, because the functional significance of a 4- to 8-point deficit is not understood. In principle, a small deficit in an IQ test, which reflects diverse cognitive competences, could indicate significant impairment in one or two specific domains of cognitive function. Detailed assessments of specific domains would be needed to address this issue.

258

REFERENCES

Barkley, R.A. Attention deficit disorder with hyperactivity. In: Mash, E.J., and Terdal, L.G., eds. *Behavioral Assessment of Childhood Disorders.* 2d ed. New York: Guilford, 1988.

Bayley, N. *Bayley Scales of Infant Development.* New York: Psychological Corporation, 1969.

Bellinger, D.; Leviton, A.; Waternaux, C.; Needleman, H.; and Rabinowitz, M. Longitudinal analyses of prenatal and postnatal lead exposure and early cognitive development. *N Engl J Med* 316:1037-1043, 1987.

Bornstein, M.H., and Sigman, M.D. Continuity in mental development from infancy. *Child Dev* 57:251-274, 1986.

Colombo, J.; Mitchell, D.W.; and Horowitz, F.D. Infant visual attention in the paired-comparison paradigm: Test-retest and attention-performance relations. *Child Dev* 89:1198-1210, 1988.

Dietrich, K.N.; Krafft, K.M; Bornschein, R.L.; Hammond, P.B.; Berger, O.; Succop, P.A.; and Bier, M. Low-level fetal lead exposure effect on neurobehavioral development in early infancy. *Pediatrics* 80:721-730, 1987.

Eaton, W.O. Measuring activity level with actometers: Reliability, validity, and arm length. *Child Dev* 54:720-726, 1983.

Fagan, J.F., and McGrath, S.K. Infant recognition memory and later intelligence. *Intelligence* 5:121-130, 1981.

Fagan, J.F., and Singer, L.T. Infant recognition memory as a measure of intelligence. In: Lipsitt, L.P., ed. *Advances in Infancy Research.* Vol. II. Norwood, NJ: Ablex, 1983.

Fenson, L.; Kagan, J.; Kearsley, R.B.; and Zelazo, P.R. The developmental progression of manipulative play in the first two years. *Child Dev* 47:232-236, 1976.

Gesell, A. *Infancy and Human Growth.* New York: MacMillan, 1928.

Gladen, B.C.; Rogan, W.J.; Hardy, P.; Thullen, J.; Tingelstad, J.; and Tully, M. Development after exposure to polychlorinated biphenyls and dichlorodiphenyl dichloroethene transplacentally and through human milk. *J Pediatr* 113:991-995, 1988.

Gunderson, V.M.; Grant, K.S.; Burbacher, T.M.; Fagan, J.F. III; and Mottet, N.K. The effect of low-level prenatal methylmercury exposure on visual recognition memory in infant crab-eating macaques. *Child Dev* 57:1076-1083, 1986.

Hans, S. Methodological issues in studying the effects of maternal drug use on infant offspring. In: Greenbaum, C., and Auerbach, J., eds. *Longitudinal Studies of Infants Born at Psychological Risk.* Norwood, NJ: Ablex, in press.

Jacobson, S.W.; Fein, G.G.; Jacobson, J.L.; Schwartz, P.M.; and Dowler, J.K. The effect of PCB exposure on visual recognition memory. *Child Dev* 56:853-860, 1985.

Jacobson, J.L., and Jacobson, S.W. Developmental effects of perinatal exposure to polychlorinated biphenyls and related contaminants. In: Needleman, H.L., and Bellinger, D., eds. *Prenatal Exposure to Environmental Toxicants: Developmental Consequences.* Baltimore: Johns Hopkins University Press, in press.

Jacobson, J.L.; Jacobson, S.W.; Padgett, R.J.; Abela, M.B.; O'Neill, J.M.; and Sokol R.J. "Alternative Measures of Infant Attention in a Visual Recognition Paradigm." Paper presented at the annual meeting of the American Psychological Association, New Orleans, 1989.

Kagan, J. The determinants of attention in the infant. *Am Sci* 58:298-306, 1970.

Kail, R. Sources of age differences in speed of processing. *Child Dev* 57:969-987, 1986.

Kail, R.; Pellegrino, J.; and Carter, P. Developmental changes in mental rotation. *J Exp Child Psychol* 29:102-116, 1980.

Keating, D.P.; List, J.A.; and Merriman, W.E. Cognitive processing and cognitive ability: A multivariate investigation. *Intelligence* 9:149-170, 1985.

McCall, R.B.; Eichorn, E.H.; and Hogarty, P.S. Transitions in early mental development. *Monogr Soc Res Child Dev* 42(serial no. 171):1-94, 1977.

McCall, R.B.; Hogarty, P.S.; and Hurlburt, N. Transitions in infant sensorimotor development and the prediction of childhood IQ. *Am Psychol* 27:728-748, 1972.

Needleman, H.L.; Gunnoe, C.; Leviton, A.; Reed, R.; Peresie, H.; Maher, C.; and Barrett, P. Deficits in psychologic and classroom performance of children with elevated dentine lead levels. *N Engl J Med* 300:689-695, 1979.

O'Connor, M.J.; Brill, N.J.; and Sigman M. Alcohol use in primiparous women older than 30 years of age: Relation to infant development. *Pediatrics* 78:444-450, 1986.

Rose, S.A., and Feldman, J.F. Infant visual attention: Stability of individual differences from 6 to 8 months. *Dev Psychol* 23:490-498, 1987.

Rose, S.A.; Feldman, J.F.; Wallace, I.F.; and McCarton, C. Infant visual attention: Relation to birth status and developmental outcome during the first 5 years. *Dev Psychol* 25:560-576, 1989.

Sternberg, S. Memory scanning: Mental process revealed by reaction-time experiments. *Am Sci* 57:421-457, 1969.

Streissguth, A.P.; Barr, H.M.; Martin, D.C.; and Herman, C.S. Effects of maternal alcohol, nicotine, and caffeine use during pregnancy on infant mental and motor development at 8 months. *Alcohol Clin Exp Res* 4:152-164, 1980.

Streissguth, A.P.; Barr, H.M.; Sampson, P.D.; Parrish-Johnson, J.C.; Kirchner, G.L.; and Martin, D.C. Attention, distraction, and reaction time at age 7 years and prenatal alcohol exposure. *Neurobehav Toxicol Teratol* 8:717-725, 1986.

Streissguth, A.P.; Martin, D.C.; Barr, H.M.; Sandman, B.M.; Kirchner, G.L.; and Darby, B.L. Intrauterine alcohol and nicotine exposure: Attention and reaction time in 4-year-old children. *Dev Psychol* 20:533-541, 1984.

Zelazo, P.R. Reactivity to perceptual-cognitive events: Applications for infant assessment. In: Kearsley, R.B., and Sigel, I.E., eds. *Infants at Risk: Assessment of Cognitive Functioning*. New York: Erlbaum Associates, 1979.

AUTHORS

Joseph L. Jacobson, Ph.D.
Associate Professor

Sandra W. Jacobson, Ph.D.
Research Scientist

Psychology Department
Wayne State University
71 West Warren Avenue
Detroit, MI 48202

New Methodologies for Evaluating Residual Brain Damage in Infants Exposed to Drugs of Abuse: Objective Methods for Describing Movements, Facial Expressions, and Communicative Behaviors

Edward Z. Tronick, Marjorie Beeghly, Linda Fetters, and M. Katherine Weinberg

This chapter describes three methods for characterizing the functional organization of movements, facial expressions, and communicative gestures: (1) kinematic analysis of movement, (2) muscle and template systems for coding facial expressions, and (3) video-based coding systems to examine communicative configurations. These methods promise to assess possible residual brain damage affecting the organization of neuromotor functioning of infants and children under 2 who were exposed *in utero* to cocaine and other illicit drugs.

The chapter focuses on the control of movement because this is a primary brain function in the infant and presents a number of approaches that may be particularly relevant to the study of movement in infants exposed *in utero* to illicit drugs.

- Organization of spontaneous movements (e.g., general patterns of infant "nondirected" activity)

- Organization of instrumental movements (e.g., reaching)

- Organization of facial expressions (e.g., patterns of muscle movements controlling facial expressions)

- Organization of communicative configurations of the limbs, hands, and head (e.g., withdrawal and defensive patterns associated with stressful social interactions)

In the past, the assessment of abnormalities in movement control such as jitteriness, jerkiness, cogwheel-like movements, "funny looking" facial configurations, or asymmetries were based on clinical judgment and considered "soft" signs of neurological dysfunction. However, new technology based on infrared sensors, video recordings, and computers makes it possible to describe normal and abnormal infant movements in a more precise and objective manner. Although this technology is in a fledgling stage and, therefore, must be used cautiously, it holds great potential for detecting underlying dysfunction.

EFFECTS OF PRENATAL COCAINE EXPOSURE ON INFANT GROWTH AND DEVELOPMENT

Intrauterine Growth Retardation

Much evidence suggests that a disruption of intrauterine growth occurs in the cocaine-exposed infant. Exposed infants have higher rates of prematurity and show depressed weight, length, and head circumference (Zuckerman et al. 1989; Chasnoff and Griffith 1989). These effects remain even when use of other potentially growth-retarding substances are controlled statistically (Zuckerman et al. 1989; Ryan et al. 1987; Hadeed and Siegel 1989). Increased incidence of microcephaly also has been reported (Hadeed and Siegel 1989).

Reports of intrauterine growth retardation (IUGR) in cocaine-exposed infants raise concerns about postnatal behavior and development, because it is well documented that IUGR is associated with compromised neuromotor and socioemotional sequelae. For example, several researchers have documented that IUGR results in poor state organization, hypotonia, decreased motor maturity, and an increased number of abnormal reflexes during the newborn period (Als et al. 1976; Beeghly et al. 1988; Lester et al. 1986; Lester and Zeskind 1978). IUGR also is associated with long-term sequelae, including neurobehavioral deficits (Beeghly et al. 1988, 1990; Vohr et al. 1979), social dysfunction in infancy (Beeghly et al. 1989, 1990), preschool cognitive deficits (Walther and Ramaekers 1982), language delays (Walther and Ramaekers 1982), and poor academic performance (Henricksen et al. 1986).

Brain Damage

A number of preliminary findings are suggestive of residual brain damage to infants exposed to cocaine *in utero*. Among such effects are clinically obvious cerebral infarctions (Chasnoff et al. 1986) and clinically silent major ultrasound abnormalities in the deep brain (Dixon and Bejar 1988). Cases of perinatal cerebral infarction, seizures, intraventricular hemorrhage, and periventricular leukomalacia also have been reported (Oro and Dixon 1987; Cohen et al. 1989;

Chasnoff et al. 1986). These effects often are ascribed to the vasoconstrictive and hypertensive effects of cocaine, although direct effects associated with the drug's action on the catecholamine system should not be discounted, as Mirochnick and coworkers (in press) are beginning to demonstrate.

Neurobehavioral Deficits

Neurobehavioral functional deficits from *in utero* exposure to cocaine have been reported in neonates, including abnormal electroencephalogram (EEG) findings and abnormal visual and auditory-evoked responses (Shih et al. 1989). Disruption of brain stem function is possible because of cardiorespiratory abnormalities that occur at a higher incidence in cocaine-exposed infants compared with opiate-exposed controls (Chasnoff et al. 1989). Increased jitteriness among infants with cocaine metabolites in their urine at birth have been noted (Parker et al. 1989). In a series of important studies, Chasnoff and colleagues (1989) compared cocaine-exposed infants, opiate-exposed infants, and nonexposed infants on the Brazelton Neonatal Behavioral Assessment Scale (NBAS) (Brazelton 1984) and found increased tremulousness, poor social interactive behavior, and poor organization of behavioral states. Other neurobehavioral signs that have been found include increased irritability, high-pitched and excessive crying, jitteriness, hyperactivity, rigidity, hypertonicity, hypotonia, coarse and choreiform movements, vigorous sucking, and abnormal neuromuscular signs (Fulroth et al. 1989; Doberczak et al. 1988).

Motor Deficits

The long-term compromise of motor function is unknown. Schneider (1988) has described deficits in muscle tone, reflexes, and volitional movements in cocaine-exposed infants at 4 months of age. Furthermore, clinicians often report persistent distal hypertonia in exposed infants.

Cognitive Deficits

Unfortunately, reports related to cognitive, motoric, and neurobehavioral deficits (Chasnoff and Griffith 1989; Rodning et al. 1989; Howard 1989) are compromised by a number of serious methodological problems. The techniques used are imprecise, based on clinical judgment, often insensitive to the parameters and dimensions of concern, and only poorly quantifiable (Tronick and Beeghly, in press). Many of these problems can be resolved by new measurement systems to be reported here: kinematic analysis of movement, muscle and template systems for coding facial expressions, and video-based coding systems to examine communicative configurations. These techniques permit objective descriptions of the behaviors that are most likely to be sensitive to brain dysfunction resulting from cocaine exposure. Moreover, these measures can be readily coordinated with one another through the use of similar experimental paradigms and settings. This results in a rather complete characterization of the infant's neurobehavioral organization and the quality of the infant's interactions with the mother or other social partners.

KINEMATIC ANALYSIS

Kinematic analysis specifies components of movement in an objective, quantifiable, and precise fashion (Fetters and Todd 1987; Kluzik et al. 1990). A typical kinematic analysis system weds high-speed computer technology with high-resolution infrared sensors to track the movement of tiny infrared-emitting diodes attached to the limbs of individuals whose movements are the subject of study. Kinematic analysis has been used to develop detailed descriptions and theoretical accounts of movement and motor control for normal adults (Harris et al. 1984), normal infants (Jeannerod 1988), infants born prematurely (Claman and Zeffiro 1986), and infants with central nervous system dysfunction (Fisk and Goodale 1988).

Kinematic data describe movement, irrespective of its causation (Winter 1987), in terms of position and the derivations of position. Thus, if reaching is the movement under study, the exact positions of the wrist, elbow, and shoulder in three-dimensional space are specified. The angles of the joints as the movement occurs and the rate at which these points change also are considered. Parameters such as angular velocities and accelerations, movement unit size, pause times between movements, and others are computed. Because kinematic parameters are objective and precise, one might cautiously argue that motor dysfunction uncovered by kinematic analysis, as opposed to other forms of motor assessment, is less likely to reflect the caretaking experienced by the infant. Thus, this technology may be extremely useful for uncovering residual brain damage.

A fundamental unit of kinematic analysis is the movement unit. Brooks (1974) described continuous vs. discontinuous arm movement in monkeys with brain lesions. A single acceleration followed by a single deceleration was a characteristic of reaches for the intact monkeys, whereas the cerebellar-lesioned animals displayed multiple acceleration/deceleration units.

Fetters and Todd (1987) and Von Hofsten (1979) defined the fundamental unit of kinematic analysis in human adults and infants as the portion of movement (e.g., a reach) between one acceleration and one deceleration, or the portion of the movement between subsequent points in a curvature-speed relationship (figure 1).

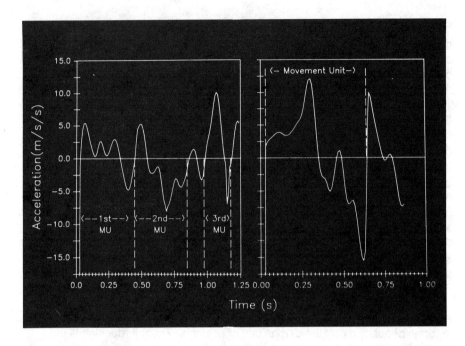

FIGURE 1. *The curvature-speed relationship is the fundamental movement unit of motor organization.*

This speed-curvature coupling also has been demonstrated in studies of adult reaching movements (Abend et al. 1982). When subjects were asked to produce curved reaches to a stationary target, they chunked their reaches into units, as defined by a decrease in speed coupled with an increase in curvature. Similar results have been found in studies of adult handwriting (Viviani and Terzuolo 1980).

Disturbances of kinematic parameters have been found to be associated with central nervous system (CNS) damage. For instance, patients suffering from cerebral vascular accidents (Lough et al. 1984) or posterior parietal lesions (Jeannerod 1988) evidence aberrant movement during reaching tasks. Kinematic parameters of patients with parietal lesions are distinguishable from those of patients with frontal lobe lesions, cerebellar lesions, and premotor cortex lesions (Claman and Zeffiro 1986; Fisk and Goodale 1988) or those of normals.

Movement organization has been studied in the developing infant. Thelen (1982) studied kicking and Fetters and Todd (1987) studied reaching. From 7 to 12 months of age in normal full-term infants, the number of movement units decreases from 2.87 to 2.33, the straightness ratio (i.e., the distance the hand travels compared with the shortest distance to the target) decreases from 2.05 to 1.71; the percentage of the total reach that is made up by the first movement unit increases from .48 to .63; and the total duration remains constant at approximately 1.209 sec. These findings (Fetters and Todd 1987) demonstrate that early reaches in the young infant include multiple units, with the number of units decreasing with maturity. Thus, jerky stop-start actions give way to one smooth, continuous acceleration, followed by a single deceleration. A mature reach, which is achieved early in the second year of life, is characterized by a single movement unit with only one stop-start action. This suggests that a lower number of movement units reflects greater control of the reaching movement. Thus, counting and timing movement units offers an important quantitative measure of changes of control or coordination. Clearly, this advance in understanding allows for a precise description of clinically useful patterns such as jerkiness, tremulousness, and cogwheel forms of movement that heretofore have been described only subjectively.

In a recent study of healthy preterm infants at 7, 9, and 12 months of age (corrected), Fetters and Todd (1987) demonstrated subtle differences in the movement strategies of healthy preterm infants compared with normal full-terms. As a group, healthy preterms are considered to be at low risk for developmental problems compared with less healthy preterm infants. Using kinematic analysis, these investigators found that preterms had a greater number of movement units in their reaches compared with full-term controls, even though, as in controls, the number of movement units in their reaches decreased from 3.15 to 2.54. In addition, as in controls, the straightness ratio of these preterm reaches increased from 2.13 to 1.56, and the duration was relatively constant at approximately 1.215 seconds. Unlike the full-term infants, however, the proportion of the reach made up by the first movement unit was unchanged from 7 to 13 months and made up only 48 percent of their reaches at 12 months. Thus, although the number of movement units within reaches decreased as the preterm infants got older, they did not elongate the first unit; that is, preterm reaching, even at 1 year of age, was characterized by multiple units of similar duration. These differences in neuromotor organization indicate a significant compromise of the healthy preterm infant's neuromotor functioning. Yet these subtle abnormalities are typically undetected by conventional methods of developmental assessment.

Long-term effects of brain dysfunction were demonstrated using kinematic analysis in a study of five children, ages 7 to 12, with cerebral palsy (Kluzik et al. 1990). In this study, an infant reaching for a target was compared before and immediately after physical therapy treatment. Kluzik and colleagues found that the reaches of these moderately to severely involved spastic children could be described as slow, jerky in quality, and curvilinear in path. Before treatment, the children averaged 3.7 movement units; the average duration of reach was 1,692 ms; and the straightness ratio was 1.2. By comparison, age-matched controls typically perform this movement with a single movement in 300 to 600 ms (Kluzik et al. 1990). Following treatment, the number of movement units decreased to 2.7, and average duration decreased to 1,267 ms (both statistically significant). Furthermore, the duration of the first movement unit in relation to the entire duration of the reach was significantly greater following treatment. This indicates that the reach was becoming characterized by a single movement unit (a single stop-start action), which is typical of mature, well-controlled reaching movements. The length the hand traveled (straightness) and the extent to which associated reactions occurred did not differ significantly after treatment.

Kinematic analysis is clearly a major advance over more clinical assessments of neuromotor functioning that rely on observer judgment and experience. While behavioral measures are effective in describing major forms of dysfunction, kinematic analysis detects subtle forms of dysfunction that are indicative of brain damage. Kinematic analysis has the additional advantage of being able to provide these data in both structured contexts (i.e., the examiner assisting the infant in organizing the task) and unstructured settings (i.e., tasks requiring self-organization by the infant). This advantage is critical because cocaine-exposed babies appear to have most difficulty when testing requires self-organization, self-initiation, and followthrough (Rodning et al. 1989). Furthermore, kinematic methods yield operational definitions of measures and data that are sensitive to even minor levels of dysfunction and therapeutic change. These qualities make kinematic analysis an extremely likely candidate for detecting any existing neuromotor dysfunction associated with brain damage in cocaine-exposed infants.

Paradigms for Eliciting Movements

A typical kinematic analysis is the WATSMART Version 2.7 (Northern Digital Company). The WATSMART is a noncontact, nonintrusive optoelectric system capable of recording high-speed kinematic motion as well as high-resolution static displacements (figure 2). It is also capable of rendering three-dimensional graphic displays of infrared light-emitting diodes (IREDs) in space. The IREDs are tracked simultaneously by two highly accurate infrared sensors (cameras) placed on a track approximately 6 feet above the seated subject and at approximately a 90-degree angle to each other and a 45-degree angle to the plane of movement. The accuracy is valid over the full 33-degree vertical and horizontal fields of view (45 degrees diagonal). The WATSMART cameras are initially calibrated in relation to the test area using a 1m cube fixed grid with 24 IREDs embedded at known locations. As long as neither the cameras nor the work station are disturbed, the system is reliable and accurate. The WATSMART is used in conjunction with a PC Limited System 200 computer (Dell Computer Corporation), an IBM AT clone.

The IREDs are fired sequentially by the central controller unit via a lightweight strobe attached to the chair back (Scholz 1989). As the subject moves, the

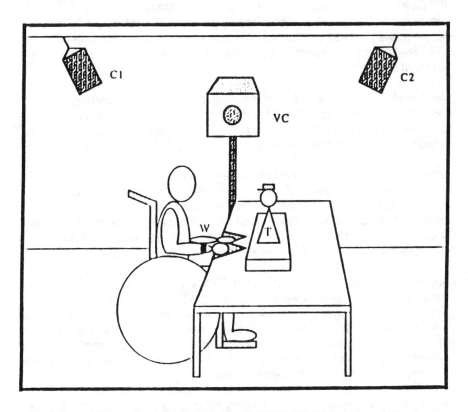

FIGURE 2. *Diagrammatic sketch of the WATSMART laboratory setup for assessing adult movement*

KEY: C1 and C2= infrared sensors; VC=video camera; T=target; W=wrist IRED marker instantaneous position of each marker is digitized at a rate of 200 Hz, with a resolution of approximately 1.0 mm. Any occluded points are flagged, and the data are interpolated, if necessary, for the occluded points. Raw data are converted to three-dimensional coordinates for graphic display of movement by use of a direct linear transformation algorithm (Scholz 1989). When care is taken to reduce reflected light in the measurement area and to prevent rotation of the IREDs away from the cameras, highly reliable recordings of position ($r > .99$; error<0.5 degree) can be obtained using WATSMART (Scholz 1989). Reliability of movement trajectory is particularly sensitive to movement of the IREDs away from the plane of the cameras, especially at endpoints of movements (Scholz 1989). The reliability values for reproducing a fixed target length rotated in three-dimensional space are below 2 mm. This means that the WATSMART system reproduces the absolute length of the moving ruler with errors of 2 mm or less.

Additional videotaping of reaching movements enhances interpretation of WATSMART recordings. The video data are coupled with a time-code generator to record the precise time of movements. Systems based solely on video technology are now available.

Procedures for eliciting scorable movements can begin in the newborn period and continue longitudinally. During the newborn period, spontaneous movements can be elicited with inanimate visual and auditory stimuli, such as a rattle, and/or with animate stimuli, such as the examiner's face and voice. Of course, special attention must be paid to the newborn's behavioral state because it is likely to modify the quality of the movements observed.

Importantly, these same procedures can be used over the course of development because they will continue to be effective in eliciting spontaneous and instrumental movements, as well as facial expressions and communicative configurations. In older infants, reaches can be elicited easily with an object placed in front of the child seated in a high chair. Spontaneous movements can be elicited when the infant is sitting or lying without the use of an object or when interacting with an adult in face-to-face play.

We expect that normal infant movements will contain fewer movement units and decreased peak velocity in comparison with the movements of drug-exposed infants. In particular, we expect that the movements of cocaine-exposed infants will (1) be made up of a greater number of movement units (i.e., less smooth); (2) be less oriented toward the midline/target (i.e., less accurate/less directed); (3) have more minor accelerations and decelerations not large enough to be considered movement units (i.e, fine tremor); (4) evidence higher velocity movements; and (5) show a greater number of associated head movements. In other words, it is expected that normal infant movements will be quantified as smooth, well-oriented, and controlled compared with the movements of cocaine-exposed infants, which will contain many stop-start actions.

FACIAL EXPRESSIONS ANALYSIS

Methodologies are now available for objectively coding facial expressions (Ekman and Friesen 1978; Izard 1979; Izard et al. 1980). Facial expressions are a crucial component of the infant's communicative capacities. They provide caretakers with information necessary for the successful meeting of the infant's homeostatic and developmental requirements (Tronick 1989). Survival and development depend significantly, therefore, on the integrity of this signaling system. Reflecting this adaptive function, large areas of the brain are devoted to the control of facial expressions. Indeed, one might argue that no other system shows the variety and subtlety of movement patterns as early in development as does the facial musculature and that it may be the most developed of the infant's motor systems (Izard 1971). Thus, although not traditionally viewed as an assessment domain, analyses of the integrity and organization of facial expressions may prove to be especially fruitful.

Most facial measurement systems can be loosely grouped into two categories: template-based systems and anatomically comprehensive systems. Template-based systems, such as Izard's Maximally Discriminative Facial Movement Coding System (MAX) (Izard 1979) and System for Identifying Affect Expressions by Holistic Judgements (AFFEX) (Izard et al. 1980), identify patterns of facial muscle movements that have been empirically or theoretically linked to discrete emotions.

Anatomically comprehensive systems, such as Ekman and Friesen's Facial Action Coding System (FACS) (Ekman and Friesen 1978), code emotionally significant facial movements as well as any other facial behavior, regardless of its relation to affect. Both types of scoring systems are designed to eliminate subjective bias in identifying emotional expressions by focusing on distinct facial muscle configurations in specific areas of the face.

Izard's MAX and AFFEX systems are designed specifically for use with young children. The basic assumption is that infant emotions are expressed in organized patterns of facial movements. The emotions identified by MAX and AFFEX include interest-excitement, enjoyment-joy, surprise-astonishment, sadness-dejection, anger-rage, disgust-contempt, fear-terror, shame-shyness, discomfort-pain, or distress-anguish. To score these emotions, coders look for

271

anatomical changes in the musculature of three regions of the face: the forehead/eyebrows/nasal root region, the eyes/nose/cheeks region, and the mouth/lips/chin region. Coders using the AFFEX system make judgments about the presence of emotions from the pattern of the entire face at once, whereas coders using MAX need to complete three runs of each video segment to score each facial region separately.

The objectivity of the two systems stems from the fact that coders make judgments regarding the presence or absence of clearly defined facial movements. They do not make judgments based on their perception of the emotional content of the expression or on the context in which the expression occurs. Furthermore, because each of the fundamental emotions is defined in terms of a specific set of facial movements, they can be differentiated from each other, as well as from blends of emotions or from facial patterns not specified by MAX or AFFEX.

Ekman and Friesen's FACS is designed to score the facial expressions of adults. FACS is more comprehensive than MAX and AFFEX, recording all observable facial muscle movements, regardless of their importance in determining emotional expressions. The system distinguishes 24 discrete action units, 20 miscellaneous facial actions, and 14 action units designating head and eye positions. The system identifies six emotions—joy, surprise, sadness, anger, disgust, and fear—by analyzing the muscle movements in the forehead/eyebrows/nasal root region, the eyes/nose/cheeks region, and the mouth/lips/chin region. Recently, FACS has been adapted for use with infants. Oster's (1990) BABY FACS is designed to precisely describe facial expressions at each stage of development and to determine the affective meaning of these expressions by taking into account their antecedents and behavioral correlates.

The major disadvantage of FACS is that its comprehensiveness makes it more time-consuming than the MAX or AFFEX systems. Nevertheless, because FACS codes all facial movements and does not specify *a priori* which facial patterns are significant, the system can be used to evaluate the role of facial movements that are not obviously or necessarily emotional. Moreover, it is precise enough to evaluate variations in timing, intensity, and sequencing of the components that make up facial expressions (Campos et al. 1983).

Methodological advances in facial-expression scoring have been instrumental in investigating the importance and function of emotions and their development from infancy to adulthood. Research during infancy has relied heavily on the use of MAX and AFFEX and has emphasized the developmental emergence and function of emotions. This work indicates that certain facial expressions are present at birth, whereas others become functional later in development. Furthermore, these facial expressions tend to occur in response to particular events and are remarkably similar to the facial expressions of adults. Research also has established that mothers and other adults are sensitive to these emotional displays, even when the infant is very young and in the absence of contextual cues (Campos et al. 1983).

To date, these coding systems have not often been employed with clinical populations such as drug-exposed infants, even though they could readily be used to address issues of concern. For example, are exposed infants able to control their facial musculature in a manner that results in fully formed and well-organized expressions, or do they show dysfunctional patterns (e.g., asymmetries)? Do they lack particular expressions? Is the timing of the different components that make up an expression well organized, or do these infants evidence problems in controlling movements in a simultaneous and sequential fashion? Do they evidence normal relations between facial expressions and environmental events, or do they respond with expressions that are inappropriate and dysfunctional (e.g., distress faces in response to normal interactive play)? It is critical to note that dysfunction in the ability to modulate facial expressions is likely to reflect underlying damage to the systems controlling these expressions. Such dysfunction also would distort the infant's communicative abilities and, consequently, the ability of others to interact with the infant.

Paradigms for Eliciting Facial Expressions

Criteria for paradigms useful in studying the organization of facial expressions in cocaine-exposed infants include (1) availability of normative data, (2) likelihood that the paradigm will elicit a wide range of normal facial expressions, and (3) ability to stress the infant's current developmental capacities to bring out underlying differences. Only the latter criterion requires some elaboration. In general, dysfunction is more evident in a stressed than in an unstressed system. A dysfunctional child in a standard paradigm may perform within normal limits when the task is easy or well structured. When a task becomes difficult or places more demands on the child for self-regulation and self-initiation, however, previously unnoticed problems may become evident. For instance, facial expressions may become asymmetrical only when an infant is highly aroused. In support of this hypothesis, recall that cocaine-exposed infants appear to perform within normal limits on well-structured cognitive tasks, yet perform significantly below agemates on more unstructured tasks, which require more self-regulation and self-initiation (Rodning et al. 1989).

Three assessment paradigms satisfy these criteria:

1. Normal and stressful face-to-face interactions between adults and infants 1 year of age or younger

2. Ainsworth and colleagues' (1978) Strange Situation paradigm for children 1 year and older

3. Unstructured, structured, and distorted interactive play involving children 2 years of age and older

Face-to-Face Paradigm

The face-to-face paradigm is a sequence of three episodes in which a normal social interaction is followed by a perturbated interaction and then another normal social interaction. In the normal conditions, mothers are simply instructed to play with the infant. Although the nature of the perturbated interactions varies from study to study, the two most common distortions include having the mother (1) remain still-faced and unresponsive (Tronick et al. 1978) or (2) assume a withdrawn, depressed countenance (Cohn and Tronick 1983). In the still-face condition, mothers are told to look at the infant with a neutral face and not to touch or talk to the infant. In the depressed condition, mothers are told to speak in a monotone, to minimize movement and touch, and to act tired and depressed. The still-face has an advantage over the simulated depression condition because it is more easily standardized. The length of each episode varies across studies, with an average duration of 2 to 3 minutes.

The typical face-to-face laboratory consists of a video studio and an adjoining equipment room. The studio is equipped with an infant seat mounted on a table, an adjustable stool for the mother, two cameras, a microphone, and an intercom (figure 3). The infant is seated in the infant seat placed on a table surrounded by an alcove of curtains. The mother sits on the adjustable stool in front of the infant. One camera is focused on the infant and one on the mother. Both video pictures are transmitted through a digital timer and split-screen generator into a single videorecorder to produce simultaneous frontal views of the mother and the infant. The digital timer, split-screen generator, and videorecorder are located in the adjoining equipment room in which the experimenter times the episodes and gives the mother instructions via the intercom (Tronick et al. 1980). The setup and camera angles produce extremely clear recordings of the infants' and the adults' facial expressions and gestural behaviors.

Normative behavioral data for infant-mother interaction and the still-face are available (Tronick 1989). Weinberg and Tronick (1991a), Malatesta and

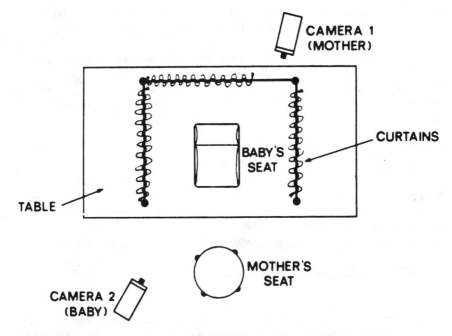

FIGURE 3. *Diagrammatic sketch of the face-to-face laboratory setup*

colleagues (1989), Oster and Ekman (1978), Cohn and Tronick (1983), Izard and colleagues (1980), and Tronick and Weinberg (1990a) present data on facial expression coding for children from birth to ages 2 years and older. In these reports, normal infants display a wide range of facial expressions representing well-organized, dynamically changing configurations of movements that are specific to environmental events. For example, normal infants predominantly display Joy and Interest faces in normal interactions but Anger, Sad, and Interest faces to the still-face (Weinberg and Tronick 1991a) (table 1). Whether cocaine-exposed infants show well-organized facial expressions in response to specific events is unknown. Evaluation of the integrity of these functions in different environmental situations would be extremely important.

Ainsworth's Strange Situation

The Ainsworth Strange Situation (Ainsworth et al. 1978) is a standardized laboratory procedure designed for 12- to 18-month-old infants and their mothers. Its purpose is to assess the quality of the infant's attachment to the mother and to evaluate the infant's ability to use the mother as a resource

TABLE 1. *Proportion of time infants displayed each AFFEX-coded facial expression during play 1, the still-face, and play 2*

Proportions of each facial expression

Facial expression*	Play 1	Still-Face	Play 2
Joy	.26[a]†	.06[b]	.32[c]
Interest	.60[a]	.72[b]	.51[c]
Sadness	.00[a]	.04[b]	.03[c]
Anger	.04[a]	.07[b]	.06[b]

*AFFEX codes are mutually exclusive.
†Different superscripts are significantly different from each other at p<.001.

SOURCE: Weinberg and Tronick (1991a)

("secure base") for coping with stress. Attachment theory posits that forming a secure attachment relationship with the mother is a major, age-appropriate task of late infancy. Moreover, it contends that the quality of the infant's attachment to his or her mother predicts to the quality of the child's developmental outcome (Ainsworth et al. 1978).

The Strange Situation consists of eight increasingly stressful episodes arranged in a standard sequence (table 2). The procedure assesses how the infant uses his or her mother as a secure base for exploration in an unfamiliar environment and how he or she responds to the appearance of a stranger, to separations from and subsequent reunions with the mother, and to attempts by the mother and the stranger to soothe him or her (figure 4). The entire procedure is videotaped and takes approximately 25 minutes.

Although a large body of research attests to the validity and reliability of Strange Situation behavior, coded according to attachment constructs (Ainsworth et al. 1978), investigators have not typically assessed the organization of facial expressions per se using this paradigm. However, the Strange Situation elicits a rich array of infant facial expressions and behaviors. For best results, input from two cameras should be used to obtain clear views of the mobile infant's face. For example, Weinberg and Tronick (1991b) have demonstrated that 1-year-olds display a wide range of facial expressions in the Strange Situation that occur reliably in response to specific episodes and contexts. Analyzing the

TABLE 2. *Summary of episodes of the strange situation*

Number of Episodes	Persons Present	Duration	Brief Description of Action
1	Mother, baby, and observer	30 sec	Observer introduces mother and baby to experimental room, then leaves.
2	Mother and baby	3 min	Mother is nonparticipant while baby explores; if necessary, play is stimulated after 2 minutes.
3	Stranger, mother, and baby	3 min	Stranger enters. First minute: Stranger silent. Second minute: Stranger converses with mother. Third minute: Stranger approaches baby. After 3 minutes mother leaves unobtrusively.
4	Stranger and baby	3 min or less[a]	First separation episode. Stranger's behavior is geared to that of baby.
5	Mother and baby	3 min or more[b]	First reunion episode. Mother greets and/ or comforts baby, then tries to settle baby again in play. Mother then leaves, saying "bye-bye."
6	Baby	3 min or less[a]	Second separation episode.
7	Stranger and baby	3 min or less[a]	Continuation of second separation. Stranger enters and gears behavior to that of baby.
8	Mother and baby	3 min	Second reunion episode. Mother enters, then greets and picks baby up. Meanwhile stranger leaves unobtrusively.

[a]Episode is curtailed if the baby is unduly distressed.
[b]Episode is prolonged if more time is required for the baby to become reinvolved in play.

SOURCE: Ainsworth et al. 1978, copyright 1978, Erlbaum

facial expressions of infants exposed to cocaine in this standard context would allow comparison of the development and organization of facial configurations of this sample with those of nonexposed children.

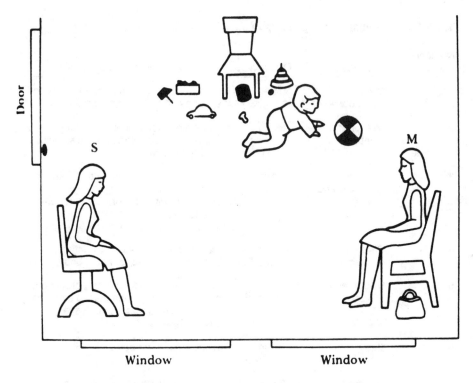

FIGURE 4. *Diagrammatic sketch of Ainsworth's Strange Situation*

KEY: S=stranger; M=mother

Play Paradigms

Play paradigms are quite numerous (Rubin et al. 1983). Children's play has long been regarded as a powerful index of toddlers' cognitive-motivational competence and affective expressiveness (Piaget 1962; Vygotsky 1978). Play is a salient and meaningful activity for most toddlers—an important means by which they explore the environment and form concepts about objects, events, causality, and interpersonal relationships (Bruner 1964, 1972).

In many play paradigms, the examiner typically seats the child and mother/adult on the floor of a laboratory playroom with a box of standard, age-appropriate toys. The dyad then is invited to play with the toys. In general, mothers are instructed to play with the child "as you normally would at home." In some studies, maternal behavior is constrained with the instructions not to direct the child's play but to participate in play and be responsive to any requests for help or social interaction. The dyad's play behavior is videotaped (15 to 30 minutes) from behind one-way mirrors. Facial expressions (and other behaviors) may be coded from these video recordings.

Contextual issues need to be considered in the design of play-assessment paradigms, because they have been demonstrated to affect children's play performance and affective involvement in systematic ways. For instance, children tend to exhibit more enthusiasm and higher object play maturity when interacting with an involved (as opposed to a passive) adult partner. Similarly, modeling paradigms elicit higher levels of play maturity and affective involvement for many children than do free-play procedures (McCune-Nicolich and Fenson 1984). However, not all children respond to structure with improved performance: Children with socioemotional delays and behavior problems appear to perform better in unstructured conditions (Kennedy et al. 1991).

Among the available play paradigms described in the extant literature (Rubin et al. 1983), three play procedures have proven useful for eliciting a wide range of infant facial expressions, especially when used in combination with each other. These paradigms, taken together, include structured as well as unstructured phases and vary in the level of stress they introduce.

Free Play. During unstructured play with an older partner, children's age-appropriate social, emotional, and cognitive functioning can be observed (Beeghly et al. 1989). Moreover, children initiate, organize, and sustain play activities during free play, allowing a glimpse of their self-regulatory capacities. Facial expressions and overall assessments of child competence and well-being also are measured in this context. As children show greater enthusiasm and produce developmentally more mature forms of play behavior when playing with an actively involved adult, including an interested, nondirective adult partner is recommended.

Structured Social Play. Structured play paradigms involving social turntaking games are useful for measuring developmental changes in children's social interactive skills. Ross and Lollis (1987) demonstrated significant age-related increases in toddlers' (9 to 18 months) ability to participate actively in social games with adults during late infancy and toddlerhood. They used a structured turntaking procedure with two phases: (1) establishment of reciprocal turntaking games with standard objects and (2) an interruption period involving a pause in adult behavior analogous to the still-face condition of the face-to-face paradigm (described above). Children's ability to initiate and sustain turntaking as well as their verbal and behavioral attempts to regulate and reestablish turntaking were measured. Furthermore, affective expressions can be expected to vary widely in this paradigm.

Self-Regulatory Play Paradigm. The Self-Regulatory Play Paradigm is a structured, five-phase social play procedure (Beeghly et al., in preparation) designed to assess toddlers' ability to initiate, maintain, and regulate/reestablish social interaction with an adult. In the first phase, the mother plays naturally with her child for 5 minutes. In the second phase, an unfamiliar adult then establishes reciprocal turntaking games with the child for 5 minutes. After a 30-second pause, a 2-minute interruption phase follows, during which the adult's behavior, affect, and vocalizations become completely noncontingent with the child. The adult scrambles toys in a somewhat disorganized manner while vocalizing and producing positive affect. Following this phase, the adult pauses for 30 seconds and then attempts to reestablish turntaking games with the child for an additional 5 minutes. In the final phase, the mother again plays with her child for 5 minutes, as in phase 1. The content and organization of children's affective, social-communicative, and behavioral responses during each segment are coded.

We recommend that these three play paradigms be used in conjunction with each other, because together they (1) include structured as well as unstructured components, (2) vary in the level of stress they introduce, and (3) are powerful elicitors of a wide variation in the affective expressions of the child, making children's self-regulatory and social-communicative abilities readily apparent. In addition, qualitative aspects of children's play performance can be measured (e.g., quality of responsiveness, cost of attention) that are not directly tapped in standardized psychometric tests. Thus, play assessments may discriminate high- and low-risk groups of children better than psychometric tests. Rodning and colleagues (1989) reported that children exposed to multiple drugs of abuse *in utero* exhibited representational play less frequently and less coherently during unstructured free play than controls. In contrast, these drug-exposed children performed within the normal range on standardized psychometric tests of sensorimotor development.

COMMUNICATIVE CONFIGURATIONS

In addition to facial expressions, communicative behaviors are well organized and available to exacting description. Investigators hypothesize that a "natural" relation between communicative behaviors and facial expressions exists (Cohn and Tronick 1983; Gaensbauer et al. 1979; Tronick et al. 1980). Recently, Weinberg and Tronick (1991a) demonstrated that facial expressions and communicative behaviors co-occur in a reliable, highly organized fashion.

Communicative configurations may be used to evaluate the effects of cocaine exposure on infant socioemotional development.

Because communicative configurations are most easily elicited in the same paradigms that are used for eliciting facial expressions alone, no additional data collection is required to evaluate their organization. Thus, the organization and timing of facial expressions, communicative behaviors, and combinations of both can be evaluated. Similarly, the relations of facial expressions, communicative behaviors, and combinations of both to external events can be examined.

Several researchers have developed scoring systems that cluster behaviors and facial expressions into communicative configurations (Cohn and Tronick 1983; Gaensbauer et al. 1979; Tronick et al. 1980). These scoring systems combine information about facial and vocal expressions, posture, gaze, and type of activity on an *a priori* basis. Matias and colleagues (1989), however, have reported strong correlations between detailed codes of behavior, including facial expressions, and Beebe and Gerstman (1980) have found that behaviors and facial expressions change as "packages" as a function of changes of rhythm in mother-infant interactions. Furthermore, Brazelton and colleagues (1974) found that the newborn's alert face is accompanied by smooth movements, eyes oriented toward mother, and fleeting smiles, grimaces, and vocalizations. Periods of withdrawal, on the other hand, are characterized by glazed or dull expressions, little movement, and face and eyes oriented away from the mother. In addition, Fogel and Hannan (1985) have speculated that some discrete hand movements may be associated with particular arousal states. These authors found that pointing tends to occur before or after mouthing and vocalizations, curling of fingers during vocalizations, and spreading of fingers when the infant is looking away from the mother.

Weinberg and Tronick (1991) examined the relations among the modalities of face, voice, gesture, gaze, and self-regulatory and withdrawal behaviors that typically occur in normal and perturbated interactions of mothers and infants. As noted, normal interactions typically elicit positive expressions, elicit whereas perturbated interactions (e.g., the mother holding a still-face) often elicit negative affective states. Coding of these interactions used systems designed to separately characterize facial expressions, gestures, self-comforting behaviors, vocalizations, and gaze (Tronick and Weinberg 1990b). These codes are presented in abbreviated form in table 3. They can be used with any high-quality videorecording of infant behavior. Coding is best carried out by coders trained on only one or a few of the codes. This results in highly reliable and objective coding.

TABLE 3. *The Infant Regulatory Scoring System (IRSS)*

Social engagement	The infant looks at or glances at the mother's face.
Object engagement	The infant looks at or manipulates an object for 2 seconds or more.
Scans	The infant briefly glances at objects or around the laboratory without focusing on anything for longer than 2 seconds.
Signals/solicitations	<u>Vocalizations</u>: The infant signals the mother by vocalizing with neutral/positive, fussy, or crying vocalizations. <u>Gestures</u>: The infant signals the mother by gesturing to be picked up or by moving his or her arms in an organized manner in the direction of the mother (e.g., banging his or her arms or kicking his or her legs).
Oral behavior/ self-comforting	The infant self-comforts by sucking on his or her body (e.g., thumb sucking) or sucking on an object (e.g., the chair strap).
Escape/get away	The infant attempts to distance himself or herself from the mother by turning, twisting, or arching his or her body.
Distress indicators	The infant exhibits behaviors that indicate distress such as spitting up, hiccupping, or heavy breathing.
Inhibition/ freezing	The infant inhibits his or her perceptual, motor, and/ or attentional processes to minimize engagement with the mother and the surroundings.

SOURCE: Weinberg and Tronick (1991a)

Weinberg and Tronick (1991a) found that in both normal and perturbated interactions (i.e., still-face), 6-month-old infants' behaviors were strongly related to one another and to facial expressions (coded by Izard's AFFEX system; table 4). Specifically, facial expressions of joy were most likely to occur when the infant was looking at the mother, positively vocalizing, and mouthing a body part. Together these behaviors formed a coherent configuration of positive person-oriented behaviors. This characterization was supported further by the finding that AFFEX joy was unlikely to co-occur with behaviors that exclude positive social engagement such as fussy vocalizations, crying, and escape/get away. Facial expressions of interest tended to co-occur with sustained and brief exploration of objects and with mouthing objects. AFFEX interest was unlikely to co-occur with behaviors indicative of a positive, socially oriented engagement (e.g., positive vocalizations) and with behaviors indicative of social disengagement (e.g., crying or attempts to escape/get away). These data suggest that the affective configuration of interest is characterized by an active engagement with the inanimate environment.

TABLE 4. *Likely and unlikely affective action configurations*

Type	Likely Configurations	Unlikely Configurations
1	Facial expression of joy Look at mother Positive vocalizations Mouthing body part	Facial expression of joy Look at objects Scans Fussy vocalizations Crying Mouthing objects Pick-me-up gestures Escape/get away
2	Facial expression of interest Look at objects Scans Mouthing objects	Facial expression of interest Look at mother Mouthing body part Escape/get away
3	Facial expression of sadness Fussy vocalizations	Facial expression of sadness Positive vocalizations
4	Facial expression of anger Scans Fussy vocalizations Crying Pick-me-up gestures Escape/get away	Facial expression of anger Look at objects Positive vocalizations Gestural signals Distress indicators

SOURCE: Weinberg and Tronick (1991a)

Facial expressions of sadness were primarily associated with fussy vocalizations. Furthermore, infants displaying sadness were unlikely to look at either the mother or objects and to vocalize in a fussy manner or cry. Thus, this configuration reflected a passive withdrawn state characterized by reduced involvement with both people and objects and by low levels of activity. Facial expressions of anger, on the other hand, were associated with several active behaviors such as scans, fussy vocalizations, fullblown crying, pick-me-up gestures, and attempts to escape/get away. Together these behaviors reflect a negative affective state characterized by behaviors that function to actively disengage the infant from both the mother and the inanimate environment. This characterization was further confirmed by the finding that AFFEX anger is unlikely to co-occur with looking at objects, indicative of engagement with the inanimate environment, or with gestural signals and positive vocalizations, behaviors indicative of a positive social engagement. This study supports the assumption that highly organized communicative configurations exist during infancy. Based on this research, one can hypothesize that cocaine-exposed infants will evidence disorganized communicative configurations and relations to stimulus events.

CONCLUSION

Until recently, investigators have regarded the control of movement as closed to objective scrutiny, although they have long recognized it as a central dimension of infant functioning. In this chapter, three objective, reliable methods of assessing movement control are described that open up new ways of uncovering possible forms of brain dysfunction in infants: (1) kinematic analysis of movement, which taps the organization of both spontaneous and instrumental movements; (2) muscle and template-based systems for coding facial expressions, which objectively measure patterns of movements controlling facial expressions; and (3) video-based coding systems to examine configurations of communicative behavior and affect. All these methods tap movement patterns that provide critical indices of the functional organization of the CNS. Moreover, these techniques provide objective descriptions of movement patterns that are most likely to be sensitive to brain dysfunction resulting from cocaine exposure.

In addition, specific paradigms for eliciting movement patterns are described for use with these three assessment methods. With the exception of kinematic analysis, none of these paradigms was originally designed to assess movement control in infants and young children. Yet, each of these well-known, standardized paradigms allows a full and rich characterization of the child's movement in a few settings and in a limited timeframe.

Moreover, to the extent that one observes infants in interaction with their mothers in these paradigms, one also can use these procedures to evaluate with precision the quality of the mother-child interaction. This is crucial, because the mother-infant relationship is a major determinant of the child's functioning and developmental outcome when considered in conjunction with the integrity of the child's CNS (Tronick 1989).

By offering increased precision and objectivity to the assessment of movement control, the three methods described in this chapter may revolutionize our ability to detect and quantify brain dysfunction in early childhood. It is our belief that these methods hold great promise for the assessment of infants and young child exposed *in utero* to cocaine or other illicit substances.

REFERENCES

Abend, W.; Bizzi, E.; and Morasso, P. Human arm trajectory formation. *Brain* 105:331-348, 1982.

Ainsworth, M.S.; Blehar, M.C.; Waters, E.; and Wall, S. *Patterns of Attachment: A Psychological Study of the Strange Situation.* Hillsdale, NJ: Lawrence Erlbaum, 1978.

Als, H.; Tronick, E.; Adamson, L.; and Brazelton, T.B. The behavior of the full term yet underweight newborn infant. *Dev Med Child Neurol* 18:590-602, 1976.

Beebe, B., and Gerstman, L.J. The "packaging" of maternal stimulation in relation to infant facial-visual engagement: A case study at four months. *Merrill-Palmer Q* 26(4):321-339, 1980.

Beeghly, M.; Brown, R.; Scott-Sutherland, J.; and Tronick, E.Z. ."The Self-Regulatory Play Paradigm," in preparation.

Beeghly, M.; Flannery, K.; Birss, S.; Jernberg, E.; Turiano, D.; and Barrett, D. Cognitive and psychosocial development of small for gestational age (SGA) infants: A follow-up study. *Soc Res Dev Abstr.* 6:189, 1989.

Beeghly, M.; Nugent, J.K.; Burrows, E.; and Brazelton, T.B. Effects of intrauterine growth retardation (IUGR) on infant behavior and development in the family. *Infant Behav Dev* (special ICIS issue) 11:21, 1988.

Beeghly, M.; Vo, D.; Burrows, E.; and Brazelton, T.B. Social and task related behavior of fullterm small for gestational age (SGA) infants at two years. *Infant Behav Dev* (special ICIS issue) 13:266, 1990.

Beeghly, M.; Weiss-Perry, B.; and Cicchetti, D. Structural and affective dimensions of play behavior in children with Down syndrome. *Infant Behav Dev* 2(2):257-277, 1989.

Brazelton, T.B. *Neonatal Behavioral Assessment Scale.* 2d ed. Philadelphia: J.B. Lippincott, 1984.

Brazelton, T.B.; Koslowski, B.; and Main, M. The origins of reciprocity: The early mother-infant interaction. In: Lewis, M., and Rosenblum, L.A., eds. *The Effect of the Infant on its Caregiver.* New York: Wiley, 1974. pp. 49-76.

Brooks, V.B. Some examples of programmed limbs movements. *Brain Res* 71:299-308, 1974.

Bruner, J. The course of cognitive growth. *Am Psychol* 19:1-15, 1964.

Bruner, J. Nature and uses of immaturity. *Am Psychol* 27:687-708, 1972.

Campos, J.J.; Barrett, K.C.; Lamb, M.; Goldsmith, H.; and Stenberg, C. Socioemotional development. In: Haith, M., and Campos, J.J., eds. *Infancy and Developmental Psychobiology,* Vol. II. New York: Wiley, 1983. pp. 789-800.

Chasnoff, I.J.; Bussey, M.E.; Savich, R.; and Stack, C.M. Perinatal cerebral infarction and maternal cocaine use. *J Pediatr* 198:456-459, 1986.

Chasnoff, I.J., and Griffith, D.R. Cocaine exposed infants: two year follow up. *Pediatr Res* 24:249, 1989.

Chasnoff, I.J.; Hunt, C.E.; Kletter, R.; and Kaplan, D. Prenatal cocaine exposure is associated with respiratory pattern abnormalities. *AJDC* 143:583-588, 1989.

Claman, D.L., and Zeffiro, T.A. Motor consequences of posterior parietal lobe injury. *Neurosci Abstr* 12:972, 1986.

Cohen, H.; deMarruis, P.; deSilva, M.; Gelber, J.; Laungani, S.; and Glass, L. Cranialsonography in infants of alkaloidal cocaine ("crack") abusing mothers. *Pediatr Res* 551, 1989.

Cohn, J., and Tronick, E. Three-month-old infants' reaction to simulated maternal depression. *Child Dev* 54:185-193, 1983.

Dixon, S.D., and Bejar, R. Brain lesions in cocaine and methamphetamine exposed neonates. *Pediatr Res* 23:359, 1988.

Doberczak, T.M.; Shanzer, S.; and Kandall, S.R. Neonatal effects of cocaine abuse in pregnancy. *Pediatr Res* 23:359A, 1988.

Ekman, P., and Friesen, W. *Facial Action Coding System.* Palo Alto, CA: Consulting Psychologists Press, 1978.

Fetters, L., and Todd, J. Quantitative assessment of infant reaching movements. *J Motor Behav* 19:147-166, 1987.

Fisk, J.D., and Goodale, M.A. The effects of unilateral brain damage on visually guided reaching: Hemispheric differences in the nature of the deficit. *Exper Brain Res* 72:425-435, 1988.

Fogel, A., and Hannan, E.T. Manual actions of nine- to fifteen-week-old infants during face-to-face interaction with their mothers. *Child Dev* 56:1271-1279, 1985.

Fulroth, R.F.; Phillips, B.; and Durant, D.J. Perinatal outcome of infants exposed to cocaine and/or heroin in utero. *AJDC* 143:905-910, 1989.

Gaensbauer, T.J.; Mrazek, D.; and Emde, R.N. Patterning of emotional response in a playroom laboratory setting. *Infant Behav Dev* 2:163-178, 1979.

Hadeed, A.J., and Siegel, S. R. Maternal cocaine use during pregnancy: Effect on the newborn infant. *Pediatrics* 84:205-210, 1989.

Harris, S.; Swanson, M.; Andrews, M.; Sells, C.; Robinson, N.; Bennett, F.; and Chandler, L. Predictive validity of the "Movement Assessment of Infants." *J Dev Behav Pediatr* 5:336-342, 1984.

Henricksen, L.; Skinhoj, K.; and Anderson, G. Delayed growth and reduced intelligence in 9-17 yearly intrauterine growth retarded children compared with their monozygous co-twins. *Acta Paediatr Scand* 75:31, 1986.

Howard J. Long-term development of infants exposed prenatally to drugs. *Special Currents: Cocaine Babies.* Ross Labs, 1989.

Izard, C.E. *The Face of Emotion.* New York: Appleton-Century-Crofts, 1971.

Izard, C.E. *The Maximally Discriminative Facial Movement Coding System (MAX).* Newark, DE: University of Delaware, Instructional Resources Center, 1979.

Izard, C.E.; Dougherty, L.M.; and Hembree, E.A. *A System for Identifying Affect Expressions by Holistic Judgments (AFFEX).* Newark, DE: University of Delaware, Instructional Resources Center, 1980.

Izard, C.E.; Huebner, R.R.; Risser, D.; McGinnes, G.C.; and Doughterty, L.M. The young infant's ability to produce discrete emotion expressions. *Dev Psychol* 16(2):132-140, 1980.

Jeannerod, J. *The Neural and Behavioral Organization of Goal-Directed Movements.* Oxford: Clarendon Press, 1988.

Kennedy, M.; Sheridan, M.; Radlinski, S.; and Beeghly, M. Play-language relationships in young children with developmental delays: Implications for assessment. *J Speech Hearing Res* 34:112-122, 1991.

Kluzik, J.; Fetters, L.; and Coryell, J. Quantitation of control: A preliminary study of effects of neurodevelopmental treatment on reaching in children with spastic cerebral palsy. *Phys Ther* 70:1-14, 1990.

Lester, B.M.; Garcia-Coll, C.T.; Valcarcel, M.; Hoffman, J.; and Brazelton, T.B. Effects of atypical patterns of fetal growth on newborn (NBAS) behavior. *Child Dev* 57:1-19, 1986.

Lester, B.M., and Zeskind, P.S. Brazelton scale and physical size correlates of neonatal cry features. *Infant Behav Dev* 1:393, 1978.

Lough, S.; Wing, A.M.; Fraser, C.; and Jenner, J.R. Measurement of recovery of function in the hemiparetic upper limb following stroke: A preliminary report. *Hum Mov Sci* 3:247-256, 1984.

Malatesta, C.Z.; Culver, C.; Tesman; and Shepard, B. The development of emotion expression during the first two years of life. *Monog Soc Res Child Dev* 54(1-2):1-103, 1989.

Matias, R.; Cohn, J.F.; and Ross, S. A comparison of two systems to code infants' affective expressions. *Dev Psychol* 25(2):483-489, 1989.

287

McCune-Nicolich, L., and Fenson, L. Methodological issues in studying early play. In: Yawkey, T., and Pellegrini, A., eds. *Child's Play: Developmental and Applied.* Hillsdale, NJ: Erlbaum, 1984. pp. 81-104.

Mirochnick, M.; Meyer, J.; Cole, J.; Herren, T.; and Zuckerman, B. Circulating catecholamines in cocaine-exposed neonates: A pilot study. *J Pediatr,* in press.

Oro, A.S., and Dixon, S.D. Perinatal cocaine and methamphetamine exposure: Maternal and neonatal correlates. *J Pediatr* 3:571-578, 1987.

Oster, H. "Baby FACS vs. MAX: The Case for an Empirical Coding System." Paper presented at the International Conference on Infant Studies. Montreal, Canada, 1990.

Oster, H., and Ekman, P. Facial behavior in child development. *Minnesota Symp Child Psychol* 11:231-276, 1978.

Parker, S.; Zuckerman, B.; Bauchner, H.; Frank, D.; Vinci, R.; and Cabral, H. Jitteriness in full-term neonates. *Pediatrics* 1989.

Piaget, J. *Play, Dreams, and Imitation in Childhood.* New York: Norton, 1962.

Rodning, C.; Beckwith, L.; and Howard, J. Characteristics of attachment organization and play organization in prenatally drug-exposed toddlers. *Dev Psychopathol* 1:277-289, 1989.

Ross, H., and Lollis, S. Communication within infant social games. *Dev Psychol* 23:241-248, 1987.

Rubin, K.; Fein, G.; and Vandenberg, B. Play. In: Hetherington, M., ed. *Carmichael's Manual of Child Psychology.* Vol. IV. New York: Wiley, 1983.

Ryan, L.; Ehrlich, S.; and Finnegan, L. Cocaine abuse in pregnancy: Effects on the fetus and newborn. *Neurotox Teratol* 9:295-299, 1987.

Schneider, J.W. Motor assessment and parent education beyond the newborn period. In: Chasnoff, I.J., ed. *Drugs, Alcohol, Pregnancy, and Parenting.* Dordrecht: Kluwer Academic Publishers, 1988.

Scholtz, J. Reliability and validity of the WATSMART three-dimensional optoelectric motion analysis system. *Phys Ther* 68:321-327, 1989.

Shih, L.; Cone-Wesson, B.; Reddix, B.; and Wu, P.Y.K. Effect of maternal cocaine abuse on the neonatal auditory system. *Pediatr Res* 264A, 1989.

Thelen, E. Kicking, rocking and waving: Contextual analysis of rhythmical stereotypes in normal human infants. *Anim Behav* 29:3-11, 1982.

Tronick, E.Z. Emotions and emotional communication in infants. *Am Psychol* 44(2):112-119, 1989.

Tronick, E.; Als, H.; Adamson, L.; Wise, S.; and Brazelton, T.B. The infant's response to entrapment between contradictory messages in face-to-face interaction. *Am Acad Child Psychiatr* 1-13, 1978.

Tronick, E.; Als, H.; and Brazelton, T.B. Monadic phases: A structural descriptive analysis of infant-mother face-to-face interaction. *Merrill Palmer Q* 1(26):3-24, 1980.

Tronick, E.Z., and Beeghly, M. Effects of prenatal exposure to cocaine on newborn behavior and development: A critical review. In: *Drug-Exposed Children Ages 2 to 5: Identifying Their Needs and Planning for Early Intervention.* Monographs of the Proceedings of the First Issues Forum of the Office for Substance Abuse Prevention (OSAP), in press.

Tronick, E.Z., and Weinberg, M.K. "Stability of Coping and Emotions in 6-Month-Olds." Paper presented at the International Conference on Infant Studies. Montreal, Canada, 1990a.

Tronick, E.Z., and Weinberg, M.K. "The Infant Regulatory Scoring System (IRSS)." Unpublished manuscript, Children's Hospital/Harvard Medical School, Boston, 1990b.

Viviani, P., and Terzuolo, C. Space-time invariance in learned skills. In: Stelmach, G.E., and Requin, J., eds. *Tutorials in Major Behavior.* Amsterdam: North-Holland, 1980.

Vohr, B.; Oh, W.; Rosenfield, A.G.; and Cowett, R.M. The preterm small-for-gestational-age infant: A two-year follow-up study. *Am J Obstet Gynecol* 133:425, 1979.

Von Hofsten, C. Development of visually directed reaching: The approach phase. *J Hum Mov Stud* 5:160-178, 1979.

Vygotsky, L. *Mind in Society.* Cambridge, MA: Harvard University Press, 1978.

Walther, F.J., and Ramaekers, L.H.J. Language development at the age of 3 years of infants malnourished in utero. *Neuropediatrics* 13:77, 1982.

Weinberg, M.K., and Tronick, E.Z. Affective configurations in 6-month-old infants. Under review, 1991a.

Weinberg, M.K., and Tronick, E.Z. "Stability of Infant Social and Coping Behaviors and Affective Displays Between 6 Months and 1 Year in Age-Appropriate Situations." Paper presented at the Society for Research in Child Development. Seattle, Washington, 1991b.

Winter, D.A. *Motor Control of Human Gait.* Waterloo, Ontario, Canada: University of Waterloo Press, Dana Porter Library, 1987.

Zuckerman, B.; Frank, D.; Hingson, R.; Amaro, H.; Levenson, S.; Kayne, H.; Parker, S.; Vinci, R.; Aboagye, K.; Fried, L.; Cabral, H.; Timperi, R.; and Bauchner, H. Effects of maternal marijuana and cocaine use on fetal growth. *N Engl J Med* 320:762-768, 1989.

AUTHORS

Edward Z. Tronick, Ph.D.
Associate Professor of Pediatrics
Harvard Medical School
Chief
Child Development Unit

Marjorie Beeghly, Ph.D.
Assistant Professor
Harvard Medical School
Research Director
Child Development Unit

M. Katherine Weinberg, M.S.
Research Director
Child Development Unit

The Children's Hospital
300 Longwood Avenue
Boston, MA 02115

Linda Fetters, Ph.D.
Associate Professor of Physical Therapy
Sargent College
Boston University
One University Road
Boston MA 02215

Rationale and Methodologies for Developing Nonhuman Primate Models of Prenatal Drug Exposure

Stephen J. Suomi and J. Dee Higley

BACKGROUND AND RATIONALE

The recent escalation of cocaine abuse and addiction has increased awareness of a difficult and growing problem. Because many cocaine users are females of childbearing age, the number of infants exposed prenatally to cocaine has reached epidemic proportions. General estimates of the percentage of all infants exposed prenatally to cocaine in the United States range from about 15 to 20 percent of the total infant population (Chasnoff et al. 1990; Frank et al. 1988), with some childbearing populations at much greater risk to abuse drugs during pregnancy than others (Amaro et al. 1989; Zuckerman et al. 1989). In some areas of the Nation, nearly 50 percent of the females who give birth report or test positive for recent cocaine use at time of delivery (Osterloh and Lee 1989; Amaro et al. 1990). Closely paralleling this epidemic is the recent increase in female polydrug use and the continued problem of female addiction to other drugs such as opiates and alcohol (Osterloh and Lee 1989; Edelin et al. 1988; Krug 1989), further increasing the risk to developing fetuses of exposure to harmful substances. Given the sheer number of infants and children that have been or will be affected by prenatal exposure, the diverse number of medical and psychological problems that these infants tend to show, and the relative ignorance of long-term outcomes of prenatal drug exposure, it seems imperative that these children be studied extensively to develop effective treatment and prevention programs.

Although to date there are few if any long-term studies of children exposed prenatally to cocaine, recent studies have examined neonates or performed short-term followup investigations of infants exposed *in utero* to cocaine and other abused drugs. Postnatal clinical reports of these infants indicate that they present a diverse range of medical and psychological problems, depending in part on whether additional illicit drugs were used, on the type of illicit drug and frequency of abuse by the pregnant mother, and the timing and duration of prenatal exposure. These postnatal problems include a variety of behavioral and temperamental deficits, with wide interindividual differences in severity (Chasnoff and Griffith 1989; Cherukuri et al. 1988; Kaye et al. 1989; Kopp 1983).

Predicting outcomes and establishing cause-effect relationships between human prenatal drug exposure and neonatal deficits can be highly problematic, given the numerous uncontrolled and confounding variables that can potentially affect vulnerability and specific outcomes. Cocaine users, for example, may differ from nonusers in terms of their nutritional state, weight gain during pregnancy, and the amount of prenatal care they receive. Each of these variables also produces its own effects on the growing fetus, thereby posing an ethical dilemma when constructing suitable control groups. More importantly, however, failure to obtain accurate information about the time course and dosage of drug use by pregnant women adds substantial error variance to the data, as well as making it difficult to pinpoint those exposure periods in which the fetus is most sensitive to insult. Finally, interactions between drugs also must be taken into account. Cocaine users frequently use other licit (e.g., nicotine, alcohol) and illicit drugs in combination. Extensive use of illicit and licit drugs already is known to increase fetal risk.

Because many of these variables cannot be readily controlled in human settings for both ethical and practical reasons, some investigators have turned to animal models to address these issues. These researchers have been able to show that when animal subjects are exposed during pregnancy to abused drugs under highly controlled experimental conditions, physical and behavioral anomalies result in the exposed offspring that resemble many of the symptoms seen in drug-exposed human infants (e.g., Henderson and McMillen 1990; Inouye et al. 1985; Spear et al. 1989; Bowden et al. 1983). Thus, animal models can be developed that provide the needed control over extraneous variables, allowing researchers to establish cause-effect relationships and assess both short- and long-term outcomes after prenatal exposure to illicit drugs. Of course, the validity and utility of any animal model depend ultimately on the degree to which the findings from the animal model generalize to the human phenomenon in question (Harlow et al. 1972; Suomi and Immelmann 1983). Some of the most compelling animal models have used nonhuman primates, humankind's closest biological relatives.

To date, few if any investigators have begun to establish any nonhuman primate models explicitly designed to examine the short- or long-term physiological, cognitive, or social-emotional consequences of prenatal exposure to cocaine. However, this is not to say that such models could not be readily developed. On the contrary, the current database regarding nonhuman primate biobehavioral development and the state-of-the-art experimental designs and

292

methodologies now available to primate researchers strongly suggest that such models are quite feasible and are apt to be of considerable significance in advancing basic knowledge at the human level.

There are several areas in which carefully developed nonhuman primate models of prenatal drug exposure could make significant contributions to knowledge regarding the human phenomena. First, nonhuman primate models could provide information regarding effects of prenatal drug exposure on the fetus prior to birth and on neonatal reflex and response patterns of prenatally exposed infants shortly after birth. Second, appropriate nonhuman primate models could be used to assess possible cognitive, social, and emotional deficits as well as to evaluate the efficacy of various postnatal intervention efforts during late infancy and juvenile periods, for which well-established normative developmental milestones already exist for several nonhuman primate species. Finally, because most nonhuman primate species mature several times faster than *Homo sapiens*, it is feasible to carry out long-term longitudinal studies of prenatally exposed individuals through puberty and into the next generation. These studies could be conducted prospectively within a 4- or 5-year period, modeling a developmental transition that would be very difficult and extraordinarily time-consuming to study systematically in human adolescents and young adults who have been prenatally exposed to cocaine and/or other abused substances. In the sections that follow, each of these areas is addressed in detail.

PRIMATE MODELS INVESTIGATING PRENATAL AND PERINATAL EFFECTS OF DRUG EXPOSURE

As mentioned previously, one of the strongest arguments favoring the development of animal models of prenatal drug exposure involves the opportunity to manipulate systematically the frequency, dose level, and period of prenatal exposure under highly controlled conditions and to compare the consequences of such manipulations with nonexposed fetuses whose mothers are otherwise maintained under identical conditions of diet, housing, etc. Prospective studies of this type should enable investigators to establish causal dose/timing-outcome relationships, especially if they were to use nonhuman primate species for which there exists a large normative database regarding the timing and sequence of prenatal development (Kemnitz et al. 1984). Several different techniques for exposing fetuses of different gestational ages to precise quantities of specific toxins have been developed in recent years. Although a detailed discussion of such techniques is beyond the scope of this chapter, it is clear that appropriate methodologies for simulating prenatal exposure to cocaine at predetermined gestational ages, frequencies, and dosages now exist and could be used in nonhuman primate models.

A range of prenatal and perinatal outcome measures also exists that would be relevant for a primate model of prenatal cocaine exposure. Most of these measures have been developed either to document species-normative patterns of fetal growth and maturation or to characterize the effects of different maternal diets (e.g., those low in protein or high in cholesterol) or maternal exposure to environmental toxins (e.g., PCBs or dioxin) during pregnancy. Standardized sets of teratological measures of organ and tissue growth, differentiation, and/ or degeneration typically are obtained in fetuses at specified gestational ages in many of these studies (e.g., Uno et al. 1990). Other studies have used ultrasonic techniques to characterize fetal development throughout the entire pregnancy; many of these investigations have included evaluations of postnatal viability as well. For a few nonhuman primate species, such as rhesus monkeys (*Macaca mulatta*), the extant literature is sufficiently detailed to provide a solid basis for characterizing and evaluating any adverse consequences of various schedules and levels of prenatal exposure to cocaine.

In addition to these physical growth measures, there is an expanding database concerning normative patterns of neonatal reflex and behavioral development in several nonhuman primate species. Some of these data come from extensive longitudinal studies of newborns under carefully controlled and standardized nursery rearing and test conditions, for example, the infant test battery developed at the University of Washington Primate Center (Ruppenthal 1986), which is standardized for pigtail macaques, crab-eating macaques, and baboons. Other neonatal assessment instruments have been taken directly from the human neonate and infant literature and adapted for other primate species. For example, Schneider (1984, 1987) has modified the Brazelton Neonatal Behavioral Assessment Scale (Brazelton 1973), perhaps the most widely used behavioral and reflex assessment device in the human infant clinical literature, for use with rhesus monkeys, whereas Bard and colleagues (1990) have standardized the same assessment scales for use with nursery-reared chimpanzee neonates. These standardized test batteries have been used to detect behavioral abnormalities in rhesus monkey neonates prenatally exposed to very low levels of environmental toxins (Levin et al. 1988) and prenatally exposed to a noise stressor (e.g., Schneider et al. 1991), as well as differentiating premature from full-term infants in terms of reflex capabilities and predominant state patterns (Bard et al. 1990). Such abnormalities in neonatal response patterns, typically below the threshold of detection using more traditional neurological tests, also have been shown to be predictive of various cognitive and behavioral deficits emerging later in life (Levin et al. 1988; Schneider et al. 1991).

It seems likely that these neonatal test batteries could be readily used to characterize and quantify neonatal reflex and behavioral deficits resulting from various degrees of prenatal drug exposure in nonhuman primate subjects. Moreover, at least some of these neonatal assessment batteries have been directly derived from assessment instruments developed and standardized for use with human infant clinical populations should greatly facilitate possible cross-species comparisons. On the one hand, such comparisons already have been useful in establishing the validity of nonhuman primate models in detecting the consequences of prenatal insults (e.g., exposure to environmental toxins) that yield similar adverse consequences in the human case. On the other hand, the use of similar or identical dependent measures in the primate model could be employed to identify those specific outcomes in the human case that can be linked directly to prenatal cocaine exposure rather than to other potentially confounding factors.

Finally, many of the above-described sets of prenatal measures and neonatal assessments already have been demonstrated to be sensitive to several of the factors that are likely to be relevant for cocaine-abusing pregnant women. This fact can be exploited in generating interactive models that go beyond "direct" evaluation of "pure" prenatal cocaine exposure effects. In other words, it should be possible to model not only specific schedules and levels of prenatal cocaine exposure but also other factors such as diet, maternal age and size, stress during pregnancy, or prenatal exposure to other drugs (alcohol, nicotine, etc.) in prospective nonhuman primate studies. Carefully constructed multifactor experimental designs could be used to evaluate the relative contributions of these other factors to prenatal and neonatal outcomes among cocaine-exposed subjects as well as to identify possible interactive or synergistic effects of various combinations of these different risk factors. Such multiple-risk studies could readily complement the findings from "direct effect" models in which the only independent variable involved differential prenatal exposure to cocaine. Thus, carefully designed studies using nonhuman primate models have the potential to isolate fetal and perinatal effects of prenatal cocaine exposure and to specify various interaction/synergistic patterns involving other specific risk factors likely to be relevant in a large proportion of the cases contributing to the human drug abuse epidemic.

PRIMATE MODELS OF INFANT AND CHILDHOOD EFFECTS

Perhaps the most valuable contributions that nonhuman primate models of prenatal drug abuse could provide involve studies focusing on developmental processes in infancy and childhood. It is here where primate models are most likely to make unique contributions to knowledge regarding the human condition, in large part because the ethical and practical limitations on both evaluative and intervention research with human infants and children are enormous, often reflecting social policy issues and restrictions more than matters of rigorous experimental design. For example, there can be numerous hurdles to overcome in obtaining blood samples or other physiological measures from human neonates or infants. Various legal complications may arise when identifying mothers as cocaine users and/or their infants as cocaine addicted.

Moreover, one of the most significant problems in the research on human infants exposed to cocaine *in utero* concerns followup assessments to monitor developmental trends. Not only is postnatal drug exposure a potential confounding variable, but also tracking of these infants can be extremely difficult because mothers are unwilling subjects or are no longer in the same area. In contrast, the strongest impact of primate models at this level (i.e., infant and childhood effects) is on the generation of a detailed and stable database of developmental effects. An enormous body of knowledge has been accumulated regarding species-normative patterns of physical, physiological, cognitive, social, and emotional development from infancy to puberty in several nonhuman primate species. Moreover, much is known about how such normative developmental patterns can be influenced by a variety of postnatal environmental circumstances, stresses, and insults as well as how faithfully such patterns generalize to *Homo sapiens*.

Over the past 30 years, major progress has been made in documenting the developmental changes, understanding the underlying processes, and specifying the parallels with human cognitive development in several primate species, including rhesus monkeys and pigtail macaques and chimpanzees. Although some of the earlier test instruments were designed specifically for each nonhuman primate species being investigated, most of the current efforts to study cognitive development in nonhuman primates use measures either taken directly from the human literature or demonstrated to produce findings that parallel those from human studies.

For example, Schneider and colleagues (e.g., Schneider 1987; Schneider et al. 1991) have developed a rhesus monkey version of the Bayley Scales of Infant Development (Bayley 1969), one of the most widely used instruments for assessing cognitive, motor, and social-emotional capabilities in human toddlers, and Bard (in preparation) has developed a comparable version of the Bayley Scales for young chimpanzees. Gunderson and colleagues (Gunderson and Sackett 1984; Gunderson et al. 1989) have modified for young pigtail macaques the procedure developed by Fantz (1964) for testing the visual perception capabilities and emergence of novelty preferences of human infants. A variety of investigators (e.g., Parker 1977; Wise et al. 1974) have demonstrated that Old World monkeys and great apes go through the same early stages of cognitive development in the same invariant order as Piaget (1951) has described for human infants and young children.

These and other well-established procedures for assessing cognitive development in a variety of nonhuman primate species could be used in developmental studies of prenatally exposed infants, with the twin advantages of (1) well-established developmental norms, facilitating the detection of exposure effects and/or interactions, and (2) clear-cut generality to specific aspects of human cognitive development, facilitating cross-species comparisons and extrapolation of patterns of results. In fact, virtually all the new human infant measures described by Jacobson and Jacobson (this volume) and by Tronick and colleagues (this volume) could be used in such primate models.

In a similar vein, the well-established literature on social and emotional development in different species of nonhuman primates, particularly with respect to mother-infant attachment bonds and emerging relationships with peers, lends itself well to use in potential primate models of prenatal drug exposure. Not only is there a solid base of knowledge regarding species-normative patterns of social-emotional development, but also a huge body of data exists regarding the consequences of rearing under varying conditions of social deprivation as well as the efficacy of various experimental interventions or "therapies" designed to reverse the effects of early social deprivation (e.g., Mitchell 1970; Suomi 1982), and the efficacy of various experimental interventions or "therapies" designed to reverse the effects of early social deprivation (e.g., Suomi and Harlow 1972; Novak and Harlow 1975). Some of the conditions of early social deprivation in primates bear striking resemblance to many of the socially impoverished environments faced by all too many offspring of human substance-abusing mothers, again facilitating the development of primate models that can model potentially relevant aspects of the human condition. Moreover, as was the case for measures of cognitive development, most of the dependent measures commonly employed in studies of primate social-emotional development—observational scoring systems using predetermined behavioral categories, rating scales, Q-sort procedures, and physiological indices of emotional state (e.g., heart rate patterns and cortisol levels)—also are being used in studies of social-emotional development in human infants, toddlers, and preschool children, enhancing the opportunities for cross-species comparisons.

LONGITUDINAL EFFECTS OF PRENATAL DRUG EXPOSURE

Nonhuman primate models using monkeys can provide yet another unique opportunity to understand the long-term consequences of prenatal drug exposure. Given the relative rate at which monkeys and humans develop, it seems likely that substantial information can be obtained on the long-term effects of prenatal cocaine exposure in monkeys prior to actually observing the patterns that might develop in the human population. In this regard, nonhuman primate work may be predictive of these later human problems and may enable researchers to plan appropriate interventions or treatments in advance of the developing disorders.

Several questions are of critical importance in regard to these long-term developmental considerations. The first concerns the patterns of deficit seen in adolescence and early adulthood. Is there a gradual decline, a continuation, or an increase in the social and cognitive problems that appear in early development? A longitudinal focus may reveal the extent to which the developing system can accommodate prenatal insults either naturally or through specifically designed interventions.

Of particular concern is the extent to which new deficits may appear, perhaps associated with some of the major biological and social markers of adolescence (e.g., puberty and sexual activity). The early-experience literature concerning nonhuman primates is replete with examples in which very early experiences continue to inflict damage on animals into adulthood. Monkeys reared in isolation during the first 6 months of life, for example, typically exhibit new deficits that are related to reproduction and parental care as they pass through adolescence and into adulthood (Harlow et al. 1966; Suomi 1982).

Longitudinal studies of abuse (both substance and physical abuse) often reveal cascading multigenerational patterns in which offspring carry on the abuse of their parents and in turn pass it along to their offspring. These findings have broad implications not only in the social and political spheres but also in terms of the cost as measured both economically and in lost lives. It is therefore critical to determine the precise link, if any, between prenatal cocaine exposure and subsequent cocaine abuse. Are cocaine-exposed offspring more vulnerable to developing a pattern of abuse in adolescence and adulthood and, if so, is this a reflection of greater sensitivity to the drug? At present, these questions may best be answered with research on nonhuman primates.

EFFECTS OF ENVIRONMENTAL CHALLENGES

Recent studies of primate social-emotional development have highlighted two basic principles that seem likely to be highly relevant for evaluation of the consequences of prenatal drug exposure in humans and in primate models. First, it is clear that many at-risk subjects whose behavior and emotional expressions appear completely normal under stable and familiar environmental

298

circumstances display major deficits under conditions of stress. For example, rhesus monkey infants reared during the first 6 months of life without mothers but with access to peers, and then placed into normal monkey groups, generally develop relatively normal social behavioral repertoires and emotional expressions in terms of patterns of peer play, relative position in the group-dominance hierarchy, reproductive and subsequent parental behavior, and socialization of emotions. However, if peer-reared monkeys are briefly separated from their social group, they exhibit far more severe biobehavioral reactions—higher levels of disturbance behavior, higher and more stable heart rates, higher levels of plasma cortisol and adrenocorticotropic hormone (ACTH), and greater monoamine turnover—than their mother-reared counterparts (e.g., Higley and Suomi 1989). Other primate studies focusing on other at-risk subgroups of subjects (e.g., Novak and Harlow 1979) suggest that this pattern may represent a widespread general principle: that aberrant behavioral and physiological responses to challenging and/or stressful situations may be largely masked under stable, familiar conditions. Anecdotal reports of young children prenatally exposed to cocaine suggest a similar pattern of extreme emotional response to novel or stressful environments (e.g., entry into preschool) in some children who appear to be perfectly normal in home settings. Those investigators contemplating development of primate models of prenatal drug exposure thus might consider testing their subjects in a variety of different settings as they are growing up.

CONCLUSIONS

To date, there has been relatively little effort devoted to the creation of animal models of prenatal cocaine exposure that use nonhuman primates as subjects. However, the development of such primate models would appear to be important and timely, because of their potential for major contribution to understanding the human condition and developing effective intervention strategies and therapies. Carefully controlled studies with nonhuman primates could enable investigators to pinpoint the effects of prenatal cocaine exposure on physical growth, physiological processes, and cognitive and social-emotional development from birth to maturity as well as to explore the consequences of interactions with other drugs or postnatal challenges. Although longitudinal studies using nonhuman primates tend to be more expensive and time-consuming than studies using rodents or other nonprimate animals, the degree to which the physical, physiological, cognitive, and social-emotional processes in nonhuman primates generalize to *Homo sapiens* is unique. Thus, the time appears ripe for the development of viable primate models of prenatal cocaine exposure.

REFERENCES

Amaro, H.; Fried, L.E.; Cabral, H.; and Zuckerman, B. Violence during pregnancy and substance use. *Am J Public Health* 80:575-579, 1990.

Amaro, H.; Zuckerman, B.; and Cabral, H. Drug use among adolescent mothers: Profile of risk. *Pediatrics* 84:144-151, 1989.

Bard, K.A. "Bayley Testing of Infant Chimpanzees," in preparation.

Bard, K.A.; Platzman, K.A.; and Lester, B.M. Comparisons of neurobehavioral integrity in chimpanzee and human neonates. *Am J Primatol* 20:3-4, 1990.

Bayley, N. *Bayley Scales of Infant Development.* New York: Psychological Corporation, 1969.

Bowdon, D.M.; Weathersbee, S.K.; Clarren, S.K.; Fahrenbruch, B.L.; Goodlin, B.L.; and Caffery, S.A. A periodic dosing model of fetal alcohol syndrome in pigtail macaques (Macaca nemestrina). *Am J Primatol* 4:143-157, 1983.

Brazelton, T.B. *Neonatal Behavioral Assessment Scale.* Philadelphia: Lippincott, 1973.

Chasnoff, I.J., and Griffith, D.R. Cocaine: Clinical studies of pregnancy and the newborn. *Ann N Y Acad Sci* 562:260-266, 1989.

Chasnoff, I.J.; Landress, H.J.; and Barrett, M.E. The prevalence of illicit-drug or alcohol abuse during pregnancy and discrepancies in mandatory reporting in Pinellas County, Florida. *N Engl J Med* 322:102-106, 1990.

Cherukuri, R.; Minkoff, H.; Feldman, J.; Parekh, A.; and Glass, L. A cohort study of alkaloidal cocaine ("crack") in pregnancy. *Obstet Gynecol* 72:147-151, 1988.

Edelin, K.C.; Gouganious, L.; Golar, K.; Oellerich, D.; Kyei-Aboagye, K.; and Hamid, A. Methadone maintenance in pregnancy: Consequences to care and outcome. *Obstet Gynecol* 71:399-404, 1988.

Fantz, R.L. Visual experience in infants: Decreased attention to familiar patterns relative to novel ones. *Science* 146:668-670, 1964.

Frank, D.A.; Zuckerman, B.; Amaro, H.; Aboagye, K.; Bauchner, H.; Cabral, H.; Fried, L.; Hingson, R.; Kayne, H.; Levenson, S.M.; Parker, S.; Reece, H.; and Vinci, R. Cocaine use during pregnancy: Prevalence and correlates. *Pediatrics* 82:888-895, 1988.

Gunderson, V.M.; Grant-Webster, K.S.; and Sackett, G.P. Deficits in visual recognition in low birth weight infant pigtail monkeys. *Child Dev* 60:119-127, 1989.

Gunderson, V.M., and Sackett, G.P. Development of pattern recognition in infant pigtail macaques (M. nemestrina). *Dev Psychol* 20:418-426, 1984.

Harlow, H.F.; Gluck, J.P.; and Suomi, S.J. Generalization of behavioral data between nonhuman and human animals. *Am Psychol* 27:709-716, 1972.

Harlow, H.F.; Harlow, M.K.; Dodsworth, R.O.; and Arling, G.L. Maternal behavior of monkeys deprived of mothering and peer associations in infancy. *Proc Am Phil Soc* 110:58-66, 1966.

Henderson, M.G., and McMillen, B.A. Effects of prenatal exposure to cocaine or related drugs on rat development and neurological indices. *Brain Res Bull* 14:207-212, 1990.

Higley, J.D., and Suomi, S.J. Temperamental reactivity in nonhuman primates. In: Kownstamm, G.A.; Bates, J.E.; and Rothbard, M.K., eds. *Handbook of Temperament in Children.* New York: Wiley, 1989. pp. 153-157.

Inouye, R.N.; Kokich, V.G.; Clarren, S.K.; and Bowden, D.M. Fetal alcohol syndrome: An examination of craniofacial dysmorphology in Macaca nemestrina. *J Med Primatol* 14:35-48, 1985.

Kaye, K.L.; Elkind, L.; Goldberg, D.; and Tytun, A. Birth outcomes for infants of drug abusing mothers. *N Y State J Med* 89:256-261, 1989.

Kemnitz, J.W.; Houser, W.D.; Eisele, S.G.; Engle, M.J.; Perelman, R.H.; and Farrell, P.M. Pregnancy and fetal development in the rhesus monkey. I. Maternal metabolism and fetal growth. In: Nathanielsz, P.W., and Parer, J.T., eds. *Research in Perinatal Medicine.* Ithaca, NY: Perinatology Press, 1984. pp. 1-25.

Kopp, C. Risk factors in development. In: Mussen, P.H. *Handbook of Child Psychiatry.* New York: Wiley, 1983. pp. 1081-1188.

Krug, S.E. Cocaine abuse: Historical, epidemiologic, and clinical perspective for pediatricians. *Adv Pediatr* 36:369-406, 1989.

Levin, E.D.; Schneider, M.L.; Ferguson, S.A.; Schantz, S.L.; and Bowman, R.E. Behavioral effects of lead exposure in rhesus monkeys. *Dev Psychobiol* 21:371-382, 1988.

Mitchell, G.D. Abnormal behavior in primates. In: Sackett, G.P., ed. *Primate Behaviors, Vol. 1.* New York: Academic Press, 1970. pp. 196-253.

Novak, M.A., and Harlow, H.F. Social recovery of monkeys isolated for the first year of life. 2. Long-term assessment. *Dev Psychol* 15:50-61, 1979.

Novak, M.A., and Harlow, H.F. Social recovery of monkeys isolated for the first year of life. 1. Rehabilitation and therapy. *Dev Psychol* 11:453-465, 1975.

Osterloh, J.D., and Lee, B.L. Urine drug screening in mothers and newborns. *Am J Dis Child* 143:791-793, 1989.

Parker, S.T. Piaget's sensory-motor series in an infant macaque: A model for comparing unstereotyped behavior and intelligence in human and nonhuman primates. In: Chevalier-Skolnikoff, S., and Poirier, F., eds. *Primate Biosocial Development* New York: Garland Press, 1977. pp. 87-102.

Piaget, J. *The Child's Perception of Physical Causality.* London: Routledge & Kegan Paul, 1951.

Ruppenthal, G.C. Infant primate research laboratory. Research Protocols Guide. Seattle, WA: CDMR, University of Washington, 1986.

Schneider, M.L. "Neonatal Assessment in Rhesus Monkeys." Master's thesis, University of Wisconsin-Madison, 1984.

Schneider, M.L. "A Rhesus Monkey Model of Human Individual Differences." Doctoral dissertation, University of Wisconsin-Madison, 1987.

Schneider, M.L.; Kraemer, G.W.; and Suomi, S.J. The effects of vestibular-proprioceptive stimulation on motor maturation and response to challenge in rhesus monkey infants. *J Occ Ther Res* 11:135-154, 1991.

Spear, L.P.; Kirstein, C.L.; and Frambes, N.A. Cocaine effects on the developing central nervous system: Behavioral, psychopharmacological, and neurochemical studies. *Ann N Y Acad Sci* 562:290-307, 1989.

Suomi, S.J. Abnormal behavior and primate models of psychopathology. In: Fobes, J.L., and King, J.E., eds. *Primate Behavior.* New York: Academic Press, 1982. pp. 171-215.

Suomi, S.J., and Harlow, H.F. Social rehabilitation of isolate-reared monkeys. *Dev Psychol* 6:487-496, 1972.

Suomi, S.J., and Immelmann, K. On the process and product of cross-species generalization. In: Rajecki, D.W., ed. *Studying Man Studying Animals.* New York: Plenum Press, 1983. pp. 203-223.

Uno, H.; Lohmiller, L.; Thieme, C.; Kemnizt, J.W.; Engle, M.J.; Roecker, E.B.; and Farrell, P.M. Brain damage induced by prenatal exposure to dexamethasone in fetal rhesus macaques. I. Hippocampus. *Dev Brain Res* 53:157-167, 1990.

Wise, K.L.; Wise, L.A.; and Zimmermann, R.R. Piagetian object permanence in the infant rhesus monkey. *Dev Psychol* 10:429-437, 1974.

Zuckerman, B.; Frank, D.A.; Hingson, R.; Amaro, H.; Levenson, S.; Parker S.; Vinci, R.; Aboagye, K.; Fried, L.; Cabral, H.; Timperi, R.; and Banchner, H. Effects of maternal marijuana and cocaine use on fetal growth. *N Engl J Med* 320:762-768, 1989.

AUTHORS

Stephen J. Suomi, Ph.D.
Chief
Laboratory of Comparative Ethology
National Institute of Child Health and Human Development
Building 31, Room B2B15
Bethesda, MD 20892

J. Dee Higley, Ph.D.
Staff Fellow
Laboratory of Clinical Studies—Primate Unit
National Institute on Alcohol Abuse and Alcoholism
National Institutes of Health Animal Center
P.O. Box 289
Poolesville, MD 20837

Discussion: Measurement of Drug-Induced Delays in Learning and Cognition and Social and Emotional Development

Sheldon B. Sparber

INTRODUCTION

This monograph critically evaluates methodological aspects of research into the potential deleterious consequences of prenatal exposure to drugs of abuse, including clinical research and research with animal models. The problems associated with this research, which uses evaluative and analytical techniques drawn from traditional clinical and basic sciences, are complex. Superimposed upon specialized, often divergent, disciplinary approaches to developmental issues is the special need to incorporate principles of pharmacological sciences, including drug disposition and pharmacodynamics, whether studies are retrospective or prospective, animal or clinical. The three preceding chapters (Jacobson and Jacobson, Tronick and colleagues, Suomi and Higley) offer insight into how future research strategies might improve the clinical assessment of drug-exposed children and primates. This chapter discusses the potential special problems one may expect to encounter in interdisciplinary research, which seems to be the hallmark of developmental pharmacology/toxicology studies. For example:

1. How should one separate causal from correlational relationships in such studies? Is the agent directly responsible for outcomes; is undernutrition secondary to withdrawal; or is infection caused by dirty needles responsible for developmental dysfunction?

2. Are databases from previous studies on normal and severely affected subjects reliable enough to use in place of contemporaneous controls, especially for assessing seemingly subtle impairment?

3. When and how should one account for the magnitude and duration, as well as time during development, when drug exposure occurs?

4. How can one separate the direct effects of drug exposure on the developing subject from the indirect effects of early experience with the lifestyles of drug-abusing parents and/or maternal behaviors that may be altered by drugs? Direct drug effects on the child prenatally as well as indirectly through modification of caretakers' behavior must be considered in the design, execution, and interpretation of studies of the effect of prenatal exposure to illicit drugs.

These are a few additional factors that should be considered by the interested reader contemplating future utility of the methods being suggested by the researchers in this section. These issues are by no means unique to the chapters under discussion, but they are necessary considerations if one wishes to derive meaningful and interpretable data from developmental drug studies in general.

ASSESSMENT OF TERATOGENIC EFFECTS

Jacobson and Jacobson's chapter focuses, in part, on the strengths and weaknesses of the Bayley Scales of Infant Development for assessing developmental milestones in normal infants and those exposed to various insults *in utero*, including alcohol, lead, and PCBs, among others. While they acknowledge the Bayley's sensitivity for assessing milestones, they argue that its principal drawback is that it does not tap into "specific domains" designed to assess attention, fine motor coordination, precursors to language, etc., to determine the reason(s) why an infant may not make a motoric response (e.g., pull a string to obtain a plastic ring). Is it because the subject cannot form the proper "means-end" relationship, because of a sensory or attention impairment, or because the stimulus may not be sufficiently reinforcing? This inability to accurately predict cognitive performance in early childhood may occur in part because the Bayley provides a more global analysis of subcomponents of behavior such as information processing, which may be assessed independently only later in development. One possible way to evaluate information processing is by using the Fagan Visual Recognition Memory Test. A specific behavior, such as eye gaze toward a visual target, is the dependent variable assessed. Jacobson and Jacobson reported its effectiveness in detecting consequences of exposure to PCBs in human infants and to methylmercury in laboratory monkeys. The Fagan appears to have better predictive validity than the Bayley for performance during the early school years of 4 to 7 years of age. Poor performance on the Fagan could reflect deficits or dysfunction within one or more so-called domains on which visual recognition performance depends. For example, methylmercury is known to affect the visual cortex as a primary site for inducing lesions, tunnel vision and blindness being one of the earliest signs of poisoning in older children and adults. Although fetal methylmercury poisoning is associated with central nervous system (CNS) lesions of a more diffuse nature, poor performance on the Fagan by children exposed to this neurotoxin could reflect such a sensory (i.e., visual) impairment. Alternatively, poor performance on the Fagan could reflect a difference in reinforcement efficacy of the target photos presented to exposed and control subjects. Lastly, poor performance could be due to an actual deficit in information processing, which is necessary for the ability to discriminate a novel from a familiar target. It is posssible that a combination of the above impairments could result from a developmental insult. As described, the Fagan will not discriminate these and other possibilities. However, the procedure could easily be modified to incorporate tests for such possibilities, and therein lies one of its strengths.

The Fagan also "taps" into a domain that may be associated with the level of cognitive function, namely, novelty preference or attention. The age when a child is tested may be a critical variable when considering either the Bayley, the Fagan, or any other assessment instrument. A significant delay or enhancement of functional maturation caused by exposure to a drug during development theoretically can affect a child's level of interest (i.e., attentiveness) or motor capacity (i.e., responsiveness, thereby affecting performance, relative to age-matched control subjects. While the Bayley may be sensitive to teratogenic insult when used at 6 to 12 months of age, Jacobson and Jacobson suggest that the Fagan has greater predictive validity when used at 6 to 7 months of age. They also suggest the use of the McCarthy scales and Stanford-Binet IQ tests for assessing preschool-age children because they comprise a series of subtests focusing on specific domains, such as block building, pictorial memory, draw-a-design, counting, and sorting. Such a multidimensional assessment, they argue, is important for detecting specific aspects of cognitive function/dysfunction in exposed infants and may offer clues as to "underlying neurochemical or neuroanatomical mechanisms."

By the time the child reaches school age, a more focused type of cognitive testing protocol may be useful. This might include evaluating short-term memory through a visual search and recognition task, spatial reasoning ability, and sustained attention and activity level. While most of these abilities are assessed through interactive computer-based systems of analysis that use a visual modality, other sensory systems (e.g., auditory or somatosensory) could be developed to evaluate more specific sensory domains. Protocols of this type provide greater objectivity than conventional clinical judgments, and interinstitutional reliability should be good to excellent.

There are limitations to focused cognitive testing, however. If deficits are seen prior to the ages of 4 to 5, they will be difficult to interpret because even children not exposed to drugs may have difficulty performing focused tasks. Secondly, for successful completion of these tasks, "numerous abilities are required." Thus, it becomes difficult to sort out the factors that determine whether the test item was passed or failed.

The most sensitive and reliable measure may be straightforward measures of motor activity, social-play analysis, and attention prior to age 2 and very elementary speech and language tests measuring processes such as onset time and articulation through the ages of 3 to 4. Beyond this age more cognitive tests involving reaction time and information processing efficiency may be used.

OBJECTIVE METHODS FOR DESCRIBING MOVEMENT, FACIAL EXPRESSIONS, AND COMMUNICATIVE BEHAVIORS

In their chapter, Tronick and colleagues present arguments favoring the notion that four different classes of movement by infants, when objectively measured, will be of potential utility for assessing altered organization of neuromotor function representing residual brain damage. They classify such behaviors as (1) spontaneous or "nondirected activity"; (2) instrumental movements, implying they are goal-directed and altered by their consequences; (3) facial expression as the external analog of anger (and perhaps other "emotions"); and (4) combinations of movements of limbs, head, etc., that are interpreted as the infant's expression or communication defensive patterns and/or stress.

Tronick and colleagues describe new technologies for objectively, rather than subjectively, measuring these movements to replace past reliance on clinical judgments. Such judgments were not easily quantifiable and thus must vary greatly from institution to institution, or from person to person within the same institution. They also make the point that numerous reports of intrauterine growth retardation (IUGR) and prematurity in cocaine-exposed infants, for example, imply that there should also be evidence of disrupted motor function during the period of infancy. Since IUGR (degree not specified) has been shown to be associated with sundry cognitive and other behavioral dysfunctions during preschool and school years, the implication is that any other variable that causes IUGR (e.g., illicit drug use by pregnant women) should also cause or be associated with later dysfunction.

When overt signs of acute brain trauma, such as cocaine-associated cerebrovascular accidents and seizures, are considered, it should not be surprising if one or more of the four categories of motor behaviors described by

Tronick and coworkers is also deemed to be different from "normal." Indeed, such neurobehavioral assessments, carried out longitudinally, may be invaluable in diagnosing and judging the prognosis, as well as the effectiveness, of any treatment interventions chosen for such infants. They argue, perhaps rightly so, that the reports of altered neurobehavioral function in children exposed to various drugs of abuse, mainly cocaine, are "compromised by serious methodological issues," mainly reliance upon subjective, clinical judgments. The new methods they propose, including kinematic movement analyses, templates for coding facial expressions, and coding systems for "communicative configurations" based on video recordings, may offer more objective alternatives. Tronick and colleagues describe the results of such kinematic analyses of otherwise healthy preterm infants, which revealed that the number of "movement units" decreased when they reached for objects, as is seen during development of healthy full-term infants. However, movement units, straightness ratios, and other measures, such as movement duration, showed subtle differences compared with full-term infants of the same age.

Because kinematic analyses allowed such a demonstration of small differences in neuromotor organization up to 1 year of age, which otherwise would go undetected by more conventional clinical judgments, Tronick and colleagues believe the method detected "a significant compromise of the healthy preterm infant's neuromotor functioning." Whether these observations indicate biologically nonsignificant, transient delays or are predictive of impending, long-term or permanent dysfunction that will translate into one or more developmental or adult disabilities remains an important research issue that deserves further attention.

Other techniques, such as the use of templates for coding facial expressions and coding systems for communicative configurations, are more subjectively scored and/or interpreted, regardless of whether videotapes or computer spreadsheets are used for analyses. Sufficient numbers of well-trained individuals and appropriate interrater reliabilities will need to be established as these techniques continue to be used.

The concept of using an "unmasking" manipulation, such as stressing or "increasing task demands" by stretching the limitations of a system to determine if a dysfunction first exists and then tracking the return to baseline, should provide useful information about possible drug-induced behavioral deficits. This approach has been used successfully in animal behavioral teratology laboratories. Tronick and coworkers make an important point that "a dysfunctional child in a standard paradigm may perform quite 'normally' when a task is easy. However, when a task becomes difficult, previously unnoticed problems may become evident."

In conclusion, this author was impressed with the potential utility of kinematic analyses of motor behavior for tapping brain function of specific regions and objectively determining the "mechanism" of altered motor behavior. Many of the dependent variables used to assess motor behavior may be influenced by nonmotoric factors that can be manipulated and controlled systematically in this procedure. For example, a drug-exposed infant may be unable to perceive or be attracted to an object placed within its reach because of motivational factors or sensory, cerebellar, extrapyramidal, or neuromuscular dysfunction. Kinematic analysis has great potential to aid in the diagnosis of these deficits, test the effectiveness of treatment interventions, and/or give insight into the prognosis of infants at risk for subtle behavioral or cognitive dysfunctions because of passive exposure to drugs or other insults *in utero* or during early postnatal development.

DEVELOPING NONHUMAN PRIMATE MODELS

In their chapter, Suomi and Higley argue for the utilization of infrahuman primates for research into the possible later effects of exposure during development to illicit, abused drugs (e.g., cocaine) on physiological, cognitive, or social-emotional variables. Primates are chosen because these species are "our closest biological relatives" and because infrahuman primates can be assessed before birth and shortly after birth, as well as during adolescence, in adulthood, and perhaps across generations. The use of primates instead of human subjects for developmental drug studies cannot be criticized. Well-designed studies with limited numbers of primate subjects can be used to confirm the reliability and validity of results obtained with greater numbers of nonprimate experimental subjects, such as those that have been carried out successfully with rodents and sheep.

Suomi and Higley describe the potential use of infrahuman primates for prenatal drug studies based on work done in their laboratory. This work utilizes ethological behavior analyses to study behaviors under naturalistic (field) conditions. Since monkeys are generally social creatures, living and foraging in troupes where dominant and subordinate adults, adolescents, and infants form social hierarchies, such an analysis offers the experimenter an opportunity to study influences on behavior and behavioral development in a more complex context than the average laboratory setting. Careful framing of specific research questions is important, however, because the behavior of subjects within a complex social group is very different than the behavior of subjects who are raised and live relatively individually. For example, when a drug manipulation is done prenatally and then primates are evaluated postnatally within a social group, a sideward glance or display of subordination could be misinterpreted as a sign of excessive aggression by one or more members of

308

the troupe. Many behaviors analyzed may be due only in part to the action of the drug per se, which then is superimposed onto a variety of other social responses occurring in the group.

SUMMARY

Methods of the type described in these three chapters promise to be useful in isolating and characterizing the type and degree of CNS deficit, if any, caused by drugs alone or in combination with many of the so-called confounding factors that are ordinarily covaried out in retrospective studies or controlled for in prospective studies. Important factors to be considered include the importance of undernutrition, infection, polydrug abuse, hypoxia, and early postnatal experience, acting alone or in concert, to affect the abilities and disabilities of at-risk infants.

AUTHOR

Sheldon B. Sparber, Ph.D.
Professor
Departments of Pharmacology, Psychiatry, and Psychology
University of Minnesota
435 Delaware Street, S.E.
Minneapolis, MN 55455

Following Drug-Exposed Infants Into Middle Childhood: Challenges to Researchers

Sydney L. Hans

INTRODUCTION

Clinical research examining the effects that drugs of abuse taken during pregnancy may have on child development has focused primarily on the neonatal period and the first 2 years of life. Because widespread interest in the effects of drug use during pregnancy is relatively new, few investigators have had the opportunity to follow samples of drug-exposed infants to school age. The purpose of this chapter is to discuss the rationale for conducting long-term followup research of drug-exposed infants and some of the challenges in executing such research.

RATIONALE FOR FOLLOWUP STUDIES

Studies that follow infants exposed *in utero* to drugs of abuse to middle childhood are essential to understand the behavioral teratological effects of such drugs. While useful information on drug-exposed children can be derived from cross-sectional research, only longitudinal investigations beginning before birth can ensure the most accurate information possible about mothers' actual drug use during pregnancy. Similarly, only longitudinal investigations can provide accurate information about other relevant variables that might be confounded with maternal drug use such as perinatal problems and early history of care.

Studies of school-age children are important to the field of human behavioral teratology regardless of the observed effects of a particular drug during infancy. The organization and meaning of behavior are different at different age periods, as are the demands placed on children by the environment at different ages. In particular, there are major shifts in behavior around the time children enter school (White 1970). Thus, the manifestations of prenatal drug exposure might take different forms at different developmental stages or be more clearly observable at different ages. While it is possible that one might observe a consistent developmental effect across age periods—such as consistently poor fine motor coordination—it is also possible that one might observe different types of effects at different ages or different degrees of effects at different ages. For example, in studying the effects of a particular drug, it is important to assess the extent to which the child recovers from the insults of perinatal drug exposure. The central nervous system retains a great degree of plasticity until fairly late in development that may allow for substantial recovery from some types of early insults (Rutter 1987a). It is also important to assess the extent to which there may be sleeper effects (Mednick 1981) that are not clearly observable until school age. Sleeper effects are plausible because many of the types of behavior typically observed during infancy—in particular the acquisition of motor and sensorimotor milestones—are highly resistant to perturbations in development (Horowitz 1989). The higher cognitive functioning processes required of the older child may be much more vulnerable to the negative effects of prenatal events or pathology in the early environment.

BACKGROUND TO RESEARCH

The observations presented in this chapter are based in large part on experience in one particular longitudinal study. For over a decade, the University of Chicago Parent Health and Child Development Project has studied longitudinally children whose mothers used methadone during pregnancy and a drug-free comparison group (Marcus et al. 1984). Participant families were recruited during the mothers' pregnancies through the obstetrical clinics at Chicago Lying-In Hospital between 1978 and 1982. Special weekly obstetrical clinics were held for drug-addicted women.

At that time the patient population in the clinics consisted primarily of lower-middle- and low-income African-American women living on the city's south side. The typical mother enrolled in the study was in her late 20s, was unmarried but living with a male partner, and had given birth to two or three previous children. The typical methadone-using mother was receiving less than 20 mg of methadone a day and occasionally used other substances.

Prior to delivery, information was gathered not only about the women's substance use but also their socioeconomic status, intellectual functioning, and mental health. The final sample of neonates available for assessment consisted of 45 methadone-exposed children and 47 comparison children. At the end of the second year of life, the sample consisted of 38 methadone-exposed children and 46 comparison children. Most of the attrition was from the methadone group, and most was due to the death or disablement of the children (Hans 1989).

The behavior of the children born into the sample was similar to that of other infants exposed to methadone who have been described in the literature (Hans et al. 1984). During the first week of life, methadone-exposed neonates differed from comparison infants in motoric and state behavior (Jeremy and Hans 1985; Hans et al., in press). Relative to comparison-group infants, they were more jerky, tremulous, tense, active, and better able to put hand in mouth. They were also more irritable and more highly aroused. By the end of the first month these differences diminished, although there was still a tendency for the methadone-exposed infants to have elevated general body tonus. Throughout the first 2 years of life, the methadone infants lagged slightly behind comparison infants in their acquisition of motor and sensorimotor milestones (Hans 1989; Hans et al. 1984). These differences were consistent but did not reach statistical significance at most ages. Methadone-exposed infants also were observed to be more active than comparison infants (primarily at 4 months of age), to have a shorter attention span (particularly at 12 months of age), and to have poorer motor coordination (Hans and Marcus 1983).

CHALLENGES TO CONDUCTING FOLLOWUP RESEARCH

In 1987 the project researchers began planning and conducting a school-age followup study of the children in the methadone study. This work presents several scientific, logistical, and ethical challenges, including (1) designing a study with a strong theoretical basis, (2) using research strategies that might illuminate causal antecedents of children's behavioral problems, (3) maintaining contact with the participants over time, (4) maintaining positive, mutually beneficial relationships with participant families, (5) protecting the rights of the participants, and (6) generating "useful" information. A discussion of these challenges follows.

Theoretical Framework

Human behavioral teratology is a scientific discipline in its infancy. Most research in the field to date has been atheoretical in its design. Typically, studies have assessed children exposed to drugs using standardized instruments that, while appropriate to a particular age of interest, were not chosen to test specific hypotheses. For example, in the project's research on methadone-exposed infants, there are now several sets of data using the Neonatal Behavioral Assessment Scale and the Bayley Scales of Infant Development; there are also several data sets using standardized intelligence tests in preschool followup studies. The scientific strength of relying on standard measures is the production of a set of replicated findings from multiple samples (Hans et al. 1984). Yet, as the discipline begins to develop, investigators increasingly should be choosing measures that allow them to test specific hypotheses. In designing followup studies, there are several sources from which hypotheses can come:

- Studies of the behavior of drug-exposed infants
- Clinical case reports of drug-exposed children
- Cross-sectional reports of children with drug-using parents
- Studies of animal behavior
- Studies of animal neurochemistry and neuroanatomy
- Followup studies of children exposed to other substances
- Followup studies of children from other high-risk groups

In designing the study of school-age methadone-exposed children, there were several of these sources of information from which to draw ideas. First were the project's infancy findings indicating motor dyscoordination and attentional problems in drug-exposed infants. Second, while there were no previous longitudinal data on school-age methadone-exposed children, several investigators (Kaltenbach et al. 1978; Strauss et al. 1979; Lifshitz et al. 1985; Wilson et al. 1979) had reported followup data on the development of opioid-exposed children in the preschool years. In these studies opioid-exposed children were reported to be more active, to have poorer fine motor coordination, and to have less well-focused attention than comparison children. These findings of poor attention, high activity, and soft neurological signs, including motor dyscoordination, were intriguing because they suggested that *in utero* exposure to opioid drugs might result in symptoms of attention deficit hyperactivity disorder (ADHD) (American Psychiatric Association 1987).

Hypothesizing that methadone-exposed children develop disorders of attention is not inconsistent with data on followup of children exposed to other substances. In particular, Streissguth and colleagues (1986) found a pattern of neurobehavioral deficits related to prenatal alcohol exposure that includes memory and attention deficits similar to those observed in children with attention deficit disorders.

Thus, this followup study focused on the hypothesis that children exposed prenatally to methadone might display symptoms of attention deficit disorder at school age. The project researchers decided to develop an assessment battery that would focus on the assessment of ADHD from a multifaceted, multiobserver approach.

In the research on methadone, the following types of assessments were planned:

313

- A psychiatric interview was chosen to establish clinical criteria for ADHD as reported by the mother and the child.

- Teacher rating scales were chosen that focused on aspects of attention and hyperactivity.

- An intelligence scale was included to be able to make differential diagnoses of various learning and attentional problems.

- A continuous performance test was chosen to be able to finely quantify aspects of sustained attention and to separate aspects of attentional dysfunctioning related to impulsivity from those related to processing errors.

- A neurological assessment was selected to look clinically at a variety of large and fine motor skills.

- A battery of electronically scored fine motor and tremor assessments was chosen to provide quantified measures of fine motor dysfunctioning.

The attention deficit hypothesis thus guided the choice of instruments. It also could have guided the experimental design. For example, one might have wished to build in a comparison group of hyperactive children or children with other types of learning disabilities. Such a strategy has been useful in other high-risk research focusing on attention deficit; Nuechterlein (1983) was able to clarify the nature of attention deficits in children at risk for schizophrenia by comparing them with clinically hyperactive children.

Strategies for Illuminating Causal Antecedents of Behavior Problems

Perhaps the single most difficult methodological issue confronting those in the field of human behavioral teratology is trying to understand causal factors without being able to implement experimental research designs. Because clinical researchers have no control over mothers' use of substances during pregnancy and no control of children's rearing environment after birth, no human study will ever provide definitive evidence about the behavioral teratological effects of a drug. While it would be inappropriate to hold human studies up to the standards of animal research, it is nevertheless desirable for clinical investigators to try to identify the most plausible sources of behavioral problems in children from drug-using families. Much of the research on drug-exposed infants has made the mistake of assuming that, because mothers in their drug and comparison groups have been matched on a limited number of demographic variables, any differences between drug-exposed infants and comparison groups are due to teratological factors. Yet there are many alternative causal factors that might explain such differences, including increased incidence of perinatal complications in drug-exposed children, a poor child-rearing environment provided by drug-using families, and the genetic transmission of behavior problems found in drug-using parents (Aylward 1982; Marcus and Hans 1982). The numbers of nonteratological causal explanations for behavioral problems in children of drug-using parents only become greater as children reach school age.

Several techniques are available for illuminating the plausibility of alternative causal factors in human behavioral teratology studies. One such technique is the inclusion of multiple control groups in a study. Possible comparison groups in addition to unexposed infants might be drug-exposed children in adoptive homes or children of drug-using mothers who were drug-free during pregnancy.

The most important technique for looking at nonteratological causal factors is inclusion of measures that assess such possible factors. In followup work, the project researchers have chosen to look extensively at sources of variation in the child's rearing experience, specifically exploring:

- Family stressors
- Maternal mental health
- Family interpersonal relationships
- Childrearing values held by the mother
- Children's perception of their parents
- Mother's style of interaction with the child

Child outcome measures need to be carefully analyzed not only in relation to maternal drug use but also to measures of nonteratological factors. It is particularly important to look at the interaction between drug exposure and other factors. For example, one needs to explore questions of whether drug effects occur only in the presence of other risk factors such as impoverished environment or in children of only one sex. Interactions between drug exposure and environmental factors might lead to theories that drug exposure sensitizes children to the effects of poor environments (Hans 1989) and that particular environmental conditions can protect children from the effects of prenatal biological insult environments (Rutter 1987b).

Maintaining Contact With Participants Over Time

The relatively unstable lifestyle of many drug-using families often makes tracking their whereabouts over time a difficult task. Telephone service is intermittent in drug-using households. Families change residences frequently. Women may live in the homes of different friends and relatives at different times. Mail may not be reliably received in dangerous neighborhoods.

315

To maintain contact with participants over time, it is important for researchers to have information on how to locate the mother's entire social network. In this methadone study, files are maintained of participant names and addresses and of the names and addresses of other family members and friends. For drug-using mothers, it is also important to keep information on the drug abuse treatment facilities at which they have previously received treatment.

Between assessment sessions, project researchers try to make periodic contacts with families, either through a friendly telephone call or a card in the mail. If mail is returned undelivered, other family members and friends are contacted to locate the participant before the "trail grows cold."

When there are difficulties contacting other family members, staff members have often relied on locating information available in computer data banks. While access to different types of information will vary in different localities, there are many types of data banks that are open to the public and others to which researchers may be able to achieve access by going through appropriate institutional channels or by obtaining appropriate consent in advance from families. Examples of data banks that might prove useful in locating families include telephone listings, voter registration records, birth and death records, public aid records, public housing records, postal records, child welfare records, driver's license records, and school enrollment information.

Maintaining Positive, Mutually Beneficial Relationships With Participants

Another major challenge to working with drug-using families is helping them feel positive about their experience in the research project. If families do not feel positively toward the research project, sample attrition will be high. In work with drug-using families, project researchers have used many techniques for creating a positive experience for families. In scheduling appointments the families' schedules are accommodated. If families desire, they are picked up at their homes by a driver and transported to the project site. The staff will routinely wait 2 hours after the scheduled appointment time for late families to arrive. Children and parents are always given generous positive feedback during the interview and testing sessions. Mothers and children are offered snacks during research sessions. Photographs of the children are taken at each session to give to the parents, and during the school-age assessments families are given copies of videotapes made when their children were infants. At the end of each session, the children select a present for themselves, and mothers receive monetary compensation for their time. Greeting cards are sent to parents on birthdays (their own and the children's) and on holidays (particularly Mother's Day).

Most of the feelings family members have toward the research project come from the characteristics of the research staff members with whom they interact in the research sessions. In working with African-American families, African-American staff members are hired so that the families will feel comfortable. But more important than staff members' racial or ethnic identity is their capacity to be sensitive to the types of difficulties experienced by parents, by individuals living in poverty, and by those addicted to drugs. For most parents and children in this research, having the opportunity to talk about themselves to an interested person is a unique and positive experience. Yet for such an experience to be a positive one, staff members must be warm and have a genuine interest in and respect for the families. Their attitudes are ultimately what families sense. Consistently communicating respect to families can be difficult when a mother repeatedly makes staff members wait, arrives for sessions while "under the influence," is evasive in her communication, or manipulates the staff member to meet her own needs. School-age children can similarly try the patience of the staff through their oppositional behavior. Staff members need to be patient and flexible.

While staff characteristics are at the core of the relationship that develops between families and the research project, the underlying model of the research and the selection of instruments also play a role in how the family experiences the research project. Human behavioral teratology research is based on a developmental psychopathology model. Many of the research questions and hypotheses in the field focus on problem behavior in problem families. Yet to barrage parents with questions about their own and their children's problems may alienate and insult them. Questioning children about problems in their own behavior and problems in their families is similarly intimidating to them. In this pilot work using psychiatric interviews, researchers became concerned that such a negative approach damaged rapport between researcher and participant. It is normal for adults and children, particularly those who have not sought help for a problem, to respond in a defensive and evasive manner to the kinds of questions included in such interviews. There also was concern that results of research relying primarily on a pathological model, as has much research on poor children and children from minority populations (McLoyd 1990), would produce overly simplistic conclusions that ignore the complexity and dignity of the participants' lives. Therefore, staff members made an effort to alter some of the research protocols to include more positive material on the achievements of children and their families and to make the theoretical perspective somewhat more positive by considering children's adaptive skills and the factors that protect children and foster their resilience (Garmezy and Masten 1986).

Ultimately, the most important part of showing respect to families lies in seeing that the research benefits not only the researcher but also the families. Benefits may come to some mothers and children from the positive stimulation of participating in the research project or in the form of financial compensation. Alternatively, benefits may need to come from direct efforts of the research staff to help families with their individual needs. Researchers working with drug-using families—even researchers not working in a clinic setting—must be prepared to see that families receive help with their problems. Helping families receive help is not only an ethical responsibility but also a key to maintaining positive relationships with families and ultimately to minimizing sample attrition. It is important that the research team includes a member who is able to consider the needs of these families and to make appropriate referrals when it is apparent that the family is not being adequately helped by existing services. It is also a good practice to review each case periodically to determine whether any action needs to be undertaken. In this project's experience with the methadone study, the types of problems experienced by families become increasingly complex as the children become older and the availability of appropriate referrals becomes more difficult. Investigators need to have available appropriate and affordable referrals for child and adult medical problems, domestic violence and other family problems, legal problems, child behavior problems, acquired immunodeficiency syndrome (AIDS) counseling and testing, and educational problems.

Protecting the Rights of Participants

While all clinical researchers must deal with the ethical issues of informed consent and confidentiality, these issues are particularly challenging when working with drug-using families and become increasingly complex as the children under study become older.

In research with school-age children it is important to explain the research not only to the parents but also to the child. Before beginning assessment, one must explain clearly to children what procedures they will be experiencing. The children should have the opportunity to explore the assessment room and any apparatus with which they will be working and to meet the examiners. In clinical research, it is also important that both parents and children understand that what they say will be treated with confidentiality and to understand the limits of such confidentiality. In general terms, the limits of confidentiality are when it appears that the child or someone else may be hurt (Taylor and Adelman 1989).

In working with school-age children, protecting confidentiality is not always easy or natural. Seemingly trivial breaches of confidentiality are potentially harmful to the child. For example, it might be tempting casually to report to the parent a "cute" comment the child made about some aspect of family life. Yet such an offhand comment might embarrass the child if he or she discovers it was reported and might cause the child to lose trust in the researcher. Parents who discover from the researcher that children reported freely on aspects of family life might also feel that the child violated aspects of family privacy and reprimand or punish the child for his or her discussions with the researcher.

There are two basic ways in which the researcher may need to break confidentiality: (1) breaking confidentiality with the family and reporting information to outside authorities and (2) breaking confidentiality with the child and reporting information to the parent.

Researchers may be mandated by law to report information on child abuse and neglect to the State. Such obligations to report supersede the confidentiality of the researcher-participant relationship and probably supersede Federal certificates of researcher confidentiality such as those granted by the National Institute on Drug Abuse (NIDA). In this project, in cases where child abuse or neglect appear clear, researchers always first discuss with the parent the need to make a report. Then the staff members plan with the parent how such a report will be made and offer to accompany the family through the process. Project experience teaches that parents recognize their need for help and ultimately are grateful for the intervention. The project has never lost a family to followup because of intervening in such a manner.

The researcher is also morally obligated to break confidentiality in situations in which the child or someone else is likely to get hurt, for example, when the child reports suicidal thoughts. It is often very difficult to decide when a problem is serious enough to warrant breaking the important promise of confidentiality. In this work staff have discovered that there is rarely a clear-cut situation in which confidentiality should be broken. For example, is the danger to the child who is experimenting with alcohol at age 10 great enough to warrant breaking confidentiality and telling the parent? Sometimes the staff has concerns about whether reporting a problem behavior to a particular parent will truly help the child or only place him or her at increased danger of abuse from an erratic parent. In any situation where a staff member breaks confidentiality by reporting to the parent, the staff member first discusses the problem with the child, who usually will indicate a willingness to report himself or herself to the parent or to discuss the matter jointly with the parent. The staff always tries to minimize the negative consequences of the disclosure by considering in advance possible plans of action that might be recommended to the parent.

Generating Useful Information

Finally, scientists working with clinical populations need to be cognizant of their obligation to provide not only scientifically interesting information but also information that will be useful to those providing services to the population under study—in this case, drug-using families with children. While most clinical studies of drug-exposed infants and children were initiated to provide enlightenment about teratological effects of particular substances, their greatest value may ultimately lie in suggesting ways of helping children affected by drug abuse.

It is a challenge to most scientists to conduct and report research in a manner that will be truly useful to those working directly with families. Yet those in the fields of public policy, medicine, social work, and education are making decisions every day about how to intervene with drug-using families, how and when to treat disabilities experienced by drug-exposed children, whether drug-using parents are capable of caring for their children, and which families should receive limited prevention and intervention resources. To make such decisions, those professionals need better information about the nature of problematic outcomes to be expected in children exposed to various drugs and about the antecedents and correlates of such problems. The types of questions raised by those conducting human behavioral teratology work and those in the helping professions are related but may be different in subtle ways. For example, while the scientist may typically ask whether drug-exposed children have poorer mean scores on a particular intelligence scale than comparison children, the helping professional needs to know what proportion of drug-exposed children have scores on that intelligence scale that are problematic and need intervention. While the scientist may report that drug exposure has a teratological effect on the child, causing biological damage that is manifested in problematic behavior, the helping professional needs to know what aspects of the child's environment help to ameliorate such teratological effects or to exacerbate them. In designing studies and reporting results it is a challenge, but a worthwhile one, for scientists to consider the potential use of their data to those in the helping professions.

CONCLUSION

Long-term followup studies of drug-exposed children are essential for truly understanding the behavioral teratological effects of drugs on human populations. Yet conducting these studies presents many challenges to the researcher. Some of these challenges are the scientific and logistical ones of designing and conducting good research in a difficult and "messy" field with a sometimes difficult population. Others are the more human and ethical challenges of working with families in a manner that benefits them directly through their participation in the research and that will ultimately be of use to others trying to help the population under study.

REFERENCES

Aylward, G.P. Methadone outcome studies: Is it more than the methadone? *J Pediatr* 10:214-215, 1982.

American Psychiatric Association. *Diagnostic and Statistical Manual of Mental Disorders.* 3d ed. Washington, DC: American Psychiatric Association, 1987.

Garmezy, N., and Masten, A.S. Stress, competence, and resilience: Common frontiers for therapist and psychopathologist. *Behav Ther* 17:500-521, 1986.

Hans, S.L. Developmental consequences of prenatal exposure to methadone. *Ann N Y Acad Sci* 562:195-207, 1989.

Hans, S.L.; Jeremy, R.J.; and Henson, L.G. The development of children exposed in utero to opioid drugs. In: Greenbaum, C.W., and Auerbach, J.G., eds. *Longitudinal Studies of Children at Risk: Cross-National Perspectives.* Norwood, NJ: Ablex Press, in press.

Hans, S.L., and Marcus, J. Motor and attentional behavior in infants of methadone maintained women. In: Harris, L.S., ed. *Problems of Drug Dependence 1982: Proceedings of the 44th Annual Scientific Meeting, The Committee on Problems of Drug Dependence, Inc.* National Institute on Drug Abuse Research Monograph 43. DHHS Pub. No. (ADM)83-1264. Washington, DC: U.S. Govt. Print. Off., 1983. pp. 287-293.

Hans, S.L.; Marcus, J.; Jeremy, R.J.; and Auerbach, J.G. Neurobehavioral development of children exposed in utero to opioid drugs. In: Yanai, J., ed. *Neurobehavioral Teratology.* Amsterdam: Elsevier, 1984. pp. 249-273.

Horowitz, F.D. "The Concept of Risk: A Re-Evaluation." Paper presented at the meeting of the Society for Research in Child Development, Kansas City, MO, April 1989.

Jeremy, R.J., and Hans, S.L. Behavior of neonates exposed in utero to methadone as assessed on the Brazelton scale. *Infant Behav Dev* 8:323-336, 1985.

Kaltenbach, K.; Graziani, L.J.; and Finnegan, L.P. Development of children born to women who received methadone during pregnancy. *Pediatr Res* 12:372, 1978.

Lifshitz, M.H.; Wilson, G.S.; Smith, E.O'B.; and Desmond, M.M. Factors affecting head growth and intellectual function in children of drug addicts. *J Pediatr* 75:269-274, 1985.

Marcus, J., and Hans, S.L. A methodological model to study the effects of toxins on child development. *Neurobehav Toxicol Teratol* 4:483-487, 1982.

Marcus, J.; Hans, S.L.; Patterson, C.B.; and Morris, A.J. A longitudinal study of offspring born to methadone-maintained women. I. Design, methodology, and description of women's resources for functioning. *Am J Drug Alcohol Abuse* 10:135-160, 1984.

McLoyd, V.C. Minority children: Introduction to the special issue. *Child Dev* 61:263-267, 1990.

Mednick, S.A. Methods of prospective, longitudinal research. In: Mednick, S.A., and Baert, A.E., eds. *Prospective Longitudinal Research: An Empirical Basis for the Primary Prevention of Psychosocial Disorders.* Oxford: Oxford University Press, 1981. pp. 11-15.

Nuechterlein, K.H. Signal detection in vigilance tasks and behavioral attributes among offspring of schizophrenic mothers and among hyperactive children. *J Abnorm Psychol* 92:4-28, 1983.

Rutter, M. Continuities and discontinuities from infancy. In: Osofsky, J.D., ed. *Handbook of Infant Development.* 2d ed. New York: Wiley, 1987a. pp. 1256-1296.

Rutter, M. Psychosocial resilience and protective mechanisms. *Am J Orthopsychiatry* 57:316-331, 1987b.

Strauss, M.E.; Lessen-Firestone, J.K.; Chavez, C.J.; and Stryker, J.C. Children of methadone-treated women at five years of age. *Pharmacol Biochem Behav* 11:3-6, 1979.

Streissguth, A.P.; Barr, H.M.; Sampson, P.D.; Parrish-Johnson, J.C.; Kirchner, G.L.; and Martin, D.C. Attention, distraction and reaction time at age 7 years and prenatal alcohol exposure. *Neurobehav Toxicol Teratol* 8:717-725, 1986.

Taylor, L., and Adelman, H.S. Reframing the confidentiality dilemma to work in children's best interests. *Professional Psychol Res Practice* 20:79-83, 1989.

White, S.H. Some general outlines of the matrix of developmental changes between five and seven years. *Bull Orton Soc* 20:41-57, 1970.

Wilson, G.S.; McCreary, R.; Kean, J.; and Baxter, J.C. The development of preschool children of heroin-addicted mothers: A controlled study. *J Pediatr* 63:135-141, 1979.

ACKNOWLEDGMENT

The followup study described in this chapter is supported by National Institute on Drug Abuse grant DA-05396.

AUTHOR

Sydney L. Hans, Ph.D.
Research Associate (Associate Professor)
Department of Psychiatry
University of Chicago
Box 411
5841 South Maryland Avenue
Chicago, IL 60637

Patterns of Growth and Development in Narcotic-Exposed Children

Marta H. Lifschitz and Geraldine S. Wilson

INTRODUCTION

Low birth weight is the most frequent and clearly documented adverse outcome associated with gestational exposure to narcotics and other toxic addictive substances, including nicotine, alcohol, marijuana, and cocaine. While decreased birth weight can be attributed primarily to impaired fetal growth, an increased occurrence of premature birth, as reported with maternal use of heroin and cocaine, may also play a role (Zelson et al. 1971; Wilson et al. 1973; Oro and Dixon 1987). The persistence of effects of maternal narcotic use on growth beyond the perinatal period has been suggested by several investigators (Wilson et al. 1973, 1979; Chasnoff et al. 1980; Bauman and Levine 1986; Hans 1989), while others have reported normal postnatal growth (Strauss et al. 1979; Rosen and Johnson 1982, 1985). To date, clinical studies have failed to establish a direct relationship between narcotic use during pregnancy and growth. The investigation of drug-abusing women and their offspring has been compromised by a variety of both practical and theoretical issues. Longitudinal studies of children exposed to illicit drugs during pregnancy are few in number, and many have serious methodological limitations. The initial cohort is often small and the rate of attrition is high. In addition, the history of drug exposure is poorly documented, and the issue of polydrug use is often ignored. Comparison groups are absent from early studies and, when included, are often poorly defined. Unfortunately, the techniques of data analysis are often inadequate for the interpretation of multifactorial outcome effects.

One purpose of this chapter is to review longitudinal studies of postnatal growth and its relationship to cognitive development in children prenatally exposed to narcotics. The second aim is to discuss methodologic issues regarding stability of outcome measures across time and the relative impact of direct drug effects within the context of other measures known to influence somatic growth.

WEIGHT AND LENGTH AT BIRTH

A well-established finding in infants of heroin-addicted mothers is a high incidence of low birth weight. Early studies of drug-exposed pregnancies failed to differentiate the small-for-gestational-age (SGA) or growth-retarded infant from the preterm infant of less than 37 weeks of gestation. Differentiation between premature birth and growth retardation is important because the conditions differ in terms of causative mechanisms, perinatal complications, and postnatal growth patterns.

The question of causal relationship between specific drug exposure and impaired fetal growth must be analyzed within the context of a multitude of variables that are known to affect fetal size. Impaired intrauterine growth has been associated with poor maternal weight gain, maternal undernutrition, absence of prenatal care, preeclampsia, chronic maternal illness, unmarried status, intrauterine infections (Miller and Hassanein 1973), smoking (Longo 1982), and heavy alcohol consumption (Streissguth et al. 1989). Many of these factors are common during the pregnancy of the drug-abusing woman (Finnegan et al. 1972; Naeye et al. 1973). Fetal and postnatal growth are also influenced by race (Wilcox 1981), maternal age (Goldstein 1971), and sex of the infant (Wingerd and Schoen 1974).

In one of the largest perinatal studies, reviewing 384 births to heroin addicts over a 10-year period, Zelson and colleagues (1971) found a 50-percent incidence of low birth weight (<2,500 g). The hospital incidence for the same period was 15 percent. Forty percent of the low birth weight infants born to addicted women were SGA. No prospective studies of comparable size have been conducted to enable an examination of nutritional, hormonal, biochemical, and biologic variables as they interact with maternal drug use.

The introduction of methadone treatment added a new dimension to the study of fetal exposure to narcotics. Early experience indicated that involvement in treatment programs resulted in modification of risk factors associated with illicit drug use (Finnegan et al. 1972). However, subsequent studies failed to show consistent improvement in pregnancy outcome or birth size.

Similar rates of low birth weight in infants of 45 heroin addicts and 46 methadone-treated women (44.4 percent and 47.8 percent, respectively) were interpreted by Zelson and coworkers (1973) as indicating that narcotics, either methadone or heroin, adversely affected fetal growth. These researchers observed a tendency for birth weight to increase relative to the duration of methadone treatment but did not analyze the contribution of associated social, biologic, or health variables.

324

Kandall and colleagues (1976) concluded that methadone administration during pregnancy appeared to correct heroin-associated fetal growth retardation in a dose-dependent manner. While they studied a large sample (337 neonates) by group comparisons of variables that might influence birth weight, the study had two weaknesses: Data were largely retrospective, and the contribution of each potentially confounding factor (maternal age, prenatal care, and race) was analyzed separately rather than in a multivariate model.

The prospective study by Wilson and colleagues (1981) of 39 methadone-treated women and 29 untreated heroin addicts enrolled during pregnancy showed no improvement in birth size with methadone treatment despite improved nutrition and compliance with prenatal care. They postulated that continued polydrug use by the methadone-treated mothers may have affected birth size, although birth weight and length were unaffected in Chasnoff and colleagues' study (1982) of polydrug users who were not exposed to opiates. Analysis of covariance was applied to Wilson's prospective cohort to investigate the effect of drug addiction on length at birth (Lifschitz et al. 1983). Although infants in both treated and untreated drug groups were shorter than the comparison group, when group means were adjusted for sex, race, prenatal care, weight gain during pregnancy, maternal nutrition, prenatal risk, and smoking, they no longer differed significantly. This suggests that the growth impairment observed in infants born to narcotic-dependent women is unrelated to action of the narcotic but secondary to the adverse social and health factors commonly associated with addiction. These findings are confirmed by a larger study of 220 infants born to methadone-maintained mothers that utilized regression analysis to demonstrate that three variables (number of prenatal visits, gestational stage at first prenatal care visit, and the interval of the pregnancy during which the woman received prenatal care) contribute significant increments to the proportion of variance with respect to birth weight (Suffet and Brotman 1984). Methadone dose at the time of delivery was not a significant factor.

HEAD SIZE AT BIRTH

Small head size was reported in a descriptive study of 67 heroin-exposed neonates (Vargas et al. 1975). The head circumference of 25 (39 percent) of the infants was below the 10th percentile for gestational age; 15 of these infants were also SGA. Although these observations were retrospective and uncontrolled, they suggested the need for further research because of the serious implications of impaired brain growth for future cognitive development.

There is evidence that the period of most rapid brain growth occurs prenatally in the human; peak growth occurs about the time of birth, and cell division ends about 5 to 6 months after birth (Winick 1969). Severe malnutrition of the mother during famine conditions results in reductions of weight, length, and head circumference at birth (Stein and Susser 1975). Data from the Dutch famine indicated that fetal weight gain is particularly related to maternal diet during the last trimester of pregnancy, the critical period for myelination in the human brain (Winick 1969). Reduced head size (microencephaly) at birth also may be related to intrauterine infections, a relatively common complication of pregnancy in narcotic-dependent women (Volpe 1987; Naeye et al. 1973).

Literature on narcotic-exposed infants yields almost no information about their head growth before the era of methadone treatment. Chasnoff and colleagues (1980) first reported that mean head circumference at birth was low (at the 5th percentile) in 15 methadone-exposed infants, while birth weight and length were at the 10th percentile. Controls were not included. Rosen and Johnson (1982) then reported a differential effect of methadone on head growth in a prospective study of 62 infants. Although their mean birth weight did not differ significantly from that of the 32 comparison infants, the incidence of microencephaly (head size below the 3rd percentile) was increased in methadone-exposed infants (p<0.001). Multiple-regression analyses were performed to determine the contribution of other factors to developmental outcome; head size at birth, however, was not included (Rosen and Johnson 1982). In a controlled study of 39 infants whose mothers were maintained on low-dose methadone without evidence of other drug use, mean head circumference was significantly less than that of controls after adjustment for confounding variables (Chasnoff et al. 1982). A study by Lifschitz and colleagues (1985), which included heroin-exposed infants and infants born to a heterogeneous group of polydrug-abusing methadone-maintained mothers, also demonstrated significant differences in mean head size at birth between drug groups and controls. The preliminary correlation analysis showed a strong inverse relationship between a quantitative estimate of narcotic exposure and head size at birth that appeared to substantiate Chasnoff's impression that opiate exposure directly affected fetal head growth. However, narcotic exposure lost its significance after adjustment for confounding variables. Unlike Rosen, Lifschitz and coworkers were unable to demonstrate an increased incidence of microencephaly at birth.

The studies reviewed suggest, but fail to demonstrate conclusively, a causal relationship between prenatal exposure to narcotics (or associated factors) and impaired fetal head growth. In part, the inability to confirm the adverse effects of maternal narcotic use may be related to small sample size. A recent study that prospectively ascertained cocaine and marijuana use in a general prenatal care sample of 1,226 mother-infant dyads, indicated that each of the drugs was independently associated with impaired fetal growth when other potentially confounding variables were analytically controlled (Zuckerman et al. 1989).

POSTNATAL LINEAR GROWTH

Early descriptive studies of infants of heroin addicts suggested the existence of long-term effects of linear growth (Wilson et al. 1973). Wilson (1975) observed that infants born to narcotic-addicted mothers not only demonstrated a high rate of intrauterine growth retardation but also showed postnatal growth disturbance; some children with appropriate measurements at birth subsequently fell below normative levels. Although birth measurements were appropriate for gestational age in 28 of 29 neonates delivered to methadone-maintained mothers, 25 percent of them showed growth disturbance postnatally. The decline in growth rate was usually evident by 6 months.

Both intrauterine and postnatal growth are known to be affected by a variety of factors, the most important of which is genetic potential. Parental stature is the predominant influence on children's growth (Wingerd and Schoen 1974). The consideration of other factors is not likely to be meaningful unless parental height is taken into account. In Wingerd and Schoen's sample, parental height alone accounted for 88.6 percent of the variation in height at 5 years of age. Maternal parity has been shown to exert a marked influence on growth. First-born babies are smaller at birth but grow faster during the first 3 months of postnatal life. By 1 year of age, they have usually shifted growth curves; and, by 5 and 7 years, they are taller than subsequent offspring (Prentice et al. 1987; Wingerd and Schoen 1974; Goldstein 1971). Although an American study did not document the importance of socioeconomic factors as determinants of growth (Wingerd and Schoen 1974), a British report showed that by 7 years of age, children born to mothers of low socioeconomic status were shorter than those of higher socioeconomic class. Emotional deprivation and physical neglect or abuse are commonly associated with failure to thrive and may result in permanent linear growth impairment (Altemeier et al. 1985). The age of the mother at the time of birth also plays a role. By 7 years of age, children of mothers under 25 years at delivery were smaller than children born to mothers who were 25 years or over (Goldstein 1971).

The rate of growth is a very important factor to consider in growth studies. During early infancy, the infant shifts from a growth rate that is predominantly determined by intrauterine conditions to one that reflects genetic background. Infants achieve their genetically determined channel of growth by 4 to 18 months (Smith et al. 1976; Sorva et al. 1989). Low-birth-weight infants tend to remain shorter than average (Goldstein 1971). When Kimble and colleagues (1982) studied the growth of infants who weighed below 1,500 g at birth and were appropriate for gestational age, they found that between the ages of 1 and 3 years the growth curve paralleled, but fell below, that of normal children. Because a substantial percentage of those infants can be expected to fall below the 5th percentile on the National Center for Health Statistics growth charts (National Center for Health Statistics 1976), special growth curves for infants born prematurely have been designed (Keen and Pearse 1988). These findings reaffirm the need to consider the length of gestation in any study that investigates growth.

Growth among SGA infants is markedly diverse during the first 6 months of postnatal life. Some infants catch up rapidly, while others continue to grow at a slow rate into childhood and remain small (Ounsted et al. 1988; Fitzhardinge and Steven 1972). Animal experiments have suggested that the capacity for catchup growth after a period of induced growth deficiency seems to be limited to early life. There may be a critical period during which the number of cells sets the stage for future growth (Winick 1969). Naeye and coworkers (1973) suggested that heroin directly attenuated growth. They demonstrated that the small size of organs in infants exposed to heroin in the third trimester of pregnancy resulted mainly from a subnormal number of cells, whereas undernutrition during pregnancy in nonaddicted women restricted the size of individual cells as well as their number. If cell numbers are indeed decreased, infants of heroin-addicted mothers would not be expected to show catchup growth. An early, cross-sectional study supported this assumption (Wilson et al. 1979). Although this study controlled for several environmental and demographic factors, it was limited by a retrospective collection of perinatal and early childhood data; and it was not possible to trace many factors that may potentially affect growth. Information on parental height, growth trajectory, and health history is lacking; therefore, the results are inconclusive.

A preliminary uncontrolled study of 15 methadone-exposed infants reported that early growth was depressed (mean birth weight and length at the 10th percentile), after which the growth rate accelerated by 4 to 6 months (Chasnoff et al. 1980). The researchers postulated that the early growth impairment could have resulted from the direct effect of methadone on the hypothalamic hypophyseal axis of the newborn, as suggested by animal studies (Friedler 1978). However, no hormonal or neurochemical studies were performed to substantiate this suggestion, nor were factors such as maternal nutritional status or genetic background considered. The accelerated growth pattern in these infants could reflect catchup growth after a period of in utero nutritional deprivation or a shift in percentiles as determined genetically. In a cross-sectional study of 70 preschool children exposed prenatally to methadone and 70 controls matched for sociodemographic variables, there was a tendency for drug-exposed children who had shown signs of withdrawal at birth to have lower preschool weight and height (Bauman and Levine 1986). Growth was not reported for the controls. Worthy of consideration is a longitudinal study of 30 methadone-exposed children and 44 comparison subjects, in which the

328

researchers found that, by 2 years of age, the exposed infants were two centimeters shorter than the comparison subjects after adjustment for sex (Hans 1989). The analysis considered socioeconomic status, maternal intellectual performance, pregnancy and birth complications, and birth weight, but it failed to include the most important predictive factor, midparental height, as an independent variable.

The Houston longitudinal study found that after 3 months of age the length of heroin-exposed and methadone-exposed subjects did not differ significantly from that of drug-free controls (Wilson et al. 1981). At 3 years, mean height was similar for all three groups (figures 1 and 2). The incidence of short stature (height below the 10th percentile) was doubled in the drug-exposed groups (23 percent for the heroin, 26 percent for the methadone, and 11 percent for the comparison) but was not statistically significant (Lifschitz et al. 1983). Of the 13 children with short stature at 3 years, only 3 had been SGA at birth. The remaining SGA infants achieved catchup in length by 6 months, a pattern usually seen in infants who suffer intrauterine growth retardation (Fitzhardinge and Steven 1972).

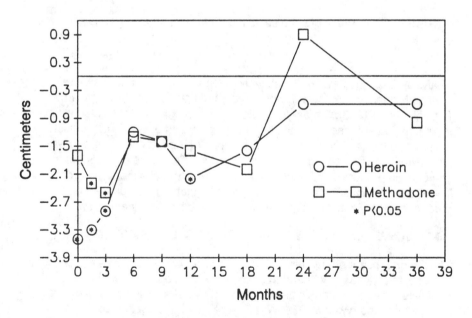

FIGURE 1. *Deviance of unadjusted length from comparison group mean, drug-exposed males (0 line=comparison group mean)*

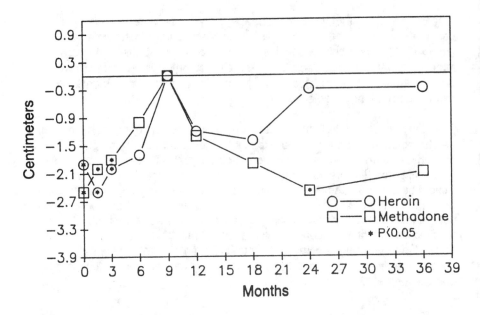

FIGURE 2. *Deviance of unadjusted length from comparison group mean, drug-exposed females*

Analysis of variance was used to investigate the interaction of narcotic exposure during pregnancy with factors widely accepted as affecting linear growth (Lifschitz et al. 1983). Three-year height was significantly associated with birth length, midparental height, and maternal cigarette smoking. When adjusted for these three factors and race, the mean height of the methadone group was significantly lower than that of the heroin group. The adjusted height of the comparison group did not differ significantly from that of either drug group. These data do not substantiate the hypothesis that narcotic use during pregnancy has direct long-term detrimental effects on postnatal growth.

POSTNATAL HEAD GROWTH AND INTELLECTUAL FUNCTION

The major concern about chronic exposure to narcotics during gestation is the potential toxicity to the vulnerable brain of the developing fetus. It has been postulated that neurotransmitter function may be altered and that brain growth may be impaired (Wilson 1975; Wilson et al. 1979; Rosen and Johnson 1985; Hans 1989). Winick (1970) has reported that brain size in severe malnutrition is reduced proportionally to head circumference, raising the possibility that narcotic-exposed children with impaired postnatal head growth are at risk for permanent neurologic and intellectual sequelae.

Studies of SGA babies who were not exposed to drugs suggest ongoing neurodevelopmental problems related to poor head growth. A report on a small sample of full-term SGA female children found that those whose head circumference was below the 10th percentile at 1 year had lower intelligence quotient (IQ) at school age than those whose head size had reached the 25th percentile or above (Babson and Henderson 1974). Ounsted and coworkers (1988) studied prospectively a large sample of SGA infants and a group of controls who were adequate for gestational age (AGA). From the age of 2 months onward, the SGA group showed evidence of neurological delay. Positive associations were found between changes in somatic measures and neurological scores from birth through 6 months; infants who grew faster also matured faster during this period and vice versa. In addition, significantly positive correlations existed for both head circumference and height with developmental scores at 7 years. These were due mainly to an association between small size and low scores rather than larger children and higher scores. The extrapolation of these data to the drug-exposed children might imply that lack of catchup head growth during the first 6 months of life in children who were SGA at birth would predict poor neurodevelopmental outcome. In the authors' experience, however, most of the narcotic-exposed infants followed to the preschool age demonstrated an accelerated rate of head growth during the first 3 months of postnatal life (figures 3 and 4). By 3 years of age, the mean head measurements were similar and fell below the 50th percentile for all three groups. Although head circumferences below the 10th percentile occurred more commonly among children of narcotic-dependent women (six heroin, 24 percent; six methadone, 23 percent; and five comparison, 12 percent), the difference was not statistically significant (Lifschitz et al. 1985).

Tracking individual growth curves provides insight into the inconsistent growth patterns of this population and the inability to predict outcome from a single data point. In one study, only 2 of the 17 preschool children with small head size had shown small heads at birth (one heroin, one comparison) (Lifschitz et al. 1985). These data indicate that, in narcotic-exposed children, deceleration of head growth may occur postnatally. In fact, in five of the six heroin-exposed children with small heads at 3 years, the decline in the rate of head growth began after the first year of life. The trend toward postnatal deceleration of head growth observed in narcotic-exposed children may have important clinical implications; the small size of the sample, however, hinders its statistical strength and precludes firm conclusions. Regression analysis determined that perinatal and genetic variables were more predictive of preschool head size than postnatal environmental factors. Birth weight, intrapartum risk score, and race (head size adjusted for age and sex was largest for blacks and smallest for Hispanics) were significantly associated with outcome.

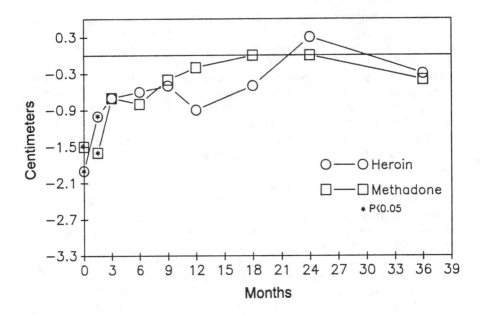

FIGURE 3. *Deviance of unadjusted head circumference from comparison group mean, drug-exposed males*

Contrary to expectations, in the Houston study, preschool head size was not significantly related to intellectual performance. Regression analysis indicated that cognitive abilities were best predicted by environmental factors, as measured by the Home Observation for Measurement of Environment score (Bradley and Caldwell 1977), along with two prenatal variables—the amount of prenatal care, and the prenatal risk score. Intellectual performance did not correlate with the amount of prenatal exposure to narcotics; however, low cognitive scores were significantly more frequent in the heroin group. Five (20 percent) of the 25 heroin-exposed children were functioning in the retarded range, a sevenfold increase over the expected rate in the general population.

A consistently higher incidence of head circumference below the third percentile was seen in a group of methadone-exposed children studied longitudinally by Rosen and Johnson (1985). At 3 years, there were no differences in mental development between children in the methadone-exposed and the comparison group; lower scores were more prevalent, however, among the methadone group. In contrast with the Houston study, measurement of head circumference did correlate with mental performance. Furthermore, cluster analysis documented that children exposed to methadone overwhelmingly (85 percent)

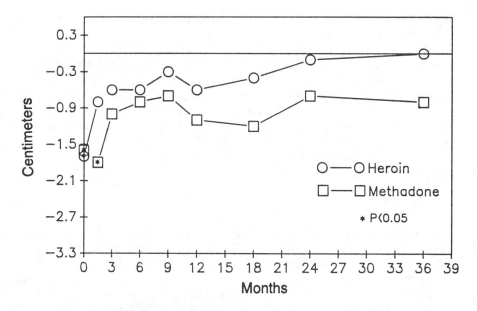

FIGURE 4. *Deviance of unadjusted head circumference from comparison group mean, drug-exposed females*

constituted the group with the weakest outcome. This cluster consisted of children who had the lowest developmental scores, mean head circumferences in the sixth percentile, and higher number of referrals for educational or developmental problems.

Another prospective study of infants exposed to methadone indicated that, when compared to unexposed controls at 2 years of age, the study subjects were shorter and had smaller head circumference and less favorable developmental scores (Hans 1989). Hans used an interesting analytical model; the sample was dichotomized into high- and low-risk groups, and drug effects were examined within risk groups using analysis of variance. Methadone-exposed infants lagged behind the comparison infants in all three categories of risk: socioeconomic status, maternal IQ, and pregnancy and birth complications. Head circumference at 2 years was strongly correlated with complications of pregnancy and birth. In contrast with the Houston study, Hans found an independent drug effect. Although cognitive development did not differ significantly between groups, examination of infants raised in families at the lowest socioeconomic levels indicated clear differences in mental scores between methadone-exposed and unexposed infants. The researcher suggested that methadone exposure may increase the vulnerability of children to the effects of an impoverished environment.

Although there is no consensus that narcotic exposure during gestation affects head growth and intellectual development directly, there is general agreement that the combination of maternal narcotic and polydrug use, poor maternal health, and obstetrical and birth complications do affect the developing fetus. Furthermore, a vulnerable infant, who often must undergo narcotic withdrawal during the first few months of life and "catch up" physically and developmentally in a suboptimal environment, is undoubtedly at risk for impaired postnatal growth and development.

COMMENTS

Despite increasingly numerous reports on the consequences of chronic narcotic use during pregnancy, little is known of the long-lasting effects of these substances on the exposed child.

As in any other area of research, the studies on fetal exposure to drugs have undergone the following evolution. The report of an isolated clinical finding is immediately followed by small, cross-sectional studies, then by larger retrospective reports in an attempt to sort out prevalence rates of specific adverse effects. Occurrences of new findings are compared to the prevalence rate of the same condition in the general population. Then, carefully designed and controlled cohort studies are reported, most of which are retrospective. Several animal models are developed. Investigators in the basic sciences follow the clinical literature, attempting to elucidate mechanisms by which drug exposure may adversely affect the fetus. Although animal experiments have proven useful, particularly because of their ability to randomize the sample and obtain longitudinal data without struggling with issues of attrition, their importance is ultimately limited by the insoluble problems of extrapolation of results to humans. At this time, clinical investigators have collected enough pilot data to warrant prospective, controlled, long-term studies. The design of such clinical studies will be "flawed" from inception by a variety of methodologic issues. Ethically, drug-dependent pregnant women cannot be randomized into treatment and nontreatment groups. Once in contact with health care professionals, every effort is made to improve the milieu of the drug user and her fetus. This is accomplished by improving her access to and utilization of medical care and other support systems, thereby promoting a healthier lifestyle with alterations of drug use through counseling or chemical detoxification. These interventions involve changes in the most important independent variable to be examined: drug use.

A second major design problem relates to the vast number of confounding variables that must be considered in the analyses of long-term effects of drug use during pregnancy. The more carefully researchers plan analyses to control for confounding variable, the larger the requirements for sample size.

In attempts to improve the ability to distinguish the effects of pregnancy drug use on outcome, some recent studies made use of new statistical approaches (e.g., cluster analyses and dichotomy of the sample). These and other creative models should be used to define direct and indirect fetal and child risks of chronic maternal drug abuse. Longitudinal studies are costly and difficult to perform because of the high attrition rate of the sample. Changing patterns of drug abuse complicate study design and outcome. Knowledge of long-term outcome in children exposed to specific substances during gestation may be substantially enhanced by monographs such as this, which seek to develop a consensus on such issues as criteria for patient inclusion; methods of documenting drug exposure; methods for identifying and reporting critical sociodemographic data, both prenatally and longitudinally; and outcome measures sensitive to suspected problems.

A strong argument could be made for collaborative investigation of long-term effects of maternal drug use. A multicentered project that provides a statistically powerful sample, standard protocol, and support services needed to prevent attrition would be the ideal means by which to answer today's questions. It is clear that a very large population must be studied over an extended period of time to definitively address the expected outcome of drug-exposed children and determine which factors (social or biologic) are most predictive of outcome. Thus far, data have been derived primarily from large inner-city hospitals, since smaller centers caring for a limited number of drug-dependent subjects have been unable to effectively compete for funding. Inclusion of small centers would broaden the database and make the population more representative of society.

The authors' experience with drug-dependent women in Houston suggests that compliance may be more readily achieved in a "small community" setting. While New York and Detroit nurseries were caring for hundreds of drug-exposed babies annually, in Houston, only 70 drug-addicted women delivered over a 2-year period. The county hospital serving the entire Houston metropolitan area became the center for the obstetrical care of pregnant addicts. While the research team networked closely with drug treatment programs, the center focused on the addict's pregnancy rather than on her addiction. Drug treatment or direct drug counseling were not provided, but every effort was made to refer each subject to the most appropriate treatment program. It became apparent that these mothers wore their "white hat" in the clinic, leaving their "black hat" for the treatment program.

A prime factor in achieving long-term compliance appeared to be the continuity of supportive services by project staff, beginning with first contact during pregnancy. A staff member (nurse, social worker, and/or physician) saw the mother at each appointed visit, responded to all phone calls and drop-in visits, and vigorously pursued missed appointments. A close working relationship developed with those subjects who availed themselves of prenatal care. The relationship with women first presenting in labor was more tenuous; in most instances, efforts were directed toward engaging family members, who frequently became primary caretakers. For the majority of participants, the "bonding" with project staff appeared to motivate them to cooperate. For the recalcitrant few, frequent contact by phone or home visit and "pick up and delivery" for all protocol sessions were effective.

The authors believe that the type of participation needed from families involved in such comprehensive studies necessitates more than token cooperation, which is most effectively accomplished by giving the participants something in return. Experience suggests that the staff's concern and availability were essential to the project's success and more effective than monetary rewards.

SUMMARY

The results of the studies reviewed indicate that intrauterine growth is adversely affected by drug use during pregnancy. Whether the impairment is a direct effect of narcotic exposure or is the result of the interaction of deleterious health, environmental, and socioeconomic factors closely associated with the lifestyle of the woman who abuses drugs cannot be determined at present.

Reports on the long-term effects of drug use on growth and intellectual functioning in the offspring of women who abuse drugs are not consistent. While some studies indicate that most of the exposed infants exhibit catchup growth by 6 months of age (Lifschitz et al. 1983, 1985), one methodologically strong study suggests that methadone may have a small direct teratogenic effect reflected in reduced head size at 2 years of age (Hans 1989). Unexplained is the pattern of growth deceleration observed in some narcotic-exposed children (Lifschitz et al. 1983, 1985).

The few available reports on long-term outcome concur that narcotic-exposed children have a high incidence of behavioral and learning problems (Strauss et al. 1979; Rosen and Johnson 1985; Wilson 1989), but population studies have been too small to demonstrate that they differ significantly from controls. There is a suggestion that narcotic use during pregnancy promotes a biological vulnerability to adverse environments, manifested in the neurobehavioral and intellectual areas.

REFERENCES

Altemeier, W.A. III; O'Connor, S.M.; Sherrod, K.B.; and Vietze, P.M.
Prospective study of antecedents for nonorganic failure to thrive. *J Pediatr*
106:360-365, 1985.

Babson, S.G., and Henderson, N.B. Fetal undergrowth: Relation of head
growth to later intellectual performance. *Pediatrics* 53:890-894, 1974.

Bauman, P.S., and Levine, S.A. The development of children of drug addicts.
Int J Addict 21:849-863, 1986.

Bradley, R.H., and Caldwell, B.M. Home observation for measurement of the
environment: A validation study of screening efficiency. *Am J Ment Defic*
81:417-420, 1977.

Chasnoff, I.J.; Hatcher, R.; and Burns, W.J. Early growth patterns of
methadone-addicted infants. *Am J Dis Child* 134:1049-1051, 1980.

Chasnoff, I.J.; Hatcher, R.; and Burns, W.J. Polydrug- and methadone-addicted
newborn: A continuum of impairment? *Pediatrics* 70:210-213, 1982.

Finnegan, L.P.; Connaughton, J.F.; Emich, J.P.; and Wieland, W.F.
Comprehensive care of the pregnant addict and its effect on maternal and
infant outcome. *Contemp Drug Prob* 1:795-809, 1972.

Fitzhardinge, P.M., and Steven, F.M. The small-for-dates infant: Later growth
patterns. *Pediatrics* 49:671-681, 1972.

Friedler, G. Pregestational administration of morphine sulfate to female mice:
Long-term effects on the development of subsequent progeny. *J Pharmacol
Exp Ther* 205:33-39, 1978.

Goldstein, H. Factors influencing the height of seven year old children: Results
from the National Child Development Study. *Hum Biol* 43:92-111, 1971.

Hans, S.L. Developmental consequences of prenatal exposure to methadone.
Ann N Y Acad Sci 562:195-207, 1989.

Kandall, S.R.; Albin, S.; Lowinson, J.; Berle, B.; Eidelman, A.I.; and Gartner,
L.M. Differential effects of maternal heroin and methadone use on
birthweight. *Pediatrics* 58:681-685, 1976.

Keen, D.V., and Pearse, R.G. Weight, length, and head circumference curves
for boys and girls of between 20 and 42 weeks gestation. *Arch Dis Child*
63(10 Spec No):1170-1172, 1988.

Kimble, K.J.; Ariagno, R.L.; Stevenson, D.K.; and Sunshine, P. Growth to age 3
years among very low-birth weight sequelae-free survivors of modern
neonatal intensive care. *J Pediatr* 100:622-624, 1982.

Lifschitz, M.H.; Wilson, G.S.; Smith, E.O.; and Desmond, M.M. Fetal and
postnatal growth of children born to narcotic-dependent women. *J Pediatr*
102:686-691, 1983.

Lifschitz, M.H.; Wilson, G.S.; Smith, E.O.; and Desmond, M.M. Factors
affecting head growth and intellectual function in children of drug addicts.
Pediatrics 75:269-274, 1985.

Longo, L.D. Some health consequences of maternal smoking: Issues without
answers. *Birth Defects* 18:13-31, 1982.

Miller, H.C., and Hassanein, K. Fetal malnutrition in white newborn infants: Maternal factors. *Pediatrics* 52:504-512, 1973.

Naeye, R.L.; Blanc, W.; Leblanc, W.; and Khatamee, M.A. Fetal complications of maternal heroin addiction: Abnormal growth, infections, and episodes of stress. *J Pediatr* 83:1055-1061, 1973.

National Center for Health Statistics: NCHS growth charts 1976. *Monthly Vital Statistics Report*, Vol. 25, No. 3, Suppl (HRA), 76-1120. Rockville, MD: Health Resources Administration, 1976.

Oro, A.S., and Dixon, S.D. Perinatal cocaine and methamphetamine exposure: Maternal and neonatal correlates. *J Pediatr* 111:571-578, 1987.

Ounsted, M.; Moar, V.A.; and Scott, A. Neurological development of small-for-gestational age babies during the first year of life. *Early Hum Dev* 16:163-172, 1988.

Prentice, A.; Cole, T.J.; and Whitehead, R.C. Impaired growth in infants born to mothers of very high parity. *Hum Nutr Clin Nutr* 5:319-325, 1987.

Rosen, T.S., and Johnson, H.L. Children of methadone-maintained mothers: Follow-up at 18 months of age. *J Pediatr* 101:192-196, 1982.

Rosen, T.S., and Johnson, H.L. Long-term effects of prenatal methadone maintenance. In: Pinkert, T.M., ed. *Current Research on the Consequences of Maternal Drug Abuse.* National Institute on Drug Abuse Research Monograph 59. DHHS Pub. No. (ADM)87-1400. Washington, DC: Supt. of Docs., U.S. Govt. Print. Off., 1985. pp. 73-83.

Smith, D.W.; Troy, W.; and McCann, J.J. Shifting linear growth during infancy and the genetics of growth in infancy. *J Pediatr* 89:225-230, 1976.

Sorva, R.; Tolppanen, E.M.; Lankinen, S.; and Perheentupa, J. Growth evaluation: Parent and child specific height standards. *Arch Dis Child* 64:1483-1487, 1989.

Stein, Z., and Susser, M. The Dutch famine, 1944-1945, and the reproductive process. I. Effects of six indices at birth. *Pediatr Res* 9:70-76, 1975.

Strauss, M.E.; Lessen-Firestone, J.K.; Chavez, C.J.; and Stryker, J.C. Children of methadone-treated women at five years of age. *Pharmacol Biochem Behav* [Suppl]11:3-6, 1979.

Streissguth, A.P.; Sampson, P.D.; and Barr, H.M. Neurobehavioral dose-response effects of prenatal alcohol exposure in humans from infancy to adulthood. *Ann N Y Acad Sci* 562:145-158, 1989.

Suffet, M.A., and Brotman, R. A comprehensive care program for pregnant addicts: Obstetrical, neonatal, and child development outcomes. *Int J Addict* 19(2):199-219, 1984.

Vargas, G.C.; Pildes, R.S.; and Vidyasagar, D. Effect of maternal heroin addiction on 67 liveborn neonates. *Clin Pediatr* 14:751-757, 1975.

Volpe, J.J. *Neurology of the Newborn.* 2d ed. Philadelphia, PA: W.B. Saunders Co., 1987.

Wilcox, A.J. Birth weight, gestation, and the fetal growth curve. *Am J Obstet Gynecol* 139:863-867, 1981.

Wilson, G.S. Somatic growth effects of perinatal addiction. *Addict Dis Int J* 2(2):333-345, 1975.

Wilson, G.S. Clinical studies of infants and children exposed prenatally to heroin. *Ann N Y Acad Sci* 562:183-194, 1989.

Wilson, G.S.; Desmond, M.M.; and Verniaud, W.M. Early development of infants of heroin-addicted mothers. *Am J Dis Child* 126:457-462, 1973.

Wilson, G.S.; Desmond, M.M.; and Wait, R.B. Follow-up of methadone-treated and untreated narcotic-dependent women and their infants: Health, developmental, and social implications. *J Pediatr* 98:716-722, 1981.

Wilson, G.S.; McCreary, R.; Kean, J.; and Baxter, J.C. The development of preschool children of heroin-addicted mothers: A controlled study. *Pediatrics* 63:135-141, 1979.

Wingerd, J., and Schoen, E.J. Factors influencing length at birth and height at five years. *Pediatrics* 53:737-741, 1974.

Winick, M. Malnutrition and brain development. *J Pediatr* 74:667-679, 1969.

Winick, M. Nutrition and mental development. *Med Clin North Am* 54:1413-1429, 1970.

Zelson, C.; Rubio, E.; and Wasserman, E. Neonatal narcotic addiction: 10 year observation. *Pediatrics* 48:178-189, 1971.

Zelson, C.; Sook, J.L.; and Casalino, M. Neonatal narcotic addiction: Comparative effects of maternal intake of heroin and methadone. *N Engl J Med* 289:1216-1220, 1973.

Zuckerman, B.; Frank, D.A.; Hingson, R.; Amaro, H.; Levenson, S.M.; Kayne, H.; Parker, S.; Vinci, R.; Aboagye, K.; Fried, L.E.; Cabral, H.; Timperi, R.; and Bauchner, H. Effects of maternal marijuana and cocaine use on fetal growth. *N Engl J Med* 320:762-768, 1989.

ACKNOWLEDGMENTS

The work described in this chapter was supported by National Institute on Drug Abuse grant DA-00915, by the American Legion, and by the USDA/ARS, Children's Nutrition Research Center, Baylor College of Medicine, Houston, TX.

AUTHORS

Marta H. Lifschitz, M.D.
Assistant Professor of Pediatrics

Geraldine S. Wilson, M.D.
Associate Professor of Pediatrics

Baylor College of Medicine
Meyer Center for Developmental Pediatrics
8080 North Stadium Drive, Suite 2300
Houston, TX 77054

Integrity of Psychopathology Diagnoses Across the Lifespan

Patricia Cohen and Judith S. Brook

INTRODUCTION

This chapter addresses two aspects of diagnoses of psychopathology: (1) measurement issues, including the age at which they can first be assessed with some reliability, and (2) the persistence of serious problems from one period of life to the next, covering the span from early childhood to early adulthood. The three diagnostic groups covered in some detail are attention deficit/hyperactivity disorder (ADHD), conduct disorder, and anxiety disorders; however, the evidence will often need to be taken from studies of symptoms rather than studies of the whole syndrome. Because clear criteria for diagnoses of psychopathology in childhood are a very recent phenomena, little information is as yet available on persistence over more than a very short span of time. Therefore, in addition to a brief synopsis of the literature on each syndrome, this chapter presents data on persistence of disorders from early childhood through young adulthood from the Children in the Community (CIC) study as representative of the state of current knowledge on these topics. In light of the fact that investigations of the risk of psychopathology associated with prenatal drug exposure are likely to examine children selected for risk status rather than those who are service-seeking, this chapter focuses on epidemiological studies of children rather than on clinical populations; although, in some cases, the latter may represent the only current evidence. Neither the reliability of the diagnosis nor the level of stability over time is independent of the source of the diagnostic information; it usually will be necessary to identify ages at which parent, child, teacher, or observer may produce sound assessment of each syndrome.

MEASUREMENT OF PSYCHOPATHOLOGY IN CHILDREN

Symptom Checklists and Screening Measures of Children's Problems

A major issue in the assessment of children is deciding who will provide the information regarding children's symptoms, impairment, and functional level. As shown in a comprehensive review by Achenbach and colleagues (1987), the various sources of this information—parents, children, teachers, or mental health professionals—usually agree rather little on either symptoms or diagnoses, especially in populations not actively seeking treatment. Direct observations of children likewise are frequently discrepant from information from other sources. The most widely recommended solution to this problem of disagreement is to seek information from as many sources as possible. Which sources are available are a function partly of the age of the child and partly of the particular population being studied. Parents are the primary source of such information about infancy and early childhood, and it is well established that mothers are more likely to note and report problems than are fathers. At these ages, observational data also may be feasible for at least some problems. For children in middle childhood, it is widely agreed that data from teachers should be used to supplement reports from parents. By late childhood and adolescence, reliable and useful information can and should be obtained from the children themselves, as well as from their parents. As children enter junior and senior high school, it is less likely that detailed description of symptoms and problems will be obtainable from schools.

One important consideration in the selection of assessment measures is the availability of some kind of normative data based on the instruments. Table 1 presents scaled or screening measures of psychopathology in children as reported by parents, teachers, or self-report. These may be described as established instruments in the sense that at least some normative information is available. The Richman scales (Richman et al. 1982) have been used in epidemiological studies in the United States and in the United Kingdom. As can be seen by the relatively few items in the Behaviour Checklist, they cover a broad spectrum with little room for discrimination of specific types of problems. The other measures in table 1 include more specific measures of types of problems, as well as an overall score. The Child Behavior Checklist (CBCL) (Achenbach and Edelbrock 1983) has been developed with special forms for the preschool age groups and is the single most thoroughly normed instrument.

In administering self-report measures to younger children, it is generally necessary to have an interviewer or teacher read the items aloud. Only two self-report measures attempt to cover more than a single domain of problems: the CBCL and the Children's Self-Report Psychiatric Rating Scale (CSPR) (Beitchman et al. 1985). The CBCL self-report version covers material approximately parallel to that covered in the parent and teacher report versions. The CSPR Scale is more global, having been developed to discriminate broadly between community and mental health treatment samples. A recent book on the assessment of children (Rutter et al. 1988) provides more detail on most of these instruments, as well as a discussion of issues to be considered in their selection.

TABLE 1. *Checklists and questionnaires for assessing symptoms of psychopathology in children*

Title, Author	Number of Items	Ages Covered		
		Parent Report	Teacher Report	Self-Report
Behaviour Checklist (Richman et al. 1982)	12	3-6		
Preschool Behavior Questionnaire (Behar 1977)	36	3-6		
Behavior Problems Checklist (Quay 1983)	89	5-17	5-17	
Conners Parent (Teacher) Rating Scale (Conners 1969)[*]	93 (39)	6-14	4-12	
Child Behavior Checklist (Achenbach and Edelbrock 1983)	126-138	2-18	6-16	11-18
Revised Children's Manifest Anxiety Scale (Reynolds and Paget 1981)	62			6-19
Children's Depression Inventory (Kovaks 1981)	27			8-17
Short Children's Depression Inventory (Carlson and Cantwell 1980)	13			7-17
Children's Self-Report Psychiatric Rating Scale (Beitchman et al. 1985)	33			7-12
Self-Reported Antisocial Behavior (Loeber et al., in press)	33			6-14

[*]See also Goyette et al. 1978.

Interviews for Diagnosing Psychopathology in Children

Over the past decade there has been an effort to develop psychiatric diagnostic instruments for children that utilize interviews of parents and children. These interviews have several properties that commend their use:

1. They emphasize problems at the severe end of the distribution.

2. They include probes for functional significance, severity of distress, frequency and duration, and associated impairment that should improve the quality of the responses.

3. They permit the counting of children with problems and thus can be more immediately translated into service needs.

4. They encourage identification of risk factors in an epidemiological framework, thus allowing for relevant indices, such as attributable risk.

5. They allow fairly fine differentiation of the nature of the problem.

6. They permit flexible analytic models because they can yield scaled measures as well as diagnoses.

Perhaps their greatest drawback is that they are relatively time-consuming. Interviews in different populations, given in their entirety to cover all potential diagnoses, range between 45 minutes and over 2 hours. Furthermore, the current evidence casts doubt on the validity of the information obtained by interviews of children under the age of 9 or 10 that is not corroborated through interviews of parents or teachers.

Current diagnostic instruments attempt to cover all diagnostic criteria explicitly, and most are available in versions matching the DSM-III-R criteria, and perhaps even anticipating some DSM-IV changes. The most popular semistructured interview designed for administration by clinicians is the Kiddie-Schedule for Affective Disorders and Schizophrenia (K-SADS) (Chambers et al. 1985), which exists in at least one relatively recent version. However, the evidence that such semistructured clinical interviews are superior to fully structured interviews is entirely lacking; and, for most research purposes, the use of one of the structured interviews designed for administration by clinicians or trained lay interviewers may be advisable.

The two most popular such instruments are the Diagnostic Interview for Children and Adolescents (DICA) (Reich et al. 1982) and the Diagnostic Interview Schedule for Children (DISC) (Costello et al. 1984). Another instrument that requires more clinical inference by the interviewer is the Child Assessment Schedule (CAS) (Hodges et al. 1982). Each of these interview schedules obtains parallel information from parent and child interviews, and each has been subject to several revisions and field trials. The DISC has a revised and expanded version covering DSM-III-R and most likely DSM-IV diagnostic criteria (DISC-2.1) (Shaffer et al. 1991). This interview is being used in the four-site national study of large random samples of children sponsored by the National Institute of Mental Health.

Age Considerations in the Assessment of Three Fairly Prevalent Diagnoses

ADHD. It is probable that children showing very extreme levels of hyperactivity and distractibility can be identified in the preschool years and even in infancy with some reliability. Nevertheless, ADHD ordinarily is detected unambiguously only when children enter the more structured demands of school, and most children with ADHD have such a problem from at least the first grade. Problems often intensify as the demands of school increase, and children are most often brought to treatment centers between the ages of 8 and 12. Identification of the problem in a single site—the school only or the home only— is not unusual; therefore, reliable assessment of the problem often may involve discrepant information from parent and teacher. Furthermore, confirmation of the diagnosis by observation in a clinic setting is usually not possible, as the novel setting and one-to-one interaction often minimizes these problems, even in children with severe problems. Children usually are not considered to be very good at self-reporting these problems before the late childhood years, when they develop the perspective for comparison with other children and awareness of difficulties with teachers or other adults.

By middle to late adolescence, ADHD is rarely diagnosed, although the general problems of hyperactivity, impulsivity, and poor concentration are far from absent in the adult population. It is probable that as opportunities to "niche pick" increase in these years, those with this disorder find settings in which the problems are not so distressing, handicapping, or liable to produce failure.

Anxiety Disorders. Clear extremes of anxious withdrawal, especially from novel stimuli, are present in some children by age 2. Extreme levels of anxiety usually are identified in the nursery years by parent report and may be confirmed by structured observation. Fears and anxieties are very common in prepubertal children, and it is probable that the necessary perspective for assessing whether one's problems are atypically severe develops only gradually in the late childhood years. Mothers are the principal source of diagnostic information in the early elementary school years; in general, it cannot be assumed that teachers are particularly attentive to these problems. It is the belief of some researchers that self-report is the primary relevant source of information by age 10 or 11; however, empirical evidence on the relative validity of information from different sources for anxiety disorders at these ages is still lacking. In the postpubertal years, self-report should be considered essential to the diagnosis.

During the elementary school years, the most debilitating manifestations of anxiety are probably (1) avoidant disorder, in which the child avoids everyone unfamiliar; (2) separation anxiety, in which the child clings to a parent both inside and outside the house; and (3) school phobia. By midadolescence, the forms of anxiety appear to be more similar to adult problems, with social phobia, a mix of anxious and depressive symptoms, and physiological manifestations of anxiety becoming more prominent.

Conduct Disorder. Diagnosable conduct disorder, which requires clearly antisocial and often illegal behavior, requires a development level and access to independent action that rarely appears before middle childhood. However, precursors of this syndrome, including aggression toward people or objects and defiance, are measurable by parent report even at nursery school ages. Information on these problems may be obtained from teachers, parents, or from self-report during the elementary school years. By adolescence, it appears that the youth is likely to be the best source of information regarding illegal and antisocial activities. In adulthood, the kinds of activities generally change to fit the adult environment, and the problem is called antisocial personality disorder, presumably because it is by that time a fairly stable trait-like behavior pattern.

PERSISTENCE OF SYNDROMES FROM BIRTH TO ADULTHOOD

As noted, the diagnostic criteria for childhood psychopathology have been spelled out clearly only in the last decade; as yet, little information is available on clearly defined syndromes. Because the major large-sample source of such information is the DISC-based longitudinal CIC study of randomly sampled children in two upstate New York counties (Cohen and Brook 1987; Velez et al. 1989), these age-specific diagnostic stabilities will be reported as representative of current estimates. For diagnostic measures, the odds ratio contrasts diagnosis at followup for those initially diagnosed compared with those children not initially diagnosed. In addition, major reviews of the stability of symptoms or problems that are relevant to the diagnostic groups are cited, as well as findings from relevant individual longitudinal studies of symptom or problem measures.

The fact of statistically significant and sometimes impressive levels of problem persistence should not be taken to imply the absence of change or the presence of stable underlying qualities in the child that may be expressed differently at different ages (Clarke and Clarke 1984). Rather, as in all physical and behavioral patterns, large amounts of change in relative position of individual children are to be expected; and the presence of excess risk for future problems of a similar kind cannot be taken to be equivalent to a negative prognosis for most children exhibiting these problems. In general, as in the case of measured intelligence, stability from very early childhood to late childhood, adolescence, or adulthood is likely to be modest. Stability can be expected to decline as a function of the magnitude of the interval over which it is measured, as a function of changes in the source or kind of information, and as a function of major changes in the setting of the assessed individuals.

Persistence From Early to Middle Childhood

ADHD. Relatively little information on the outcome of preschool attention/ hyperactivity problems is available. Recent data from the CIC showed that the odds of having diagnosable ADHD at ages 10 to 13 were about 4 1/2 times as great (odds ratio=4.62) if the children were identified by mothers as having such problems at ages 2 to 4. Table 2 provides a summary of CIC stability data.

Anxiety. Trait anxiety (i.e., anxiety measured as a continuous variable) is among the most stable of behavioral patterns in early childhood. However, observational and laboratory data gathered by Kagan and colleagues (1989) over the span from 14 months to age 4 found no stability in anxious/withdrawn behavior from the earliest assessments to the 4-year assessments, although children who showed extreme levels of anxious behavior both at 14 months and at 20 months were more likely to show anxious patterns at age 4. In the CIC data, anxiety as reported by mothers of 2- to 4-year-olds was quite stable, with a correlation over 8 years of .4. Nevertheless, the relationship between early anxiety and diagnosable anxiety disorder in late childhood based on combined mother and child interviews was not significant.

TABLE 2. *Odds ratios for subsequent diagnosis for children with and without earlier diagnosis*

	Age Span Covered		
	Early to Middle Childhood (2-4 to 10-12) (n=385)	Middle Childhood to Adolescence (5-10 to 13-18) (n=444)	Adolescence to Young Adulthood (16-18 to 19-21) (n=208)
ADHD	4.6	11.2	16.9
Overanxious disorder	—	7.8	11.8
Conduct disorder	3.7	19.3	18.2

NOTE: All data are taken from the CIC Project. All table odds ratios are statistically significant using the .01 criterion.

Conduct Disorder. A review of the stability of aggressive behavior by Olweus (1979) concluded that the aggressive component of conduct disorder is as stable as is intelligence. More recent research by Richman and coworkers (1982) reported that children presenting aggressive or management problems at age 4 were much more likely to show conduct disorder symptoms at age 8. In the CIC data, children who presented aggressive or management problems at ages 1 through 4 had an odds of diagnosable conduct disorder 8 years later, nearly 4 times that of those who did not show such early problems (3.7 odds ratio).

Persistence From Middle Childhood to Adolescence

ADHD. Because the diagnostic criteria for ADHD require onset of symptoms in the earliest school years, children obtaining the diagnosis in late childhood or adolescence must necessarily have had the diagnosis at earlier assessment. Therefore, if diagnostic criteria are strictly followed, the odds for persistent diagnosis compared to the odds for new diagnosis must be infinite. If this restriction is ignored, some data are available on diagnostic stability. Huessy and colleagues (1973) found that 37 of 64 children identified as in the top 20 percent in these symptoms in the second grade were still in the top 20 percent 3 years later, yielding an odds ratio of about 7. In the CIC study, the odds of ADHD in adolescence was 11 times as large for children with this diagnosis in middle to late childhood (odds=11.2).

Anxiety. In the CIC project data, the odds of overanxious disorder in adolescence was about eight times as great for children receiving such a diagnosis in middle to late childhood (odds=7.8).

Conduct Disorder. It has long been known that early onset of antisocial behavior is a risk factor for higher stability of such behavior. Among the many studies investigating aggression and delinquent behaviors, Roff and Wirt (1984) showed the correlation of late grade school predelinquency or aggression with adolescent delinquency to be in the range of .25 to .30. Eron and Huesmann (1984) found the stability of aggression from age 8 to age 19 to be .42. In fact, aggression at age 8 predicted aggression at age 30 (r=.25).

In the CIC data, the odds of a diagnosable conduct disorder in adolescence was 19 times as great if the child had such a diagnosis in middle to late childhood (odds=19.3).

Persistence From Adolescence to Adulthood

Since some of the early followup studies of children showing delinquent behaviors in childhood and adolescence, it has been known that most adult antisocial behavior is preceded by these earlier behaviors (Robins 1966). Sampling a more representative population, Roff and Wirt (1984) showed both adolescent aggression and adolescent delinquency to be correlated with adult criminality (r=.24 and .41, respectively).

In the CIC data, the odds ratios for young adult diagnosis (ages 19 to 21) for those with an earlier adolescent diagnosis (ages 16 to 18) compared to those without an earlier adolescent diagnosis were 16.9 for ADHD, 11.8 for overanxious disorder, and 18.2 for conduct disorder. Taken as a whole, as shown in table 2, the stability of diagnosis tends to increase over the span from early childhood to adulthood.

Heterotypic Integrity: Progressions From One Diagnosable Disorder to Another

In many cases it is suspected or known that the presence of a certain diagnosis at one age predisposes the individual to develop another diagnosis at a subsequent age. Some of these hypothetical or empirical connections were mentioned earlier, such as the possible connections between the anxiety disorders and especially those between child separation anxiety or school refusal and adult agoraphobia. Although this review does not attempt to cover the current evidence on heterotypic progressions, the topic is an important one and also raises some methodological and substantive issues that are only currently being addressed. It has long been known that children diagnosed with ADHD are likely to appear in subsequent years with frank conduct disorder or delinquent behaviors. As Quay and colleagues (1987) point out, the difficulty is that there is a very high comorbidity between these two diagnoses throughout childhood, and what appears to be a progression may only be the changing face of comorbidity. To sort out heterotypic continuities, it is necessary to differentiate between children with and without signs of comorbidity.

Another common area for comorbidity in childhood psychopathology is major depression. Several recent epidemiological studies covering middle to late childhood through adolescence have found that all cases of major depression at these ages had at least one comorbid condition, among which conduct disorder and opposition/defiant disorder are probably the most likely (for a review of these cohorts, see Costello 1989).

Perhaps particularly relevant for this monograph, conduct disorder has long been known to be an antecedent risk factor for substance abuse in adolescence. CIC data also show that aggressive and behavioral management problems at ages 5 to 10 are risks for adolescent drug use (Brook et al. 1989).

Perinatal or Early Risks for Later Manifestation of Psychopathology

Finally, modest stability of a given syndrome from early childhood should not be taken to imply that the effects of early risks, including prenatal or perinatal problems, may not emerge newly after early childhood. For the most part, evidence of "sleeper effects" of traumatic events (i.e., problems appearing at a later period without evidence of immediate problem) is sparse. However, there are reasons to think that certain kinds of biological insults, whether genetic, congenital, or occurring early in life, may first be manifest when the relevant brain structures are called into use. For example, it is hypothesized that schizophrenia may manifest almost entirely postpubertally because that is the first time the prefrontal cortex is an active influence on behavior. Similarly, in the CIC study, perinatal problems predicted newly manifest syndromes in late childhood and adolescence, presumably for similar reasons (Cohen et al. 1989).

REFERENCES

Achenbach, T.M., and Edelbrock, C.S. *Manual for the Child Behavior Checklist and Revised Child Behavior Profile.* Burlington, VT: University of Vermont, Department of Psychiatry, 1983.

Achenbach, T.M.; McConaughy, S.H.; and Howell, C.T. Child/adolescent behavioral and emotional problems: Implications of cross-informant correlations for situational specificity. *Psychol Bull* 101:213-232, 1987.

Behar, L.B. The Preschool Behavior Questionnaire. *J Abnorm Child Psychol* 5:265-275, 1977.

Beitchman, J.H.; Raman, S.; Carlson, J.; Clegg, M.; and Kruidenier, B. The development and validation of the children's self-report psychiatric rating scale. *J Am Acad Child Psychiatry* 24:413-428, 1985.

Brook, J.S.; Nomura, C.; and Cohen, P. Prenatal, perinatal, and early childhood risk factors and drug involvement in adolescence. *Genet Soc Gen Psychol Monogr* 115:221-241, 1989.

Carlson, G., and Cantwell, D.P. A survey of depressive symptoms, syndrome and disorder in a child psychiatric population. *J Child Psychol Psychiatry* 21:19-25, 1980.

Chambers, W.; Puig-Antich, J.; Hirsch, M.; Paez, P.; Ambrosini, P.J.; Tabrizi, M.A.; and Davies, M. The assessment of affective disorders in children and adolescents by semi-structured interview: Test-retest reliability of the K-SADS-P. *Arch Gen Psychiatry* 42:696-702, 1985.

Clarke, A.D.B., and Clarke, A.M. Constancy and change in the growth of human characteristics. *J Child Psychol Psychiatry* 25:191-210, 1984.

Cohen, P., and Brook, J.S. Family factors related to the persistence of psychopathology in childhood and adolescence. *Psychiatry* 50:631-638, 1987.

Cohen, P.; Velez, C.N.; Brook, J.S.; and Smith, J. Mechanisms of the relationship between perinatal problems, early childhood illness, and psychopathology in late childhood and adolescence. *Child Dev* 60:701-709, 1989.

Conners, C.K. A teacher rating scale for use in drug studies with children. *Am J Psychiatry* 126:884-888, 1969.

Costello, A.J.; Edelbrock, C.; Dulcan, M.K.; Kalas, R.; and Klaric, S.H. "Development and Testing of the NIMH Diagnostic Interview Schedule for Children in a Clinic Population." Final report (Contract No. RFP-DB-81-0027) Rockville, MD. Center for Epidemiologic Studies, National Institute of Mental Health, 1984.

Costello, E.J. Developments in child psychiatric epidemiology. *J Am Acad Child Adolesc Psychiatry* 28:848-852, 1989.

Eron, L.D., and Huesman, L.R. The relation of prosocial behavior to the development of aggression and psychopathology. *Aggressive Behav* 10(3):201-211, 1984.

Goyette, C.H.; Conners, C.K.; and Ulrich, R.F. Normative data on Revised Conners Parent and Teacher Rating Scales. *J Abnorm Child Psychol* 6:221-236, 1978.

Hodges, K.; McKnew, D.; Cytryn, L.; Stern, L.; and Kline, J. The Child Assessment Schedule (CAS) diagnostic interview: A report on reliability and validity. *J Am Acad Child Psychiatry* 21:468-473, 1982.

Huessy, H.R.; Marshall, C.D; and Gendron, R.A. Five hundred children followed from grade 2 through grade 5 for the prevalence of behavior disorder. *Paedo Psychiatry* 39:301-309, 1973.

Kagan, J.; Reznick, J.S.; and Gibbons, J. Inhibited and uninhibited types of children. *Child Dev* 60:838-845, 1989.

Kovaks, M. Rating scales to assess depression in school-aged children. *Acta Paedopsychiatry* 46:305-315, 1981.

Loeber, R.; Stouthamer-Loeber, M.; and Van Kammen, W.B. Development of a new measure of self-reported antisocial behavior for young children: Prevalence and reliability. In: Klein, M.W., ed. *Self-Report Methodology in Criminological Research*. Boston: Kluwer-Nijhoff, in press.

Olweus, D. Stability of aggressive reaction patterns in males: A review. *Psychol Bull* 86:852-875, 1979.

Quay, H.C. A dimensional approach to behavior disorder: The Revised Behavior Problem Checklist. *Sch Psychol Rev* 12:244-249, 1983.

Quay, H.C.; Routh, D.K.; and Shapiro, S.K. Psychopathology of childhood: From description to validation. *Annu Rev Psychol* 38:491-532, 1987.

Reich, W.; Herjanic, B.; Welner, Z.; and Gandhy, P.R. Development of a structured psychiatric interview for children: Agreement of diagnosis comparing parent and child. *J Abnorm Child Psychol* 10:325-336, 1982.

Reynolds, C.R., and Paget, K.D. Factor analysis of the Revised Children's Manifest Anxiety Scale for blacks, whites, males and females with a national normative sample. *J Consult Clin Psychol* 44:352-359, 1981.

Richman, N.; Stevenson, J.; and Graham, P. *Preschool to School: A Behavioural Study.* London: Academic Press, 1982.

Robins, L.N. *Deviant Children Grown Up.* Baltimore, MD: Williams and Wilkins, 1966.

Roff, J.D., and Wirt, R.D. Childhood social adjustment, adolescent status, and young adult mental health. *Am J Orthopsychiatry* 54:595-602, 1984.

Rutter, M.; Tuma, A.H.; and Lann, I.S., eds. *Assessment and Diagnosis in Child Psychopathology.* New York: Guilford Press, 1988. 477 pp.

Shaffer, D.; Fisher, P.; Piacintini, J.; Schwab-Stone, M.; and Wicks, J. *Diagnostic Interview Schedule for Children: DISC 2.1.* New York: Division of Child and Adolescent Psychiatry, Columbia University College of Physicians and Surgeons, 1991.

Velez, C.N.; Johnson, J.; and Cohen, P. The Children in the Community Project: Longitudinal analyses of selected risk factors for childhood psychopathology. *J Am Acad Child Adolesc Psychiatry* 28:861-864, 1989.

ACKNOWLEDGMENT

The CIC Project was supported by National Institute of Mental Health Grant MH-36971 to Patricia Cohen, Principal Investigator, and by National Institute on Drug Abuse grant DA-03188 to Judith Brook, Principal Investigator.

AUTHORS

Patricia Cohen, Ph.D.
Professor of Clinical Epidemiology and Psychiatry
Columbia University School of Public Health and
  College of Physicians and Surgeons
Research Scientist
New York State Psychiatric Institute
Box 47
722 West 168 Street
New York, NY 10032

Judith S. Brook, Ed.D.
Professor of Psychiatry
Mount Sinai School of Medicine
Department of Psychiatry
New York Medical College
Valhalla, NY 10595

Discussion: Drug Effects—A Search for Mechanisms

Barry Zuckerman

INTRODUCTION

Three of the chapters in this monograph (Lifschitz and Wilson; Hans; Cohen and Brook) highlight the relationship between social and biologic factors, issues regarding the measurement of psychopathology, and strategies to maintain contact with and protect the rights of subjects. The ability to determine the validity of a relationship between prenatal drug exposure and long-term outcomes will be increased if a mechanism is identified that helps to explain the association. This chapter focuses on possible mechanisms by which maternal drug use during pregnancy may alter the subsequent growth and development of the exposed child and reemphasizes the vital importance of considering the social environment as a covariable in any study concerning long-term outcomes.

MODELS OF DEVELOPMENT

How does maternal drug use affect the exposed fetus? It is particularly difficult to attribute a long-term outcome to any prenatal event, including attributing later psychopathology to prenatal drug exposure. The closer the exposure to the measurement of outcome, the greater the ability to make causal inference. A nosology of psychopathology or a predictive assessment of behavioral functioning during infancy would help increase understanding of the impact of prenatal drug exposure. It is unlikely that psychopathology during later childhood or adolescence can be caused solely by *in utero* drug exposure. The information presented by Cohen and Brook (this volume) regarding the measurement of psychopathology and behavior disorders in school-age children and adolescents is helpful because measures in infancy are not available.

Early theories of child development implied that poor developmental outcome was the result of a single risk factor (e.g. hypoxia, prematurity, or in the present case, *in utero* exposure to psychoactive drugs) thought to affect the central nervous system (CNS). This approach is called the main-effect model of development and implies a linear cause-and-effect relationship between risk and outcome. Information to support this model was based on retrospective studies of children with significant neurologic problems who had high rates of perinatal problems. Prospective studies, however, showed developmental outcomes to be largely unpredictable solely by the presence or degree of a biologic insult. Rather, children's development could best be understood by a transactional model of development that describes a dynamic interplay between the environment and the child, so that the child is shaped by the environment and the environment is actively modified by the child (Sameroff and Chandler 1975).

Available information, much of it in a preliminary stage, provides clues to aspects of the dynamic interplay that may contribute to the later functioning of drug-exposed infants. These clues to possible mechanisms include biologic vulnerabilities within the CNS from the direct and indirect effects of prenatal drug(s) and social factors in the child's environment. This chapter focuses primarily on prenatal cocaine exposure because its use among pregnant women is increasing and because, although much information is available about cocaine, little is known about its effects on the fetus.

POSSIBLE MECHANISMS

Cocaine can affect the fetus by both direct and indirect mechanisms. Cocaine's primary action is to prevent the reuptake of norepinephrine, epinephrine, and dopamine at presynaptic sites. This leads to increases in CNS and peripheral catecholamine concentrations. Alterations in these neurotransmitters could directly affect the developing CNS. Peripherally, these changes result in increased temperature, increased heart rate, and vasoconstriction. Vasoconstriction of the placental vessels and subsequent fetal hypoxia is an indirect mechanism of cocaine's effect on the fetus. Because most mothers who use cocaine also smoke cigarettes and marijuana, cocaine may exacerbate the known hypoxia associated with marijuana and cigarette smoking, thereby inducing a cumulative hypoxic effect.

BIOLOGIC VULNERABILITIES ATTRIBUTABLE TO INDIRECT EFFECTS

Growth

Examining growth parameters of newborns exposed to cocaine *in utero* provides information regarding indirect mechanisms. Anthropometric assessments of body composition and proportionality provide important information regarding the mechanisms of growth impairment, as well as prognosis for future growth (Frisancho et al. 1977; Harrison et al. 1983;

Georgieff et al. 1988; Miller and Merrit 1979; Villar and Belizan 1982) and may shed light on some unanswered questions identified by Lifschitz and Wilson (this volume).

Frank and colleagues (1990) assessed fat and lean body mass by measuring fat folds and mean upper arm muscle circumference in the nonfat area of the upper arm, respectively. The study found that marijuana, like cigarettes, depresses indicators of lean body mass while sparing fat deposition, consistent with a hypoxic or other nonnutritional mechanism (Frisancho et al. 1977). This finding remained after controlling for maternal cigarette use and nutritional status and is consistent with studies showing that marijuana smoking produces hypoxia at the pulmonary level (Clapp et al. 1986; Abrams et al. 1985; Niederreither et al. 1985). In addition, marijuana elevates carbon monoxide to levels higher than those attained by smoking cigarettes (Wu et al. 1988).

Cocaine, on the other hand, is associated with indicators of both depressed neonatal fat stores and lean body mass (Frank et al. 1990), a pattern commonly associated with maternal malnutrition (Frisancho et al. 1977; Harrison et al. 1983). This finding remained even after nutritional markers such as maternal weight for height at conception and pregnancy weight gain were analytically controlled. It is possible that transfer of nutrients to the fetus is impaired due to vasoconstriction caused by cocaine, regardless of maternal nutritional status. In addition, cocaine also may diminish birth weight by increasing fetal metabolism through its effect on the sympathetic nervous system.

Among neonates, body proportionality is measured by the ponderal index (weight in grams/length in cm^3 x 100), which is thought to indicate timing of prenatal insults and also may be related to postnatal growth (Miller and Merritt 1979; Villar and Belizan 1982). A low ponderal index (a long, thin newborn) indicates reduced soft tissue mass with relative sparing of linear growth, reflecting fetal malnutrition in the third trimester. In contrast, infants whose birth weights are depressed and ponderal indices are normal (symmetrically growth-retarded newborns) suffer impairment of linear growth that suggests an early and/or chronic process starting early in gestation.

Frank and colleagues (1990) have shown that positive urine assays for marijuana and cocaine during pregnancy are both associated with a symmetrical pattern of intrauterine growth retardation, suggesting a chronic prenatal insult. Cocaine-exposed infants also had smaller head circumferences. Newborns from other study populations with symmetrical growth retardation have poorer postneonatal growth and development than infants with either asymmetrical intrauterine growth retardation or normal intrauterine growth, particularly if head circumference is also depressed (Holms et al. 1977; Davies et al. 1979; Villar et al. 1984). Whether this will also be true for marijuana- and cocaine-exposed newborns is unknown.

Central Nervous System

Another indirect mechanism that may contribute to long-term outcome are the lesions that are seen as echolucencies and echodensities in the CNS associated with prenatal cocaine/amphetamine exposure (Dixon and Bejar 1989). It is known that extensive intraventricular (Grade III and/or IV hemorrhage), but not echodensities (including small cysts among premature infants), is associated with poor neurodevelopmental outcome (Bennett et al. 1990). However, in cocaine-exposed infants, the locations of these lesions are different than those found among asphyxiated infants; whether these lesions are clinically important is unknown. Among cocaine-exposed infants, the lesions tend to be located in the frontal lobe and basal ganglia. It is postulated that this distribution is attributable to early development of musculature in the blood vessels leading to these regions. Thus, subsequent impairments among cocaine-exposed newborns may involve frontal-lobe dysfunction (such as higher level cognitive functions, perceptual motor tasks, and/or affective states) and may be different from those shown for premature or asphyxiated infants. New or different assessments may need to be developed and/or considered to detect the functional consequences of these lesions.

BIOLOGIC VULNERABILITIES ATTRIBUTABLE TO DIRECT EFFECTS

Cocaine's direct effect on the fetal brain may be influenced by many factors, including maternal metabolism of cocaine and changing lipid concentration of the developing fetal brain. Cholinesterase is the primary enzyme that metabolizes cocaine. Cholinesterase levels are usually low in pregnant women and fetuses, thereby decreasing the metabolism of cocaine and increasing duration of exposure during pregnancy. However, in an investigation determining cholinesterase levels during pregnancy starting at preconception until 3 months postpartum, cholinesterase levels did not decrease for all women, and for some women it actually increased (Evans et al. 1988). Women with high cholinesterase levels metabolize cocaine more quickly, thereby decreasing duration of exposure to the fetus and decreasing potential CNS impairment. Thus, some maternal-fetal units may be relatively less vulnerable to the detrimental effects of cocaine than others.

In animals, administration of cocaine results in higher concentrations in the adult brain than in the fetal brain (Wiggins et al. 1989). Because cocaine is lipophilic, this may be due to the increased lipid content of the adult brain. Thus, it is possible that cocaine's concentration in the fetal brain may increase during gestation as the lipid concentration of the brain increases.

A direct effect of cocaine on the brain may be due to its ability to alter neurotransmitters. This possibility is supported by changes in neurobehavioral (Chasnoff et al. 1985) and cardiac functioning (van der Bor et al. 1990) in cocaine-exposed newborns. To assess the effects of prenatal cocaine exposure on catecholamine physiology, Mirochnick and coworkers (in press) conducted a preliminary investigation to determine circulating levels of catecholamines in neonates and their relationship to neurobehavioral functioning. Among full-term, appropriate-for-gestational-age infants, the catecholamine precursor dihydroxyphenylalanine (DOPA) was increased in cocaine-exposed (n=12) compared with unexposed newborns (n=8). Circulating DOPA is believed to be derived substantially from sympathetic neurons, so that measurement of circulating DOPA may reflect neuronal catecholamine biosynthesis (Eisenhofer et al. 1986).

There were no statistically significant differences in norepinephrine (NE) and dopamine concentrations among the cocaine-exposed comparison subjects in the Microchnick study. However, inspection of the norepinephrine results suggests a trend to increased NE concentrations in the cocaine-exposed group. One member of the control group had an NE concentration several times higher than any other infant in the control group. Had this outlier been removed, NE concentrations in the cocaine-exposed newborns would have been almost twice that in the control infants and would have approached statistical significance in the small study population. Among the cocaine-exposed infants, those with high NE concentrations were least responsive to auditory and visual stimuli (orientation subscale) as measured by the Neonatal Behavioral Assessment Scale. This finding raises the possibility that this behavioral disturbance, which has been shown in other studies of cocaine-exposed newborns (e.g., Chasnoff et al. 1985), may be mediated in part by elevated levels of NE. However, measurements were made on blood and do not necessarily indicate changes in the CNS. Although it is possible that catecholamine changes shown in this preliminary study are attributable entirely to chronic stress associated with cocaine-induced vasoconstriction and hypoxia in utero, a study of 2-month-old infants showed increased levels of circulating NE, suggesting ongoing disturbance in the catecholamine systems (Ward et al. 1989). Further investigations are needed to determine whether the catecholamines and their metabolites are elevated in the CNS.

The impact of increased levels of neurotransmitters on the developing CNS raises important questions regarding long-term CNS effects, including diagnoses associated with alterations of these neurotransmitters such as attention deficit/hyperactivity disorder (ADHD) (Raskin et al. 1984) and depression (Gold et al. 1988). Because females suffer higher rates of depression compared to males, females may be more vulnerable to the direct effects of cocaine on the CNS. A study of rats exposed to cocaine showed increased rates of brain functional activity among females (but not males) especially in the cingulate cortex and the ventral tegmental area, which have high concentrations of dopaminergic synapses (Weiss et al. 1981). With this possibility in mind, Frank and Zuckerman (unpublished data) reanalyzed neonatal neurodevelopmental assessment data among newborns exposed prenatally to cocaine. Prior analysis combining both male and female neonates had not shown any difference between cocaine-exposed and nonexposed infants. This preliminary reanalysis showed poorer neurodevelopmental scores, as measured by the Neurologic and Adaptive Capacity Scale developed by Amiel Tison, among cocaine-exposed female infants compared with nonexposed female infants. The differences remained when confounding variables were controlled. No difference was seen between exposed and nonexposed males.

These preliminary data suggest that catecholamine activity may be increased in cocaine-exposed newborns and may be associated with concurrent neurobehavioral abnormalities. Longitudinal studies are needed to delineate the nature, magnitude, and duration of the relationship among prenatal cocaine exposure, catecholamine physiology, and long-term child functioning, including psychopathology. Analysis of cocaine-exposed infants should be stratified by gender to avoid missing significant association due to potential differential vulnerabilities to cocaine in the CNS. Global outcome measures such as cognitive performance, developmental quotients, or psychiatric diagnoses may not identify prenatal effects of cocaine. The potential impact on the CNS of neurotransmitter alterations or small localized hemorrhages suggests specific outcome measures such as regulation of attentional states, problems with information processing, or the ability to regulate affect or anxiety.

SOCIAL ENVIRONMENT

Prospective studies of biologically at-risk newborns during the past 20 years highlight the importance of a good social environment in optimizing development in the face of biologic vulnerabilities. This protective effect of the social environment is consistent with the transactional model of development in predicting children's development (Sameroff and Chandler 1975). For example, among an extensively studied group of premature infants, intelligence quotient (IQ) scores at 7 years of age were lower among infants who at 1 month of age were neurologically immature as indicated by a decreased amount of an electroencephalogram (EEG) pattern called trace alternans. However, among infants with low trace alternans, responsive caretaking (measured by direct observation) resulted in an IQ similar to infants who were not neurologically immature (Beckwith and Parmalee 1986). Thus, responsive caretaking appeared to be a protective factor for premature children with biologic vulnerability. In another study, children with equivalent levels of perinatal stress had better outcomes if their families had a high level of stability. It was only the combination of high perinatal stress and low family stability that impaired children's developmental functioning (Werner 1989). The importance of the environment in modifying perinatal risk factors also has been shown in studies of drug-exposed infants. Hans (this volume) found that only when prenatal methadone exposure was combined with low social class could impaired development be demonstrated compared with a control group. Lifschitz and colleagues (1985) also showed that the quality of the postnatal environment, and not the amount of maternal opiate use, appeared to be the more important determinant of outcome among opiate-exposed infants. The transactional model of development predicts that the biologic vulnerability created by *in utero* cocaine exposure can be highly modified or exacerbated by social factors.

Unfortunately, drug- and alcohol-abusing mothers are at high risk for dysfunctional caretaking. Because of the highly addictive nature of cocaine, it is likely that cocaine addiction causes significant disturbances in mothering behavior. At this time, little information on caregiving characteristics of cocaine-using women is available.

As part of an ongoing study of health behaviors and psychosocial characteristics of young mothers, Greer and Zuckerman (unpublished data) evaluated caregiving behaviors in the homes of 35 young mothers when their children were approximately 1 year of age. The Home Observation for Measurement of the Environment was used to assess the social and physical environment of the home, and the Nursing Child Assessment Teaching Scale was used to evaluate the responsiveness and sensitivity of the mother-child relationship. These assessments were done by an observer who was blind to the mother's drug use and other psychosocial characteristics. Inspection of the data showed the scores of two mothers to be more deviant than were the scores of the remainder of the group. Further exploration revealed that these two mothers were the only cocaine users in the sample. The two cocaine-using mothers provided less nurturing and attentive home environments and were less responsive and supportive in interactions with their infants compared with the other mothers. For example, one of the mothers' involvement and interaction with her 1-year-old son was minimal, except for shouting at him. In response to the examiner's request to ask her son to build a tower of three blocks, she said: "Do this," building the tower herself and then returning to her breakfast and cigarette. The child, however, did receive stimulation and support from a 3-year-old brother, an 8-year-old cousin, and his father. These case reports are consistent with clinical observation and need to be replicated with studies of larger sample sizes.

Mothers usually do not use drugs in isolation. The father of the baby, friends, and even grandparents are likely to be drug users. This drug-using environment is likely to involve violence, including women being victims of violence during their pregnancy (Amaro et al. 1990). Children born into this type of environment are most likely at an increased risk of physical abuse. Even if the child is not directly abused, being reared in a violent, dangerous environment that involves witnessing violence may have important physiologic, behavioral, and emotional consequences (van der Kilk 1988).

Although Hans (this volume) points out that children of drug-using parents may be at high risk for ADHD because of a direct effect of cocaine on the CNS, the social environment also may contribute to this outcome. For example, maternal depression may contribute to the development of short attention span in children. The depressed mother's tendency to initiate and terminate more frequently their children's interaction with objects was associated with a shorter attention span in her child. Because depression is a common comorbidity of cocaine abuse, this social interactive mechanism may contribute to symptoms associated with ADHD.

NEED FOR MATERNAL-CHILD CENTERS

It is important to determine the long-term effects and associated mechanisms of prenatal cocaine use. In the process, understanding of brain behavior relationships also may be improved. An important but unanswered question is whether good caretaking will help compensate for cocaine-induced direct or indirect biological vulnerability. However, the likelihood of good caretaking without comprehensive intervention for drug-using mothers and their children is unlikely because of cocaine's significant adverse effect on behavior and functioning.

The last National Institute on Drug Abuse technical review conference on perinatal drug use was held approximately 5 years ago. Unfortunately, the scientific community is only slightly more knowledgeable now than it was then. The Nation is experiencing an epidemic of perinatal drug use without reliable knowledge of the prevalence of such use, the short-term and long-term impact of these drugs, and the most effective treatment strategies. There are also an inadequate number of researchers trained in investigating perinatal drug effects. To effectively move the field ahead, one to four mother-child centers devoted to research, training of investigators and clinicians, and clinical care need to be developed. A service component is an important part of such centers because the ability to conduct longitudinal studies of the long-term effects of drugs depends on maintaining a study population. For drug-using mothers and their infants, this is best accomplished in the context of a comprehensive service program. Without such a focused and extensive commitment, the ability to understand and help drug-exposed infants and their parents will remain limited.

REFERENCES

Abrams, R.M.; Cook, C.E.; Davis, K.H.; Niederreither, K.; Jaeger, M.J.; and Szeto, H.H. Plasma D-9-tetrahydrocannabinol in pregnant sheep and fetus after inhalation of smoke from a marijuana cigarette. *Alcohol Drug Res* 6:361-369, 1985.

Amaro, H.; Fried, L.E.; Cabral, H.; and Zuckerman, B. Violence during pregnancy and substance use. *Am J Public Health* 80:575-579, 1990.

Beckwith, L., and Parmalee, A. EEG patterns in preterm infants, home environment, and later I.Q. *Child Dev* 57:777-789, 1986.

Bennett, F.C.; Silver, G.; Leung E.J.; and Mack. L.A. Periventricular echodensities detected by cranial ultrasonography: Usefulness in predicting neurodevelopmental outcome in low birthweight, preterm infants. *Pediatrics* 85:400-404, 1990.

Chasnoff, I.J.; Burns, W.J.; Schnoll, S.H.; and Burns, K.A. Cocaine use in pregnancy. *N Engl J Med* 313:666-669, 1985.

Clapp, J.J.; Wesley, M.; Cooke, R.; Pekals, R.; and Holstein, C. The effects of marijuana smoke on gas exchange in ovine pregnancy. *Alcohol Drug Res* 7:85-92, 1986.

Davies, D.P.; Platts, P.; Pritchard, J.M.; and Wilkinson, P.W. Nutritional status of light-for-date infants at birth and its influence on early postnatal growth. *Arch Dis Child* 54:703-706, 1979.

Dixon, S.D., and Bejar, R. Echoencephalographic findings in neonates associated with maternal cocaine and methamphetamine use: Incidence and clinical correlates. *J Pediatr* 115:770-778, 1989.

Eisenhofer, G.; Goldstein, D.S.; Stull, R.; Keiser, H.R.; Sunderland, T.; Murphy, D.L.; and Kopin, I.J. Simultaneous liquid-chromatographic determination of 3,4-dihydroxyphenylglycol, catecholamines and 3,4-dihydroxyphenylalanine in plasma, and their responses to inhibition of monoamine oxidase. *Clin Chem* 32:2030-2033, 1986.

Evans, R.T.; O'Callaghan, F.; and Norman, A. A longitudinal study of cholinesterase changes in pregnancy. *Clin Chem* 34:2249-2252, 1988.

Frank, D.A.; Bauchner, H.; Parker, S.; Huber, A.M.; Kyei-Aboagye, K.; Cabral, H.; and Zuckerman, B. Neonatal body proportionality and body composition following in utero exposure to cocaine and marijuana. *J Pediatr* 117:662-626, 1990.

Frisancho, A.R.; Klayman, J.E.; and Matos, J. Newborn body composition and its relationship to linear growth. *Am J Clin Nutr* 30:704-711, 1977.

Georgieff, M.K.; Sasanow, S.R.; Chockalingam, U.M.; and Pereira, G.R. A comparison of the mid-arm circumference/head circumference ratio and ponderal index for the evaluation of newborn infants after abnormal intrauterine growth. *Acta Paediatr Scand* 77:214-219, 1988.

Gold, P.W.; Goodwin, F.K.; and Chrousos, G.P. Clinical and biochemical manifestations of depression: Relation to the neurobiology of stress (part 1). *N Engl J Med* 319:348-353, 1988.

Harrison, G.G.; Branson R.S.; and Vaucher, Y.E. Association of maternal smoking with body composition of the newborn. *Am J Clin Nutr* 38:757-762, 1983.

Holms, G.E.; Miller, H.C.; Hassanein, K.; Lansky, S.B.; and Goggin, J.E. Postnatal somatic growth in infants with atypical fetal growth patterns. *Am J Dis Child* 131:1078-1083, 1977.

Lifschitz, M.H.; Wilson, G.S.; Smith, E.O.; and Desmond, M.M. Factors affecting head growth and intellectual function in children of drug addicts. *Pediatrics* 75:269-274, 1985.

Miller, H.C., and Merrit, T.A. *Fetal Growth in Humans.* Chicago: Year Book Publishers, 1979.

Mirochnick, M.; Meyer, J.; Cole, J.; Herren, T.; and Zuckerman, B. Circulating catecholamines in cocaine-exposed neonates: A pilot study. *Pediatrics,* in press.

Niederreither, K.; Jaeger, M.C.; and Abrams, R.M. Cardiopulmonary effects of marijuana and delta-9-tetrahydrocannabinol in sheep. *Res Commun Substances Abuse* 6:87-98, 1985.

Raskin, L.A.; Shaywitz, S.E.; Shaywitz, B.A.; Anderson, G.M.; and Cohen, D. Neurochemical correlates of attention deficit disorder. *Pediatr Clin North Am* 31:387-396, 1984.

Sameroff, A., and Chandler, M. Reproductive risk and the continuum of caretaking casualty. In: Horowitz, F., Hetherington, M.; and Scarr-Salanatek, S., eds. *Review of Child Development Research.* Chicago: University of Chicago Press, 1975. pp. 187-244.

van der Bor, M.; Walther, F.J.; and Ebrahimi, M. Decreased cardiac output in infants of mothers who abused cocaine. *Pediatrics* 85:30-32, 1990.

van der Kilk, B. The trauma spectrum: The interaction of biological and social events in the genesis of the trauma response. *J Traumatic Stress* 1:273-290, 1988.

Villar, J., and Belizan, J.M. The timing factor in the pathophysiology of the intrauterine growth retardation syndrome. *Obstet Gynecol Surv* 37:499-506, 1982.

Villar, J.; Smerigilio, V.; Martorell, R.; Brown, C.H.; and Klein, R.E. Heterogeneous growth and mental development of intrauterine growth-related infants during the first 3 years of life. *Pediatrics* 74:783-791, 1984.

Ward, S.L.D.; Bautista, D.B.; Buckley, S.; Schuetz, S.; Wachsman, L.; Bean, X.; and Warburton, D. Circulating catecholamines and adrenoreceptors in infants of cocaine abusing mothers. *Pediatr Res* 25:74A, 1989.

Weiss, J.M.; Goodman, P.A.; Losito, P.G.; Corrigan, S.; Charry, J.; and Bailey, W. Behavioral depression produced by an uncontrolled stressor: Relation to norepinephrine, dopamine and serotonin levels in various regions of the rat brain. *Brain Res Rev* 3:167-205, 1981.

Werner, E. Children of the Garden Island. *Sci Am* 106:9-14, 1989.

Wiggins, R.C.; Rolsten, C.; Ruiz, B.; and Davis, C.M. Pharmacokinetics of cocaine: Basic studies of route, dosage, pregnancy and lactation. *Neurotoxicology* 10:367-382, 1989.

Wu, T.C.; Taskin, D.P.; Djahed, B.; and Rose, J.E. Pulmonary hazards of smoking marijuana as compared to tobacco. *N Engl J Med* 318:347-351, 1988.

ACKNOWLEDGMENT

Support for the work described in this chapter was provided by the Harris Foundation.

AUTHOR

Barry Zuckerman, M.D.
Professor of Pediatrics
Department of Pediatrics and Public Health
Boston University School of Medicine
Director
Division of Developmental and Behavioral Pediatrics
Boston City Hospital
Talbot 214
818 Harrison Avenue
Boston, MA 02118

National
Institute on
Drug
Abuse

MONOGRAPH SERIES

While limited supplies last, single copies of the monographs may be obtained
free of charge from the National Clearinghouse for Alcohol and Drug
Information (NCADI). Please contact NCADI also for information about
availability of coming issues and other publications of the National Institute on
Drug Abuse relevant to drug abuse research.

Additional copies may be purchased from the U.S. Government Printing Office
(GPO) and/or the National Technical Information Service (NTIS) as indicated.
NTIS prices are for paper copy; add $3 handling charge for each order.
Microfiche copies are also available from NTIS. Prices from either source are
subject to change.

Addresses are:

NCADI
National Clearinghouse for Alcohol and Drug Information
P.O. Box 2345
Rockville, MD 20852
(301) 468-2600
(800) 729-6686

GPO
Superintendent of Documents
U.S. Government Printing Office
Washington, DC 20402
(202) 275-2981

NTIS
National Technical Information Service
U.S. Department of Commerce
Springfield, VA 22161
(703) 487-4650

*For information on availability of NIDA Research Monographs 1 through 24
(1975-1979) and others not listed, write to NIDA, Community and Professional
Education Branch, Room 10A-54, 5600 Fishers Lane, Rockville, MD 20857.*

25 BEHAVIORAL ANALYSIS AND TREATMENT OF SUBSTANCE ABUSE.
Norman A. Krasnegor, Ph.D., ed.
GPO out of stock   NCADI out of stock
                                             NTIS PB #80-112428/AS $31

26 THE BEHAVIORAL ASPECTS OF SMOKING. Norman A. Krasnegor,
Ph.D., ed. (reprint from 1979 Surgeon General's Report on Smoking and
Health)
GPO out of stock   NTIS PB #80-118755/AS $23

30 THEORIES ON DRUG ABUSE: SELECTED CONTEMPORARY
PERSPECTIVES. Dan J. Lettieri, Ph.D.; Mollie Sayers; and Helen W. Pearson,
eds.
GPO out of stock   NCADI out of stock
                                             Not available from NTIS

31 MARIJUANA RESEARCH FINDINGS: 1980. Robert C. Petersen, Ph.D.,
ed.
GPO out of stock   NTIS PB #80-215171/AS $31

32 GC/MS ASSAYS FOR ABUSED DRUGS IN BODY FLUIDS. Rodger L.
Foltz, Ph.D.; Allison F. Fentiman, Jr., Ph.D.; and Ruth B. Foltz, eds.
GPO out of stock   NCADI out of stock
                                             NTIS PB #81-133746/AS $31

36 NEW APPROACHES TO TREATMENT OF CHRONIC PAIN: A REVIEW
OF MULTIDISCIPLINARY PAIN CLINICS AND PAIN CENTERS. Lorenz K.Y.
Ng, M.D., ed.
GPO out of stock   NCADI out of stock
                                             NTIS PB #81-240913/AS $31

37 BEHAVIORAL PHARMACOLOGY OF HUMAN DRUG DEPENDENCE.
Travis Thompson, Ph.D., and Chris E. Johanson, Ph.D., eds.
GPO out of stock   NCADI out of stock
                                             NTIS PB #82-136961/AS $39

38 DRUG ABUSE AND THE AMERICAN ADOLESCENT. Dan J. Lettieri,
Ph.D., and Jacqueline P. Ludford, M.S., eds. A RAUS Review Report.
GPO out of stock   NCADI out of stock
                                             NTIS PB #82-148198/AS $23

40 ADOLESCENT MARIJUANA ABUSERS AND THEIR FAMILIES. Herbert Hendin, M.D; Ann Pollinger, Ph.D.; Richard Ulman, Ph.D.; and Arthur Carr, Ph.D., eds.
GPO out of stock   NCADI out of stock
                                     NTIS PB #82-133117/AS $23

42 THE ANALYSIS OF CANNABINOIDS IN BIOLOGICAL FLUIDS. Richard L. Hawks, Ph.D., ed.
GPO out of stock   NTIS PB #83-136044/AS $23

44 MARIJUANA EFFECTS ON THE ENDOCRINE AND REPRODUCTIVE SYSTEMS. Monique C. Braude, Ph.D., and Jacqueline P. Ludford, M.S., eds. A RAUS Review Report.
GPO out of stock   NCADI out of stock
                                     NTIS PB #85-150563/AS $23

45 CONTEMPORARY RESEARCH IN PAIN AND ANALGESIA, 1983. Roger M. Brown, Ph.D.; Theodore M. Pinkert, M.D., J.D.; and Jacqueline P. Ludford, M.S. eds. A RAUS Review Report.
GPO out of stock   NCADI out of stock
                                     NTIS PB #84-184670/AS $17

46 BEHAVIORAL INTERVENTION TECHNIQUES IN DRUG ABUSE TREATMENT. John Grabowski, Ph.D.; Maxine L. Stitzer, Ph.D.; and Jack E. Henningfield, Ph.D., eds.
GPO out of stock   NCADI out of stock
                                     NTIS PB #84-184688/AS $23

47 PREVENTING ADOLESCENT DRUG ABUSE: INTERVENTION STRATEGIES. Thomas J. Glynn, Ph.D.; Carl G. Leukefeld, D.S.W.; and Jacqueline P. Ludford, M.S., eds. A RAUS Review Report.
GPO out of stock   NCADI out of stock
                                     NTIS PB #85-159663/AS $31

48 MEASUREMENT IN THE ANALYSIS AND TREATMENT OF SMOKING BEHAVIOR. John Grabowski, Ph.D., and Catherine Bell, M.S., eds.
GPO out of stock   NCADI out of stock
                                     NTIS PB #84-145184/AS $23

50 COCAINE: PHARMACOLOGY, EFFECTS, AND TREATMENT OF ABUSE. John Grabowski, Ph.D., ed.
GPO Stock #017-024-01214-9 $4   NTIS PB #85-150381/AS $23

51 DRUG ABUSE TREATMENT EVALUATION: STRATEGIES, PROGRESS, AND PROSPECTS. Frank M. Tims, Ph.D., ed.
GPO out of stock   NTIS PB #85-150365/AS $23

52 TESTING DRUGS FOR PHYSICAL DEPENDENCE POTENTIAL AND ABUSE LIABILITY. Joseph V. Brady, Ph.D., and Scott E. Lukas, Ph.D., eds.
GPO out of stock   NTIS PB #85-150373/AS $23

53 PHARMACOLOGICAL ADJUNCTS IN SMOKING CESSATION. John Grabowski, Ph.D., and Sharon M. Hall, Ph.D., eds.
GPO out of stock   NCADI out of stock
                                             NTIS PB #89-123186/AS $23

54 MECHANISMS OF TOLERANCE AND DEPENDENCE. Charles Wm. Sharp, Ph.D., ed.
GPO out of stock   NCADI out of stock
                                             NTIS PB #89-103279/AS $39

55 PROBLEMS OF DRUG DEPENDENCE, 1984: PROCEEDINGS OF THE 46TH ANNUAL SCIENTIFIC MEETING, THE COMMITTEE ON PROBLEMS OF DRUG DEPENDENCE, INC. Louis S. Harris, Ph.D., ed.
GPO out of stock   NCADI out of stock
                                             NTIS PB #89-123194/AS $45

56 ETIOLOGY OF DRUG ABUSE: IMPLICATIONS FOR PREVENTION. Coryl LaRue Jones, Ph.D., and Robert J. Battjes, D.S.W., eds.
GPO Stock #017-024-01250-5 $6.50   NTIS PB #89-123160/AS $31

57 SELF-REPORT METHODS OF ESTIMATING DRUG USE: MEETING CURRENT CHALLENGES TO VALIDITY. Beatrice A. Rouse, Ph.D.; Nicholas J. Kozel, M.S.; and Louise G. Richards, Ph.D., eds.
GPO out of stock   NTIS PB #88-248083/AS $23

58 PROGRESS IN THE DEVELOPMENT OF COST-EFFECTIVE TREATMENT FOR DRUG ABUSERS. Rebecca S. Ashery, D.S.W., ed.
GPO out of stock   NTIS PB #89-125017/AS $23

59 CURRENT RESEARCH ON THE CONSEQUENCES OF MATERNAL DRUG ABUSE. Theodore M. Pinkert, M.D., J.D., ed.
GPO out of stock   NTIS PB #89-125025/AS $23

60 PRENATAL DRUG EXPOSURE: KINETICS AND DYNAMICS. C. Nora Chiang, Ph.D., and Charles C. Lee, Ph.D., eds.
GPO out of stock   NTIS PB #89-124564/AS $23

61 COCAINE USE IN AMERICA: EPIDEMIOLOGIC AND CLINICAL PERSPECTIVES. Nicholas J. Kozel, M.S., and Edgar H. Adams, M.S., eds.
GPO out of stock   NTIS PB #89-131866/AS $31

62 NEUROSCIENCE METHODS IN DRUG ABUSE RESEARCH. Roger M. Brown, Ph.D.; David P. Friedman, Ph.D.; and Yuth Nimit, Ph.D., eds.
GPO out of stock   NCADI out of stock
                                            NTIS PB #89-130660/AS $23

63 PREVENTION RESEARCH: DETERRING DRUG ABUSE AMONG CHILDREN AND ADOLESCENTS. Catherine S. Bell, M.S., and Robert Battjes, D.S.W., eds.
GPO out of stock   NTIS PB #89-103287/AS $31

64 PHENCYCLIDINE: AN UPDATE. Doris H. Clouet, Ph.D., ed.
GPO out of stock   NTIS PB #89-131858/AS $31

65 WOMEN AND DRUGS: A NEW ERA FOR RESEARCH. Barbara A. Ray, Ph.D., and Monique C. Braude, Ph.D., eds.
GPO Stock #017-024-01283-1 $3.50   NTIS PB #89-130637/AS $23

66 GENETIC AND BIOLOGICAL MARKERS IN DRUG ABUSE AND ALCOHOLISM. Monique C. Braude, Ph.D., and Helen M. Chao, Ph.D., eds.
GPO out of stock   NCADI out of stock
                                            NTIS PB #89-134423/AS $23

68 STRATEGIES FOR RESEARCH ON THE INTERACTIONS OF DRUGS OF ABUSE. Monique C. Braude, Ph.D., and Harold M. Ginzburg, M.D., J.D., M.P.H., eds.
GPO out of stock   NCADI out of stock
                                            NTIS PB #89-134936/AS $31

69 OPIOID PEPTIDES: MEDICINAL CHEMISTRY. Rao S. Rapaka, Ph.D.; Gene Barnett, Ph.D.; and Richard L. Hawks, Ph.D., eds.
GPO out of stock   NTIS PB #89-158422/AS $39

70 OPIOID PEPTIDES: MOLECULAR PHARMACOLOGY, BIOSYNTHESIS, AND ANALYSIS. Rao S. Rapaka, Ph.D., and Richard L. Hawks, Ph.D., eds.
GPO out of stock   NTIS PB #89-158430/AS $45

71 OPIATE RECEPTOR SUBTYPES AND BRAIN FUNCTION. Roger M. Brown, Ph.D.; Doris H. Clouet, Ph.D.; and David P. Friedman, Ph.D., eds.
GPO out of stock   NTIS PB #89-151955/AS $31

72 RELAPSE AND RECOVERY IN DRUG ABUSE. Frank M. Tims, Ph.D., and Carl G. Leukefeld, D.S.W., eds.
GPO Stock #017-024-01302-1 $6   NTIS PB #89-151963/AS $31

73 URINE TESTING FOR DRUGS OF ABUSE. Richard L. Hawks, Ph.D., and C. Nora Chiang, Ph.D., eds.
GPO Stock #017-024-01313-7 $3.75   NTIS PB #89-151971/AS $23

74 NEUROBIOLOGY OF BEHAVIORAL CONTROL IN DRUG ABUSE. Stephen I. Szara, M.D., D.Sc., ed.
GPO Stock #017-024-01314-5 $3.75   NTIS PB #89-151989/AS $23

75 PROGRESS IN OPIOID RESEARCH. PROCEEDINGS OF THE 1986 INTERNATIONAL NARCOTICS RESEARCH CONFERENCE. John W. Holaday, Ph.D.; Ping-Yee Law, Ph.D.; and Albert Herz, M.D., eds.
GPO out of stock   NCADI out of stock
                                    Not available from NTIS

76 PROBLEMS OF DRUG DEPENDENCE, 1986: PROCEEDINGS OF THE 48TH ANNUAL SCIENTIFIC MEETING, THE COMMITTEE ON PROBLEMS OF DRUG DEPENDENCE, INC. Louis S. Harris, Ph.D., ed.
GPO out of stock   NCADI out of stock
                                    NTIS PB #88-208111/AS $53

77 ADOLESCENT DRUG ABUSE: ANALYSES OF TREATMENT RESEARCH. Elizabeth R. Rahdert, Ph.D., and John Grabowski, Ph.D., eds.
GPO Stock #017-024-01348-0 $4   NCADI out of stock
                                    NTIS PB #89-125488/AS $23

78 THE ROLE OF NEUROPLASTICITY IN THE RESPONSE TO DRUGS. David P. Friedman, Ph.D., and Doris H. Clouet, Ph.D., eds.
GPO out of stock   NTIS PB #88-245683/AS $31

79 STRUCTURE-ACTIVITY RELATIONSHIPS OF THE CANNABINOIDS. Rao S. Rapaka, Ph.D., and Alexandros Makriyannis, Ph.D., eds.
GPO out of stock   NTIS PB #89-109201/AS $31

80 NEEDLE SHARING AMONG INTRAVENOUS DRUG ABUSERS: NATIONAL AND INTERNATIONAL PERSPECTIVES. Robert J. Battjes, D.S.W., and Roy W. Pickens, Ph.D., eds.
GPO out of stock   NTIS PB #88-236138/AS $31

81 PROBLEMS OF DRUG DEPENDENCE, 1987: PROCEEDINGS OF THE 49TH ANNUAL SCIENTIFIC MEETING, THE COMMITTEE ON PROBLEMS OF DRUG DEPENDENCE, INC. Louis S. Harris, Ph.D., ed.
GPO Stock #017-024-01354-4 $17   NTIS PB #89-109227/AS
                                          Contact NTIS for price

82 OPIOIDS IN THE HIPPOCAMPUS. Jacqueline F. McGinty, Ph.D., and David P. Friedman, Ph.D., eds.
GPO out of stock   NTIS PB #88-245691/AS $23

83 HEALTH HAZARDS OF NITRITE INHALANTS. Harry W. Haverkos, M.D., and John A. Dougherty, Ph.D., eds.
GPO out of stock   NTIS PB #89-125496/AS $23

84 LEARNING FACTORS IN SUBSTANCE ABUSE. Barbara A. Ray, Ph.D., ed.
GPO Stock #017-024-01353-6 $6   NTIS PB #89-125504/AS $31

85 EPIDEMIOLOGY OF INHALANT ABUSE: AN UPDATE. Raquel A. Crider, Ph.D., and Beatrice A. Rouse, Ph.D., eds.
GPO Stock #017-024-01360-9 $5.50   NTIS PB #89-123178/AS $31

86 COMPULSORY TREATMENT OF DRUG ABUSE: RESEARCH AND CLINICAL PRACTICE. Carl G. Leukefeld, D.S.W., and Frank M. Tims, Ph.D., eds.
GPO Stock #017-024-01352-8 $7.50   NTIS PB #89-151997/AS $31

87 OPIOID PEPTIDES: AN UPDATE. Rao S. Rapaka, Ph.D., and Bhola N. Dhawan, M.D., eds.
GPO Stock #017-024-01366-8 $7   NTIS PB #89-158430/AS $45

88 MECHANISMS OF COCAINE ABUSE AND TOXICITY. Doris H. Clouet, Ph.D.; Khursheed Asghar, Ph.D.; and Roger M. Brown, Ph.D., eds.
GPO Stock #017-024-01359-5 $11   NTIS PB #89-125512/AS $39

89 BIOLOGICAL VULNERABILTY TO DRUG ABUSE. Roy W. Pickens, Ph.D., and Dace S. Svikis, B.A., eds.
GPO Stock #017-022-01054-2 $5   NTIS PB #89-125520/AS $23

90 PROBLEMS OF DRUG DEPENDENCE, 1988: PROCEEDINGS OF THE 50TH ANNUAL SCIENTIFIC MEETING, THE COMMITTEE ON PROBLEMS OF DRUG DEPENDENCE, INC. Louis S. Harris, Ph.D., ed.
GPO Stock #017-024-01362-5 $17

91 DRUGS IN THE WORKPLACE: RESEARCH AND EVALUATION DATA. Steven W. Gust, Ph.D., and J. Michael Walsh, Ph.D., eds.
GPO Stock #017-024-01384-6 $10   NTIS PB #90-147257/AS $39

92 TESTING FOR ABUSE LIABILITY OF DRUGS IN HUMANS. Marian W. Fischman, Ph.D., and Nancy K. Mello, Ph.D., eds.
GPO Stock #017-024-01379-0 $12   NTIS PB #90-148933/AS $45

93 AIDS AND INTRAVENOUS DRUG USE: FUTURE DIRECTIONS FOR COMMUNITY-BASED PREVENTION RESEARCH. C.G. Leukefeld, D.S.W.; R.J. Battjes, D.S.W.; and Z. Amsel, D.Sc., eds.
GPO Stock #017-024-01388-9 $10   NTIS PB #90-148941/AS $39

94 PHARMACOLOGY AND TOXICOLOGY OF AMPHETAMINE AND RELATED DESIGNER DRUGS. Khursheed Asghar, Ph.D., and Errol De Souza, Ph.D., eds.
GPO Stock #017-024-01386-2 $11   NTIS PB #90-148958/AS $39

95 PROBLEMS OF DRUG DEPENDENCE, 1989: PROCEEDINGS OF THE 51ST ANNUAL SCIENTIFIC MEETING, THE COMMITTEE ON PROBLEMS OF DRUG DEPENDENCE, INC. Louis S. Harris, Ph.D., ed.
GPO Stock #017-024-01399-4 $21   NTIS PB #90-237660/AS $67

96 DRUGS OF ABUSE: CHEMISTRY, PHARMACOLOGY, IMMUNOLOGY, AND AIDS. Phuong Thi Kim Pham, Ph.D., and Kenner Rice, Ph.D., eds.
GPO Stock #017-024-01403-6 $8   NTIS PB #90-237678/AS $31

97 NEUROBIOLOGY OF DRUG ABUSE: LEARNING AND MEMORY. Lynda Erinoff, Ph.D., ed.
GPO Stock #017-024-01404-4 $8   NTIS PB #90-237686/AS $31

98 THE COLLECTION AND INTERPRETATION OF DATA FROM HIDDEN POPULATIONS. Elizabeth Y. Lambert, M.S., ed.
GPO Stock #017-024-01407-9 $4.75   NTIS PB #90-237694/AS $23

99 RESEARCH FINDINGS ON SMOKING OF ABUSED SUBSTANCES. C. Nora Chiang, Ph.D., and Richard L. Hawks, Ph.D., eds.
GPO Stock #017-024-01412-5 $5   NTIS PB #91-141119 $23

100 DRUGS IN THE WORKPLACE: RESEARCH AND EVALUATION DATA. VOL. II. Steven W. Gust, Ph.D., and J. Michael Walsh, Ph.D., eds.

101 RESIDUAL EFFECTS OF ABUSED DRUGS ON BEHAVIOR. John W. Spencer, Ph.D., and John J. Boren, Ph.D., eds.
GPO Stock #017-024-01426-7 $6   NTIS PB #91-172858/AS $31

102 ANABOLIC STEROID ABUSE. Geraline C. Lin, Ph.D., and Lynda Erinoff, Ph.D., eds.
GPO Stock #017-024-01425-7 $8   NTIS PB #91-172866/AS $31

103 DRUGS AND VIOLENCE: CAUSES, CORRELATES, AND CONSEQUENCES. Mario De La Rosa, Ph.D.; Elizabeth Y. Lambert, M.S.; and Bernard Gropper, Ph.D., eds.
GPO Stock #017-024-01427-3 $9   NTIS PB #91-172841/AS $31

104 PSYCHOTHERAPY AND COUNSELING IN THE TREATMENT OF DRUG ABUSE. Lisa Simon Onken, Ph.D., and Jack D. Blaine, M.D., eds.
GPO Stock #017-024-01429-0 $4   NTIS PB #91-172874/AS $23

105 PROBLEMS OF DRUG DEPENDENCE, 1990: PROCEEDINGS OF THE 52ND ANNUAL SCIENTIFIC MEETING, THE COMMITTEE ON PROBLEMS OF DRUG DEPENDENCE, INC. Louis S. Harris, Ph.D., ed.
GPO Stock #017-024-01435-4 $22

106 IMPROVING DRUG ABUSE TREATMENT. Roy W. Pickens, Ph.D.; Carl G. Leukefeld, D.S.W.; and Charles R. Schuster, Ph.D., eds.
GPO Stock #017-024-01439-7 $12

107 DRUG ABUSE PREVENTION INTERVENTION RESEARCH: METHODOLOGICAL ISSUES. Carl G. Leukefeld, D.S.W., and William J. Bukoski, Ph.D., eds.
GPO Stock #017-024-01441-9 $9

108 CARDIOVASCULAR TOXICITY OF COCAINE: UNDERLYING MECHANISMS. Pushpa V. Thadani, Ph.D., ed.
GPO Stock #017-024-01446-0

109 LONGITUDINAL STUDIES OF HIV INFECTION IN INTRAVENOUS DRUG USERS: METHODOLOGICAL ISSUES IN NATURAL HISTORY RESEARCH. Peter Hartsock, Dr.P.H., and Sander G. Genser, M.D., M.P.H., eds.
GPO Stock #017-024-01445-1